r: William Shen
: 沈維賢

: J.B. Heaton & N.D. Turton
: J · B · 希頓、N · D · 陶頓
ors : Wong Kwun & Lam Sheung Chau
: 黃均、林相周

Consultant: Prof Benjamin T'sou (PhD., F.I.L.)
: 鄒嘉彥教授
: Wong Yuk Lun
: 黃玉麟

朗文常用英語正誤詞

LONGMAN ENGLISH-CHINESE DICTIONARY OF COMMON ERRORS

J.B. Heaton and N.D. Turton

E
編
Ed
編輯

朗文常用英語
正誤詞典

LONGMAN ENGLISH-CHINESE DICTIONARY OF COMMON ERRORS

J.B. Heaton and N.D. Turton

Longman朗文

Published by
Longman Asia Limited
18/F., Cornwall House
Taikoo Place
979 King's Road
Quarry Bay
Hong Kong
Tel: 2811 8168
Fax: 2565 7440
Telex: 73051 LGHK HX

朗文出版亞洲有限公司
香港鰂魚涌英皇道 979 號
太古坊康和大廈十八樓
電話：2811 8168
圖文傳真：2565 7440
電傳：73051 LGHK HX

First published 1990
Fourth impression 1996
一九九〇年初版
一九九六年第四次印刷

ISBN 962 359 041 5

Produced by Longman Asia Limited
Printed in Hong Kong
SWT/04

The publisher's policy is to use **paper manufactured from sustainable forests**

本詞典編譯顧問: 鄒嘉彥博士簡介

美國哈佛大學語言學碩士、美國伯克萊加州大學語言學博士、英國語言學會會士 (F.I.L.)、美國語言學會會員、香港語言學會創會主席

曾任美國加州大學助理教授、澳洲大學副教授、香港大學教授、香港城市理工學院語言系系主任等職

現任香港城市理工學院助理院長、語言學講座教授

曾在歐、美、亞洲各地發表並出版有關語言學及應用語言學著作數十種

前　言

中國人學英語所遇的困難和常犯的錯誤是多方面的，其犖犖大端者，如用詞，如搭配，如句法結構；而搭配方面又可分動詞與前置詞（如說“與 ... 不同”，本應是 differ **from**，但常誤作 differ **to**）、名詞與前置詞（如說廉價購得某物，本應是 buy something **in a sale**，但常誤作 **on a sale**）、動詞與名詞（如說“收拾行李”，本應是 pack one's **suitcases**，但常誤作 pack one's **luggage**）、形容詞與前置詞（如說“對某人很友善'，本應是 be kind **to** someone，但常誤作 be kind **with** someone）、形容詞與名詞（如本應說 He asked me **a lot of** questions，但常誤作 He asked me **many** questions）等等。此外還有可數與不可數名詞的區別（如本應說 improve one's **knowledge** of English，但常誤用了 **knowledges**）、冠詞 the 之用與不用（如 Himalayas 之前不能缺了 **the**，而 Mount Everest 之前卻誤加了 **the**；play chess 是對的，但 play piano/guitar 就不對）。

以上種種都是中國人學英文感到不易解決的困難，而有一些更是中國人常犯的錯誤，譬如，中國學生往往會說：“How to spell 'squirrel'?”（見本書 149 頁）或者，“I would really appreciate if you could let me have her address as soon as possible.”（見本書 27 頁）。他們又會受到中文句法的影響，說出“We all were delighted when we heard the news.”（見本書 14 頁）這樣的話。說到“移民”，他們弄不清該用 immigration 還是 emigration 才是。

對中國人來說，尤其頭痛的是，以上的許多難點不知查什麼書才能解決。像“How to spell 'squirrel'?”這樣的錯誤，就是花許多時間去查，也未必能從一般詞典或文法書上找出答案。

細心的讀者不難發現，譯者不僅具有豐富的翻譯經驗，而且具有豐富的英語教學經驗。為了照顧不熟識文法的讀者，譯者有意避開生僻的文法術語，而另作通俗的解釋；有一些過於公式化或過於簡化的地方，也不厭其詳地加以解釋，務求做到深入淺出，通俗易懂。

如果你能找到原文詞典來對照，你還會看出，為了使本書對中國讀者更具針對性、實用性和準確性，編譯者付出了幾許心血。

朗文出版（遠東）有限公司
辭書/翻譯出版部
一九九零年九月

Contents 目 錄

How to use the dictionary

This book provides learners of English with a quick and easy way of avoiding or correcting their mistakes. When writing an essay or the answers to an exercise, the learner often wishes to use a particular word or phrase but feels uncertain about its correct usage. For example, which is correct: 'succeed **to do** something' or 'succeed **in doing** something'; '**do** a mistake' or '**make** a mistake'; 'He has **much** money' or 'He has **a lot of** money'? Searching for this information in dictionaries and grammar books can take a great deal of time. By referring to the ***Longman Dictionary of Common Errors***, the user can find the required information within seconds, and in order to ensure quick and easy reference, great care has been taken to keep the explanatory note at the end of each entry as brief and simple as possible. It must be stressed, therefore, that the ***Longman Dictionary of Common Errors*** is not intended as a comprehensive grammar book. It has the very practical aim of providing all the information required to avoid or correct a particular error, and no more.

如何使用本詞典

本詞典能幫助學習英語的人士, 以事半功倍之效, 避免或改正學習中所犯的錯誤。寫英文或做作業時, 初學者希望用某個詞或片語, 但是對其正確用法往往心中無數。例如, succeed **to do** something 和 succeed **in doing** something, 究竟哪一個正確? 應用 **do** a mistake 還是 **make** a mistake? 而 He has **much** money 和 He has **a lot of** money, 到底是哪一句對? 從詞典和語法書中尋找這類解釋要費很多時間, 但查閱本詞典, 用不着一分鐘就能迎刃而解。為了確保查閱快而方便, 編纂時力求每一個詞條末尾的解釋盡可能做到簡單明瞭。因此, 必須着重說明本詞典不是一部綜合性的文法書; 它只是從實用的目的出發, 就如何避免或糾正某一錯誤提供所需的詳盡解釋而已。

How to find an error quickly

This dictionary is arranged in alphabetical order: the entries beginning with **a** are to be found at the front of the book and the entries beginning with **z** at the back. To help you find an entry quickly, there is a word in heavy type at the top of each page. The word at the top of a left-hand page shows the first entry on that page; the word at the top of a right-hand page shows the last entry on that page.

如何很快查出錯誤

本詞典按字母順序編排: 從書前面的字母 **a** 詞條開始到後面的字母 **z** 詞條結尾。為了便於很快查到詞條, 書中每頁上首都印有粗體詞: 左頁上首的詞表明該頁中的第一個詞條, 右頁上首的詞即是該頁中的最後一個詞條。

Where to look

An entry that is made up of more than one word is treated as if it were a single word. For example, the entry for **go out** is placed after **goods** and before **gossip**, not at **go**.

如何着手查找

由一個詞以上組成的詞條按一個整體詞處理。例如, 詞條 **go out** 排在 **goods** 之後 **gossip** 之前, 不和 **go** 排在一起, 如下例:

goods 1 × The goods was not delivered in time.
√ **The goods were not delivered in time.**
Goods is a plural noun and takes a plural verb.
2 × He had very little money and very few goods.
√ **He had very little money and very few possessions.**
goods = things for sale: 'leather goods'
possessions = all the things a person owns

go out × As soon as the bus stopped, he went out.
√ **As soon as the bus stopped, he got off.**
get on/off a bus/train/plane etc.

gossip × She told me gossips about all her relations.
√ **She told me a lot of gossip about all her relations.**
gossip (uncountable) = talk concerned with people's private lives
Note also: 'bits/pieces of gossip'

As a basic guideline, you are advised to look for information in this dictionary in the same way as in any other dictionary. For example, if you are in doubt about whether to write 'marry someone' or 'marry **with** someone', you should look for the relevant information at the entry for **marry**, not at **with**. Similarly, if you feel uncertain about which is correct–'**in** guarantee' or '**under** guarantee'–you should turn to **guarantee**, not **in** or **under**.

查閱本詞典的基本方法一如任何其他詞典。例如, 要知道究竟是用 marry someone 還是 marry **with** someone 時, 應查詞條 **marry** 不查 with。同樣, 如果沒有把握該用 **in** guarantee 還是 **under** guarantee, 應查 guarantee, 不查 **in** 也不查 **under**, 如下例:

guarantee 2 × May I remind you that the cassette recorder is still in guarantee.
√ **May I remind you that the cassette recorder is still under guarantee.**
(be) under guarantee, NOT **in**

In each of these cases, the entry is located at the keyword. This is the most important word in a group of words which regularly occur together. Therefore the entry for **in spite of** is to be found at **spite**, the entry for **of/on your own accord** at **accord**, and the entry for **do/make a mistake** at **mistake**.

從上述兩例來看, 詞條選自詞語中最重要的組成部分, 即基本詞。因此, 要查 **in spite of** 須找詞條 **spite,** 要找 **of/on your own accord** 須查 **accord,** 要查 **do/make a mistake** 須找 **mistake,** 如下例:

mistake 2 × I rarely do more than three mistakes in an essay.
✓ **I rarely make more than three mistakes in an essay.**
make a mistake, NOT **do**

On the other hand, if you want to know what is wrong with 'I went **out** the room' or '**at** 1984', you should turn to **out** (not **go** or **room**) or **at** (not **1984**). In these cases, there is no fixed group of words and there is therefore no keyword. Again, the user should follow standard dictionary practice.

另一方面, 如果要知道 I went **out** the room 或 **at** 1984 錯在什麼地方, 那就應查 **out** 和 **at,** 不查 **go** 和 **room,** 也不查 **1984**, 因為這兩例中沒有固定的詞組, 也就沒有基本詞。再說一遍, 讀者應參照一般詞典慣例, 如下例:

out 2 × I felt very cold when I went out the room.
✓ **I felt very cold when I went out of the room.**
Out is an adverb. 'Alan went out, leaving just the two of us in the room.'
Out of is a preposition.
Note that in informal conversation, **out** is sometimes used instead of **out of**: 'I saw someone jump out the window.'

Examining an entry

An entry usually has three parts. As an example, look at the entry for **noise.** The first part is a sentence containing the error. It is printed in ordinary type and has a cross (×) next to it. Beneath this, in heavy type and marked with a tick (✓), is the correct sentence. In many cases, the user will see the mistake when he or she compares the two sentences but there is also a brief explanation at the end of the entry. As already mentioned, this has been kept as short as possible and concentrates on the particular problem underlying the error.

如何查看詞條

詞條通常有三個部分, 以 **noise** 這一詞條為例, 第一部分是錯句, 用正常字體印刷, 句前打上 × 號。錯句下面是正句, 用粗體印刷, 前面是 ✓ 號。在許多情況下, 讀者看了兩句就會知道錯誤所在。儘管如此, 詞條末尾還有個簡短的解釋。如前所述, 解釋力求簡短扼要, 針對錯誤根源, 如下例:

noise	× I turned on the radio but there was no noise. √ **I turned on the radio but there was no sound.** **noise** = loud unpleasant sounds: 'The noise of the traffic gave me a headache.' **sound** = something noticed by the ear: 'the sound of a guitar', 'the sound of a car engine'

Sub-entries

Sometimes a single word or phrase can produce two or more types of error. In these cases, the entry will be divided into several sub-entries, each dealing with a particular error, and having its own number.

Grammatical errors generally come before errors involving usage or meaning, and errors which are very common are usually placed before those which occur less frequently.

分詞條

有時候一個詞或一個片語可能產生兩種或兩種以上的錯誤。遇到這類情況，詞條分成幾個分詞條，每個分詞條涉及一種錯誤，有獨立的編號。一般來說，文法錯誤安排在用法錯誤或意思錯誤之前，常犯錯誤通常放在不常犯錯誤之前，如下例:

no matter	**1**	× No matter he tries hard, he never succeeds in passing. √ **No matter how hard he tries, he never succeeds in passing.** **no matter how** much he studies/often he goes/well he plays etc. + main clause
	2	× No matter the recession, sales remained high. √ **In spite of the recession, sales remained high.** **No matter** is ALWAYS followed by a **wh-** word: 'No matter what they did, they couldn't put the fire out.'

When a sub-entry consists of a cross-reference, this always come last.

分詞條所包括的互見條目總是放在最後，如下例:

according to	**1**	× According to me, we should spend more money on education. √ **In my opinion, we should spend more money on education.** **According to** cannot be followed by **me** or **us**
	2	See OPINION

When a cross-reference is made to a particular sub-entry, the number of the sub-entry is shown.

互見條目涉及某一分詞條時, 均標明分詞條編號。

invitation See AGREE 5

However, when the cross-reference is to both or all of the sub-entries at a headword, then no number is given.

然而, 互見條目涉及詞目詞的兩個或全部分詞條時, 則不再標明編號。

evening See AFTERNOON

Cross-references

You will find a number of cross-references in the dictionary. The purpose of these cross-references is simply to help you find the information you are looking for. For example, in the case of **do/make a mistake**, if you turn to **do** instead of **mistake**, you will find a cross-reference to **mistake**. Similarly, if you want to know what is wrong with **reach an aim** and look under **reach**, you will be directed to the entry at **aim**.

互見條目

詞典裡有一些互見條目, 旨在幫助讀者查到所要找的解答。例如, 遇到 **do/make a mistake** 這種情況時, 如果你先查的是 **do**, 詞典就會告訴你參見 **mistake**。同樣, 要是你想知道 **reach an aim** 錯在哪裡而去查了 **reach,** 詞典就會指示你去查 **aim** 詞條。

reach 2 See AIM 2

Cross-references also help to avoid a lot of repetition in the dictionary. For example, when a small group of words such as **dozen/hundred/thousand/million** or **spring/summer/autumn/winter** follow the same rule or pattern, this is explained just once–at **hundred** and **summer**. If you look up one of the other words in the group, you will find a cross-reference to the entry where the explanation is given.

互見條目也有助於避免詞典中的內容重複。例如, 遇到 **dozen/hundred/thousand/million** 或者 **spring/summer/autumn/winter** 這類用法和句型都相同的詞, 只在 **hundred** 和 **summer** 詞條下加以解釋, 要是查到其餘幾個詞時, 就要參見有解釋的那個詞條。

dozen See HUNDRED 2

Cross-references are also used in entries dealing with British English and American English usage. The way in which this is treated in the dictionary is described below.

互見條目也用於涉及英式英語和美式英語用法的詞條。有關這方面的處理方法說明如下:

British and American differences

Whereas speakers of British English say **aerial**, speakers of American English say **antenna**. Pairs of this type have been included in the dictionary, not because either usage is wrong or substandard but simply in order to draw attention to the differences between the two language varieties. Some students are unaware of these differences and make the stylistic mistake of switching from one variety to the other within the same piece of written work.

英美用法上的差異

講英式英語的人說 **aerial**, 講美式英語的人則說 **antenna**。本詞典之所以將這兩詞都收, 並不是因為其中有一個詞的用法錯誤, 也不是因為不合乎標準, 純粹是為了要讀者注意這兩種語體的差異。有些學生不注意這種差異, 在同一篇文字裏混用兩種語體, 犯了寫作上的文體錯誤。

In these cases, the entry is placed at the American English variant, while a cross-reference is given at the British English word. Unlike the other entries in the dictionary, no mistake is involved. Both variants are simply shown one above the other with the labels ***AmE*** and ***BrE.***

涉及英美不同用法時, 詞條按美式英語變體編排, 而詞條下互見條目的詞則是英式英語用法。與其他詞條不同的是, 這類詞條不涉及錯誤問題, 詞條下面的兩種變體一前一後, 分別標上 AmE (美式英語) 和 BrE (英式英語)。

Glossary

If an explanatory note contains a technical word which you do not understand, you should refer to the glossary of technical terms at the back of the book. It should be remembered, however, that the glossary is not intended to be comprehensive. It aims to provide sufficient information for the user to understand the notes, and no more.

術語詞彙表

如果注釋中有你不懂的術語, 可查閱書末的詞彙表。然而, 應該指出, 詞彙表無意收入全部術語, 事實上讀者已可從中理解注釋的內容。

Use by the teacher

Although designed primarily for the needs of the learner, the ***Longman Dictionary of Common Errors*** can also be used by the teacher of English in a number of ways. Some of these are outlined below.

教師如何使用本詞典

本詞典主要是為滿足學生的需要而編，但也可為英語教師提供多方面的用途，試舉例如下。

– While students are engaged in writing tasks, the teacher might walk round the classroom, briefly checking the work in progress. Instead of correcting the errors observed and explaining the reasons for their correction, the teacher could simply call students' attention to the appropriate entries in the dictionary. In this way the students become actively involved in discovering and correcting their errors themselves.
— 學生在課堂上寫作時，教師可以巡視，但不必看到錯誤就加以改正並給予解釋，而只需告訴學生參考本詞典的有關詞條，就能使學生主動地去發現和改正錯誤。

– The same technique could be used when dealing with errors after written work has been handed in. Instead of writing lengthy corrections and comments on the scripts, the teacher could simply underline the error, adding a brief reference to the appropriate dictionary entry.
— 對於學生交來的書面作業上的錯誤，也可採用同樣的方法。教師不必在學生的作業上註寫冗長的批改，而只需在錯誤底下畫線，另外再加上參見本詞典中的有關條目。

– After marking a batch of written work, the teacher might wish to select certain common errors as a focus for remedial teaching. The dictionary provides easy access to clear and concise notes which can serve as a basis for such teaching.
— 教師在批改一批書面習作後，可以選擇某些常犯錯誤作為集中的輔導教學。本詞典提供的解釋不僅查閱方便，而且簡單明瞭，有助於進行這類教學。

– Familiarity with the dictionary will also enable the teacher to predict the types of error that students are likely to make when introduced to a new grammatical or lexical item. Such awareness will be of considerable help in the preparation of effective teaching materials.
— 教師如果熟悉本詞典的內容，在向學生講授文法或詞彙上新的項目時，能夠預知學生可能要犯的錯誤，從而大大有助於準備有效的教學材料。

a **1** × I hope you all have a enjoyable stay.
√ **I hope you all have an enjoyable stay.**
(逗留期間, 我希望你們都過得愉快。)

> Always use **an** (NOT **a**) before a word beginning with a vowel sound (在元音開始的詞之前, 總是用 **an** 而不用 **a**, 例如): 'an egg', 'an envelope'.

2 × My husband is doing a MSc in civil engineering.
√ **My husband is doing an MSc in civil engineering.**
(我丈夫正在攻讀土木工程的碩士學位。)

> Use **an** (NOT **a**) before an abbreviation that begins with a vowel sound (在元音開始的縮寫詞之前用 **an** 而不用 **a**, 例如): 'an MSc' /ɛm ɛs si/, 'an MP' /ɛm pi/.

3 × Sometimes it is difficult to live a honest life.
√ **Sometimes it is difficult to live an honest life.**
(有時候要老老實實的做人也並不容易。)

> Use **an** (NOT **a**) before words beginning with **h** when the **h** is not pronounced (在不發音的 **h** 開始的詞之前用 **an** 而不用 **a**, 例如): 'an honour', 'an hour'.

4 × A bottle of milk is in the fridge.
√ **There is a bottle of milk in the fridge.**
(冰箱裏有一瓶牛奶。)
× A party will be at the language school.
√ **There will be a party at the language school.**
(語言學校將舉行一次歡聚。)

> In many sentences, the verb **be** is used to mean 'exist' or 'take place'. If the subject has not been mentioned before, it is placed immediately after the verb and the sentence begins with **there.**
> 在許多句子裏, 動詞 **be** 用來表示 exist (存在) 或 take place (舉行; 發生) 的意思。如上文未提及主語, 那麼主語應接在動詞 be 之後, 句子用 **there** 開始。

a lot of See (見) LOTS

about × I was about leaving when the telephone rang.
√ **I was about to leave when the telephone rang.**
(我正要出去, 電話鈴突然響了。)

be about+to-v
be about 後面接帶 to 的動詞。

above × There were above a hundred people in the crowd.
√ **There were over a hundred people in the crowd.**
(這人群有一百多人。)

Do not use **above** with numbers (unless referring to points on a scale) (一般不用 **above** 修飾數字, 例如): 'He is over eighty years of age,' 'I receive over twenty letters a day,' BUT (但在刻度上則可與數字連用, 例如): 'Don't let the temperature get above thirty degrees.'

above-mentioned × I would be grateful if you would send it to the address above-mentioned.
√ **I would be grateful if you would send it to the above-mentioned address.**
(如果你把東西送到上述地址, 我將不勝感謝。)

Above-mentioned ALWAYS comes before the noun it modifies (注意: **above-mentioned** 總是放在它所修飾的名詞之前, 例如): 'above-mentioned person', (上述的人) 'above-mentioned company' (上述之公司).

absent 1 × The sales manager was absent at the meeting.
√ **The sales manager was absent from the meeting.**
(銷售經理未出席會議。)

absent from, NOT **at**
absent 後接 **from**, 不接 **at**

2 × I went to her house at four o'clock but she was absent.
√ **I went to her house at four o'clock but she wasn't in.**
(我四點鐘到她家去, 但她不在。)

absent=not present at something that you are supposed to attend (注意: **absent** 指沒有出席理應到場的活動, 例如): 'absent from school'

absolutely See (見) TIRED

accept 1

× These people accept to take risks in order to succeed.

√ **These people accept the need to take risks in order to succeed.**
(為了取得成功, 這些人認為有冒險的必要。)

> **Accept** is NEVER followed by to-v
> **accept** 之後從不接帶 to 的動詞。

2

× The company will not accept to buy new machines.

√ **The company will not agree to buy new machines.**
(該公司不會同意購買新機器。)

> We **accept** a person's advice, opinion, or suggestion BUT **agree** to do something. Compare (按 **accept** 後接某人的 advice—忠告, opinion—意見或 suggestion—建議, 而 **agree** 後接 to do something, 試比較): 'I accepted her suggestion and agreed to see the doctor that evening.'

3

× To tell you the truth, I can't accept people who think about money all the time.

√ **To tell you the truth, I can't stand/bear/abide people who think about money all the time.**
(說老實話, 我受不了那些老是盤算着錢的人。)

> **cannot stand/bear/abide** = cannot tolerate (指"無法容忍"、"受不了")

accommodation

√ **AmE Accommodations in London are very expensive.**
(美式英語: 倫敦的住宿很貴。)

√ **BrE Accommodation in London is very expensive.**
(英式英語: 譯文同上)

> In British English **accommodation** (= a place to live or spend the night) is ALWAYS uncountable. In American English it can be countable.
> **accommodation** 一詞在英式英語中作"供住宿的地方"解時總是不可數名詞, 而在美式英語中則是可數名詞。

accord

× People think he resigned on his own accord.

√ **People think he resigned of his own accord.**
(人們認為他是自願辭職的。)

of your own accord, NOT **on**
of your own accord 中的 **of** 不可用 **on** 替代。

according to 1 × According to me, we should spend more money on education.
√ **In my opinion, we should spend more money on education.**
(我的意見是我們應在教育上多花一些錢。)

According to cannot be followed by **me** or **us**.
中文 "按照我(們)的意見" 不能用 **according to me (us)** 來表達, 換句話說, **according to** 不能後接 **me** 或 **us**。

2 See (見) OPINION

accuse × Some unemployed men accuse women for taking their jobs.
√ **Some unemployed men accuse women of taking their jobs.**
(有些失業的男子責怪婦女搶去了他們的工作。)

accuse someone **of** something, NOT **for**
accuse someone **of** something 中的 **of** 不可用 **for** 替代。

accustomed 1 × Having lived in England for two years, I am now accustomed myself to the cold weather.
√ **Having lived in England for two years, I am now accustomed to the cold weather.**
(我在英國住了兩年, 對寒冷的天氣已經習慣。)

be/grow accustomed to something OR **accustom** oneself **to** something
中文 "習慣於" 可用 **be/grow accustomed to** (something) 或用 **accustom** oneself **to** (something) 來表達
Compare (比較) 'He soon grew accustomed to the harsh working conditions.' 'He soon accustomed himself to the harsh working conditions.'
Note the more informal alternative (注意口語體的用法): 'He soon got used to the harsh working conditions.'

2 × It took me six months to get accustomed with the climate.
√ **It took me six months to get accustomed to the climate.**
(我過了六個月才適應這裏的氣候。)

> **get accustomed to** something, NOT **with**
> **get accustomed to** 中的 **to** 不可用 **with** 替代。

3 × Where I come from, we are not accustomed to see so many things in the shops.
√ **Where I come from, we are not accustomed to seeing so many things in the shops.**
(在我的家鄉, 我們從來沒有見過像這裏商店賣的那許多東西。)

> **be accustomed to** + v-ing
> **be accustomed to** 後接帶 "-ing" 的動詞。

actual × We'd like to know more about the actual crisis, not the economic problems of the past.
√ **We'd like to know more about the present/current crisis, not the economic problems of the past.**
(我們想更多地了解當前的危機, 而不是過去的經濟問題。)

> **actual** = real (as opposed to 'guessed', 'supposed', etc.) (注意 **actual** 相當於 real, 意義和 guessed [猜測的], supposed [假設的] 相反, 例如): 'People think he is over fifty but his actual age is forty-eight.' (人們都以為他五十多歲, 可是他的實際年齡是四十八。)
> **present/current** = happening or existing now (指目前正在發生的或現有的)

admire × How I admire you; I wish I could make my hair curl like that.
√ **How I envy you; I wish I could make my hair curl like that.**
(真羡慕你! 我多希望能有那麼一頭鬈髮!)

> **admire** = to think of or look at with pleasure and respect (意為 "欽佩", "佩服", 例如): 'You may not like him, but you've got to admire his persistence.'
> **envy** = to wish you had the same things or qualities of another person (意為 "羡慕")

advice **1** × I adviced him to tell the police.
√ **I advised him to tell the police.**
(我勸他去報告警方。)

> **Advice** /əd'vaɪs/ is a noun.
> **advice** 是名詞。
> **Advise** /əd'vaɪz/ is a verb.
> **advise** 是動詞。

2 × She gave me a good advice.
√ **She gave me some good advice.**
(她給我出了好主意。)

> **Advice** is an uncountable noun.
> **advice** 是不可數名詞, 前面不能用不定冠詞 "a".
> Note the alternative (注意: 也可以說): 'She gave me a good piece of advice.'

advise × I asked my lawyer for her advise.
√ **I asked my lawyer for her advice.**
(我向我的律師徵詢意見。)

> **Advise** is a verb.
> **advise** 是動詞。
> **Advice** is a noun.
> **advice** 是名詞。

aerial See (見) ANTENNA

affect × It's a magazine about computers and their affects on our lives.
√ **It's a magazine about computers and their effects on our lives.**
(這是一本有關電腦的雜誌, 其中也探討電腦對我們生活的影響。)

> **Affect** (WITH **aff**) is a verb. To **affect** something is to have an **effect** on it (注意 **affect** 是動詞。To **affect** something 相當於 to have an effect on it, 例如): 'Smoking affects your health.' (吸煙影響健康。) (=Smoking has an effect on your health. ——吸煙對健康有影響。)

afford 1 × A newspaper can be afforded by most people.
√ **Most people can afford a newspaper.**
(大多數人買得起報紙。)

> **Afford** is rarely used in the passive.
> **afford** 很少用被動語態。

2 × My father couldn't afford paying for my education.
√ **My father couldn't afford to pay for my education.**
(我父親無力負擔我的教育費用。)

> **afford (to do)** something.
> **afford** 後接 (**to do**) something。

3 × My father couldn't afford himself to lend me any money.
√ **My father couldn't afford to lend me any money.**
(我父親無力借錢給我。)

> **Afford** is NOT a reflexive verb.
> **afford** 不是反身動詞, 不能説 afford oneself.

4 × I want to get my coat back because I can't afford the money for a new one.
√ **I want to get my coat back because I can't afford (to buy) a new one.**
(我要取回我的上衣, 因為我無錢買新的。)

> **Money** is rarely used as an object of **afford.**
> **money** 很少用作 **afford** 的受詞。

afraid × The road to the airport was very busy and we were afraid to miss the plane.
√ **The road to the airport was very busy and we were afraid of missing the plane.**
(通往機場的那條路交通擁擠, 我們擔心趕不上飛機。)

> **be afraid to do** something = be unwilling to do something because you are frightened (指因害怕而不敢做某事, 例如): 'She was afraid to eat it in case it was poisonous.'
> **be afraid of doing** something = be worried or anxious about something which might happen (指擔心或憂慮某事可能發生)

after 1 × The flight had been very pleasant until a man sitting after me started to shout.
√ **The flight had been very pleasant until a man sitting behind me started to shout.**
(起飛後, 旅途一直很舒適, 但後來有個坐在我背後的男子突然大喊大叫起來。)

after = following in time or order (指時間或順序的先後, 例如): 'I'll see you after lunch.' 'Remember to put a full stop after the last word.'
behind = at the back of (指在背後)

2 × After a week we're going to Italy.
√ **In a week's time we're going to Italy.**
(一星期後我們去意大利。)

in a week OR (或) **in a week's time** = after or at the end of a week (指一星期後或在週末)

3 × Most of the people on the bus were after sixty.
√ **Most of the people on the bus were over sixty.**
(公共汽車上大多數人都年過六十。)

The preposition **over** is used with ages (and numbers) to mean 'more than'.
前置詞 **over** 和年紀, 數字連用時作 more than (超過) 解。

4 × I promised to meet George at the exhibition a week after.
√ **I promised to meet George at the exhibition a week later.**
(我答應了一星期後在展覽會上會晤喬治。)

The use of **after** as an adverb (in place of **later**) is very colloquial and is likely to be regarded as non-standard by careful users.
after 作為副詞用來代替 **later** 純屬口語體, 用詞謹慎的人可能認為這樣用不合標準。

5 √ **AmE A police car arrived within minutes and soon after, an ambulance came.**
(美式英語: 一輛警車在幾分鐘內到達, 隨後不久開來了救護車。)

√ **BrE A police car arrived within minutes and soon afterwards, an ambulance came.**
(英式英語: 譯文同上)

> In British English the use of **after** as an adverb (in place of **afterwards**) is common in informal usage but is regarded by careful users as non-standard.
> 在英式英語中, **after** 用作副詞來代替 **afterwards,** 這在口語體的用法中很常見, 但用詞謹慎的人則認為不合標準。

6 × After you will leave, we will write to you every day.
√ **After you leave/have left, we will write to you every day.**
(你走後我們將每天給你寫信。)

> **After** is followed by the present simple tense (or present perfect) for future reference, NOT **shall/will** + verb.
> 在 **after** 引導的子句裏用一般現在式或現在完成式來表示將來, 但不用 **shall/will** + 動詞。

after all × After all, I'd like to thank you all for coming here today.
√ **Finally, I'd like to thank you all for coming here today.**
(最後, 我感謝各位今天的光臨。)

> Use **after all** when (1) you want to introduce an idea which seems to contradict something which has been said before (注意 **after all** 用來指 1. 你要提出的想法看來和前面已說的事情相違反, 例如): 'They had planned to go by train, but they went by car after all.'
> (2) you want to remind someone of a fact which they should consider (2. 你想提醒某人應考慮一件事, 例如): 'I'm not surprised you're tired. After all, you were working all night.'
> **finally** = to conclude (最後)

afternoon 1 × The afternoon I met them at the hotel and we went to the beach.
√ **In the afternoon I met them at the hotel and we went to the beach.**
(下午, 我在旅館跟他們會合, 隨即一起去了海濱。)

in the morning/afternoon/evening
指在早上/下午/晚上, 用 **in the morning/afternoon/evening。**
Compare (比較): 'The next afternoon I met them again.'

2 × On the afternoon we have two hours of classes.
√ **In the afternoon we have two hours of classes.**
(我們下午上兩小時課。)

When talking about a particular afternoon, use **on.**
When speaking generally, use **in**: **on the afternon/ morning/evening of** 3rd July BUT **in the morning/afternoon/evening.**
on 用來指一個特定的下午 (早上/晚上), 例如: **on the afternoon(morning/evening) of** 3rd July; **in** 用來泛指, 例如: **in the morning/afternoon/evening.**

age × I met a group of youngsters at my age in Trafalgar Square.
√ **I met a group of youngsters (of) my own age in Trafalgar Square.**
(我在特拉法加廣場遇見一群和我同齡的年青人。)

(of) my own age, NOT **at**
與我同齡是 **of my own age**, 不是 **at my age**。
(編譯者按: at one's age 作 "在我這個年紀" 解。如 'At my age, driving a car is difficult.'——以我的年紀來說, 駕駛汽車很困難。)

agenda × In the left-hand pocket you will find a little red agenda that I need urgently.
√ **In the left-hand pocket you will find a little red diary that I need urgently.**
(在左手口袋裏, 你會找到一本我急需的紅色小記事簿。)

agenda = a list of topics for discussion at a meeting (指會議上討論的一系列議題)
diary = a book in which a person writes appointments or things to be remembered (指用來記下約會或其他事項的日記簿。)

ages × The glasses haven't been washed since ages.
√ **The glasses haven't been washed for ages.**
(這副眼鏡很久很久沒有清洗了。)

See (見) SINCE 2

ago 1 × It is a month ago since I left Germany.
√ **It is a month since I left Germany.**
√ **I left Germany a month ago.**
(我離開德國已有一個月了。)

> Do not use **ago** before **since.**
> 在 **since** 之前不用 **ago**。

2 × I'm writing in reply to your letter that I've received two days ago.
√ **I'm writing in reply to your letter that I received two days ago.**
(我現在寫信回覆你兩天前的來函。)

> The present perfect tense is NOT used with words showing past time such as **yesterday, last week, a year ago.**
> 諸如 **yesterday**、**last week**、**a year ago** 之類表示過去時間的詞, 不用現在完成式。

3 × The inspector asked to see his ticket, as I had done a few minutes ago.
√ **The inspector asked to see his ticket, as I had done a few minutes before.**
(查票員要求看他的票, 而我幾分鐘之前也問過他要看他的票。)

> **Ago** is used to indicate a period in the past that is measured from the present moment.
> **ago** 用以指從現在算起的一段過去了的時間。
> **Before** is used to indicate an earlier period that is measured from a point in the past.
> **before** 用以指從過去某一點算起的一段更早的時間。
> **a few minutes ago** = before now (比現在早)
> **a few minutes before** = before then (比過去某一時間更早)

4 × The accident happened at ten years ago.
√ **The accident happened ten years ago.**
(這事故發生在十年前。)

> Do not use **at** to introduce a time expression with **ago.**
> 用 **ago** 表示時間的詞 (如上句的 "十年"), 不與 **at** 連用。

agree 1 × Unfortunately not many people agreed helping us.
√ **Unfortunately not many people agreed to help us.**
(可惜沒有多少人肯幫我們。)

> **agree** + to-v
> **agree** 後接帶 to 的動詞

2 × I don't agree the people who say women should stay at home.
√ **I don't agree with people who say women should stay at home.**
(有些人說婦女應待在家裏, 我不同意他們的意見。)

> **agree with** someone or something = have the same opinion as
> **agree** 一詞作 "同意" 解, 但如說同意某人的意見或同意某事, 應用 **agree with**。

3 × In many ways I agree to his statement.
√ **In many ways I agree with his statement.**
(我在許多方面同意他的主張。)

> **agree with** = have the same opinion as (持有相同的意見, 例如): 'I fully agree with you/your opinion.'
> **agree to** = be willing to accept or allow something (願意接受某事或允許某事發生): 'The bank manager has agreed to our request for a loan.'

4 × In some ways I am agree with those who want stricter punishments.
√ **In some ways I agree with those who want stricter punishments.**
(我在某些方面同意那些主張從嚴懲處的人的意見。)

> **Agree** is a verb, NOT an adjective.
> **agree** 是動詞, 不是形容詞, 前面不能加動詞 be。

5 × Although I didn't really like him, I agreed his invitation.
√ **Although I didn't really like him, I accepted his invitation.**
(說真的, 我不太喜歡他, 但還是接受了他的邀請。)

> **accept** an invitation, NOT **agree**
> 接受邀請, 不説 **agree** an invitation, 應把 **agree** 改為 **accept**。

agreed × We were both agreed with him.
√ **We both agreed with him.**
(我們兩人都同意他的意見。)

> **Agreed** cannot be used as an adjective when it is followed by **with.** Compare (注意 **agreed** 後接 **with** 時, 不能用作形容詞, 試比較): 'When it comes to the question of finance, we are all agreed.' (=have the same opinion 意見相同)

aid × Many more will die unless there is an increase in foreign aids.
√ **Many more will die unless there is an increase in foreign aid.**
(要是不增加外國援助, 更多的人就會死亡。)

> **Aid** (=support or help) is an uncountable noun.
> **aid** 作 support (支持) 或 help (幫助)解時是不可數名詞。

aim 1 × I started to learn English with the aim to become a teacher.
√ **I started to learn English with the aim of becoming a teacher.**
(我開始學習英語的目的是要當教師。)

> **with the aim of**+v-ing
> **with the aim of** 後接帶 "-ing" 的動詞
> Note however (然而請注意): 'My aim is to become a teacher.'

2 × Everybody should be given the chance to reach their aims.
√ **Everybody should be given the chance to achieve their aims.**
(人人都應有機會達到自己的目標。)

> **achieve an aim,** NOT **reach**
> **achieve an aim** 中的 **achieve** 不可用 **reach** 替代。

alive 1 × Every alive creature in the sea is affected by pollution.
√ **Every living creature in the sea is affected by pollution.**
(海裏的生物全都受到污染。)

> **Alive** is a predicative adjective which usually comes after the verb, e.g. (注意: **alive** 是個敍述形容詞, 這類形容詞往往放在動詞後面, 例如): "The three fish in the bottle were still alive."
> **Living** is an attributive adjective which always comes before a noun it modifies, e.g. (注意: **living** 是個修飾形容詞, 總是放在所修飾的名詞之前, 例如): "living relatives" (仍然在世的親屬)

2 × Our teacher, Mr Collins, is very alive.
√ **Our teacher, Mr Collins, is very lively.**
(我們的老師柯林斯先生很活躍。)

> **alive** = not dead (rarely modified)
> **alive** 意為未死, 很少受副詞之類的詞所修飾
> **lively** = full of energy and action
> **lively** 的意思是富有生氣和活力

all 1 × I like all the kinds of music.
√ **I like all kinds of music.**
(我喜歡各種音樂。)

> Do not use **the** after **all** when the reference is general. Compare (泛指時不要在 **all** 後面用 **the**, 試比較): 'I like all kinds of fruit.' (general reference 泛指) 'I like all the kinds of fruit that my wife likes.' (specific reference 特指)

2 × We all were delighted when we heard the news.
√ **We were all delighted when we heard the news.**
(我們聽到這消息都很高興。)
× We all must try to find a solution to the problem.
√ **We must all try to find a solution to the problem.**
(我們必須同心協力找出解決問題的辦法。)

> **All** ususlly goes immediately after the (first) auxiliary verb (注意: **all** 通常緊接在 [第一個] 助動詞之後, 例如):

'You should all pass the exam if you work hard.' 'They have all been working hard.' When there is no auxiliary verb, **all** is placed immediately before the main verb (句中不用助動詞時, **all** 緊接在主動詞之前): 'They all passed the exam.' However, when the main verb is **be, all** is placed immediately after it (然而, 如果主動詞是 **be, all** 緊接在 **be** 之後): 'The letters are all on your desk.' (這些信都在你的書桌上。)

3 × All of us didn't want to go to bed.
√ **None of us wanted to go to bed.**
(我們誰也不想睡覺。)

Use **none of** with an affirmative verb, NOT **all of** with a negative verb.
none of 之後用肯定式動詞, **all of** 之後不用否定式動詞。

4 × I was alone in the house as all my parents were at work.
√ **I was alone in the house as both my parents were at work.**
(由於我父母都去了工作, 我一個人在家。)

All is used for three or more people or things.
all 用於三個或三個以上的人或物。
Both is used for two people or things.
both 用於兩個人或物。

5 × If you sit down and listen, I will explain all the situation.
√ **If you sit down and listen, I will explain the whole situation.**
(如果你們坐下來聽, 我會把整個情況說清楚。)
× He spent all the journey talking about accidents.
√ **He spent the whole/entire journey talking about accidents.**
(他一路上都在談論各種事故。)

All is rarely used with the singular form of a countable noun. Compare (**all** 很少用來修飾可數名詞的單數, 試比較): 'All the walls have been painted green.' (plural 複數) 'The whole wall has been painted green.' (singular 單數)

allow

× It is not allowed to talk in the library.
√ **People are not allowed to talk in the library.**
√ **Talking in the library is not allowed.**
(圖書館裏不准談話。)

> **It** is NOT used as a preparatory subject before **allow**.
> 在 **allow** 前面, 不用 "**it**" 作為句子的形式主語。換句話說, 表達 "不准" 這個意思, 不用 "It is not allowed" 這種句型。

all right

× The man was covered in blood but the woman was allright.
√ **The man was covered in blood but the woman was all right.**
(那男的渾身是血, 女的情況尚好。)
× I hope you are feeling alright now.
√ **I hope you are feeling all right now.**
(我希望你現在感到身體好了。)

> **Allright** (one word) does not exist. Note that, although it is widely used, **alright** (one **l**) is considered non-standard by careful users of British English.
> **allright** (作為一個詞) 的寫法是錯誤的。請注意: **alright** (一個 **l**) 的寫法雖然很常見, 但使用英式英語較謹慎的人認為不合標準。

almost

× The suitcase almost was too heavy to lift.
√ **The suitcase was almost too heavy to lift.**
(手提箱重得幾乎提不起來。)

> When there is no auxiliary verb, **almost** is placed immediately before the main verb (句中沒有助動詞時, **almost** 緊接在主動詞之前, 例如): 'She almost fell over.' However, when the main verb is **be, almost** is placed immediately after it (然而, 如果主動詞是 **be, almost** 則緊接在 **be** 之後, 例如): 'He is almost blind' Otherwise **almost** goes immediately after the (first) auxiliary verb (在其他場合, **almost** 總是緊接在第一個助動詞之後, 例如): 'I had almost finished the letter when the telephone rang.'

alone 1

× I think I will buy a dog because sometimes I feel alone.
√ **I think I will buy a dog because sometimes I feel lonely.**
(我想買一條狗, 因為我有時感到孤獨。)

> **alone** = by yourself (not with anyone) (指獨自, 沒跟人在一起, 例如): 'I've thought about getting married, but I prefer living alone.'
> **lonely** = sad because you are alone (指孤獨)

2 × A child learns a lot by doing things alone.
√ **A child learns a lot by doing things on his or her own.**
(孩子靠自己動手做事學到很多東西。)

> **alone** = without other people present (指獨自, 沒有其他人在場)
> **on one's own** = without anyone's help or supervision; independently (指沒有別人的幫助和指導; 獨立地, 例如): 'He built the car all on his own.'

already 1 × I think my English has improved a bit allready.
√ **I think my English has improved a bit already.**
(我認為我的英語已有一點進步。)

> **already** = by now (此刻已經, 例如): 'The plane has already taken off.'
> **all ready** = all prepared (一切準備就緒, 例如): 'The suitcases are all ready to take out to the taxi.'
> **Allready** (one word) does not exist.
> **allready** 作為一個詞是不存在的

2 × Most of the food is cold already when you get it.
√ **Most of the food is already cold when you get it.**
(吃的東西到你手的時候, 大都已經涼了。)

> When there is no auxiliary verb, **already** is usually placed immediately before the main verb (句中沒有助動詞時, **already** 通常緊放在主動詞之前, 例如): 'They already know.' However, when the main verb is **be, already** is usually placed immediately after it (然而 如果主動詞是 **be, already** 通常緊接在 **be** 之後。例如): 'They are already aware of the problem.' Otherwise **already** goes immediately after the (first) auxiliary verb (在其他場合, **already** 緊接在第一個助動詞之後, 例如): 'They have already discussed the various solutions.'

alright See (見) ALL RIGHT

also 1 × Of course, there also are people who steal because they are greedy.
√ **Of course, there are also people who steal because they are greedy.**
(當然也有人因貪婪而偷竊。)
× We also would like to be given more fresh food.
√ **We would also like to be given more fresh food.**
(我們也想得到更多的新鮮食品。)

> **Also** usually goes immediately after the (first) auxiliary verb (注意: **also** 通常緊接在 [第一個] 助動詞之後, 例如): 'I would also like to play squash if I had the time.' When there is no auxiliary verb, **also** is placed immediately before the main verb (如果句中沒有助動詞時, **also** 緊接在主動詞之前, 例如): 'I also play tennis in the summer.' However, when the main verb is **be, also** is placed immediately after it (然而, 如果主動詞是 **be, also** 緊接在 **be** 之後, 例如): 'I am also interested in golf.'

2 × I don't like your climate and I don't like English food also.
√ **I don't like your climate and I don't like English food either.**
(我不喜歡你們那裏的氣候, 也不喜歡英國的食物。)

> In a negative clause use **either**, NOT **also**.
> 在否定句裏用 **either**, 不用 **also**.

alternate √ **AmE We decided to make alternate arrangements in case the hotel was fully booked.**
√ **BrE We decided to make alternative arrangements in case the hotel was fully booked.**
(我們決定作出另外的安排以防旅館客房已經訂滿。)

> **alternate** = (1) happening in turn, first one then the other (先是這事, 後是那事輪流發生, 例如): 'alternate periods of sun and rain' (2) every second (day, week, etc. 每隔一秒、一天、一週等, 例如): 'Our local football team plays at home on alternate Saturdays.'
> **alternative** = (of two or more things) that may be used, had, done, etc., instead of another; other (指在兩個或兩個以上的事物中, 可用一個代替另一個; 其他的)
> Note that in American English **alternate** can also be used with the same meaning as **alternative.** (但在美式英語中, alternate 可作 alternative 那樣使用, 意思相同。)

alternatively × In Sweden many wives and husbands stay at home alternatively to look after their children.

√ **In Sweden many wives and husbands stay at home alternately to look after their children.**
(在瑞典不少夫婦輪流待在家裏照顧孩子。)

> **alternatively** = another possibility is (指另一種可能性, 例如): 'I thought we'd stay at home. Alternatively, you might like to go for a walk.' (我想我們可以留在家裏, 要不然, 也許你願意出去散散步。)
> **alternately** = in turns, first one then the other (輪流地, 先是這個, 後是那個)

although **1** × Although I was frightened, but I couldn't scream.

√ **Although I was frightened, I couldn't scream.**
(雖然我很害怕, 但是我當時無法喊出來。)

> When the subordinate clause begins with **although,** the main clause does not usually begin with **but** or **yet.**
> 子句以 **although** 開始時, 主句通常不以 **but**, 也不以 **yet** 開始。

2 × Although the problem with the car, we enjoyed the journey very much.

√ **In spite of/Despite the problem with the car, we enjoyed the journey very much.**
(儘管汽車有些毛病, 我們旅途上還是玩得很愉快。)

> **In spite of/Despite** are prepositions and are usually followed by a noun or noun phrase. **Although** is a conjunction and must therefore be followed by a clause. Note the alternative (**in spite of** 和 **despite** 是前置詞, 通常後接名詞或名詞片語。**although** 是連接詞, 引導一個子句。注意: 上面可以另一種方式表達, 例如): 'Although we had a problem with the car, we enjoyed the journey very much.'

3 × Even although he couldn't swim, he jumped straight into the water.

√ **Even though he couldn't swim, he jumped straight into the water.**
(即使他不會游泳, 他也逕直跳入水中。)

When **even** is used like this to give emphasis, it is followed by **though,** NOT **although.**
even 這種用法是為了加強語氣, 後接 **though**, 不接 **although**。

altogether × He put the knives altogether in the middle of the table.
√ **He put the knives all together in the middle of the table.**
(他把這些小刀全都放在桌子中央。)

altogether = completely or thoroughly (完全地或徹底地, 例如): 'I'm not altogether sure what to do.'
all together = together in a group (全部、總共、在一起)

always **1** × I have always the feeling that she enjoys teaching us.
√ **I always have the feeling that she enjoys teaching us.**
(我總覺得她喜歡當我們的老師。)

When there is no auxiliary verb, **always** is placed immediately before the main verb (句中如沒有助動詞, **always** 應放在主動詞之前, 例如): 'She always arrives late.' (她老是遲到。) However, when the main verb is **be, always** is placed immediately after it (如主動詞是 **be,** 則 **always** 應放在 **be** 之後, 例如): 'He is always in a bad mood.' (他的情緒總是不好。) Otherwise **always** goes immediately after the (first) auxiliary verb (在其他情況下, **always** 緊接在 [第一個] 助動詞之後, 例如): 'You should always take care when crossing the road.' (什麼時候過馬路都要小心。)

2 × He is the most boring man I've always known.
√ **He is the most boring man I've ever known.**
(在我認識的人當中, 他最令人煩悶的了。)

always = all the time; at all times; every time (總是, 始終, 時時, 無論何時, 例如): 'Have you always lived in London?' 'Whenever I start singing, she always laughs.'
ever = at any time (無論何時, 隨時, 曾經, 例如): 'Have you ever been to Paris?'

3 × While he was writing the letter, he always scratched his chin.
√ **While he was writing the letter, he kept scratching his chin.**
(他一邊寫信, 一邊不停地搔下巴。)

> **always** = (1) at all times; all the time (一直, 始終, 時時): 'She always has a lot of work to do.'
> (2) every time (每次): 'Why do you always ask the same questions?'
> **keep** + v-ing = do something repeatedly
> **keep** 一詞如後接 "-ing" 形式結尾的動詞(如上句 kept scratching), 則此片語帶 "不斷地做下去" 的意思。

a.m. See (見) O'CLOCK 3

amount 1 × The amount of accidents is steadily increasing.
√ **The number of accidents is steadily increasing.**
(事故的次數不斷增加。)

> **amount** is used with uncountable nouns, e.g., an amount of money. With most plurals it is better to use **number.**
> **amount** 一般與不可數名詞連用, 例如 an amount of money (money 為不可數名詞, 無複數)。當與大多數的複數名詞連用時, 應以 **number** 代替 amount 為佳。

2 × Large amounts of money is required.
√ **Large amounts of money are required.**
(目前需要大筆大筆的錢。)

> The verb should agree with the subject "amounts", not with "money", which together with "of" is an attributive adjective modifying "amounts".
> **amounts** 是複數名詞, 在本句中是真正的主語, 所以動詞也應用複數的 **are**, 動詞的數不應據不可數名詞的 money 而用 **is**, 因為 money 在本句與 of 連用, 只是修飾 amounts 的一個修飾語, 而非主語。

an × I had never visited an hospital before.
√ **I had never visited a hospital before.**
(我以前從未去過醫院。)

Use **a** (NOT **an**) before a word beginning with **h**, unless the **h** is not pronounce: 'a house', 'a half' BUT 'an hour', 'an honour'.
在以 **h** 開始的詞之前用 **a**, 不用 **an**, 但是不 發音的 **h** 除外, 例如: 'a house' (一幢房子), 'a half' (一半)。但說 'an hour' (一小時), 'an honour' (一種榮譽)。
Note that **an** may also be used before a word beginning with **h** when the syllable it introduces is unstressed (注意: 在以 **h** 開始的詞前, 如果 **h** 構成的音節不重讀, 也可用 **an**, 例如): 'an historical novel'. However, this usage is usually regarded as old-fashioned nowadays. (然而, 這種用法現被視為舊的用法。)

and **1** × The magazine has many and beautiful photographs.
✓ **The magazine has many beautiful photographs.**
(這本雜誌有許多好看的照片。)

many + adjective + noun WITHOUT **and**
在 **many** 和形容詞, 名詞之間不可插入 **and**。

2 × She was carrying a long and green umbrella.
✓ **She was carrying a long green umbrella.**
(她拿着一把長柄的綠色雨傘。)

Two adjectives coming before a noun are not usually separated by **and** unless (1) they are both colours (名詞之前如有兩個形容詞, 則兩個形容詞中間不加 **and**, 除非 1. 兩個形容詞都是顏色詞, 例如): 'a red and green umbrella', (2) they are both materials (2. 這兩個形容詞都是帶物質性的, 例如): 'a gold and silver bracelet', (3) they describe similar or related qualities (3. 這兩形容詞都顯示類似或相關的性質, 例如): 'a cold (and) windy day'.

3 × The problem was that he didn't have any money and clothes.
✓ **The problem was that he didn't have any money or clothes.**
(問題是他既沒有錢也沒有衣服。)

Use **and** when the sentence is affirmative (肯定句中用 **and**, 例如): 'He had a pen and a ruler.' Use **or** when the sentence is negative (否定句中用 **or**, 例如): 'He didn't have a pen or a ruler.' Note, however, the use of **and** when the two items are considered as a single thing (但應注意, 如兩物視為一整體者, 則可用 **and**, 例如): 'He didn't want any fish and chips.'

4 × She said she couldn't remember who she was and where she lived.
√ **She said she couldn't remember who she was or where she lived.**
(她說她記不清她是誰和住在哪裏。)

Use **and** when the sentence is affirmative (肯定句中用 **and**, 例如): 'She smokes and drinks.' Use **or** when the sentence is negative (否定句中用 **or**, 例如): 'She never smokes or drinks.'
Note, however, the use of **and** when the two actions are closely connected or happen at the same time (但應注意, 如兩個動詞的意思緊密相關或其動作同時發生, 則可用 and, 例如): 'She never drinks and drives.'

5 × Rollo Martins was a very good writer and he was not famous.
√ **Rollo Martins was a very good writer but he was not famous.**
(羅洛・馬丁斯是位優秀作家, 只是不甚著名。)

Do not use **and** to link clauses which contain contrasting ideas (不要用 **and** 去連接兩個表示對比含義的子句, 例如): 'He hates her but wants to marry her.' (NOT (不用) **and**) Otherwise (否則): 'He loves her and wants to marry her.' (not (不用) **but**)

announcement × On almost every page there were announcements for cigarettes and tobacco.
√ **On almost every page there were advertisements for cigarettes and tobacco.**
(幾乎每一頁上都有香煙和煙草的廣告。)

announcement = the act of making something known publicly, especially by means of radio, television, or newspapers (指公佈, 尤指通過廣播、電視或報紙宣佈, 例如): 'Following the announcement of her marriage to the Prince of Wales, Lady Diana was pursued by crowds of journalists.'
advertisement = a film, broadcast, newspaper item, poster, etc., designed to persuade the public to buy, use, or hire something (指電影、廣播、報紙上的廣告)

another 1 × Rio has another important sights such as the famous football stadium.
√ **Rio has other important sights such as the famous football stadium.**
(里約熱內盧還有其他許多可觀光的地方, 例如著名的足球場。)

> **another** + singular (**another** 後接單數名詞, 例如): 'another mistake'
> **other** + plural (**other** 則接複數名詞, 例如): 'other mistakes'

2 × My mother loved her old sewing machine, but on her birthday my father bought her another new one.
√ **My mother loved her old sewing machine, but on her birthday my father bought her a new one.**
(我母親喜歡她那台舊縫紉機, 但我父親在她生日那天給她買了一台新的。)

> Compare: 'another new one' (= a second new one: i.e. she now has two new sewing machines)
> 'a new one' (= one new sewing machine)
> 注意: 錯句中用的 another new one 意為 "第二台新縫紉機", 因而全句的意思變成: "母親原來已有一台新縫紉機, 現在又得了另一台新的, 總共有兩台新縫紉機"; 而 "a new one" 只是指 "一台新的" 而已。

answer 1 × They still can't find an answer for this problem.
√ **They still can't find an answer to this problem.**
(他們依然找不到這個問題的答案。)

> **an answer to** a problem or question, NOT **for**
> **an answer to** a problem or question 中的 **to** 不可用 **for** 替代。

2 × I don't think we will ever be able to answer to these questions correctly.
√ **I don't think we will ever be able to answer these questions correctly.**
(我認為我們將永遠無法正確回答這些問題。)
× I'm sorry that I didn't answer to your letter earlier but I've been very busy.
√ **I'm sorry that I didn't answer your letter earlier but I've been very busy.**
(抱歉的是我未能早一點給你回信, 但是我一直很忙。)

answer someone or something WITHOUT **to**
answer 作動詞用直接跟某人或某事物, 不再用 to。

antenna √ **AmE The radio won't work if the antenna is broken.**
(美式英語: 如果天線壞了, 收音機就失靈。)
√ **BrE The radio won't work if the aerial is broken.**
(英式英語: 譯文同上)

Note that in British English **antenna** usually means 'a long, thin, sensitive organ, commonly found in pairs, on the heads of some insects and other animals'.
(注意: 英式英語中, **antenna** 通常解作一些昆蟲、動物頭上的 "觸角")

anxious × We were anxious for knowing whether he had arrived safely.
√ **We were anxious to know whether he had arrived safely.**
(我們急於想知道他是否已安全到達。)

anxious + to-v, NOT + **for** v-ing
anxious 之後用帶 **to** 的動詞, 而不用 **for** 後接帶 "-ing" 的動詞這種結構形式。
Compare (比較): 'Both parents were anxious for/about the child's safety.' (= worried about 擔心)

any × When he asked if he could use the telephone, he was told that the family didn't have any.
√ **When he asked if he could use the telephone, he was told that the family didn't have one.**
(他問能否使用電話, 當時得到的回答是這家沒有電話。)

Do not use **any** as a pronoun for a singular countable noun. Compare (不要用 **any** 作為代詞來代替單數可數名詞。比較): 'He asked for some help but nobody gave him any.' (**help** is an uncountable noun 按: **help** 是不可數名詞) 'She wanted to borrow some books but nobody would lend her any.' (**books** is a plural countable noun 按: **books** 是複數可數名詞) 'I need a new typewriter but I can't afford one.' (**typewriter** is a singular countable noun 按: **typewriter** 是單數可數名詞)

anything See (見) SOMETHING

anywhere See (見) SOMEWHERE

apart from

× Apart of a few minor problems, the trip was a great success.

√ **Apart from a few minor problems, the trip was a great success.**
(除了一些小問題外, 這次旅程非常成功。)

> **apart from,** NOT **of**
> **apart from** 中的 **from** 不可用 **of** 替代。

apartment

√ **AmE I'm renting a small apartment in Paris.**
(美式英語: 我在巴黎租了一套小公寓。)

√ **BrE I'm renting a small flat in Paris.**
(英式英語: 譯文同上)

> **Apartment** is chiefly American English.
> **apartment** 主要用於美式英語。
> **Flat** is more common in British English.
> **flat** 在英式英語中較常見。

apologize **1**

× The waiter was made to apologize my father for being so rude to him.

√ **The waiter was made to apologize to my father for being so rude to him.**
(那侍者因對我父親無禮不得不向他道歉。)

> **apologize to** someone (**for** something)
> **apologize to** 後接某人, **apologize for** 後接某事。

2

× She insisted on apologizing her husband's behaviour.

√ **She insisted on apologizing for her husband's behaviour.**
(她堅持要為她丈夫的行為表示歉意。)

> **apologize to** (someone) **for** (doing) something
> **apologize to** 後接某人, **apologize for** 後接 (做) 某事。

appreciate

× I would really appreciate if you could let me have her address as soon as possible.

√ **I would really appreciate it if you could let me have her address as soon as possible.**

(如果你能盡早把她的地址給我, 將不勝感謝。)

> **appreciate + it + if/when** clause (**appreciate** 後接 **it** 再接由 **if** 或 **when** 引導的子句, 例如): 'We really appreciated it when she offered to help.'

approach

× He approached to my table and took a seat opposite me.

√ **He approached my table and took a seat opposite me.**

(他走近我的桌子, 在我對面坐下。)

> **approach** someone or something WITHOUT **to**
> 作動詞用的 **approach** 如接某人或某事物, 不應用 **to**。

approve

× I personally do not approve to the image of women as housewives.

√ **I personally do not approve of the image of women as housewives.**

(我個人不贊成婦女只能當家庭主婦。)

× Some husbands do not approve the idea of their wives having a job.

√ **Some husbands do not approve of the idea of their wives having a job.**

(有些丈夫不贊成他們的妻子外出工作。)

> **approve of** something = think it is good
> approve of 作 "贊成" 解。錯句沒有用 **of**, 則作 "批准" 解, 如 approve the bill (批准該項法案)。

armchair

× She was sitting on a big armchair.

√ **She was sitting in a big armchair.**

(她坐在一張很大的扶手椅裏。)

> **sit on** a chair BUT **sit in** an armchair
> **sit on** 後接 a chair, 而 **sit in** 則後接 an armchair。

arrival

× At his arrival in Vienna, he was surprised not to find his friend.

√ **On his arrival in Vienna, he was surprised not to find his friend.**

(他到達維也納後想不到未找到他的朋友。)

> **on/upon** someone's arrival, NOT **at**
> **on/upon** someone's arrival 中 **on** 或 **upon** 不可用 **at** 替代。

arrive 1

× She arrived the station just in time to catch the train.
√ **She arrived at the station just in time to catch the train.**
(她剛好及時趕到車站, 乘上火車。)
× We arrived to the hotel in time for dinner.
√ **We arrived at the hotel in time for dinner.**
(我們及時到達旅館吃飯。)

> **arrive at** a building, station, airport, etc.
> **arrive** 是個不及物動詞, 若指到達一些較小的地方, 如 building、station、airport 等後應接 **at**。
> See also (見) HOME

2

× I arrived to London on 21st May.
√ **I arrived in London on 21st May.**
(我在五月二十一日到達倫敦。)
× When he arrived at Vienna, he was told that his aunt had died.
√ **When he arrived in Vienna, he was told that his aunt had died.**
(他到達維也納時, 獲悉他姑母去世了。)

> **arrive in** a country, city, etc.
> 若指到達大的地方, 如 country, city 等, **arrive** 後應接 **in**。

as 1

× It looked very fragile and so I handled it as china.
√ **It looked very fragile and so I handled it like china.**
(這東西看來容易破碎, 所以我把它當作瓷器看待。)
× He started to cry as a hungry baby.
√ **He started to cry like a hungry baby.**
(他開始像餓極了的嬰兒那樣哭喊。)

> When the intended meaning is 'as if he/she/they etc. were', use **like,** NOT **as.**
> 如要表達 "as if he/she/they were" 這層意思, 應用 **like**, 不能用 **as**。

(as) **2** × I prefer eating fresh things as tomatoes and lettuce.
√ **I prefer eating fresh things like tomatoes and lettuce.**
√ **I prefer eating fresh things such as tomatoes and lettuce.**
(我喜歡吃像番茄和西生菜那樣的新鮮蔬菜。)

> Examples of a class or category (e.g. 'fresh things') are introduced by **such as** or **like.**
> 介紹某類東西, 如上句的 "新鮮蔬菜", 用 **such as** 或 **like**。

3 × As I decided to learn English, I didn't know how difficult it would be.
√ **When I decided to learn English, I didn't know how difficult it would be.**
(我在決定學英語時還不知道會有多難。)

> If the verb in the main clause describes a state or condition ('I didn't know'), the subordinate clause describing an action or event ('I decided to learn English') begins with **when,** NOT **as.**
> 如果主句裏的動詞表示狀態或條件 (如 'I didn't know'), 那麼表示行動或事件 (如 'I decided to learn English') 的 子句裏要用 **when**, 不用 **as**。

4 × That night he thought there was nothing better as to be home again.
√ **That night he thought there was nothing better than to be home again.**
(那天晚上他覺得重返自己的家比什麼都幸福。)

> comparative adjective/adverb + **than,** NOT **as**
> 比較級形容詞/副詞之後用 **than**, 不用 **as**。

5 × As I know you are interested in ballet, that's why I decided to write to you about the performance.
√ **As I know you are interested in ballet, I decided to write to you about the performance.**
(因為我知道你對芭蕾舞感興趣, 我才決定寫信告訴你這次的演出情況。)

When the subordinate clause begins with **as,** the main clause cannot begin with **that's why.** Note the alternative (子句用了 **as**, 主句不能再以 **that's why** 開始, 注意另一種說法): 'I know you are interested in ballet, and that's why I decided to write to you about the performance.'

6 × As I can remember, I left the coat in the cupboard in my room.
√ **As far as I can remember, I left the coat in the cupboard in my room.**
(我記得, 我把上衣放在我房間的衣櫃裏。)

as/so far as I (can) remember (就我記憶所及)

7 See (見) THAT 4

ashamed × I always feel ashamed when I have to speak in public.
√ **I always feel embarrassed when I have to speak in public.**
(我不得不在公開場合講話時總是感到很彆扭。)

ashamed = feeling guilt and disgust for yourself (感到羞恥、慚愧, 例如): 'How can you admit to stealing from your own mother without feeling ashamed?'
embarrassed = feeling socially uncomfortable or anxious (在人們面前感到侷促不安)

ask 1 × He asked her a glass of water.
√ **He asked her for a glass of water.**
(他向她要了一杯水。)

ask (someone) **for** something = ask to be given something
指向人要東西, 用 **ask** 某人 **for** 某物, 在"東西"之前要加 **for**

2 × I asked to the man if he knew the way to the airport.
√ **I asked the man if he knew the way to the airport.**
(我問那人是否知道去機場的路。)

> **ask** someone something WITHOUT **to**
> 在表達向某人問某事的意思時, 説 ask someone something, 不可用 **to**。

3 × He asked for watching television.
√ **He asked if he could watch television.**
(他問能否看電視。)

> Use **ask** + **if** clause when reporting a request.
> 表達請求時用 **ask** 再接 **if** 子句。

4 × She asked me what was the time.
√ **She asked me what the time was.**
(她當時問我那是幾點鐘。)

> When the object of the sentence is a **wh-** clause, the subject and the verb in the **wh-** clause do not change places.
> 如果句中的受詞是 who、when、what、where 一類的子句, 子句裏的主語和動詞不互換位置。

as long as **1** × I'll go with you as long as I won't have to sing.
√ **I'll go with you as long as I don't have to sing.**
(只要我不用唱歌, 我跟你一起去。)

> After **as long as** (= if), use the present simple tense for future reference, NOT **shall/will** + verb.
> 在 **as long as** 用作 if 解時, 子句裏不用 **shall/will** 表示將來意思, 而用一般現在式。

2 × He wants me to send him all the newspapers because he doesn't want to miss anything as long as he's out of the country.
√ **He wants me to send him all the newspapers because he doesn't want to miss anything while he's out of the country.**
(他要我把所有的報紙給他寄去, 因為他不在家鄉期間也不願漏掉任何消息。)

> **as long as** = (1) for (NOT during) a length of time (指 "一段時間", 不指 "在此期間," 例如): 'You can stay here as long as you like.' 'You can stay here as long as three weeks but no longer.'
> (2) provided that (作 "只要" 解, 例如): 'You can stay as long as you keep quiet.' (只要你保持安靜你可以留在這裏。)

as soon as

× I'll pay you as soon as I will receive the parcel.
√ **I'll pay you as soon as I receive the parcel.**
(我一收到包裹就付錢給你。)

After **as soon as,** use the present simple tense for future reference, NOT **shall/will** + verb.
在 **as soon as** 引導的子句裏, 用一般現在式表示將來含義, 不用 **shall/will** 再接動詞。

as though

× I felt as though if somebody had kicked me.
√ **I felt as if somebody had kicked me.**
√ **I felt as though somebody had kicked me.**
(我感到好像有人踢我。)

Use **as if** OR **as though.**
用 **as if** 或用 **as though**, 但不用 **as though if**。

astonishment

× The old man shook his head astonishedly.
√ **The old man shook his head in astonishment.**
(那老人驚訝地搖頭。)

Astonishedly does not exist. This meaning is expressed by the phrase **in astonishment.**
英語並沒有 **astonishedly** 這個字, 這層意思應用 **in astonishment** 的片語來表達。

as well

× When he reached her house, he noticed that there were no lights on. He couldn't see her car as well.
√ **When he reached her house, he noticed that there were no lights on. He couldn't see her car either.**
(他到達她家時, 發現屋內沒有燈光, 也看不到她的汽車。)

As well is rarely used in a negative clause.
as well 很少用於否定句。

as well as

× Each week he wrote her three letters, as well as telephoned her.
√ **Each week he wrote her three letters, as well as telephoning her.**
(他每星期除了打電話, 還給她寫三封信。)

clause + **as well as** + v-ing
主句後如用 **as well as**, 則 **as well as** 應接帶 "-ing" 的動詞。

at **1** × It was almost midnight when we landed at France.
√ **It was almost midnight when we landed in France.**
(我們的飛機在法國着陸時幾乎已是半夜。)
× At last I can study English at London.
√ **At last I can study English in London.**
(我終於能在倫敦學習英語。)

> Use **in** (NOT **at**) before the names of countries, regions, cities, and large towns.
> 在表示國家、地區、城市和大城鎮的名字前面用 **in**, 不用 **at**。

2 × In Germany we have a lot of snow at wintertime.
√ **In Germany we have a lot of snow in wintertime.**
(德國到了冬天雪下得很多。)

> Use **in** (NOT **at**) with seasons, months, and years (在表示季節、月和年的詞前面用 **in**, 不用 **at**, 例如): 'in the summertime', 'in February', 'in 1985'.

3 × I bought the tape recorder just a week ago, at 4th December.
√ **I bought the tape recorder just a week ago, on 4th December.**
(我在十二月四日, 即一星期之前買的這個卡式錄音機。)

> Use **on** (NOT **at**) before dates.
> 在日期前面用 **on**, 不用 **at**。

4 × At about one and a half hours later I took the cake out of the oven.
√ **About one and a half hours later I took the cake out of the oven.**
(大約一個半小時以後我從烤箱裏取出蛋糕。)

> 'an hour **before**', 'a week **later**', 'two years **afterwards**' WITHOUT **at**
> 在 'an hour **before**'、'a week **later**'、'two years **afterwards**' 等詞組前, 不用 **at**。

5 See (見) AGO 4

athletic × A lot of athletic reporters write for the magazine.
√ **A lot of athletics reporters write for the magazine.**
(很多體育記者為該雜誌撰稿。)

athletic reporters = reporters who are good at running, jumping, etc. (指擅長賽跑、跳高等的記者)
athletics reporters = reporters who write about athletics (指報導體育運動的記者)

attention 1 × I told him that I wanted to read, but he didn't pay any attention at me.
√ **I told him that I wanted to read, but he didn't pay any attention to me.**
(我告訴他我要看書, 但他不予理睬。)

pay attention to a person or thing, NOT **at**
pay attention to a person or thing 中的 **to** 不可用 **at** 替代。

2 × 'You won't know what to do if you don't give attention,' she said.
√ **'You won't know what to do if you don't pay attention,' she said.**
("你如果不注意, 就不知道怎麼做," 她說。)

pay attention to someone or something OR (或說) **give** someone **your attention**
Compare (比較): 'I'd like you to give me your full attention.'

3 × The driver of the car was very young and I paid attention that he was drunk.
√ **The driver of the car was very young and I noticed that he was drunk.**
(汽車司機很年輕, 而且我注意到他喝醉了。)

pay attention (to) = watch and listen to with full concentration (指全神貫注地看和聽, 例如): 'If you don't pay attention, you won't know what to do.'
notice = see and make a mental note of (指看到並思想上予以注意, 例如): 'I noticed that someone had opened the window.'

autumn See (見) SUMMER

average × In average about ten people die every day.
√ **On average about ten people die every day.**
(每天平均約有十人死亡。)

> **on average,** NOT **in**
> **on average** 中的 **on** 不可用 **in** 替代。

avoid **1** × Some criminals use guns to avoid to be caught.
√ **Some criminals use guns to avoid being caught.**
(有些罪犯為了避免被捕而使用槍械。)

> **avoid** + v-ing
> **avoid** 後接帶 "-ing" 的動詞。

2 × He is such a nice man that you cannot avoid liking him.
√ **He is such a nice man that you cannot help liking him.**
(他為人極好, 你一定會喜歡他。)

> **cannot help** + v-ing (= cannot stop yourself from doing something) (**cannot help** 後接帶 "-ing" 的動詞意為 "不得不 …"、"不禁 …", 例如):
> 'Whenever he smiles at me, I just can't help laughing.'

3 × Some parents try to avoid their children from leaving home.
√ **Some parents try to prevent their children from leaving home.**
(有些父母設法防止孩子到外面去。)

> **avoid** + v-ing = keep or save yourself from doing something (指不讓自己做某事, 例如) 'Where possible, try to avoid drinking unboiled water.'
> **prevent** someone (**from**) + v-ing = stop someone doing something (指 "阻止別人做某事")

4 × I told him that we would be grateful if he would kindly avoid ringing our doorbell after midnight.
√ **I told him that we would be grateful if he would kindly refrain from ringing our doorbell after midnight.**
(我告訴他, 如果他在半夜不按我們的門鈴, 我們就太感謝了。)

> **avoid** = keep or save yourself from (doing something) (避免 [做某件事], 例如): 'Most film stars try to avoid being recognized when they are on holiday.'

refrain from (formal 正式用語) = stop yourself from (doing something) because other people do not like it (指不要做某件事, 以免人家不高興)
Note the phrase: 'Would/Could you kindly refrain from' + v-ing
注意 'Would/Could you kindly refrain from' 這一片語後接帶 "-ing" 形式的動詞, 意為 "請你不要 (做某事)"。

awaken

× I was awakened by the ticket inspector.
√ **I was woken up by the ticket inspector.**
(我被查票員喚醒了。)

Awakened is grammatically possible but is used only in a very formal or literary context.
awakened 在語法上講得通, 但只用於很正式的場合或文學語體。

aware

× Only those aware of the subject could join in the discussion.
√ **Only those familiar with the subject could join in the discussion.**
(只有熟悉該課題的人才能參加討論。)

aware of = conscious (of) (意識到, 例如): 'I became aware of someone following me.' 'Are you aware that the train leaves in five minutes?'
familiar with = acquainted with (指 "熟悉"、"認識", 例如): 'The aim of the course is to make you fully familiar with the latest teaching methods.'

baby

× Sitting in the next seat was a young woman who was having a baby.
√ **Sitting in the next seat was a young woman who was expecting a baby.**
(坐在旁邊座位的是一位年輕孕婦。)

have a baby = give birth (指 "分娩")
expect a baby = be pregnant (指 "懷孕")
In informal conversation **she's having a baby** can be used to mean 'she's pregnant' but it is better to use this phrase only when there is no risk of confusion.
在口語交談中, **she's having a baby** 可用作 "她已懷孕" 解, 但要表示 "她已懷孕" 這一意思, 用 she's pregnant 較恰當, 這樣沒有誤解的危險。

back **1** See (見) SIDE 1

2 See (見) RETURN 1

bad **1** × A country can be different without being better or badder than your own.
√ **A country can be different without being better or worse than your own.**
(別的國家不可能與你自己的國家相同, 即使它們貧富程度相當。)
× Despite the medicine, I started to feel more bad.
√ **Despite the medicine, I started to feel worse.**
(儘管我吃了藥, 我開始覺得更不舒服了。)

> **bad, worse, worst**
> **bad** 的形容詞比較級是 **worse,** 最高級是 **worst**。

2 × I'm afraid I speak English very bad.
√ **I'm afraid I speak English very badly.**
(對不起, 我的英語講得很不好。)

> **Bad** is an adjective.
> **bad** 是形容詞。
> **Badly** is an adverb.
> **badly** 是副詞。

baggage × All the passengers carried their own baggages.
√ **All the passengers carried their own baggage.**
(所有的旅客都自拿行李。)
× Deborah had five baggages.
√ **Deborah had five pieces of baggage.**
(狄波拉有五件行李。)

> **Baggage** is an uncountable noun.
> **baggage** 是不可數名詞, 不用複數。
> **A piece of baggage** is a single suitcase or bag.
> **a piece of baggage** 指一個手提箱或提袋。

band × The first time I played the tape recorder it 'ate' the band.
√ **The first time I played the tape recorder it 'ate' the tape.**
(我第一次開動卡式錄音機, 機器就"吃"帶子[意指磁帶卡住了]。)

> **band** = a thin flat narrow piece of material which is joined at the ends (指圈形帶子, 例如) 'Her dress had a green band round the hem.' (她的衣裙鑲有綠色邊條。) 'A band of metal was used to strengthen the joint.' (用了一個金屬圈加固接縫處。)
> **tape** = (1) a cassette tape (卡式錄音機磁帶)
> (2) a thin flat narrow piece of material (扁而狹的帶)

bath × It is not possible to take a bath along this coast because the sea is badly polluted.
√ **It is not possible to bathe along this coast because the sea is badly polluted.**
(由於海水污染嚴重, 不可能在沿岸游泳。)

> **take a bath** = wash yourself (and relax) in a bath (指洗澡)
> **bathe** = swim (游泳之意)

be 1 × Nowadays is very difficult to get a job.
√ **Nowadays it is very difficult to get a job.**
(如今很難找到工作。)

> In statements, **be** (like all other verbs) must ALWAYS have a subject. When the real subject is a to-v or v-ing structure, use the preparatory subject **it** and put the real subject later. Compare (陳述句中用動詞 **be**, 像用其他動詞一樣, 必須要有個主語。如果真正主語是帶 to 的動詞或帶 "-ing" 的動詞結構, 要用形式主語 **it**, 把真正主語移後。試比較): 'To get a job is very difficult.' 'It is very difficult to get a job.'

2 × The grammer teacher is easily to understand.
√ **The grammer teacher is easy to understand.**
(這位語法教師講課容易懂。)

> **Be** is followed by an adjective, NOT an adverb.
> **be** 後接形容詞, 不接副詞。

because 1 × Because her terrible behaviour, the flight became a nightmare.
√ **Because of her terrible behaviour, the flight became a nightmare.**
(由於她行為惡劣, 這次坐飛機的整個旅程彷彿發了一場惡夢。)

> **because of** (preposition) + noun or noun phrase
> **because of** 為前置詞,後接名詞或名詞片語。
> **because** (conjunction) + clause (按 because 為連接詞, 後接子句, 例如): 'Because she behaved terribly, the flight became a nightmare.'

2 See (見) REASON 1

become See (見) DARK, TRUE

bed 1
× His grandmother gave him some dinner and brought him to bed.
√ **His grandmother gave him some dinner and put him to bed.**
(他祖母給他吃了飯後,讓他上床睡覺。)
× When he got home, his mother put him in bed.
√ **When he got home, his mother put him to bed.**
(他到家後,他母親便打發他上床睡覺。)

> **put** (a child) **to bed**
> **put** (a child) **to bed** 中的 **to**, 不能用 **in** 替代

2
× Every morning I have to get up from my bed very early.
√ **Every morning I have to get up very early.**
(我每天早晨都要很早起床。)

> **Bed** is rarely used with **get up.** Note, however, the phrase **get out of bed** (注意: **bed** 很少和 **get up** 連用, 但請注意 **get out of bed** 這一片語, 例如): 'I got out of bed and opened the windows.'

been
× After been sent to prison, some criminals feel hatred for society.
√ **After being sent to prison, some criminals feel hatred for society.**
(有些罪犯被捕入獄後痛恨社會。)

> preposition (**after**) + v-ing
> **after** 作前置詞用時,後接帶 "-ing" 的動詞。

before 1
× On the bus he was sitting right before me.
√ **On the bus he was sitting right in front of me.**
(在公共汽車上,他就坐在我前面。)

> **Before** is used mainly when talking about time, NOT place. The most common exception is when people are talking about order or sequence (注意: **before** 主要用來表示時間,不用來表示地方。常見的例外是 **before** 也用來表示順序的先後,例如): 'She was before me in the queue.' 'I looked at the list to see whose name was before mine.' 'Two comes before three.'

2 × 'I bought the tape recorder the week before,' he said.
√ **'I bought the tape recorder last week,' he said.**
(“我上星期買了這台卡式錄音機,” 他說。)

> In direct speech, use (直接引語用) **last week/month/year.**
> In reported speech, use (間接引語用) **the week/month/year before.**

3 × The war ended over forty years before.
√ **The war ended over forty years ago.**
(大戰結束於四十多年以前。)

> **Before** is used of a period that is NOT measured from the present (注意: **before** 用於從過去算起的一段時間, 例如): 'The war ended two months before I was born.'
> **Ago** is used of a period in the past that is measured from the present moment.
> **ago** 用於從現在算起的過去一段時間。

4 See (見) EVER 2

begin × As she left the house, it began raining.
√ **As she left the house, it began to rain.**
(她出家門時天開始下雨。)

> When the subject is inanimate, **begin** is usually followed by to-v.
> 句中的主語是無生命名詞, **begin** 通常後接帶 to 的動詞。

beginning × At the beginning I thought that the switch was broken but then i discovered it was all right.
√ **At first I thought that the switch was broken but then I discovered it was all right.**
(起先我以為開關壞了, 但是後來發現它沒有壞。)

At the beginning usually refers to something that is mentioned in the **of** phrase that follows (注意: **at the beginning** 通常指它後接的 **of** 片語所述及的事, 例如): 'at the beginning of the week', 'at the beginning of the book', or to something that is mentioned in or understood from the context (或指上下文已提及或根據上下文意思已清楚的事, 例如): 'Start at the beginning and read until you get to the bottom of page three.'
At first usually refers to the first of two or more stages or steps and conveys a strong idea of sequence.
at first 指兩個或以上的階段或步驟中的第一個, 含有着重順序先後之意。

behave

× The magazine teaches parents how to behave with their children.
√ **The magazine teaches parents how to behave towards their children.**
(該雜誌告訴做父母的如何對待兒女。)

behave towards someone, NOT **with**
behave towards someone 中的 **towards** 不可用 **with** 替代。

behaviour

× We were surprised by their peculiar behaviours.
√ **We were surprised by their peculiar behaviour.**
(我們對他們的異常行為感到吃驚。)

Behaviour is an uncountable noun.
behaviour 是不可數名詞, 不能用作複數。

behind

× The school has a little garden behind of it.
√ **The school has a little garden behind it.**
(學校後面有個小花園。)

in front of someone or something BUT **behind** someone or something (WITHOUT **of**)
in front 後接 **of**, 但 **behind** 後面不用 **of**

believe

× Some people are believing that the increase in crime is because of all the unemployment.
√ **Some people believe that the increase in crime is because of all the unemployment.**
(有人認為犯罪的增加全由失業造成。)

Believe is NOT used in progressive tenses.
believe 不用進行時態。

belong 1

× The coat belongs my daughter.
√ **The coat belongs to my daughter.**
(那件外套是我女兒的。)

belong to someone
belong to 作 "屬於" 解, 後接 someone。

2

× 'Are these gloves belonging to you?' she asked.
√ **'Do these gloves belong to you?' she asked.**
("這副手套是你的嗎?" 她問道。)

Belong is NOT used in progressive tenses.
belong 不用進行時態。

3

× The car is belong to my wife
√ **The car belongs to my wife.**
(這輛汽車是我妻子的。)

Belong is a verb. NOT an adjective.
belong 不是形容詞, 而是動詞。

benefit

× I think small children can only benefit to be by the side of their parents all the time.
√ **I think small children can only benefit from being by the side of their parents all the time.**
(我認為, 小孩只有時刻在父母親身邊才能有長進。)

benefit from/by + v-ing
benefit from/by 作 "得益於; 從 … 得到好處" 解, 後接帶 "-ing" 的動詞, 例如: 'You will benefit from/by attending the course.'

besides

× My sister's boyfriend was sitting besides me.
√ **My sister's boyfriend was sitting beside me.**
(我姊姊的男朋友坐在我旁邊。)

besides = in addition to (besides 後接受詞, 作 "除 … 以外" 解, 例如): 'There were three other people there besides me.' 'Besides tennis, what other games do you play?'
beside = next to (beside 後接受詞, 作 "在 … 近旁; 在 … 旁邊" 解)

best **1** × I trust you will do your best in repairing the cassette recorder as quickly as possible.
√ **I trust you will do your best to repair the cassette recorder as quickly as possible.**
(我相信你會作出最大努力盡快把卡式錄音機修好。)

> **do your best** + to-v
> **do your best** 後接帶 to 的動詞。

2 × We all made our best to see that they enjoyed themselves.
√ **We all did our best to see that they enjoyed themselves.**
(我們都盡了最大努力讓他們過得愉快。)

> **do your best,** NOT **make**
> **do your best** 中的 **do** 不可用 **make** 替代。

better **1** × German cars are more expensive but they are more better.
√ **German cars are more expensive but they are better.**
(德國汽車較貴, 但是質量較好。)

> **good, better, best**
> **good** 的比較級為 **better**, 最高級為 **best**。

2 × You better stop smoking.
√ **You'd better stop smoking.**
(你最好停止吸煙。)

> **had better** (not) + infinitive WITHOUT **to** (注意: **had better** 後接不帶 **to** 的動詞, 例如): 'If the phone rings again, you'd better answer it .' ' You'd better not tell her if it's a secret.'

3 × 'You had better to hurry up,' she shouted.
√ **'You had better hurry up,' she shouted.**
("最好快一點," 她喊道。)

> **had better** + infinitive WITHOUT **to**
> **had better** 後接不帶 **to** 的動詞。

4 × I advised him that he should better inform the police.
√ **I advised him that he had better inform the police.**
(我勸他最好報告警方。)
× If you don't feel well, you would better not go to work.
√ **If you don't feel well, you had better not go to work.**
(如果你身體不舒服, 最好不要去上班。)

> **Had** in **had better do something** is fixed. No other word or form may be used in its place.
> **had better do something** 中的 **had** 固定不變, 不能用其他詞或形式替代。

5 × It would be better you sent me the coat.
√ **It would be better if you sent me the coat.**
(如果你把上衣給我送來, 那就更好。)

> This follows the usual pattern of conditional sentences. Compare (這種句型通常用條件句, 試比較): 'It would be very convenient if you sent me the coat.' 'I would be delighted if you sent me the coat.'

between 1 × Between all the magazines on the shelf, there was one that was very interesting.
√ **Among/Amongst all the magazines on the shelf, there was one that was very interesting.**
(架子上的雜誌有一本非常有趣。)
× He wandered silently between the passengers on the boat.
√ **He wandered silently among/amongst the passengers on the boat.**
(他在船上乘客中間默默地走來走去。)

> **Between** is used when two or more objects, people, or places are considered separately.
> **between** 用來指分別考慮的兩個或兩個以上的東西、人或地方。
> **Among/amongst** is used with three or more objects, etc., considered as a group or mass.
> **among/amongst** 用來指作為集體或整體考慮的三個或三個以上的東西等。

2 × Today's temperature will vary between 16° to 20°.
√ **Today's temperature will vary between 16° and 20°.**
(今天的氣溫約在十六至二十度之間。)

> "**between** ... **and** ...", NOT **to**
> 中文雖然說: "在 ... 至 ... 之間", 但英文是 "**between** ... **and** ...", 而不用 **to** 代替 **and**。

big **1** × I would like to remind you that I paid a big amount for this radio-cassette and I expect it to work properly.
√ **I would like to remind you that I paid a large amount for this radio-cassette and I expect it to work properly.**
(我想提醒你, 我花了一大筆錢買這台收錄音機, 我自然認為這不會有什麼毛病。)
× Quite a big number of people believe in ghosts.
√ **Quite a large number of people believe in ghosts.**
(好多人信鬼。)

> **Amount** and **number** (= quantity) are used with **small** and **large,** NOT **little** and **big**.
> (作 "數量" 解的 **amount** 和 **number** 跟 **small** 和 **large** 連用, 不用 **little** 和 **big** 作修飾。

2 × While on holiday she caught a big disease.
√ **While on holiday she caught a serious disease.**
(她在假期中患了重病。)
× Instead of having a pleasant journey, I reached my destination with a big headache.
√ **Instead of having a pleasant journey, I reached my destination with a bad/severe/terrible headache.**
(我的旅行並不愉快, 到達目的地時我頭痛得很厲害。)

> **Big** is NOT used of illnesses, aches, and pains.
> **big** 不用來修飾 illnesses (病), aches (痛) 和 pains (痛苦)。

3 × It is a big pleasure to have you all here.
√ **It is a great pleasure to have you all here.**
(承各位光臨, 非常高興。)

> **Big** and **large** are not usually used to describe abstract qualities.
> **big** 和 **large** 一般不用來修飾抽象名詞。
> **Great** is often used instead (**great** 常與抽象名詞連用, 例如): 'great happiness/sorrow/difficulty' (莫大的幸福/痛苦/困難)

bill

× After the meal, he paid for the bill.
√ **After the meal, he paid the bill.**
(吃完飯, 他付了賬。)

> One **pays for** goods and services but **pays** a (an) bill/account/debt etc.
> 因購買貨物付款或付服務費需用 **pay for**; 付賬單、賬目或債務應用 **pay**, 後面不接 **for**。

birthday

× My husband gave me this coat as a present on our last wedding birthday.
√ **My husband gave me this coat as a present on our last wedding anniversary.**
(我丈夫送給我這件大衣作為我們去年結婚紀念日的禮物。)

> **birthday** = the date on which a person was born (指生日)
> **anniversary** = the day of the year when an important event happened and on which it is remembered or celebrated (指週年紀念日)

blame

× I really don't think it was the driver's blame.
√ **I really don't think it was the driver's fault.**
(其實我認為這不是司機的過錯。)
√ **I really don't think the driver was to blame.**
(其實我認為這不能責怪司機。)

> **Blame** is NOT used after a possessive form. Compare (注意 **blame** 不用在所有格形式之後, 試比較): 'It's my fault.' 'I am to blame.'

board

× Within a week, I found myself on board of an aeroplane.
√ **Within a week, I found myself on board an aeroplane.**
(不到一星期, 我竟然登上了飛機。)

> **on board** an aircraft, ship, etc, WITHOUT **of**
> 我們說 **on board** an aircraft (飛機), ship (船) 等,
> 不說 **on board of**

body See (見) NOBODY 4

book in × We booked in a hotel in Istanbul.
√ **We booked in at a hotel in Istanbul.**
(我們預訂了伊斯坦堡一家旅館的客房。)

> In British English **book in at a hotel** means 'reserve a room'.
> 英式英語中 **book in at a hotel** 作 "預訂客房" 解。
> **book in** 是個固定詞組 (set phrase), **in** 在此作副詞用。

bored 1 × The book has no pictures and is very bored.
√ **The book has no pictures and is very boring.**
(這本書沒有圖畫, 讀起來枯燥無味。)

See (見) BORING

2 × She soon got bored of talking to him.
√ **She soon got bored with talking to him.**
(她和他談了不久就覺得厭煩。)

> **Bored with** (doing) something is the correct form. **Of** is sometimes used in informal English but is regarded by careful users as non-standard.
> **bored with** (doing) something 是正確用法, 在口語體英語中 bored 可後接 **of**, 但嚴格說來, 不合規範。

boring × We get very boring with the same dishes every day.
√ **We get very bored with the same dishes every day.**
(我們每天都吃同樣的菜, 現在已經吃厭了。)

> 'They are boring' = They bore people. (指他們/它們使人厭煩。)
> 'They are bored' = Someone/something bores them. (指他們受某人/某事所擾而感到厭煩。)
> Compare (比較): 'a boring film' (一部令人厭煩的影片) and 'a bored audience' (一羣感到厭煩的觀眾)

born

× I have been born in a town just outside Paris.
√ **I was born in a town just outside Paris.**
(我出生於巴黎郊區不遠的一個城鎮上。)

Always use '**I was born**', NOT 'I have been born' or 'I am born' or 'I borned'.
常用 '**I was born**', 不可說 'I have been born', 也不可說 'I am born' 或 'I borned'。

borrow 1

× The garage has borrowed me another car while mine is being repaired.
√ **The garage has lent me another car while mine is being repaired.**
(我的汽車正在修理, 所以修車廠借給我一輛汽車。)

borrow = take or receive (something) for a certain time, intending to return it
borrow 指向人借用某物, 過一段時間後歸還。
lend = give (someone) the use of (something) for a certain time
lend 指把某物借給他人使用一段時間。

2

× Can I borrow your bathroom, please?
√ **Can I use your bathroom, please?**
(我能否用你的衛生間?)

You can only use **borrow** with movable objects.
borrow 只用於可搬動的東西。

both 1

× Both of them were not telling the truth.
√ **Neither of them was/were telling the truth.**
(他們倆沒有一個講真話的。)

Use **neither** + affirmative verb, NOT **both** + negative verb.
表示 "兩者都不" 或 "兩者之中沒有一個" 之意可用 **neither** 後接肯定式動詞, 不用 **both** 後接否定式動詞。

2

× It is no good unless the both countries agree to stop fighting.
√ **It is no good unless both (the) countries agree to stop fighting.**
(除非這兩個國家同意停戰, 否則這樣做沒什麼用。)

× I am pleased that my both children have written to me.
√ **I am pleased that both my children have written to me.**
(我兩個孩子都給我寫信，我感到很高興。)

> **Both** comes before a determiner, NOT after it.
> **both** 用於指定詞 (如 the, my, their) 之前，而不是用於其後。

3 × Two of the biggest firms are Apple and IBM, which both are in the computer business.
√ **Two of the biggest firms are Apple and IBM, which are both in the computer business.**
√ **Two of the biggest firms are Apple and IBM, both of which are in the computer business.**
(最大的企業當中有 Apple 和 IBM 兩家，他們都經營電腦。)

> **Both** cannot be placed immediately before **be** unless it is used as a pronoun (**both** 一詞不能放在 **be** 之前，除非是用作代名詞，例如): 'Two of the biggest firms are Apple and IBM. Both are in the computer business.'

4 × Lappish is completely different from both the two Norwegian languages.
√ **Lappish is completely different from both the Norwegian languages.**
(拉布蘭語跟挪威的兩種語言截然不同。)

> Do not use **two** after **both.**
> **both** 之後不用 **two**。

5 × I'm writing this letter to tell both about my time in England.
√ **I'm writing this letter to tell you both about my time in England.**
√ **I'm writing this letter to tell both of you about my time in England.**
(我寫這封信告訴你們倆有關我在英國逗留期間的一切。)

> **Both** cannot replace a first person pronoun ('we/us') or second person pronoun ('you').
> both 一詞不能代替第一人稱代名詞 (we/us) 或第二人稱代名詞 (you)。

bother

√ **AmE I am sorry that I have to bother you about this problem.**
(美式英語**:** 很抱歉**,** 我得麻煩你這個問題。**)**

√ **BrE I am sorry that I have to bother you with this problem.**
(英式英語: 譯文同上)

> In American English, use **bother** someone **with** OR **about** something.
> (美式英語中, 用 **bother** someone, 後接 **with** 或 **about** something)
> In British English, use **bother** someone **with** something
> 英式英語中, 用 **bother** someone, 後接 **with** something。

boyfriend

See (見) FRIEND

brand

× He bought a very well-known brand of car.

√ **He bought a very well-known make of car.**
(他買了一輛名牌汽車。)

> **Brand** is used of soap, toothpaste, butter, etc.
> **brand** 用於肥皂、牙膏、黃油等。
> **Make** is used of cars, washing machines, refrigerators, etc.
> **make** 用於汽車、洗衣機、冰箱等。

breakfast

× Every morning my first job is to prepare a breakfast.

√ **Every morning my first job is to prepare (the) breakfast.**
(我每天早晨做的第一件事是準備早餐。)

> **make/prepare (the)** breakfast, NOT **a**
> 在 **make/prepare (the)** breakfast 中 **the** 可用, 也可省略, 但切忌用 **a**。

breath

× She had a very bad cold and couldn't breath properly.

√ **She had a very bad cold and couldn't breathe properly.**
(她患重感冒, 連正常呼吸都感困難。)

> **Breath**/brɛθ/ is a noun.
> **breath** 是名詞。
> **Breathe** /brið/ is a verb.
> **breathe** 是動詞。

The verb is longer than the noun both in its spelling and in its vowel sound.
動詞 **breathe** 的拼法比名詞 **breath** 多一個字母 **e**; **breathe** 中的元音 **ea** 讀長音, 而 **breath** 裡的 **ea** 發短音。

briefly

× They set out over an hour ago and so they should be here briefly.

√ **They set out over an hour ago and so they should be here shortly.**
(他們一個多小時以前就出發了, 因此他們不久應到達這裡。)

briefly =for a short time. (指短暫地)
shortly =soon (指不久、很快)

bring 1

× I am going abroad next week and would like to bring the cassette recorder with me.

√ **I am going abroad next week and would like to take the cassette recorder with me.**
(我下週出國, 要把這台卡式錄音機帶去。)

× Would you like me to bring you home?

√ **Would you like me to take you home?**
(要我送你回家嗎?)

Bring is used for movement towards the place where the speaker is, was, or intends to be, or towards the person being talked about (**bring** 作 "帶來" 解, 指朝說話人或朝被人談及的人的方向而言, 例如): 'He asked me to bring him a dictionary.' (他要我帶一本詞典給他。)
Take is used for movement in other directions.
take 作 "帶走"、"帶去" 解, 指朝其他方向而去。

2 See (見) BED 1

British

× I am sharing a room with one of my classmates. She is a British.

√ **I am sharing a room with one of my classmates. She is British.**
(我跟班上一個同學合住一個房間。她是個英國人。)

British is an adjective. Note, however, that it is used as a noun in the phrase **the British**, when this means 'the British people'.

British 是形容詞。但 **the British** 中的 **British** 自然是個名詞。**The British** 作 "英國人民" 解, 是個 collective noun (集合名詞), 因此說她是一個英國人, 應說 she is British, 而不說 she is a British 或 she is the British。

broken

× The car could not stop because its brakes were broken.
√ **The car could not stop because its brakes were not working.**
(這輛汽車停不住, 因為煞車壞了。)

broken = physically damaged (指 "本身損壞", 例如): 'a broken windscreen'
not working = not functioning properly (指 "運轉不正常" 或 "失靈")

burst

× He was so frightened that he burst in tears.
√ **He was so frightened that he burst into tears.**
(他嚇得哭了起來。)

burst into tears (流淚)/shrieks of laughter (尖聲大笑)/flames (起火燃燒), etc. 等, NOT **in** (都不用 in 來代替 into)

bus **1**

× Henry travelled to Osaka by a bus.
√ **Henry travelled to Osaka by bus.**
亨利乘公共汽車到大阪去旅行。

travel/go by bus WITHOUT **a**
在 **travel/go by** bus 這一片語中, bus 前不可用 **a**。

2

× He ran down the road and went into a bus.
√ **He ran down the road and got on a bus.**
(他沿着馬路跑, 終於上了公共汽車。)

get on/off a bus
"上公共汽車", 用 **get on** a bus; 下公共汽車則用 **get off** a bus。

business

× I'm sorry for not replying sooner but I had a business to take care of.
√ **I'm sorry for not replying sooner but I had some business to take care of.**
因事務纏身, 遲覆為歉。

> **business** (countable) (可數名詞)＝a shop, company, etc. (指 "商店", "公司" 等)
> **business** (uncountable) (不可數名詞)＝matters or duties (指 "事情" 或 "職責")

busy × In the busy time, the road is always jammed up with vehicles.
√ **During rush hour, the road is always jammed up with vehicles.**
(在繁忙時間, 這條路總是塞滿了車輛。)

> The Chinese "繁忙時間" is the equivalent of an English fixed expression, "during rush hour".
> 中文常說的 "繁忙時間" 正好等於英文的說法: "during rush hour"。

but See (見) ALTHOUGH 1

by 1 × He managed to open the lid by a screwdriver.
√ **He managed to open the lid with a screwdriver.**
(他終於用螺絲起子打開了蓋子。)

> do something **with** a tool, instrument, etc., NOT **by**
> "用某一工具做某事", 英文可說 do something **with** a tool、instrument, 其中 **with** 不可用 **by** 代替。

2 × They watch the customers by a little window.
√ **They watch the customers through a little window.**
(他們從小窗口監視顧客。)

> **watch/look/see through** a window, NOT **by**
> **watch/look/see through** a window 中的 **through** 不可用 **by** 替代。

3 × I hope you feel better by this letter reaches you.
√ **I hope you feel better by the time this letter reaches you.**
(我希望你收到這封信時已覺好點了。)

> **By** is NEVER used as a conjunction
> 錯句誤把 **by** 用作連接詞, 承接前後兩句。

call **1** × I ran to the telephone and called to the fire brigade.
√ **I ran to the telephone and called the fire brigade.**
(我跑到電話機旁, 打電話給消防隊。)

> **call/ring/telephone** a person or place WITHOUT **to**
> 給某人或某處打電話, 可用 **call** 或 **ring** 或 **telephone**, 後面不必加 **to**。

2 × Her name is called Mary.
√ **Her name is Mary.**
√ **She is called Mary.**
她名叫瑪麗。

> "to be called **x**" means to have the name **x**, and the subject of the sentence should be the people or people so named.
> "to be called" 意為 "叫甚麼名字 ", 故主語應是人。

can **1** × I can not see why the machine stopped working.
√ **I can't/cannot see why the machine stopped working.**
(我不明白機器停止運轉的原因。)

> **Can not** usually becomes **can't** (chiefly spoken, informal) or **cannot** (more formal).
> **can not** 一般寫作 **can't**, 主要用於口語, 或寫作 **cannot**, 則為較正式用語。

2 × As you can remember, I was always interested in scientific subjects.
√ **As you may remember, I was always interested in scientific subjects.**
(你可能記得, 我一向對科學題材感興趣。)
× I think you can remember me as I was the only Japanese in the group.
√ **I think you may remember me as I was the only Japanese in the group.**
(我想你可能記得我, 因為我當時在小組裏是唯一的日本人。)

> **May** is used to express possibility.
> **may** 用來表示可能性。
> **Can** is used to express ability.
> **can** 用來表示能力。

3 See (見) COULD

cancel

× The meeting has been cancelled until next Thursday.
√ **The meeting has been postponed until next Thursday.**
(會議延期至下星期四舉行。)

> **cancel** = decide that something (previously arranged) will no longer take place (指決定取消原先安排的事情)
> **postpone** = move to a later time or date (指推遲或延期)

capable

× I took the machine back to the shop but there was nobody there capable to repair it.
√ **I took the machine back to the shop but there was nobody there capable of repairing it.**
(我把機器送回那個舖子, 但是那裏沒有人會修。)

> **able** + to-v BUT **capable of** + v-ing
> **able** 後接帶 to 的動詞, 而 **capable of** 則後接帶 "-ing" 的動詞。

car

× Are you going by taxi or by your own car?
√ **Are you going by taxi or in your own car?**
√ **Are you going by taxi or by car?**
(你坐出租汽車還是自己的汽車去?)

> **go by** car BUT **go in** your (own) car
> 乘車去 **go by** car, 乘你自己的車去則用 **go in** your (own) car。

care 1

× My host family took a good care of me.
√ **My host family took good care of me.**
(我房東家裏的人都對我照顧周到。)

> **take (good/great) care of** is a set phrase, and there is no indefinite article before "(good) care".
> **take (good/great) care of** 是個固定詞組, "**care**" 之前沒有不定冠詞 (**a**)。

2

× She had to stay at home to take care after her family.
√ **She had to stay at home to take care of her family.**
(她不得不留在家裏照顧家人。)

> **look after** someone or something BUT **take care of** someone or something
> 照顧某人或照管某物可用 **look after** 或 **take care of**。

3 × If you want to lose weight you'll have to take care of what you eat.
✓ **If you want to lose weight you'll have to be careful about what you eat.**
(如果你要減輕體重, 你一定要注意飲食。)

> **take care of** = look after (**take care of** 的意思與 look after 相同, 例如): 'Who will take care of the dog while we're away?'
> **be careful about** = pay close attention to, especially to avoid doing the wrong thing
> **be careful about** 意為重視, 關切, 注意, 尤指避免做錯事。

4 × Some criminals simply don't care of being caught.
✓ **Some criminals simply don't care about being caught.**
(有些罪犯根本就不在乎被捕這回事。)

> **care about (doing)** something, NOT **of**
> **care about** (**doing**) something 中的 **about** 不可用 **of** 代替。

care for × The only thing they cared for was how to make money.
✓ **The only thing they cared about was how to make money.**
(他們唯一關心的事情是怎樣賺錢。)

> **care for** (formal) = (1) like (**care for** 作正式用語時有兩義, 1. 喜歡, 例如): 'Would you care for another drink?'
> (2) take care of (2. 照顧, 例如): 'The child was well cared for.' (usually adjectival 常用作形容詞)
> **care about** = be concerned about (關心)

careless × How wonderful it would be to be young and careless again!
✓ **How wonderful it would be to be young and carefree again!**
(要是能恢復青春, 重新過無憂無慮的生活該多好!)

> The opposite of **careless** is **careful** (**careless** 的反義詞是 **careful**, 例如): 'If you weren't so careless, you wouldn't make so many mistakes.' (如果你不是這樣粗心大意, 你不會有這麼多錯誤。)
> The opposite of **carefree** is **worried.**
> **carefree** (無憂無慮的) 的反義詞是 **worried** (憂慮的)。

carry × An ambulance arrived and carried her to the hospital.
✓ **An ambulance arrived and took her to the hospital.**
(救護車來了, 隨即把她送往醫院。)

> A vehicle **takes** a person somewhere.
> "用車輛載人到某處" 應用 **take**。(編者按, 這裏用 carry 也不能算錯, 但這個用詞屬舊式 (out-of-date), 還是改用 **take** 為佳)

case 1 × Switzerland has very little unemployment and in this case we are very lucky.
✓ **Switzerland has very little unemployment and in this respect we are very lucky.**
(瑞士很少有人失業, 我們在這方面倒是很幸運。)

> **in this/that case** = in these/those circumstances (意指 "在這種/那種情況下", 例如): 'What shall I do if there are no trains?' 'In that case go by bus.'
> **In this/that respect** = with regard to this/that point or detail (意指 "在這一/那一方面", 例如): 'The film is full of violence and in this respect is unsuitable for children.'

2 × I advise you to eat something now in case there won't be any food when we get there.
✓ **I advise you to eat something now in case there isn't any food when we get there.**
(我勸你現在吃點東西, 說不定我們到了那裏根本就找不到吃的東西。)

> After **in case,** use the present simple tense for future reference, NOT **shall/will** + verb (在 **in case** 後面, 應用一般現在式以表示將來的事, 不用 **shall/will** 的結構形式, 例如): 'Take an umbrella in case it rains.'

3 ✓ **AmE In case you need any more information, please contact me.**
(美式英語: 要是你還需要什麼資料的話, 請跟我聯絡。)
✓ **BrE If you need any more information, please contact me.**
(英式英語: 譯文同上)
✓ **AmE In case a woman goes out to work, she shouldn't have to do all the housework.**
(美式英語: 如果女士們出去工作, 她們就不應再承擔全部家務。)
✓ **BrE If a woman goes out to work, she shouldn't have to do all the housework.**
(英式英語: 譯文同上)

> This usage of **in case** is acceptable in American English but NOT in British English. Note that **if** ... can be used in both British and American English.
> **in case** 這種用法在美式英語中可以接受, 但英式英語則不用。注意 **if** 在英式和美式英語中都可用。

cause 1 × The police wanted to know the cause for the accident.
✓ **The police wanted to know the cause of the accident.**
(警方想知道事故的原因。)

> **cause of,** NOT **for** something
> 指 "... 的原因" 可用 **cause of** something, 這裡 **of** 不可用 **for** 替代。

2 × This causes that the children look for affection elsewhere.
✓ **This causes the children to look for affection elsewhere.**
(這促使孩子們到別處去尋找慈愛。)

> **cause** somebody **to do** something, NOT **cause that** 指 "促使某人做某事" 用 **cause** somebody **to do** something 這一句式, **cause** 後不接 **that** 子句。

center ✓ **AmE The cinema was in the middle of a large shopping center.**
(美式英語: 電影院位於龐大購物中心當中。)
✓ **BrE The cinema was in the middle of a large shopping centre.**
(英式英語: 譯文同上)

> **Center** is American English.
> **center** 是美式英語
> **Centre** is British English.
> **centre** 是英式英語

certain 1 × She was extremely certain that they would offer her the job.
√ **She was absolutely/quite certain that they would offer her the job.**
(她極其肯定他們會給她這份工作。)

> Although usage varies, an adjective which contains the sense 'very', 'extremely', or '100%' as part of its meaning is NOT ususally used with **very** or **extremely.**
> Examples are (雖然用法不同, 但一個本身已含有 "very—非常"、"extremely—極其" 或 "100%—百分之百地" 這類意思的形容詞通常是不能與 **very** 或 **extremely** 連用, 例如): **boiling** (=very hot 非常熱), **certain** (=very sure 十分肯定), **convinced** (=very sure 確信), **delighted** (=very pleased 非常高興), **desperate** (=very worried 十分着急), **fascinated** (=very interested (by) 極感興趣), **fine** (=very well, as in 'I feel fine' 很好), **freezing** (=very cold 非常冷), and **starving** (=very hungry 非常餓). To intensify such adjectives, use **absolutely**, NOT **very** OR **extremely.** (如要加強這類形容詞的語氣, 要用 **absolutely**, 而不用 **very** 或 **extremely**。)

2 × The present government is certain of losing the next election.
√ **The present government is certain to lose the next election.**
(本屆政府肯定會在下次選舉中落敗。)

> **certain of doing** something = feel sure that you will do something: (意指 "自己肯定會去做某事", 例如): 'John is certain of being invited.' (= John's opinion 約翰自以為如此)
> **certain to do** something = will definitely do something (意指 "肯定對方會去做某事", 例如): 'John is certain to be invited.' (=the speaker's opinion 說話者認為約翰一定如此)

certainly × I certainly will try harder the next time.
√ **I will certainly try harder the next time.**
(我下次一定更加努力。)

Certainly usually goes immediately after the (first) auxiliary verb (注意 **certainly** 通常緊接在〔第一個〕助動詞之後, 例如): 'His work has certainly improved this year.' When there is no auxiliary verb, **certainly** is placed immediately before the main verb (句中沒有助動詞時, certainly 緊放在主動詞之前, 例如): 'She certainly likes you.' However, when the main verb is **be**, **certainly** is usually placed immediately before or immediately after it. (然而, 如果主要動詞是 **be**, **certainly** 一般可緊放在主要動詞前面或後面。)

chair

× During the flight she sat on the chair behind me.
√ **During the flight she sat in the seat behind me.**
(在飛機飛行中, 她坐在我後面的座位上。

seat = a place for sitting , as found in a cinema, train, bus, etc. (指電影院、火車、公共汽車等的座位)
chair = a movable seat for one person (指可搬動的椅子)

chance 1

× The higher your qualifications, the better your chances to find a job.
√ **The higher your qualifications, the better your chances of finding a job.**
(你的資歷越高, 尋找工作的機會越好。)

chance/s of + v-ing
chance/s of 後接帶 "-ing" 的動詞。
(編譯者按: **chance** 後接 "-ing" 動詞往往強調 something is likely to happen — 很有可能發生的事, 尤指愉快和盼望的事, 如本例句。**chance** 後接帶 to 的動詞也是一種句型, 強調的是: there is an opportunity to do something — 有機會做某事, 如 The long spell of dry weather gave us a chance to paint the house.)

2

× I spent the whole morning looking for the ring but had no chance.
√ **I spent the whole morning looking for the ring but had no luck.**
(我花了整個早晨尋找那戒指, 不幸沒有找到。)

chance = the force that seems to make something happen or not happen (指 "機會", 例如): 'It was by sheer chance that I discovered he had been telling lies.'
luck = good fortune (指 "好運氣")

cheap

× The wages in Taiwan are very cheap.
√ **The wages in Taiwan are very low.**
(台灣的工資很低。)

> Use **cheap** with goods.
> 用 **cheap** (廉價的, 便宜的) 修飾 goods (貨物)。
> Use **low** with wages, costs, payments, etc.
> 用 **low** (低) 修飾 wages (工資)、costs (成本)、payments (報酬) 等。

check 1

√ **AmE I paid for the radio by check.**
(美式英語: 我買這台收音機用支票付款。)
√ **BrE I paid for the radio by cheque.**
(英式英語: 譯文同上)

2

√ **AmE Although he had invited me, he asked me to pay the check.**
(美式英語: 雖然是他邀請了我, 但是他卻要我付賬。)
√ **BrE Although he had invited me, he asked me to pay the bill.**
(英式英語: 譯文同上)

> In American English **check** means (1) 'a form instructing a bank to pay money to someone' (BrE **cheque**)
> 美式英語, check 1. 作 "支票" 解 (英式英語用 cheque)
> (2) 'a list of things bought and their price' (BrE **bill**).
> 2. 作 "賬單" 解 (英式英語用 bill)

cheerful

× The old couple are very cheerful in their new home.
√ **The old couple are very happy in their new home.**
(那對年老夫妻住在新居裡心滿意足。)

> **happy** = feeling satisfied or contented (指心滿意足, 例如): 'We're very happy with our new car.'
> **cheerful** = tending to smile and laugh, or be in good spirits (指興高彩烈, 有說有笑, 例如): 'Despite all her problems, she's always cheerful.'

choose

× Many women choose for children at an early age.
√ **Many women choose to have children at an early age.**
(許多婦女喜歡在年青時生孩子。)

choose (to do) something, NOT **for**
表示 "選擇某事物或喜歡/想/決定做某事" 要用 **choose (to do)** something, 中間不可插入 **for.**

church

× Not so long ago nearly everybody used to go to the church.
✓ **Not so long ago nearly everybody used to go to church.**
(不久以前, 差不多每個人都去做禮拜。)

Use **go to church** WITHOUT **the** when referring to church as an institution and not to one church in particular. Compare (go to church〔注意 church 前不用 the〕作 "去做禮拜" 解, 不是指 "去某教堂", 試比較): 'the church on the hill' (山上那座教堂).

circulate

× On weekdays, cars are not allowed to circulate in the centre of the city.
✓ **On weekdays, cars are not allowed to go into/enter the centre of the city.**
(在週日, 汽車不准進入市中心。)

circulate = move around in a steady stream (指 "暢通無阻", 例如): 'A one-way system has been introduced to keep the traffic circulating.' (採用單行線, 以保持車輛通行無阻。)

classic

× I prefer classic music to pop.
✓ **I prefer classical music to pop.**
(以古典音樂同流行音樂相比較, 我還是喜歡前者。)

classic = being among the best or most typical of its class; serving as a standard or model (作 "最優秀的", "經典的" 解, 例如): 'The painting is a classic example of sixteenth-century Venetian art.' (這幅畫是十六世紀威尼斯藝術的典範。)
classical music = the music of Mozart, Beethoven, etc. (作 "古典音樂" 解, 指莫扎特、貝多芬等的音樂作品)

clothing

× The women were selling second-hand clothings.
✓ **The women were selling second-hand clothing.**
(這些婦女在售賣舊衣服。)

Clothing is an uncountable noun. Note the more common alternative (**clothing** 是不可數名詞。注意較常見的另一種說法是): 'The women were selling second-hand clothes.'

cloths

× I spent the morning unpacking my cloths.
√ **I spent the morning unpacking my clothes.**
(我打開箱子, 把衣服拿出來收拾好, 花了整個上午的時間。)

In British English **cloth** /klɔθ/ = (a piece of) material made of cotton, wool, etc. (在英式英語中, cloth 作 (一塊) "布料, 毛料等" 解, 例如): 'I'm afraid I've spilled some milk. Have you got a cloth?'
clothes /kloðz/ (plural noun) = the things a person wears, such as trousers, sweaters, etc. (作 "衣服" 解, 如褲子, 羊毛衣等)

collaboration

× The police were grateful to the public for their collaboration.
√ **The police were grateful to the public for their co-operation.**
(警方對公眾的合作表示感激。)

Collaboration comes from the verb **collaborate** (= work in partnership with someone on the same task) (**collaboration** 從動詞 **collaborate** 派生而來, 指 "與人合伙做某事", 例如): 'The two writers have decided to collaborate on the biography.' (這兩位作家決定合寫那本傳記。)
Co-operation comes from the verb **co-operate** (= be willing to help someone to achieve something; be helpful).
co-operation 從動詞 **co-operate** 派生而來, 意指 "願意幫助某人完成某事", "肯協助"。

college

× After a year he decided to leave his college and get a job.
√ **After a year he decided to leave college and get a job.**
(一年後他決定離校謀職。)

Use **leave/go to college** WITHOUT a determiner when referring to college as an institution and not to one college in particular.
leave/go to college 中的 **college**, 前面不用指定詞時, 只作一般的泛指, 不特指某校。

colour 1

× The belt has the same colour as the coat.
√ **The belt is the same colour as the coat.**
(腰帶和上衣的顏色相同。)

Use **be** (NOT **have**) when describing the colour of something.
表示某物的顏色時用 **be**, 不用 **have**。

2

× I bought a blue colour shirt.
√ **I bought a blue shirt.**
(我買了一件藍襯衫。)
× The handbag is a brown colour.
√ **The handbag is brown.**
(這手提包是棕色的。)

The name of a colour ('red/blue/green' etc.) is not usually used with the noun **colour.** Note, however, the exception ('red/blue/green' etc. **in colour**) (用 red/blue/green 等表示顏色的詞後面一般不再用名詞 **colour**, 但要注意, red/blue/green 等後面可接 **in colour**, 例如): 'The handbag is brown in colour.'

coloured

× The cardigan is pink-coloured.
√ **The cardigan is pink.**
(這件開襟羊毛衫是粉紅色的。)

pink-coloured = not quite pink (指 "不完全是粉紅色的")
When talking about colours, it is usual to say simply 'It is red/blue/green' etc. Adjectives like **pink-coloured** are quite rare. They are sometimes used when you are not sure of the exact colour.
形容顏色時一般就說 It is red/blue/green 等。很少用 **pink-coloured** 這類形容詞。有時用了, 是要表示不能精確地斷定其顏色。

come 1

× The little boy was afraid of his father and didn't want to come back home.
√ **The little boy was afraid of his father and didn't want to go back home.**
(這小孩怕他父親, 因而不肯回家。)

Come is used for movement towards the place where the speaker is, was, or intends to be, or towards the person being talked about (**come** 指走向說話人或被談到的人的動作, 例如): 'Why have you come here?'

'Suddenly a tall woman came into my office.'
Go is used for movement in other directions.
go 指走往其他方向的動作。

2 × The students who are coming from Japan are hard-working.
√ **The students who come from Japan are hard-working.**
(那些日本學生很用功。)

When **come from** means 'have as a place of origin' or 'was born in', it is NEVER used in a progressive tense. However, when **come from** means 'travel from', the progressive forms can be used. Compare (**come from** 作"出生於" 解, 從來不用進行式, 但作 "從某地旅行回來" 解時則可用進行式, 試比較): 'She comes from Germany.' (=she was born in Germany) 'She is coming from Germany.' (=she is travelling from Germany)

common × Nowadays it is common that women go out to work.
√ **Nowadays it is common for women to go out to work.**
(現在婦女出去工作很普通。)

be common for someone **to do** something, NOT **that** 表示 "某人做某事是很普通的" 如用 **it is common**, 則後應接 (for someone) **to do** something。注意: **it is common** 後不接以 **that** 開始的子句。

compare × The teachers will be able to visit our schools and compare our teaching methods to their own.
√ **The teachers will be able to visit our schools and compare our teaching methods with their own.**
(教師們可到我們一些學校來參觀, 可把我們的教學方法跟他們自己的作比較。)

compare to = describe (someone or something) as being similar to (someone or something else); liken (指某人或某物與另一人另一物相似; 例如): 'She compared the child to a noisy monkey.'
compare with = examine (someone or something) in order to discover similarities with or differences from (someone or something else) (指 "通過比較找出與他人或他物的異同", 例如): 'Having compared the new dictionary with the old one, she found the new one more helpful.' (她把新舊詞典進行比較後發覺新詞典更有幫助。)

complain

× For the first time in twenty years, I have to complain on one of your products.

√ **For the first time in twenty years, I have to complain about one of your products.**
(這是我二十年來第一次不得不投訴你們的一種產品。)

× He called the waitress and started complaining over the service.

√ **He called the waitress and started complaining about the service.**
(他把女侍者叫來, 開始抱怨服務欠佳。)

> **complain about** someone or something, NOT **on** or **over**
> **complain about** someone 或 something 中的 **about** 不可用 **on** 或 **over** 替代。

completely See TIRED

comprehension

× There is not enough comprehension between our two countries.

√ **There is not enough understanding between our two countries.**
(我們兩國之間仍需取得更多的諒解。)

> **Comprehension** and **understanding** are often interchangeable when they refer to mental ability but NOT when **understanding** means 'feelings of sympathy or friendship'.
> **comprehension** 和 **understanding** 作 "理解力" 解時常可通用, 但 **understanding** 作 "同情", "友情" 解時不能和 **comprehension** 通用。

comprehensive

× The teachers are very kind and comprehensive.

√ **The teachers are very kind and understanding.**
(教師們和藹可親、通情達理。)

> **comprehensive** = including everything or almost everything; all-inclusive (指 "包羅萬象的" 、"綜合性的", 例如): 'The witness provided a comprehensive account of the accident.' (目擊者把事故的整個過程都說了。)
> **understanding** = sympathetic (指 "表示同情的, 能體諒別人的")

comprise

× The former Soviet Union comprised of fifteen union republics.
× The former Soviet Union was comprised of fifteen union republics.
√ **The former Soviet Union comprised fifteen union republics.**
(前蘇聯由十五個加盟共和國組成。)

> **comprise** something WITHOUT **of**
> **comprise** 作 "包括" 解時後接受詞, 不可用 **of**。
> Note the alternatives (注意以下幾種用法): 'The former Soviet Union **consisted of/was made up of/was composed of** fifteen union republics.'

concentrate

× I am concentrated on both speaking and writing.
√ **I am concentrating on both speaking and writing.**
(我正集中精力於說寫兩方面。)

> **concentrated**=very strong. Compare (指很濃之意, 試比較): 'The orange juice is concentrated.' (這橙汁很濃。) (=with little or no water added 只加很少的水或完全不加水)

concern

× As far as I concern, the cost of the repair is not my responsibility.
√ **As far as I am concerned, the cost of the repair is not my responsibility.**
(就我而言, 修理費多少與我無關。)

> as far as I am/he is etc. **concerned,** NOT **concern**
> as far as I am **concerned** 或 he is **concerned** 中的 **concerned** 不可用 **concern** 替代。

concerned

× The magazine is concerned about motor-cycles.
√ **The magazine is concerned with motor-cycles.**
(這雜誌是有關摩托車方面的。)

> **be concerned about** something (of people)=be anxious or worried about (something) (指對某事 "表示關切" 、"表示擔憂")
> **be concerned with** something (of a book, programme, etc.) = be about (a particular subject) (指 "與 ... 有關"、"涉及 ..."、"關於 ... 方面" 之意, 如涉及某書、某節目, 或關於某一特定的內容之類。)

conclusion

× As a conclusion, I'd like to say that everyone should be able to work if they want to.
√ **In conclusion, I'd like to say that everyone should be able to work if they want to.**
(最後, 我要說, 每一個人只要願意, 都應有工作可做。)

> **In conclusion** is a fixed phrase.
> **in conclusion** 是個固定詞組。

condition 1

× You should try to keep the car in a good condition.
√ **You should try to keep the car in good condition.**
(你應好好保養這汽車。)

> **In good/excellent/terrible condition** WITHOUT **a**, because "condition" here meaning a state of readiness for use is uncountable
> 在 **in good/excellent/terrible condition** 這一片語中, **condition** 之前不用 **a**, 因為 **condition** 在此意為 "性能良好, 隨時可以用", 是不可數名詞。

2

× The patient is in critical condition now.
√ **The patient is in a critical condition now.**
(病人現在已經病危。)

> When "**condition**" refers to a person's illness, it is a countable noun, and the article "a" is used before it.
> 如 "**condition**" 指的是疾病, 則是一個可數名詞, 前面應加冠詞 "a"。
> 編譯者按: 錯句在美式英語中不算錯。

3

× After selling his car, George is in better condition now.
√ **After selling his car, George is in better conditions now.**
(賣掉了汽車後, 喬治目前的環境好多了。)

> "**condition**" when used in singular form usually refers to the state of general health (uncountable without "a") or to a person's illness (countable with "a"), and the plural "conditions" refers to the circumstances a person is in.
> "**condition**" 用作單數時, 往往指人的一般健康狀態 (屬不可數名詞, 不用冠詞 "a") 或指人的疾病 (屬可數名詞, 需加冠詞 "a"), 而用作複數 conditions 時, 意指人的生活或經濟條件。

consider × We are considering to visit Switzerland next year.
√ **We are considering visiting Switzerland next year.**
(我們正考慮明年去瑞士旅遊。)

> **consider** + v-ing
> **consider** 後接帶 "-ing" 的動詞。

consist 1 × The house was consisting of three bedrooms, a kitchen, and a bathroom.
√ **The house consisted of three bedrooms, a kitchen, and a bathroom.**
(這房子有三間臥室、一間廚房和一間浴室。)

> **Consist of** is NOT used in progressive tenses.
> **consist of** 不用進行式。

2 × The group was consisted of ten people.
√ **The group consisted of ten people.**
(這小組有十個人。)

> **Consist of** is used only in the active.
> **consist of** 只用於主動語態。
> See also note at COMPRISE
> 參見 COMPRISE 的注意事項

consul × He had lunch with the American consulate.
√ **He had lunch with the American consul.**
(他同美國領事共進午餐。)

> **consulate** is the official building in which a consul lives or works
> **consulate** 是領事館
> **consul** is an official who represents his country overseas
> **consul** 是領事

consult √ **AmE At last we persuaded him to consult with his doctor.**
(美式英語: 最後我們説服了他去看醫生。)
√ **BrE At last we persuaded him to consult his doctor.**
(英式英語: 譯文同上)

consult with someone and **consult someone** are both acceptable in American English. However, only **consult someone** is possible in British English.
consult with someone 和 **consult someone** 在美式英語中都可用,但是英式英語中只能用 **consult someone**。

contact

× I'll contact with you by phone tomorrow.
√ **I'll contact you by phone tomorrow.**
(我明天跟你電話聯絡。)

"**contact**" is here a transitive verb meaning to get in touch with someone, and takes a direct object.
contact 一詞在本句是個及物動詞, 意為與人聯絡, 後接一直接受詞。

continual

× The canals join to form one continual waterway.
√ **The canals join to form one continuous waterway.**
(這些運河滙成一條暢通的水道。)
× A line of cars stretched continually down the motorway.
√ **A line of cars stretched continuously down the motorway.**
(一隊汽車在車道上一字排開。)

A **continual** action happens repeatedly over a long period of time, and often refers to unpleasant things (**continual** 表示長時間內反覆發生的動作, 常指不愉快的事情, 例如):
'That telephone has been ringing continually.' (那電話的鈴聲響個不停。)
A **continuous** action/performance/line is uninterrupted of without a break.
continuous 表示連續不斷或中間無停頓的行動、行為和行列。

continuous

× I grew tired of his continuous moaning.
√ **I grew tired of his continual moaning.**
(我對他斷斷續續的呻吟已覺得厭煩。)
× The meeting was continuously interrupted.
√ **The meeting was continually interrupted.**
(這會議接二連三地受到干擾。)

continuous = uninterrupted (指 "不中斷的")
continual = happening repeatedly over a long period of time (指長時期內反覆發生的行動)

contrast

× It was cold yesterday, but on the contrary it's very hot today.
√ **It was cold yesterday, but in contrast it's very hot today.**
(昨天很冷, 可是相反地, 今天卻很熱。)

> **"on the contrary"** is used to show complete disagreement with what has just been said (英語 "**on the contrary**" 這一片語表示對剛才所講的不同意, 例如): 'It was cold yesterday.'—'**On the contrary**, it was hot.' ("昨天很冷。"—"恰恰相反, 昨天很熱。")
> **"in contrast"** shows the difference between two very different facts. (英語 **in contrast** 表示兩個對立的事物或意見之間的差異)

contribute

× Oxfam and Save the Children have contributed a lot of money for the relief work.
√ **Oxfam and Save the Children have contributed a lot of money to the relief work.**
("牛津救濟委員會" 和 "拯救兒童" 這兩個組織對救濟工作捐了許多錢。)

> **contribute** (money etc.) **to** something, NOT **for**
> **contribute** (money etc) **to** something 作 "向 … 捐款等" 解時, 其中的 **to** 不可用 **for** 替代。

control

× These people want to control over our lives.
√ **These people want to control our lives.**
√ **These people want control over our lives.**
(這些人想控制我們的生活。)

> **control** something (verb) BUT **control over** something (noun)
> **control** 如作動詞用, 後接受詞; 如用作名詞, 則後接 **over** 再加受詞。

convinced 1

× I'm extremely convinced that there will not be another war.
√ **I'm absolutely/totally convinced that there will not be another war.**
(我完全相信, 今後再也不會發生戰爭了。)

> See note at CERTAIN 1
> 參見 CERTAIN 1 的註釋。

2 × I'm convinced to have left my leather coat at the hotel.
√ **I'm convinced (that) I left my leather coat at the hotel.**
(我相信我把皮外套留在旅館裏了。)

convinced (+**that**)+clause
convinced 後可接 **that** 或省略 **that**, 再接子句。

cooker × My wife is an excellent cooker.
√ **My wife is an excellent cook.**
(我太太燒菜是一流好手。)

cooker=an apparatus for cooking food (指炊事用具)
cook=a person who cooks (指廚師)

corner × I have written my address on the top right-hand corner.
√ **I have written my address in the top right-hand corner.**
(我在右上角寫了我的地址。)
× We sat on the right-hand corner of the room, near the window.
√ **We sat in the right-hand corner of the room, near the window.**
(他們坐在房間靠窗的右角。)

in the corner, NOT **on**
in the corner 中的 **in** 不可用 **on** 替代。

cost 1 × It will cost to the church a great deal to repair the roof.
√ **It will cost the church a great deal to repair the roof.**
(教堂修理屋頂要花很多錢。)

cost someone **a certain amount** WITHOUT **to**
在 **cost** someone **a certain amount** 中不用 **to**。

2 × The cassette recorder costed £200.
√ **The cassette recorder cost £200.**
(卡式錄音機的價格是 200 英鎊。)

cost, costing, cost, cost
cost 的現在分詞為 **costing**, 過去式為 **cost**, 過去分詞為 **cost.**

3 × I'll send you a cheque to cover the cost for the stamps.
√ **I'll send you a cheque to cover the cost of the stamps.**
(我將給你送上一張支票付郵費。)

> **the cost of** something, NOT **for**
> **the cost of** something 中的 **of** 不可用 **for** 替代。

4 × I will be happy to pay for the costs of the postage.
√ **I will be happy to pay for the cost of the postage.**
(我將樂於支付郵資。)

> **costs** (plural 複數) = expenses incurred in making or producing something (指生產成本, 例如): 'Our costs have doubled in the last five years as a result of the increase in oil prices.' (近五年來由於石油漲價, 我們的成本增加了一倍。)

5 × That shop was always empty because the costs were too high.
√ **That shop was always empty because the prices were too high.**
(那商店總是無人光顧, 因為商品售價太貴。)

> **cost** = the expense of doing something or having something done (指 "成本"、"代價")
> **price** = the amount of money asked for something which is for sale (指 "售價"、"標價")

6 × They agreed to repair the damage free of cost.
√ **They agreed to repair the damage free of charge.**
(他們同意免費把損壞處修好。)

> **charge** = a fee that is demanded for a service (指 "收費")
> **Free of charge** is a fixed phrase which is often used when talking about services. (指 "免收費用", 尤用於服務行業。)

7 × In London the cost of life is very expensive.
√ **In London the cost of living is very expensive.**
(倫敦的生活費用很貴。)

the cost of living, NOT **life**
the cost of living 中的 **living** 不可用 **life** 替代。

could × By reading quickly, I could finish the book before the library closed.
√ **By reading quickly, I was able to finish the book before the library closed.**
(我加快閱讀, 終於在圖書館關門之前把這本書看完。)

When talking about the successful performance of a difficult task, use **be able to,** NOT **can/could.**
be able to 用於完成一項艱難任務, 不用 **can/could**。

couple 1 × She said it wouldn't take more than couple of minutes.
√ **She said it wouldn't take more than a couple of minutes.**
(她說這花不了幾分鐘就行了。)

A couple of is a fixed phrase in British English.
a couple of 是英式英語中的固定詞組。

2 × The couple was sitting just behind me.
√ **The couple were sitting just behind me.**
(這對男女就坐在我後面。)

A **couple** (such as a husband and wife) is used with a plural verb (unless identified as one of a number of couples).
a **couple** (例如指 "夫妻") 一般後接複數動詞, 除非是指幾對中的一對。—編者按: 美式英語單複數均可, 但前後應相呼應: The couple **are** spending **their** honeymoon 或 ... **is** spending **its** honeymoon。Compare (比較): 'And tonight's winning couple is George and Dorothy Lightfoot.' (今晚獲勝的一對是喬治和陶洛姍・拉福特。)

course 1 × I am taking an intermediate course of English.
√ **I am taking an intermediate course in English.**
(我正在英語中級班上課。)

take a course in something, NOT **of**
take a course in something 中的 in 不可用 **of** 替代。

2 ✓ **AmE The boys and girls in my English course come from all over the world.**
(美式英語: 我英語班上的男女學生來自世界各地。)
✓ **BrE The boys and girls on my English course come from all over the world.**
(英式英語: 譯文同上)

crash × There was a terrible noise as the car and truck crashed each other.
✓ **There was a terrible noise as the car and truck crashed into each other.**
(汽車和貨車相撞時發出的聲音可怕極了。)
× The motorcyclist couldn't stop and crashed with the truck.
✓ **The motorcyclist couldn't stop and crashed into the truck.**
(駕駛摩托車的人煞不住車, 和貨車相撞。)

> **crash into** something, NOT (**with**) something
> **crash into** something 中的 **into** 不可省略, 也不可用 **with** 替代。

crime × We need to understand why people do these crimes.
✓ **We need to understand why people commit these crimes.**
(我們要了解, 人為什麼會犯這些罪行。)
× Somehow we must stop people from making these crimes.
✓ **Somehow we must stop people from committing these crimes.**
(我們必須設法制止人們犯這些罪行。)

> **commit a crime,** NOT **do** or **make**
> **commit a crime** 中的 **commit** 不可用 **do** 或 **make** 替代。

criticize × The report strongly criticized that the police failed to deal with drug traffickers.
✓ **The report strongly criticized the police for failing to deal with drug traffickers.**
(報告猛烈抨擊警方無力對付毒販。)

> **criticize** is a transitive verb taking a noun as a direct object, not a that-clause. The correct sentence structure is (按 **criticize** 是個及物動詞, 後應接一個直接受詞, 而不是一個帶 that 的子句。正確的句型應是): "**criticize** someone or something **for doing** something".

cry

× Mrs Jones cryed the whole trip and I had to keep holding her hand until we arrived in Rio.

√ **Mrs Jones cried the whole trip and I had to keep holding her hand until we arrived in Rio.**
(鍾斯太太在整個旅途中哭哭啼啼，我不得不一直握着她的手，直至抵達里約熱內盧。)

> **cry, crying, cried, cried**
> **cry** 的現在分詞為 **crying**，過去式為 **cried**，過去分詞為 **cried**。

cup

× We enjoyed a cup of wine with our meal.

√ **We enjoyed a glass of wine with our meal.**
(我們進餐時喝了一杯酒。)

> **a cup of** tea/coffee BUT **a glass of** wine/beer/whisky
> 一杯茶或一杯咖啡，用 **a cup of**；但如說一杯葡萄酒、啤酒或威士忌酒，則用 **a glass of**

curiosity

× Several passers-by stopped to look at the strange bicycle from curiosity.

√ **Several passers-by stopped to look at the strange bicycle out of curiosity.**
(好幾個行人停下來好奇地看看這輛稀奇古怪的自行車。)

> **do** something **out of curiosity,** NOT **from**
> **do** something **out of curiosity** 中的 **out of** 不可用 **from** 替代。

custom

× He has a custom of coughing before he speaks.

√ **He has a habit of coughing before he speaks.**
(他習慣於在講話前咳嗽幾下。)

> **Custom** is used of the established practices of a society or very large group (**custom** 用來指 "社會的風俗"、"做法"，例如): 'In Hong Kong I learned a lot about Chinese customs.' (在香港我了解不少中國風俗習慣。)
> **Habit** is used of an individual。
> **habit** 用來指 "個人的習慣"。

damage × The fire caused a lot of damages.
√ **The fire caused a lot of damage.**
(大火造成很大的損失。)
× The car crashed into a tree and suffered a severe damage.
√ **The car crashed into a tree and suffered severe damage.**
(汽車撞在一棵樹上, 損壞嚴重。)

> **Damage** is an uncountable noun.
> **damage** 是不可數名詞, 不應加不定冠詞 "a"。

dare 1 × 'How dare you to come in without knocking!' he shouted.
√ **'How dare you come in without knocking!' he shouted.**
("你怎麼敢不敲門就進來!" 他大聲叫道。)

> **how dare you/they,** etc. + infinitive WITHOUT **to**
> **how dare you/they** 等之後接不帶 **to** 的動詞。

2 × His mother thinks that somebody must have dared him steal the bicycle.
√ **His mother thinks that somebody must have dared him to steal the bicycle.**
(他母親認為必定有人慫恿他去偷自行車。)

> **dare** someone **to** do something = to challenge
> (意為: 以挑釁的口吻問對方敢不敢做某事。在表示這層意思時 **dare** 之後接帶 **to** 的動詞。)

daren't × I daren't to ask her for any more money.
√ **I daren't ask her for any more money.**
(我不敢再問她要錢。)

> **daren't/wouldn't dare**+inifinitive WITHOUT **to**
> **daren't/wouldn't dare** 後接不帶 **to** 的動詞。

dark × Soon it began to become dark and it was time to go back home.
√ **Soon it began to get dark and it was time to go back home.**
(天不久黑了下來, 是回家的時候了。)

> **get dark,** NOT **become**
> **get dark** 中的 **get** 不可用 **become** 替代。

day **1** × The bus arrived in Paris the following day morning.
√ **The bus arrived in Paris (on) the following morning.**
(第二天早晨, 長途汽車抵達巴黎。)

> Compare: 'the following day', the following morning'
> 比較: "the following day" (第二天) 和 "the following morning" (第二天早晨)。

2 × We were all very tired at the last day of our journey.
√ **We were all very tired on the last day of our journey.**
(在旅程的最後一天, 我們都感到非常疲倦。)
× I made an appointment for the following Friday. In that day I got up early so as to have plenty of time.
√ **I made an appointment for the following Friday. On that day I got up early so as to have plenty of time.**
(我在緊接着的那個星期五定了個約會。到了那一天, 我很早就起床, 以便有寬裕的時間。)

> **on** + a day or date (NOT **at** or **in**)
> 指某一天或某一日期, 應說 **on** a day 或 **on** a date, 其中的 **on** 不可換成 **at** 或 **in**, 見下例: 'on Tuesday', 'on the following day', 'on the third day', 'on 19th March' 等等。

3 See (見) MONTH

4 See (見) IN

5 See (見) OF 2

days × Unemployment is a major problem in these days.
√ **Unemployment is a major problem these days.**
(失業是目前的一個大問題。)

> 'These days' is used WITHOUT **in** or any other preposition. Note however (注意: these days 前面不用 **in** 或任何其他前置詞。但請注意): 'In those days cigarettes were much cheaper.' (在那年代, 香煙便宜得很。)

dead

× One of the passengers was dead in the accident.
√ **One of the passengers died in the acccident.**
(有一名乘客在事故中死亡。)

Dead is an adjective (按 **dead** 是形容詞, 例如): 'dead soldiers', 'Is the plant dead?'
Died is the past tense and past participle of **die**.
died 是 **die** 的過去式和過去分詞
(譯者按: dead 和 die 都可以譯作 "死", 但前者指狀態 (state), 後者指動態 (action)。使用時要注意區分, 如說 'He is dead'—這意思是他已經死了, 不再生存了。如說 'He died yesterday.' 意為他死亡這 "動作" 發生在昨日。上述句子清楚地表示死亡是發生在一事故之中, 故應用動態動詞 die。)

deal

× We have been receiving a great deal of complaints.
√ **We have been receiving a great number of complaints.**
(我們收到大量投訴。)

A great deal of is ALWAYS followed by an uncountable noun (注意: **a geat deal of** 總是後接不可數名詞, 例如): 'a great deal of money/time/meat' etc.

deal in

× The play deals in the struggle of a married couple to live their own lives.
√ **The play deals with the struggle of a married couple to live their own lives.**
(這齣戲描述一對夫妻如何為自己的生活奮鬥。)

deal in = buy and sell (作 "買賣" 解, 例如): 'The company deals in textiles.' (該公司經營紡織品。)
deal with = be about (作 "涉及"、"關於" 解)

defect

× He told me that any goods that were defect could be returned for a refund.
√ **He told me that any goods that were defective could be returned for a refund.**
(他告訴我任何有毛病的貨品都可以退款。)

Defect is a noun.
defect 是名詞。
Defective is an adjective.
defective 是形容詞。

definitively See SURELY 1

delay

× Because of the bad weather, the match was delayed for a week.

√ **Because of the bad weather, the match was postponed for a week.**
(由於天氣欠佳, 比賽延期一週。)

delay = cause to arrive, leave, or happen, at a time that is later than the one arranged (指比預先安排好的時間晚到、晚走、晚發生, 例如): 'The departure of the flight was briefly delayed.' (飛機起飛推遲了一點時間。)
postpone = move to a later time or date (意為 "延期")

delighted

× When they knew that they had won, they were very delighted.

√ **When they knew that they had won, they were absolutely delighted.**
(他們知道自己贏了, 高興得不得了。)

See note at CERTAIN 1
參見 CERTAIN 1 的註釋

delightful

× Her parents were delightful that she had won and ran over to kiss her.

√ **Her parents were delighted that she had won and ran over to kiss her.**
(她父母見她贏了非常高興, 跑過去吻她。)

delightful = causing delight (意為 "使人感到高興", 例如): 'a delightful party'
delighted = feeling delight (意為"自己感到高興")

demand

× The union demanded for more money.

√ **The union demanded more money.**
(工會要求得到更多的錢。)

demand something WITHOUT **for**
demand something 中的 **demand** 後不可接 **for**。

demonstration

× Many demonstrations have been made in recent years in protest against the level of pollution.

√ **Many demonstrations have been held in recent years in protest against the level of pollution.**
(近年來發動了多次示威遊行, 抗議嚴重污染。)

> **hold/stage a demonstration** NOT **make**
> **hold/stage a demonstration** 中的 **hold/stage** 不可用 **make** 替代。

deny × She accused him of cheating but he denied.
√ **She accused him of cheating but he denied it.**
(她指責他詐騙, 但他否認。)

> **Deny** is a transitive verb (**deny** 是一個及物動詞, 後面一定要有受詞, 例如): 'He denied it.' 'He denied that he had.'

depend 1 × Whether or not she passes is depending upon how hard she works.
× Whether or not she passes is depended upon how hard she works.
√ **Whether or not she passes depends upon how hard she works.**
(她能否及格, 那要看她用功到什麼程度。)

> **Depend (on/upon)** (= may or may not happen according to) is rarely used in progressive tenses and, as an intransitive verb, is never used in the passive voice.
> **depend (on/upon)** 意為 "視 ... 而定", 很少用進行式, 又因是不及物動詞, 也沒有被動語態。)

2 × The number of hours he worked was depend on the number of absentees.
√ **The number of hours he worked depended on the number of absentees.**
(他需要工作多少個小時, 取決於缺勤人數的多寡。)

> **Depend (on)** is a verb, NOT an adjective.
> **depend (on)** 是動詞, 不是形容詞。

dependant × Most wives don't like being dependant on their husbands.
√ **Most wives don't like being dependent on their husbands.**
(大多數妻子不喜歡依賴丈夫。)

In British English **dependant** (WITH **ant**) is a noun (英式英語中, **dependant** (以 **ant** 結尾) 是名詞, 例如): 'Do you have any other dependants, apart from your widowed mother?' (你除了寡母以外, 還有任何其他要你贍養的直系親屬嗎?)
Dependent (WITH **ent**) is an adjective.
dependent (以 **ent** 結尾) 是形容詞。

describe

× I want to describe you some of the difficulties.
√ **I want to describe to you some of the difficulties.**
(我要給你說一下其中的一些困難。)

With **describe,** the preposition **to** must ALWAYS be used before an indirect object.
describe 後接間接受詞時, 必須在間接受詞前面用 **to**。

description

× I'll send you some English food and a description on how to prepare it.
√ **I'll send you some English food and a description of how to prepare it.**
(我將給你送去一些英國食品及有關的烹飪說明。)

a description of someone or something, NOT **on**
a description of someone or something 中的 of 不可用 **on** 替代。

desire

× They came to Hong Kong because they desired for a higher standard of living.
√ **They came to Hong Kong because they desired a higher standard of living.**
(他們來香港是因為他們希望過較高水平的生活。)

desire something (verb) BUT **a desire for** something (noun) (按 **desire** 作動詞用, 可接 something, 如作名詞用, 則後面必須接 **for** 才接 something)
Compare (試比較下句): 'They came to Hong Kong because of their desire for a higher standard of living.'

desperate × It was almost midnight and his parents were getting very desperate.
√ **It was almost midnight and his parents were getting desperate.**
(時近半夜, 他的父母快感到絕望了。)

See note at CERTAIN 1
參見 CERTAIN 1 的注意事項

despite 1 × Despite the train was empty, he came and sat in front of me.
√ **Despite the train being empty, he came and sat in front of me.**
(儘管火車的車廂很空, 他卻走來坐在我面前。)

Despite is a preposition (NOT a conjunction) and cannot introduce a clause which contains a finite verb. (按 **despite** 是前置詞, 不是連接詞, 不能用來引導有限式動詞的子句。)
Note the alternative (注意可換另一種說法, 例如): 'Although the train was empty, he came and sat in front of me.'

2 × Despite of my qualifications, I couldn't get a job.
√ **Despite my qualifications, I couldn't get a job.**
(儘管我的資歷很好, 我還是找不到工作。)

despite something WITHOUT **of**
despite 後接 something, 不可用 **of**。
Note the alternative (注意可換另一種說法): **'In spite of** my qualifications, I couldn't get a job.'

destroy × This unpleasant man with his endless complaints destroyed my journey.
√ **This unpleasant man with his endless complaints ruined/spoilt my journey.**
(這個不知趣的人沒完沒了地發洩不滿, 破壞了我旅行的樂趣。)

To express the meaning 'remove the pleasure or enjoyment from', use **ruin** or **spoil,** NOT **destroy.**
在表示"破壞樂趣"這類意思時用 **ruin** 或 **spoil**, 不用 **destroy**。

detail

× Please contact Mrs Oda for further detail.
√ **Please contact Mrs Oda for further details.**
(欲知詳情, 請與奧達太太聯絡。)

further information (uncountable) BUT **further details** (countable)
“詳情” 如譯作 **further information** 則 **information** 是不可數名詞, 不能寫作 informations; 如用 **further details** 來譯, 則 **detail** 本身是可數詞, 在這裡必須加 s, 作 details。
Note, however, the fixed phrase **In detail** (但應注意, **in detail** 是固定詞組, 意亦為“詳情”, 例如): ‘Will you explain in detail what happened?’

deter

× How can we deter our leaders to use the atomic bomb?
√ **How can we deter our leaders from using the atomic bomb?**
(我們怎麼才能阻止我們的領導人使用原子彈?)

deter someone **from** + v-ing
deter someone 後接 **from**, 再接帶 “-ing” 的動詞。

dialled

√ **AmE I hurried to the telephone and dialed the police.**
(美式英語: 我急忙跑到電話機旁打電話報警。)
√ **BrE I hurried to the telephone and dialled the police.**
(英式英語: 譯文同上)

Note the spelling of **dialed** (ONLY ONE **l**) in American English and **dialled** (DOUBLE **l**) in British English.
注意美式英語中的 **dialed** 只有一個 “l”, 而英式英語中的 dialled 卻有兩個 “l”。

die

× People say she died with pneumonia.
√ **People say she died of pneumonia.**
(據說她死於肺炎。)

die of a disease, NOT **with**
die of a disease (疾病) 中的 of 不可用 **with** 替代。
(譯者按: die with 不能說是絕對錯, 只是屬古英語, 現已不用。)

differ

× My own beliefs differ to those of the church in several ways.

√ **My own beliefs differ from those of the church in several ways.**

(我自己的信仰在好些方面跟教會的不同。)

> **differ from,** NOT **to**
> **differ from** 中的 **from** 不可用 **to** 替代。

difference

× You have to make a difference between women who have to work and women who choose to work.

√ **You have to make a distinction between women who have to work and women who choose to work.**

(你必須對那些不得不工作的婦女和那些自願工作的婦女加以區別。)

> make **a distinction** between A and B = not regard or treat A and B in the same way (意為"對甲和乙採取不同的看待或對待)

different **1**

× My new school was very different than the old one.

√ **My new school was very different from/to the old one.**

(我的新學校同以前的學校有很大區別。)

> **Different than** is much less common in British English than **different from/to.** It is not usually used except to avoid awkwardness or repetition.
> 在英式英語中, 很少用 **different than,** 而常用 **different from/to.** 除非為了避免不自然的用法和重複, 才用 different than.

2

× In Argentina, Christmas celebrations are completely different as the ones in England.

√ **In Argentina, Christmas celebrations are completely different from/to the ones in England.**

(在阿根廷, 聖誕節的慶祝活動和英國的完全不同。)

> A is **different from/to** B, NOT **as.**
> A is **different from/to** B 中的 from 或 to 均不可用 **as** 代替。
> Note that careful speakers prefer **from.**
> 注意:用詞講究的人喜歡用 **from。**

3

× Opinions are more different than ever.

√ **Opinions differ more than ever.**

(意見不同, 越來越多。)

We say that people or things **differ** when we are talking about differences within a group. Compare (提到一群人或一組物件之中各不相同的時候, 常用 **differ** 這個詞來表達, 試比較): 'I asked the class and opinions differed.' (=there were many different opinions) (我向班上學生提了個問題, 他們意見紛紜。)
'I asked the class again and opinions were different this time.' (=different from the first time) (我再問問班上的學生, 這一次他們的意見不一樣了。)

difficult

× I was very difficult to make a fire in the open because of the wind.
√ **It was very difficult for me to make a fire in the open because of the wind.**
(風太大, 我很難在戶外把火生起來。)

In idiomatic English, one says: "It is difficult (for someone) to do something", but never: "Someone is difficult to do something", because it is the "something" that is difficult rather than the person who is doing it.
"某人做某事感到困難", 合乎英語習慣的說法是: "It is difficult for someone to do something", 而不是 "someone is difficult to do somethinig"。這因為, 困難的是去做某事, 而不是某人。

difficulty

× Initially I had a difficulty to understand people.
√ **Initially I had difficulty in understanding people.**
(起先我在了解別人這方面遇到困難。)

have difficulty/difficulties in+v-ing, NOT **a difficulty**
"在 ... 方面有困難" 可用 "**have difficulty/difficulties in** ..." 來表達。請注意: 1. in 之後應接帶 "-ing" 的動詞; 2. difficulty 之前不用不定冠詞 "**a**"。

dinner

× They decided to take dinner in a café.
√ **They decided to have dinner in a café.**
(他們決定在小飯館裡吃飯。)

have dinner, NOT **take**
have dinner 中的 have 一般不用 **take** 替代。

dirty

× She had fallen over in the rain and her clothes were completely dirty.
√ **She had fallen over in the rain and her clothes were very dirty.**
(她在雨中跌了一跤, 衣服弄得很髒。)

See note at TIRED
參見 tired 的注意事項

disagree 1

× Nowadays most people disagree to work very long hours.
√ **Nowadays most people refuse to work very long hours.**
(如今, 大多數人不願意做時間長的工作。)

disagree (with) = not have the same opinion/s; quarrel (指不同意; 有不同意見; 爭論, 例如): 'I tend to disagree with what you say.' 'She disagreed with him about how much they should spend.'
refuse = not do something because you are unwilling to do it (不願做; 拒做)

2

× She disagreed totally to what I said.
√ **She disagreed totally with what I said.**
(她完全不同意我的話。)

disagree with someone or something, NOT **to**
diasgree with someone or something 中 **with** 一般不用 **to** 代替。

disappeared

× When I got home I realized that one of my suitcases was disappeared.
√ **When I got home I realized that one of my suitcases had disappeared.**
(我到家才知道我的一個衣箱不見了。)

Disappeared is NOT used as an adjective. Note the alternative (按 **disappeared** 不用作形容詞。注意另一種說法): 'When I got home I realized that one of my suitcases was missing.'

disappointed

× The result was very disappointed.
√ **The result was very disappointing.**
(結果令人十分失望。)

disappointed = (of person) feeling unhappy at not seeing hopes come true (指人感到失望, 灰心, 例如): 'He was very disappointed at the result.' (他對結果感到很失望。)
disappointing = causing one to be unhappy at not seeing hopes realized. (指令人感到失望或灰心)

discount

× He bought the house at a 90% discount.
√ **He bought the house at a 10% discount.**
(他以九折的價錢買了這房子。)

Discount means a sum or percentage deducted from the price of something.
英語 discount 指某物減價出售時所減去的那個百分比。"折扣" in Chinese means the percentage of the original price remaining after the discount.
中文 "折扣" 意為扣除了所減之百分比後餘下的那個百分比。
換言之, 中文説九折, 英文是 10% discount/off/less; 照此類推, 八折, 即英文的 20% discount/off/less。

discourage

× Of course we have to discourage people to commit crimes.
√ **Of course we have to discourage people from committing crimes.**
(當然我們一定要勸止人們犯罪。)

encourage someone **to do** something BUT
discourage someone **from doing** something
encourage someone 後接 **to do** something (意為 "鼓勵某人做某事"), 而 **discourage** someone 後接 **from doing** something (意為 "勸止某人做某事")。

discuss **1**

× We're pleased that you have agreed to discuss with us.
√ **We're pleased that you have agreed to discuss the matter with us.**
(你同意和我們討論這事, 我們很高興。)

Discuss is a transitive verb.
discuss 是及物動詞。

2

× We spent almost two hours discussing about the course.
√ **We spent almost two hours discussing the course.**
(我們花了幾乎兩小時討論這課程。)

discuss something BUT **(have) a discussion about** something
discuss 作動詞用, 後緊接一受詞, 不接 about; 但如果用作名詞, 如 have a discussion, 則後接前置詞 about, 然後才接 something。

disease See (見) BIG 2

dispose × Jumble sales provide people with a good opportunity to dispose all their unwanted goods.
√ **Jumble sales provide people with a good opportunity to dispose of all their unwanted goods.**
(舊衣物義賣可給人提供一個好機會, 處理他們不再需要的東西。)

dispose of something = get rid of (作 "處理掉" 解)

distance × From the distance we could hear a fire engine.
√ **In the distance we could hear a fire engine.**
(我們能聽見遠處救火車的聲音。)

in the distance, NOT **from**
in the distance 中的 **in** 不可用 **from** 替代。

distinctive × The audience showed a distinctive lack of enthusiasm.
√ **The audience showed a distinct lack of enthusiasm.**
(觀眾的表現顯然缺乏熱情。)

distinctive = clearly marking a person or thing as different from other; characteristic (意為 "與眾不同的" "有特色的", 例如): 'It was easy to identify the German wine because of its distinctive taste.' (德國酒的味道很有特色, 很容易區別出來。)
distinct = clearly seen, heard, or sensed; noticeable (意為 "看、聽或感覺得很清楚"、"顯而易見的")

divide × For lunch and dinner we were divided in groups of ten.
√ **For lunch and dinner we were divided into groups of ten.**
(我們吃午飯和晚飯時, 按十人一組分成幾組。)

> **divide** something **into** (sections), NOT **in**
> **divide** something **into** (sections 部份) 中的 into 不可用 **in** 替代。

do 1 × 'Do you know who did write the poem?' she asked.
✓ **'Do you know who wrote the poem?' she asked.**
("你是否知道誰寫這首詩?" 她問道。)

> Do not use the auxiliary verb **do** in a dependent **wh-** clause unless the clause is negative or the intention is to provide emphasis (不要在 who-/where-/which- 等子句裡用助動詞 do, 但否定句或有意加強語氣時除外, 例如): 'We know it wasn't Monet or Manet but do you know who did paint that picture?' (我們知道這幅畫既不是莫奈也不是馬奈畫的, 你知道到底是誰畫的?)

2 × What can we do against the problem?
✓ **What can we do about the problem?**
(我們對這問題怎麼辦?)

> **do** something **about** something, NOT **against**
> **do** something **about** something 中的 about 不可用 **against** 替代。

3 See (見) CRIME, EFFORT 2, FLIGHT, JOURNEY, MISTAKE 2, PROGRESS, VISIT

doubt 1 × There is no doubt whether the government has made the right decision.
✓ **There is no doubt that the government has made the right decision.**
(毫無疑問, 政府作出了正確的決定。)

> **no doubt that,** NOT **if** or **whether**
> **no doubt that** 中的 that 不可用 **if** 或 **whether** 替代。
> Compare (試比較): 'There is no doubt that she will pass.' (她無疑會通過考試。) 'There is some doubt as to whether she will pass.' (至於她能否通過考試, 尚成疑問。)

2 × Without doubt you're tired after your journey.
✓ **No doubt you're tired after your journey.**
(我看你長途旅行以後, 一定很累了。)

Without doubt is used to express certainty.
without doubt 表示確定無疑。
No doubt is used to mean 'I think' or 'I suppose'.
no doubt 作 "I think" (我想) 或 "I suppose" (我猜想) 解。

downstairs × I was in a hurry and I forgot to bring the coat to downstairs with me.
√ **I was in a hurry and I forgot to bring the coat downstairs with me.**
(我當時很匆忙, 忘了把外衣帶下樓來。)

downstairs and **upstairs** are adverbs, not nouns. Do not use **to** or any other preposition before them.
downstairs 和 **upstairs** 是副詞, 不是名詞, 故前面不應用 **to** 或任何前置詞。

dozen See (見) HUNDRED 2

dream **1** × I have always dreamed to visit America.
√ **I have always dreamed of visiting America.**
√ **I have always dreamed that I shall visit America.**
(我一向渴望到美國去。)

Generally **dream** is followed by **of** + v-ing or **that**-clause, not by **to** + v.
動詞 **dream** 一般應後接 **of** 及帶 "-ing" 的動詞或接 **that** 子句, 而不接 **to** 及原形動詞。

2 × He has got everything he ever dreamed for.
√ **He has got everything he ever dreamed of.**
(他已經得到他渴望得到的一切。)

dream of something, NOT **for**
dream of something 中的 **of** 不可用 for 代替。

3 × I made a strange dream last night.
√ **I had a strange dream last night.**
(我昨天晚上做了一個很奇怪的夢。)

have a dream, not make a dream
have a dream 中的 have 不可用 make 代替。

dress

× Everybody arrived dressed with their smartest clothes.
√ **Everybody arrived dressed in their smartest clothes.**
(每一位到場的人都穿了自己最漂亮的衣服。)

> **(be) dressed in,** NOT **with**
> **(be) dressed in** 中的 **in** 不可用 **with** 替代。

dress up

× Even though they don't have much money, their children are always dressed up very nicely.
√ **Even though they don't have much money, their children are always dressed very nicely.**
(儘管他們的錢不多, 他們的孩子們總是穿得很好。)

> **dress up** = (1) put on fancy dress (穿上奇裝異服, 例如): 'Henry and Alice went to the party dressed up as a prince and princess.' (亨利和愛麗斯打扮得好像王子和公主那樣去參加聚會。)
> (2) put on formal or smart clothes ("穿禮服或漂亮的服裝", 例如): 'Helen has invited us to dinner but says we shouldn't bother to dress up.' (海倫邀請我們吃飯, 但說不必太講究衣著。)

drink

× He drunk too much and had lots of accidents.
√ **He drank too much and had lots of accidents.**
(他喝得太多酒, 出了不少事。)

> **drink, drinking, drank, drunk**
> **drink** 的現在分詞為 **drinking,** 過去式為 **drank**, 過去分詞為 **drunk**。

drunken

× That man who kept falling over was obviously drunken.
√ **That man who kept falling over was obviously drunk.**
(那個跌跌撞撞的漢子顯然是喝醉了。)

> **drunken** (attributive only 只用作定語形容詞, 即只能置於名詞之前) = caused by drinking too much alcohol (意為 "醉酒的", 例如): 'drunken driving' (醉後駕駛), 'a drunken brawl' (醉後吵架)
> **drunk** = having drunk too much alcohol (意為醉酒)

dull × This knife is too dull to cut the bread.
√ **This knife is too blunt to cut the bread.**
(這把刀鈍得不能切麵包。)

dull=not bright (意為 "不明亮", 例如): 'If you think it's too dull in here, I'll change the light bulb for a more powerful one.' (如果你認為這裡太暗, 我換個亮一點的燈泡。)
blunt=not sharp (意為 "不鋒利的")

during 1 × It is difficult to concentrate during such a long time.
√ **It is difficult to concentrate for such a long time.**
(要這麼長時間集中精神是很困難的。)
× The sun gives us light for the day.
√ **The sun gives us light during the day.**
(白天太陽給我們光。)

When you are talking about the time within which something happens use **during.**
指動作發生的整段時間, 可用 **during**。
When you are talking about how long something lasts use **for.**
指動作發生的時間持續多久, 可用 **for**。

2 × During waiting for the ship to leave, I met an old friend of mine.
√ **While waiting for the ship to leave, I met an old friend of mine.**
(我在等着開船, 這時候碰到了一位老朋友。)

During must be followed by a noun, noun phrase, or pronoun. Compare (**during** 一詞必須後接名詞或名詞片語或代名詞, 試比較): 'during the holiday' and 'while I was on holiday'

each 1 × In our class each of the girls are good at dancing.
√ **In our class each of the girls is good at dancing.**
(在我們班, 每一個女生都擅長舞蹈。)

each is usually singular, thus the number of the predicate is governed by 'each', rather than the noun in the 'of-phrase'.
each 一般後接單數動詞, 換言之, 上句述詞 (即句中的主要動詞) 應根據 each 而用單數, 而不是根據 of 後那個名詞。

2 × They each has a beautiful daughter.
√ **They each have beautiful daughters.**
(他們每個人的女兒都長得很漂亮。)

If '**each**' is placed after a plural subject, the number of the predicate is governed by the subject, not by the adjective 'each'.
如 **each** 在句中的位置是在一個複數主語之後, 則述詞應根據主語用複數而不是根據 each, 因 each 在句中只是一個形容詞。

easy × Life is more easier than it used to be.
√ **Life is easier than it used to be.**
(生活比過往輕鬆了。)

Two-syllable adjectives ending in **-y** form their comparatives and superlatives with **-er** and **-est** (NOT with **more** and **most**) (以 "-y" 結尾的雙音節形容詞的比較級和最高級用 **-er** 和 **-est**, 不用 **more** 和 **most** 構成, 例如): 'easy, easier, easiest', 'pretty, prettier, prettiest'.

economical × First we need to improve our economical situation.
√ **First we need to improve our economic situation.**
(我們首先需要改善我們的經濟情況。)

economic = concerned with trade, industry, economics
(指有關貿易、工業、經濟學方面的)
economical = not wasteful; money-saving (指節約的; 省儉的, 例如): 'A large packet is more economical.' (大的包裝比較合算。)

economics × The Brazilian economics seem to be improving.
√ **The Brazilian economy seems to be improving.**
(巴西的經濟情況似乎正在改善。)

economics = (1) the science of the production, distribution, and use of goods and services (指經濟學, 例如): 'students of economics'
(2) the financial aspects of something ("經濟情況", 例如): 'the economics of dairy farming' (乳品業的經濟情況)
economy = the system by which a country produces or tries to produce wealth (指國家的經濟體系)

edition

× The dictionary went through many publications.
√ **The dictionary went through many editions.**
(詞典已經出了許多版。)

edition = the total number of copies of a book produced and issued at one time (意為: 書的一次印製、發行、版)
publication = the offering for sale to the public of something printed (指把印製好的書報等向公眾銷售, 即出版)

effect 1

× I thought that the long illness would effect my chances of passing the exam.
√ **I thought that the long illness would affect my chances of passing the exam.**
(我想那次長期患病會影響我通過考試的機會。)

effect = bring about; accomplish (意為: 完成; 實現, 例如): 'The new president effected several major changes.' (新總統實施了幾項重大改革。)
affect = have an effect (on something) (指 (對某事) 產生影響)

2

× They think that stricter punishments will have the effect to reduce the amount of crime.
√ **They think that stricter punishments will have the effect of reducing the amount of crime.**
(他們認為更嚴厲的懲罰會產生一種減少犯罪的作用。)

have/produce the effect + **of** + v-ing
have/produce the effect 後接 **of**, 再加接帶 "-ing" 的動詞。

efficient

× The medicine proved very efficient.
√ **The medicine proved very effective.**
(這藥證明非常有效。)

efficient = working quickly and without waste (指 "工作效率很高", 例如): 'The more efficient the engine, the less petrol it uses.' (發動機效能越好, 汽油消耗越少。)
effective = having the desired effect (指 "有效的"、"達到預期效果的")

effort 1

× The authorities have put a lot of efforts into making the streets cleaner.

√ **The authorities have put a lot of effort into making the streets cleaner.**

(當局作了很大的努力, 使街道保持清潔。)

> **effort** (countable 可數名詞)＝a determined attempt (指 "有决心努力去做", 例如): 'Despite all his efforts, the prisoner failed to escape.' (這囚犯千方百計要逃跑, 可是沒能跑掉。)
> **effort** (uncountable 不可數名詞)＝the use of strength over a period of time; hard work (指 "要費一定的力氣去做"; "艱難的工作", 例如): 'Digging the tunnel demanded a great deal of effort.' (挖掘隧道要花很大力氣。)

2

× Little effort has been done to solve the problem.

√ **Little effort has been made to solve the problem.**

(至今未曾下多大功夫去解决這個問題。)

> **make an effort,** NOT **do**
> **make an effort** 中的 make 不可用 **do** 替代。

either

× I shall either go home to Brazil or my family will come to England.

√ **Either I shall go home to Brazil or my family will come to England.**

(不是我返回在巴西的家, 就是我的家人到英國來。)

> The position of **either** should be the same as the position of **or** (i.e. immediately before a subject, immediately before a main verb, immediately after a verb, etc.) (**either** 在句中的位置應和 **or** 的位置相同, 就是說緊放在主語或動詞之前, 或緊接在動詞之後, 等等, 例如): 'Either stay or go.' 'You should either stay or go.' 'You should stay either here or at home.' 'You should stay with either me or your uncle.'

elder

× The two ladies are twins. Can you tell which is the older?

√ **The two ladies are twins. Can you tell which is the elder?**

(這兩位女士是孿生姊妹。你說得出哪一位是年長的嗎?)

older is a comparative adjective and cannot be used as a noun.
older 是個比較級形容詞, 不能用作名詞。
elder is a noun here meaning the older member of the family.
elder 在這裏是個名詞, 指家庭裏年長的一個。

elect × Some people elect marriage partners who are totally unsuitable.
√ **Some people choose/select/pick marriage partners who are totally unsuitable.**
(有些人選擇/挑選完全不適合的伴侶結婚。)

elect = choose (someone) by voting for them (指"投票選舉", 例如): 'The committee has elected a new chairman.' (該委員會選出了新主席。)

electric **1** × My father's company imports electric goods.
√ **My father's company imports electrical goods.**
(我父親的公司做電器用品進口生意。)

Use **electric** when talking about specific things powered by electricity ('an electric fire') and **electrical** when talking about the general class of things ('electrical equipment').
electric 一詞指"用電作動力的", 例如 an electric fire (電爐); 而 electrical 卻泛指"與電有關的", 例如 electrical equipment (電機設備)。

2 × My brother is an electric engineer.
√ **My brother is an electrical engineer.**
(我兄弟是一位電機工程師。)

electric = produced by, worked by, or charged with electricity (按 **electric** 指由電產生的/引起的, 用電帶動的或帶電的, 例如): 'an electric shock', 'an electric light', 'an electric fence'
electrical = related to (the subject of) electricity
electrical 是指有關電方面的

else × Parents who go out to work have to think about something else than just children.
√ **Parents who go out to work have to think about something other than just children.**
(外出工作的父母必須想到除了孩子以外的其他事情。)

Something else cannot be followed by **than.** Compare (**something else** 不能後接 than, 比較): 'I'm tired of this conversation; let's talk about something else.' (我對這個話題已經感到厭煩了, 讓我們談談別的事情吧。)

embark

× My friend and I had just embarked the plane and were looking for our seats.

√ **My friend and I had just boarded the plane and were looking for our seats.**

(我和朋友剛登上飛機, 正在找我們的座位。)

embark (intransitive) = board a ship 指登船 (作不及物動詞): 'We embarked at Macau.' 'He embarked on the steamer the Mayflower for America.'
board a plane/train/ship
board 用以指登船、登飛機、登火車均可。

embarrassed

× He was a bit embarrassed of what he had said.

√ **He was a bit embarrassed by what he had said.**

(他對自己剛才説的話覺得有點不好意思。)

(be) embarrassed by something, NOT **of**
(be) embarrassed by something 中的 by 不可用 **of** 替代。

emphasize

× He emphasized on the need for hard work.

√ **He emphasized the need for hard work.**

(他強調了勤奮工作的必要性。)

emphasize is a transitive verb and does not take 'on'.
emphasize 是個及物動詞, 不帶 "on"。

employ

× The boys were employed to weed the garden.

√ **The boys were employed in weeding the garden.**

(那些男孩子正忙着給花園除草。)

The verb pattern here is **'be employed in doing something'**, meaning **to be busy doing something**, not 'be employed to do something'.
The first sentence above is correct if it means that "the boys were paid to weed the garden", but its meaning differs from that of the second one.
"忙於做某事" 的英語句型可用 "be employed in doing something", 而不是 "be employed to do something"。
上面那個錯句, 如用以指 "那些男孩是受僱來除草的", 則不能算錯, 只是意思與第二句不同。

end 1 × In the end, I should like to wish you all a very interesting and enjoyable stay.
√ **Finally, I should like to wish you all a very interesting and enjoyable stay.**
(最後, 祝各位在這裏逗留期間生活豐富多彩, 心情輕鬆愉快。)

in the end = the final outcome was that (指最後的結果, 例如): 'We tried lots of different medicines but they didn't do any good. In the end we had to take her to hospital.'
finally = to conclude (意為 "在結束之前")

2 × Since nobody would lend me the money, I ended asking my father for it.
√ **Since nobody would lend me the money, I ended up asking my father for it.**
(既然誰也不願借錢給我, 最後我只好跟父親要。)
× The mass meeting ended up with the singing of the national anthem.
√ **The mass meeting ended with the singing of the national anthem.**
(民眾大會最後以唱國歌結束。)

end = finish or cause (something) to finish (指完成或結束某事, 例如): 'The lessons usually end at five o'clock but some teachers end their lessons early.'
end up = (1) be forced to do something (when everything else has failed) (指別無他法時被迫做某事, 例如): 'For months she refused to pay us any rent, so we ended up taking her to court.' (2) eventually find yourself in a particular place or condition (指 "落到…境地"、"收場" 例如): 'If you don't stop smoking, you'll end up in hospital.'

energetic × Our main energetic source is nuclear power.
√ **Our main energy source is nuclear power.**
(我們的主要能源是核能。)

energetic = having energy; active (指"精力充沛的"、"有活力的", 例如): 'Does anyone feel energetic enough to go for another swim?' (誰還有力氣再去游泳?)
energy = power (指 "動力"、"能源")

engage 1

× Our son is engaged with Mary.
√ **Our son is engaged to Mary.**
(我們的兒子和瑪麗訂婚。)

> **be engaged to,** not **with**, meaning having agreed to marry.
> “訂婚” 可用英文 “**be engaged to** “來表達, 但不是 “be engaged with”。

2

× My husband gave me the coat when we engaged (to be married).
√ **My husband gave me the coat when we got engaged (to be married).**
(訂婚時, 我丈夫送給我這件大衣。)

> Here **engage** is not used as a verb but as an adjective in the form of a past participle. The verbal phrase is **get/become engaged.**
> **engage** 作 “訂婚” 解時不用作動詞, 而用作形容詞, 其形式是過去分詞 — engaged, 整個動詞片語是 **get** 或 **become engaged**。

English

× Our teacher is a typical English.
√ **Our teacher is a typical Englishwoman.**
(我們的教師是一位典型的英國婦女。)

> **the English** (=English people) but NEVER **an English**
> the English 指 “英國人”, 相當於 English people, 但從來不說 an English; 如果指 “他是個英國人”, 應說 ‘He is an Englishman.’ 或說 ‘He is English.’

enjoy 1

× I enjoy to speak foreign languages.
√ **I enjoy speaking foreign languages.**
(我喜歡講外語。)

> **enjoy** + v-ing
> **enjoy** 後接帶 “-ing” 的動詞。

2

× We were working very hard but we were enjoying.
√ **We were working very hard but we were enjoying ourselves.**
(我們工作很辛苦, 但覺得很有樂趣。)

> **enjoy** something; **enjoy** yourself
> **Enjoy** is not usually intransitive.
> **enjoy** 通常不用作不及物動詞。

3 × I really enjoy my stay in London.
√ **I am really enjoying my stay in London.**
(我在倫敦逗留期間確實很愉快。)

The present progressive tense is used because the emphasis is on the present moment. Compare (這句使用現在進行式, 是因為重點放在眼前這個時候。比較): 'I enjoy a book at bedtime and I'm really enjoying this one.' (我喜歡臨睡前看書, 對現在這一本更是愛不釋手。)

enough 1 × The time isn't enough for us to catch the next train.
√ **There isn't enough time for us to catch the next train.**
(我們沒有足夠時間趕上下一班火車。)

Enough is not usually used predicatively except when the subject is **there**, **it**, or a specific number or amount. Compare (除主語是 **there**、**it** 或一特定數目或數量外, **enough** 一般不作述語用, 試比較): 'There is enough for everyone.' 'Two pints isn't enough for all of us.'

2 × As they were busy, they did not have time enough to talk to her.
√ **As they were busy, they did not have enough time to talk to her.**
(他們因為忙, 所以沒有足夠的時間和她談話。)

enough + noun + to-v
enough 後接名詞再接帶 to 的動詞

3 × Another advantage is that flying is cheap enough.
√ **Another advantage is that flying is fairly/quite cheap.**
(另一個好處是, 搭飛機頗為便宜。)

Enough is not used to mean 'fairly' or 'quite' except in very informal speech.
除非是在非正式語體中, 否則 **enough** 不作 'fairly' (尚算) 或 'quite' (頗為) 解。

enquire × I'm writing to you to enquire for a jacket that I left at your hotel last week.
√ **I'm writing to you to enquire about a jacket that I left at your hotel last week.**
(我上星期在你們旅館留下一件夾克衫, 現特來信查詢。)

enquire about something, NOT **for**
enquire about something 中的 about 不可用 **for** 替代。
Note that **enquire** may also be spelt **inquire**.
注意 enquire 也可拼寫為 **inquire**。

enter 1 × A strange woman entered into the room and closed the window.
√ **A strange woman entered the room and closed the window.**
(一位陌生的婦人走進房間, 關上窗戶。)

enter a room, building, etc. WITHOUT **into**
說進入一個地方, 如 **enter** a room, building 等, 不用加 **into**。

2 × I entered the train in Oslo.
√ **I boarded the train in Oslo.**
√ **I got on the train in Oslo.**
(我在奧斯陸上了火車。)

board/get on a train/plane/ship
上火車、飛機、輪船用 board/get on。

entertainment × We spend our holidays there because there are always a lot of entertainments for the children.
√ **We spend our holidays there because there is always a lot of entertainment for the children.**
(我們在那裏度假, 是因為那裏一向為孩子們提供很多玩樂的節目。)

Entertainment (=all the various things that provide amusement) is an uncountable noun.
entertainment 作 "文娛節目; 娛樂活動" 解時, 是不可數名詞。

equally × In my opinion the old wooden rackets are equally as good as the new steel ones.
√ **In my opinion the old wooden rackets are (just) as good as the new steel ones.**
(在我看來, 舊的木架球拍和新的鋼架球拍一樣好。)

Equally cannot be placed before **as … as**.
在 **as … as** 之前不能用 **equally**。

equipment **1**

× They were not satisfied with the new equipments.
√ **They were not satisfied with the new equipment.**
(他們對新設備表示不滿。)

> **Equipment** is an uncountable noun.
> equipment 是不可數名詞, 不可作複數形式。

2

× It's a useful equipment and I intend to have it repaired.
√ **It's a useful piece of equipment and I intend to have it repaired.**
(這是一件有用的器具, 我打算叫人把它修好。)

> **a piece of** equipment
> 若指 "一件器具", 應說 **a piece of** equipment。

error

× I dialled the wrong number by error.
√ **I dialled the wrong number by mistake.**
(我撥錯了號碼。)

> **by mistake** BUT **in error.** Note that **by mistake** is the more common expression.
> 如說 "弄錯、做錯", 英文的 **by mistake** 和 **in error** 均可用 (不說 by error), 但兩相比較, 前者較常用。

especially

× In the south of Germany there is a different mentality. Especially the Bavarians are very lively and cheerful.
√ **In the south of Germany there is a different mentality. The Bavarians especially are very lively and cheerful.**
(在德國南部人們的心態不同, 尤其是巴伐利亞人非常活躍開朗。)
× Looking after children can be very tiring. Especially young children need a lot of attention.
√ **Looking after children can be very tiring. Young children especially need a lot of attention.**
(照料孩子非常吃力, 年幼的尤其需要加倍注意。)

> When the focus of **especially** is the subject of a sentence, **especially** is usually placed immediately after the subject.
> 如果 **especially** 指的重點是主語, 它通常緊接在主語之後。

even 1 × Some people think a mother should stay at home during the first year, even she has someone who could look after the child.

√ **Some people think a mother should stay at home during the first year, even if she has someone who could look after the child.**

(有些人認為生了孩子的母親第一年應待在家裏, 即使家裏有人能照料嬰孩也該如此。)

> **Even** is an adverb, NOT a conjunction.
> **even** 是副詞而不是連接詞。
> **even** + **if/though/when** + clause
> **even** 後接 **if/though/when** 再加接子句。

2 × Even though I paid her for the room, but I knew she would prefer to live alone.

√ **Even though I paid her for the room, I knew she would prefer to live alone.**

(即使我付這個房間的房租, 我知道她還是喜歡獨個兒住。)

> When the subordinate clause begins with **even though,** the main clause cannot begin with **but** or **yet.**
> 如果子句以 **even though** 開始, 主句不能用 **but** 或 **yet** 開始。

3 × Many people think that it even snows in Norway in the summer.

√ **Many people think that it snows in Norway even in the summer.**

(許多人認為挪威甚至在夏天也下雪。)

> When there is a danger of confusion, put **even** immediately before the word or phrase that it qualifies.
> 在有混淆的可能時, 把 **even** 緊放在它所修飾的詞或片語之前。

4 × In the future it even might be possible to work only thirty-five hours a week.

√ **In the future it might even be possible to work only thirty-five hours a week.**

(將來甚至可能每星期只工作三十五個小時。)

When the verb has more than one part, **even** is usually placed immediately after the (first) auxiliary.
句中的動詞由一個以上部分組成時, **even** 通常緊接在 (第一個) 助詞之後。

5 See (見) ALTHOUGH 3

evening See (見) AFTERNOON

ever **1** × He has ever been my hero.
√ **He has always been my hero.**
(他一直是我心目中的英雄。)

ever = at any time (作 "在任何時候" 解): 'Have you ever been to Paris?' 'If you ever do that again, I'll be very annoyed.'
always = from the very beginning until now; continuously/at all times (作 "一向" 解)

2 × She was the most unpleasant person that I had ever met before.
√ **She was the most unpleasant person that I had ever met.**
(她是我生平所遇到的最討厭的人。)

ever (used with a verb in the past perfect = at any time before then
和過去完成式動詞連用時, **ever** 作 "在此之前的任何時候" 解。

every **1** × I go to the library everyday.
√ **I go to the library every day.**
(我每天到圖書館去。)

Everyday (one word) is an adjective. (**everyday** 作為一個單詞是形容詞, 例如): 'everyday English'

2 × The shop sells every thing, from toothbrushes to radios.
√ **The shop sells everything, from toothbrushes to radios.**
(這商店從牙刷到收音機, 樣樣都賣。)
× Every thing went according to plan.
√ **Everything went according to plan.**
(一切照計劃進行。)

Every thing (two words) may be used only when the things are considered as separate items. Compare (**every thing** 作兩個詞, 用來指各別的東西, 試比較): 'Everything looked new but every (single) thing I bought turned out to be second-hand.' (所有的東西都像是新的, 但是我買的每一樣東西事實上都是二手貨。)

3 × Every one was tired of listening to her voice.
√ **Everyone was tired of listening to her voice.**
(人人聽到她的聲音都感到厭煩。)

See note at EVERYONE
見 EVERYONE 注意事項

4 × I have to visit the hospital every three week.
√ **I have to visit the hospital every three weeks.**
(每隔三個星期我就得到醫院去看病。)

'every day', 'every week' BUT 'every two days', 'every six weeks'.
指 "每天", "每星期" 用 'every day', 'every week';
指 "每兩天", "每六個星期", 用 'every two days', 'every six weeks'。

everyone × There are amusements and places of interest for everyone of you.
√ **There are amusements and places of interest for every one of you.**
(這裏有適合你們每一個人的娛樂和感興趣的地方。)

everyone = everybody (指每個人)
every one = each single one (of a group or number) (指 "一羣或一批中的每一個")
Compare (試比較):
'Everyone liked her children because every one of them was well-behaved.' (人人都喜歡她的孩子們, 因為他們個個都很乖。)

everywhere × It's a really beautiful park; there are flowers in everywhere.
√ **It's a really beautiful park; there are flowers everywhere.**
(這座公園確實很美, 到處都是鮮花。)

> Prepositions are NOT used before **everywhere** if there is no idea of movement. Compare (如果不含動作的意思, **everywhere** 前面不用前置詞, 試比較): 'Congratulations poured in from everywhere.' (從各處送來了祝賀的函電。)

evidence

× Are there any evidences that ghosts exist?
✓ **Is there any evidence that ghosts exist?**
(是否有什麼證據證明有鬼存在?)

> **Evidence** is an uncountable noun. Note also (按 **evidence** 是不可數名詞。注意也用) 'a piece/pieces of evidence' (一項/幾項證據)

examination See (見) PASS 4

except 1

× The old lady never spoke to anyone except someone came to visit her.
✓ **The old lady never spoke to anyone unless someone came to visit her.**
✓ **The old lady never spoke to anyone except when someone came to visit her.**
(老太太從來不跟任何人說話, 除非有人來探望她。)

> **Except** is a preposition (NOT a conjunction) and cannot introduce a clause containing a finite verb. **except** 是前置詞, 不是連接詞 (譯者按: 在英語口語中, except 用作連接詞並非罕見, 如 I would go, except it's too far. 也有些詞典把 except that 的子句中的 except 也視作連接詞的), 因而不能引導含有帶述詞形式的動詞的子句。

2

× She was willing to do anything except to tell me her name.
✓ **She was willing to do anything except tell me her name.**
(她怎麼都行, 就是不肯把她的名字告訴我。)

> **except** + infintive WITHOUT **to**
> **except** 後接不帶 **to** 的動詞, 如上句: '... except tell me ...'

3

× Except smoke and traffic fumes, there are several other types of pollution.
✓ **Besides/In addition to smoke and traffic fumes, there are several other types of pollution.**
(除了烟塵和車輛排出的氣體外, 還有其他的幾種污染。)

except (preposition) = not including; but not (except 是前置詞, 意為 "不包括 ... " 或 "除 ... 之外", 例如): 'She eats everything except fish.'

exception

× Every major city keeps changing and Lisbon is not an exception.
√ **Every major city keeps changing and Lisbon is no exception.**
(每一個大城市都在不斷地變, 里斯本也不例外。)

Note the phrase: **be no exception** (to something). 注意短語 **be no exception** 的用法, 如果後接名詞時, 需用前置詞 to 。

exchange

× Would it be possible to exchange this cassette recorder with a new one?
√ **Would it be possible to exchange this cassette recorder for a new one?**
(是否可能用這台錄音機換一台新的?)

exchange something **for** something, NOT **with**
exchange something **for** something (以 ... 換 ...) 中的 **for** 不可用 **with** 替代。

excited 1

× Although he was scared, he was excited to sit in a police car for the first time in his life.
√ **Although he was scared, he was excited about sitting in a police car for the first time in his life.**
(他雖然很害怕, 但也很興奮, 因為這是他生平第一次坐上警車。)

excited about + v-ing
"對 ... 感到興奮" 可用 be **excited about** something 或 about 後接帶 "-ing" 的動詞, 如上句。注意 excited 在這裏是形容詞。

2

× I felt very excited with the idea of having my own car.
√ **I felt very excited about the idea of having my own car.**
(一想到自己要擁有汽車, 心情十分興奮。)

excited about something, NOT **with**
excited about something 中的 **about** 不可用 **with** 替代。

excitement

× After all the excitements the children were tired.
√ **After all the excitement the children were tired.**
(孩子們大大地興奮了一陣以後感到累了。)

Excitement is an uncountable noun.
excitement 是不可數名詞，不可以用作複數。

exciting

× It is wonderful to be in London at last. I feel so exciting.
√ **It is wonderful to be in London at last. I feel so excited.**
(終於到了倫敦，好極了。我感到很興奮。)

'They are exciting.' = They excite people. (意為 "使人興奮〔的事物〕")
'They are excited.' = Someone/something excites them. (意為 "〔本身〕感到興奮")
Compare (試比較): 'an exciting film' and 'an excited audience'.

excuse 1

× When he got back home he excused himself and promised that he would never run away again.
√ **When he got back home he apologized and promised that he would never run away again.**
(他回到家後認錯，答應從此再不出走。)

excuse yourself = give a reason for having to leave or be absent ("說明離開或缺席理由", 例如): 'She excused herself from the meeting, saying that she was not feeling well.' (她不參加這會議，說她身體不好。)
apologize = say you are sorry for (doing) something (指 "為某事道歉")

2

× He was sorry that he had lied to her and asked her to excuse him.
√ **He was sorry that he had lied to her and asked her to forgive him.**
(他為自己說了謊向她道歉，並請她寬恕。)

Excuse is used only for minor faults and offences (**excuse** 只用於對小過失和輕度冒犯給予原諒，例如): 'I hope you'll excuse my untidy handwriting. I am trying to write this letter on a train.' (我希望你會原諒我的書寫潦草，我是在火車上寫這封信的。)
Forgive is used for all faults and offences, both minor and major.
forgive 用於原諒寬恕大小過失和冒犯。

exhausting

× I had been working hard all day and felt really exhausting.

√ **I had been working hard all day and felt really exhausted.**

(我努力工作了一整天, 實在感到精疲力盡。)

'The journey was exhausting.' = The journey made them feel very tired. (意為 "旅程使他們感到非常疲勞。")
'They were exhausted.' = They felt very tired. (意為 "他們感到非常疲勞"。)

exhaustive

× An exhausting investigation finally revealed the cause of the accident.

√ **An exhaustive investigation finally revealed the cause of the accident.**

(經過徹底的調查, 最後事故的原因清楚了。)

exhausting = causing tiredness (指 "使人疲勞", 例如): 'Pushing the car uphill was exhausting.' (把汽車推上山去使人疲勞。)
exhaustive = thorough; very careful (作 "徹底的", "非常仔細周密的" 解)

exist

× The problem of hunger has been existing for centuries.

√ **The problem of hunger has existed for centuries.**

(飢餓問題已存在幾個世紀。)

When its meaning is 'be real or be in existence', **exist** is NOT used in progressive tenses.
exist 作 "確有其事"、"存在" 解時, 不用進行式。

expect

× After a few minutes he stopped speaking and expected their reaction.

√ **After a few minutes he stopped speaking and waited for their reaction.**

(他講了幾分鐘, 停下來, 等他們反應。)

× She was standing by the reception desk, expecting a taxi.

√ **She was standing by the reception desk, waiting for a taxi.**

(她站在接待處旁邊等候計程車。)

expect = consider (something) likely (指 "期待某事可能發生", 例如): 'I expect they'll arrive late as usual. (我估計他們像往常一樣會遲到。)
wait for = stay in a place or remain inactive until something (that you have been expecting) happens (指 "待在某處等候某事發生")

expensive

× The price of this suit is quite expensive.
√ **The price of this suit is quite high.**
√ **This suit is quite expensive.**
(這套衣服的價錢很貴。)

When referring to prices, costs, fees, fares, **high** and **low** are usually used as modifiers.
提及價錢、成本、費用時, 一般用 **high** 或 **low** 這類形容詞。
Expensive and **cheap** are used to modify goods and services.
提及貨物和服務項目時, 一般用 **expensive** 或 **cheap**。

experience **1**

× She has had rich experiences in banking.
√ **She has had rich experience in banking.**
(她在銀行業務方面有很豐富的經驗。)

When used to mean knowledge or skill gained by practice, **experience** is an uncountable noun. 作 "經驗" 解時, **experience** 是個不可數名詞, 不可作複數。

2

× My own experience as a translator has been both painful and pleasant.
√ **My own experiences as a translator have been both painful and pleasant.**
(作為一個譯者, 我的體驗是有苦有樂。)

When used to mean something that has an effect on the mind and feelings, **experience** is a countable noun. 作 "經歷"、"體會" 解時, **experience** 是個可數名詞, 可用作複數。

explain

× Your teachers will explain you where you are going to stay.
√ **Your teachers will explain to you where you are going to stay.**
(你們的教師將給你們說清楚你們要去住的地方。)

explain something **to** someone
指“向什麼人解釋什麼事”，應説 **explain** something **to** someone。

explode

× The hijackers threatened to explode the plane.
√ **The hijackers threatened to blow up the plane.**
(劫機者威脅要炸毀飛機。)

People **blow up** buildings or objects; bombs **explode**.
Compare (**blow up** 用來指人“炸毀”樓房或物體，而 **explode** 用於炸彈“爆炸”，試比較): ‘They had planned to blow up the bridge but their bombs failed to explode.’ (他們原本計劃炸掉這座橋，但炸彈沒有爆炸。)

extinguish

× By that time the flames had extinguished.
√ **By that time the flames had been extinguished.**
(到那時，火已被撲滅。)

Extinguish is a transitive verb. Compare (按 **extinguish** 是及物動詞，或用作被動語態，如上句；或後接一受詞，如下句): ‘By that time the firemen had extinguished the flames.’

faceless

× When he failed to beat his opponent in the game he felt he was faceless with his friends.
√ **When he failed to beat his opponent in the game he felt he had lost face with his friends.**
(他在比賽中無法擊敗對手，感到在朋友面前沒有面子。)

faceless = without any clear character or ordinary human feelings (意為缺少個性或缺乏同情心的，例如): ‘Our life is controlled by faceless bureaucrats.’ (我們的生活受控於毫無人情味的官僚手裏。)

fact

× Despite the fact he felt guilty, he ate all his brother's sweets.
√ **Despite the fact that he felt guilty, he ate all his brother's sweets.**
(儘管他感到不對，他還是把他弟弟的糖全吃了。)

In formal writing, use **the fact that** + clause.
在正式的書面語中，用 **the fact that**，再接子句。

fairly

× Japanese cars are fairly cheaper than European ones.
√ **Japanese cars are rather cheaper than European ones.**
(日本汽車跟歐洲汽車相比便宜不少。)

> **Fairly** cannot be used with comparatives.
> **fairly** 不能和比較級連用。

faithfully See (見) SINCERELY

familiar

× I am not really familiar to the taxation laws here.
√ **I am not really familiar with the taxation laws here.**
(我對此地的稅務法不怎麼熟悉。)
× His name is not familiar with me.
√ **His name is not familiar to me.**
(我對他的名字並不熟悉。)

> **familiar to** = well known to (意為"為 … 所熟知")
> **familiar with** = knowing thoroughly (意為"對 … 十分熟悉")

familiarize

× I would like to familiarize with the latest teaching methods.
√ **I would like to familiarize myself with the latest teaching methods.**
(我希望能使自己熟悉那些最新的教學方法。)

> **familiarize** someone/oneself **with** something (意為"精通"、"熟習", familiarize 是個及物動詞, 後應接一受詞, 再接 **with**)

family

× Will you come over to my family this Sunday?
√ **Will you come over to my house/place this Sunday?**
(這個星期天到我家裏來好嗎?)

> Both **family** and **house** can be translated into Chinese as "家", but they are different in meaning. "**Family**" means a group of people related by blood or marriage while "**house**" or "**place**" here is a building a family lives in.
> 儘管 **family** 和 **house** 都可譯為"家", 但這兩個詞的詞義不同。"**family**" 意為"有血緣或婚姻關係的家庭成員"而"**house**"和"**place**"則指一家人生活在其中的居所。

fantasy × Were the voices real or just products of his fantasy?
√ **Were the voices real or just products of his imagination?**
(這些聲音是真實的, 還是他想像出來的呢?)

fantasy = a picture in the mind produced by the imagination, especially one which is very different from reality (指幻想, 尤其是脱離現實的空想, 例如): 'He lived in a world of fantasy.' (他生活在幻想的天地裏。)
imagination = (the part of the mind with) the ability to produce mental pictures (指 "想像")

far **1** × 'It's far to the nearest garage,' she said.
√ **'It's a long way to the nearest garage,' she said.**
("這裏離修車房還有很長一段路," 她說。)

In affirmative sentences, use **a long way**, NOT **far**, unless **far** is part of a phrase such as 'very far', 'awfully far', 'too far', etc. Compare (在肯定句中, 用 **a long way** 而不用 **far**, 除非用於 very far、awfully far、too far 這一類的詞組中, 試比較): 'It's quite far to the station.'

2 × When the bomb exploded, everyone tried to get as far as possible.
√ **When the bomb exploded, everyone tried to get as far away as possible.**
(炸彈爆炸時, 人人都想盡可能跑得遠一些。)

Use **away** when you want to emphasize the distance from a place.
如要強調距離遠一些, 可用 **away** 一詞。

3 × The house is two kilometres far from the school I attend.
√ **The house is two kilometres (away) from the school I attend.**
(這房子離我就讀的學校有兩公里遠。)

Far cannot be used after a unit of distance. Compare (注意 **far** 不能用在表示距離的量詞, 如 foot, metre, kilometre 之後, 試比較): 'The house is rather far from the school.' (WITHOUT unit of distance 此句沒有表示距離的量詞, 故可用 far)
'The house is about two kilometres (away) from the school.' (WITH unit of distance 此句用了表示距離的量詞, 故不能用 far)

fare

× The Cross-Harbour Tunnel fare is $10 per car.
✓ **The Cross-Harbour Tunnel toll is $10 per car.**
(每輛汽車通過海底隧道需付通行費十元。)

> **fare** = the price charged to carry a person by bus, train, taxi, plane, etc.
> **fare** 是坐公共汽車、火車、的士、飛機等的費用。
> **toll** = money paid for using a bridge, highway, canal, tunnel, etc.
> **toll** 是通過大橋、公路、運河、隧道所需付的費用。

farther

× If you need farther information, I suggest you go to the library.
✓ **If you need further information, I suggest you go to the library.**
(如果你需要更詳細的資料, 我建議你去圖書館查閱。)

> **Farther** is used only of distance (注意: **farther** 只指 "距離"): 'We had to travel farther than I had expected.' (我們的旅程比我預期的要更遠。)
> **Further** means "to a greater degree" as well as "to a greater distance". Compare (注意: **Further** 除了可解作 "更遠" 之意外, 還可指 "更大的程度"、"更多地"、"更詳盡地", 試比較:) "He can swim **further** than I." "I have nothing **further** to say."

fascinated

× I was very fascinated by the speed with which they worked.
✓ **I was (absolutely) fascinated by the speed with which they worked.**
(我對他們工作的速度之快感到 (萬分) 驚奇。)

See note at CERTAIN 1
見 CERTAIN 1 的注意事項

fault

× In my opinion both of the drivers were in fault.
✓ **In my opinion both of the drivers were at fault.**
(在我看來, 兩個司機都有過錯。)

> **be at fault**, NOT **in**
> be at fault 中的 **at** 不可用 **in** 替代。

favourable

× Our government is favourable to nuclear missiles.
✓ **Our government is in favour of nuclear missiles.**
(我國政府贊成生產核子飛彈。)

favourable = (1) approving, encouraging, or saying what someone wants to hear (指值得贊同的、令人鼓舞的、順耳的, 例如): 'a favourable report' (令人鼓舞的報告), 'a favourable reply' (令人滿意的答覆)
(2) (of conditions) advantageous (〔條件方面〕有利的, 例如): 'a favourable wind'
be in favour of = approve of (意為贊同、贊成)

favourite

× My most favourite drink is lemonade.
√ **My favourite drink is lemonade.**
(我最喜愛的飲料是檸檬水。)

An adjective which contains the sense **most** as part of its meaning cannot be used with **most**. **Favourite** means 'most preferred'.
含有 "最高級" 意思的形容詞不可與 **most** 連用。**favourite** 就有 "最喜歡的" 這個意思。

fear

× He suddenly felt fear.
√ **He suddenly felt afraid.**
(他突然感到害怕起來。)

feel afraid, NOT **feel fear**
指 "感到害怕", 應説 **feel afraid**, 而不説 **feel fear**。

fed up

× I soon became fed up of his bad temper.
√ **I soon became fed up with his bad temper.**
(我不久就受不了他的壞脾氣。)

tired of BUT **fed up with**
指 "對 ... 感到厭倦", 可用 be/get/become tired of ... , 也可用 be/get/become fed up with ...

feel 1

× As the plane took off, I felt myself very happy because I was finally going to London.
√ **As the plane took off, I felt very happy because I was finally going to London.**
(飛機起飛時, 我感到很高興, 因為我終於前往倫敦了。)

When **feel** is followed by an adjective or adjectival phrase, it is NOT used with a reflexive pronoun.
Compare (注意 **feel** 後接形容詞或形容詞短語時不用反身代詞。比較): 'I suddenly felt myself go cold.' (我忽然感到自己發冷了。)

2 × I suddenly felt someone to touch my arm.
√ **I suddenly felt someone touch my arm.**
(我突然感到有人觸及我的手臂。)

> **feel** someone/something + infinitive WITHOUT **to**
> 按 **feel** someone/something 後接不帶 **to** 的動詞。

3 × He is feeling that they have made a mistake.
√ **He feels that they have made a mistake.**
(他覺得他們弄錯了。)

> **Feel** (= think; have an opinion) is NOT used in progressive tenses. (作 "感到"、"認為" 解的 **feel** 不用進行式。)

feel like × I often feel like to change my job.
√ **I often feel like changing my job.**
(我常想換個工作。)

> **feel like** + v-ing
> 按 **feel like** 後接帶 "-ing" 的動詞, 作 "想 ... " 解。

feeling × The meeting provided a good opportunity for her to express her feeling.
√ **The meeting provided a good opportunity for her to express her feelings.**
(這會議給她提供了一個表達自己意見的好機會。)

> **express your feelings** (plural 複數) = express your views or opinions (作 "發表意見、看法" 解)

feet × In front of them was a six-feet wall.
√ **In front of them was a six-foot wall.**
(他們前面是一堵六英尺高的牆。)

See note at MONTH
見 MONTH 的注意事項

female × The way he dresses is rather female.
√ **The way he dresses is rather feminine.**
(他的穿着相當女性化。)

> **female** = (1) of the sex that produces eggs or gives birth to young (指 "女性的"、"雌的", 例如): 'a female elephant'

(2) for or made up of women or girls (指 "婦女的"、"女孩子的", 例如): 'a female choir' (女童唱詩班) **feminine** = having qualities or features considered to be suitable for a woman (指 "具有女性氣質的")

few **1** × With the few money he had been given, he bought an apple and some cheese.
√ **With the little money he had been given, he bought an apple and some cheese.**
(他用他所能得到的一點點錢買了一個蘋菓和一些乳酪。)

Few is used with plural countable nouns (按 **few** 用於複數可數名詞, 例如): 'There are very few apples left.'
Little is used with uncountable nouns.
little 用於不可數名詞。

2 × Few weeks ago I ordered a cassette recorder from your firm.
√ **A few weeks ago I ordered a cassette recorder from your firm.**
(幾星期以前, 我向貴公司訂購一台錄音機。)

a few = not many (相當於 "不多"、"幾"、"若干", 例如): 'a few (minutes/days/weeks etc.) ago'
few = hardly any (相當於 "幾乎沒有"): 'Few people die of smallpox nowadays.' (如今幾乎沒有人死於天花。)

fight × They spent the whole night fighting against the fire.
√ **They spent the whole night fighting the fire.**
(他們整個晚上都在奮力救火。)

fight a fire/flood etc. WITHOUT **against**
指 "與火災/洪水等搏鬥", 應說 **fight a** fire/flood 等, 在 **fight** 之後不可接 **against**。

film See (見) PLAY 2

find **1** × Nurses find very difficult to start a family while they are working.
√ **Nurses find it very difficult to start a family while they are working.**
(在職的護士覺得很難建立家庭。)

find + **it** + adjective + to-v
When the real object of **find** is a to-v structure, use the preparatory object **it** and put the real object later.
find it 後接形容詞再接帶 to 的動詞是個句型, 意為對做什麼事感到如何如何。可注意兩點: 一是其中 **it** 不能略去, 二是形容詞之後應接帶 to 的動詞。從文法看, **it** 只是形式受詞, 而帶 to 的動詞才是 **find** 的真正受詞。

2 × I am returning the machine so you can find what is wrong with it.
√ **I am returning the machine so you can find out what is wrong with it.**
(我把機子還給你, 以便你能找出它的毛病。)

find = discover by searching or by chance (意為 "經過一番尋找而發現" 或 "碰巧發現", 例如): 'I've looked for the cat everywhere but I can't find it.' 'I found the purse lying in a telephone box.'
find out = learn or discover (something that was previously unknown)
find out 指得悉或發現以前所不知道的事。

find out × Looking through the magazine, I found out several interesting articles.
√ **Looking through the magazine, I found several interesting articles.**
(我仔細看了這本雜誌, 找到了幾篇有趣味的文章。)

See note at FIND 2
見 FIND 2 的注意事項

fine × 'Hello, John. How are you?' 'Very fine, thank you.'
√ **'Hello, John. How are you?' 'Fine, thank you.'**
("喂, 約翰, 你好嗎?" "很好, 謝謝你。")

Fine cannot be modified by **very** when it describes how a person feels.
fine 用來表示一個人的健康情況時不能再用 very 來修飾。
See note at CERTAIN 1
見 CERTAIN 1 的注意事項

finish

× When we had finished to eat, the waiter brought the bill.

√ **When we had finished eating, the waiter brought the bill.**
(我們吃完飯後, 侍應生便遞上帳單。)

> **finish** + v-ing
> **finish** 後接帶 "-ing" 的動詞, 不可接帶 to 的動詞。

first

× At first, may I thank you for your wonderful hospitality.

√ **First (of all), may I thank you for your wonderful hospitality.**
(首先, 讓我謝謝您的盛情款待。)

> Use **at first** when you are talking about initial actions or feelings which are in contrast with something which comes later (注意: **at first** 作 "起先"、"最初" 解, 例如): 'At first I didn't want to go, but I soon changed my mind.' Use **first** and **first of all** to refer either to time (like **at first**) or to a series of actions, with the suggested contrast **next**, **then**, etc. (注意 **first** 和 **first of all** 作 "首先"、"第一" 解, 例如): 'First of all, open the windows. Then turn off the gas and, if necessary, call an ambulance.'

firstly

× I went and sat next to him. Firstly, I didn't speak. I just sat there thinking what I could say. Then I said, 'Nice day, isn't it?'

√ **I went and sat next to him. At first, I didn't speak. I just sat there thinking what I could say. Then I said, 'Nice day, isn't it?'**
(我走過去坐在他旁邊。開始的時候我沒有講話, 只坐在那裏想我能講些什麼話。後來我說, "天氣真好, 是嗎?")

× Firstly, I couldn't understand the local people at all.

√ **At first, I couldn't understand the local people at all.**
(最初我一點也不了解當地的人。)

> **Firstly** conveys a strong sense that 'secondly', 'thirdly', etc. will follow (如用 firstly 一詞, 下面往往要說 secondly (第二), thirdly (第三) 等, 例如): 'There are several reasons why I don't want to buy the car. Firstly, it is too expensive. Secondly ... '
> **At first** refers to time and suggests a contrast with something which comes later (按 **at first** 指時間先後, 用了 at first, 就包含和後來要發生的事相比較的意思, 例如): 'At first I liked the climate, but after two years I hated it.'

fish × I had never seen such brightly coloured fishes.
√ **I had never seen such brightly coloured fish.**
(我從未看過如此顏色鮮艷的魚。)

> The plural form **fishes** has almost disappeared.
> (**fishes** 這一複數形式已經不大用了。)

flat See (見) APARTMENT

flight × It was the worst flight I'd ever done.
√ **It was the worst flight I'd ever been on.**
(我坐飛機旅行數這一次最糟糕。)

> **be on a flight,** NOT **do**
> 可以說 **be on a flight**, 不可說 **do a flight**。

floor 1 × My room, 229, was in the second floor.
√ **My room, 229, was on the second floor.**
(我的房間 229 號是在二樓。)

> (be) **on** the ground/first floor etc. NOT **in**
> (be) **on** the ground/first floor etc. 中的 on 不可用 in 替代。

2 × I was just about to enter the station when someone grabbed me by the shoulders and threw me to the floor.
√ **I was just about to enter the station when someone grabbed me by the shoulders and threw me to the ground.**
(我正要進站時, 突然有人一把抓住我的肩膀, 把我推到在地上。)

> Use **floor** when talking about the inside of a building.
> Use **ground** when talking about a place outside.
> 室內的地面用 **floor**; 室外的地面用 **ground**。

food × They steal because they don't have enough money to buy foods.
√ **They steal because they don't have enough money to buy food.**
(他們之所以偷竊, 是因為沒有錢買吃的東西。)
× It is a disgrace to serve such a poor food.
√ **It is a disgrace to serve such poor food.**
(用這樣差的飯菜招待人, 簡直丟臉。)

> **Food** is always uncountable except when talking about a particular kind of food (注意: **food** 一般是不可數名詞, 除非用來指某種特殊的食物, 例如): 'baby foods' (嬰孩食品).

foot × Whenever there is a strike, we have to go to work by foot.
√ **Whenever there is a strike, we have to go to work on foot.**
(每逢發生罷工, 我們不得不步行去工作。)

> go **by car/bus/train/air** etc. BUT go **on foot**
> 指 "乘汽車/公共汽車/火車/飛機去", 用 go **by car/bus/train/air**, 而指 "步行去" 則用 go **on foot**。

for **1** × I have come to London for learning English.
√ **I have come to London to learn English.**
(我到倫敦來的目的是學英語。)

> do A (in order) **to** do B (表示做某事的目的是為了完成另一件事, 可用帶 **to** 的動詞而不用 **for**, 例如): 'They all worked hard to pass the exams.' 'She opened the door to let the cat out.'

2 × I am writing you this letter for to explain my problem.
√ **I am writing you this letter to explain my problem.**
(我給你寫這封信是要説明我所遇到的困難。)

> To express purpose, use to-v WITHOUT **for.**
> 為了表示目的, 可用帶 to 的動詞, 而無需在 to 之前加上 for。

3 × Unemployment has become a serious problem for the last few years.
√ **Unemployment has become a serious problem over/during the last few years.**
(這幾年失業已成為一個嚴重的問題。)

> Use **for** to introduce the length of time taken by an action (注意 **for** 是用來表示動作延續了多長時間, 例如): 'Unemployment has been rising for the last five years.' (近五年失業率一直在上升。)
> Use **over/during** to introduce the period of time within which an action happens. (注意: **over** 或 **during** 是用來表示動作發生的那一段時間。)

4 × I am waiting here now for an hour.
√ **I have been waiting here now for an hour.**
(我在這裏等了有一小時了。)

An action which began in the past and which is still continuing requires a present perfect tense. When the length of time taken by the action is emphasized, the progressive form is used. Note that in this sentence **now** means 'from a time in the past up to the present moment'.
如需表示一個動作從過去某一時間開始以後一直延續到現在, 可用現在完成式。如需強調發生的一段時間, 則用進行式。請注意本句所用的 now 一字, 意為"從過去某一時間起一直延續至現在這一刻"。

5 × He has been to Hong Kong for several times.
√ **He has been to Hong Kong several times.**
(他到過香港好幾回了。)

for is not used for the number of times something happens, but rather for the length of time an action takes.
for 這個詞不用以表示動作發生的次數而只說明動作延續的長度。

forbid × His father has forbidden him from going out on his own at night.
√ **His father has forbidden him to go out on his own at night.**
(他父親不准他晚上獨自出去。)

forbid someone **to do** something, NOT **from**
forbid someone 後接 **to do** something, 不可接 **from** doing something。

forbidden × In most cinemas nowadays it is forbidden to smoke.
√ **In most cinemas nowadays smoking is forbidden.**
(現在大多數的電影院都禁止吸煙。)

v-ing + **is/was forbidden**
帶 "-ing" 的動詞後接 **is/was forbidden**。
'It is forbidden to smoke' is grammatically correct but sounds unnatural.
"It is forbidden to smoke" 語法上正確, 但聽起來不自然。

force

× She had lost her car keys, so we had to open the door with force.

√ **She had lost her car keys, so we had to open the door by force.**

(她的汽車鑰匙丟失了, 所以我們只得用力硬把車門打開。)

> **do** something **by force** = use force as a means of doing or accomplishing something (指 "用暴力"、"用武力" 做或完成某事)
> Compare (比較): 'He kicked the ball with tremendous force.' (= very hard) (他用力猛踢這球。)

forever

× Nobody lives forever.

√ **Nobody lives for ever.**

(沒有人能長生不死。)

> **forever** = continually; all the time (指 "不斷地"、"始終"、"一直地", 例如): 'He is forever asking me for more pocket money.' (他老是問我要更多的零用錢。)
> **for ever** = for always (作 "永遠" 解)

forget

× She asked me not to forget telephoning her the next day.

√ **She asked me not to forget to telephone her the next day.**

(她要我別忘記第二天打電話給她。)

> Compare (比較): 'I forgot to post the letter.' (= I did not post the letter because I forgot to post it. — 我未曾寄信, 因為我忘記去寄)
> 'I forgot posting the letter.' (= I posted the letter but forgot that I had posted it. — 我把信寄了, 但是忘記我已把信寄出這件事)

forgive

× Please forgive me to be late.

√ **Please forgive me for being late.**

(請原諒我來晚了。)

> "**for** something" or "**for doing** something" is used after "**forgive/excuse** + somebody", but not after the infinitive to.
> 注意: **forgive** 或 **excuse** 與 somebody 連用之後, 應接 **for** something 或 **for doing** something, 而不接帶 to 的動詞。

free See COST 6

friend × I spent the afternoon listening to records with my girl friend.
√ **I spent the afternoon listening to records with my girlfriend.**
(我和女朋友整個下午都在聽唱片。)

girlfriend, boyfriend, NOT **girl friend, boy friend**
指 "女朋友"、"男朋友", 用 '**girlfriend**'、'**boyfriend**', 不用 **girl friend**、**boy friend**。

friendly × All the teachers are very friendly with me.
√ **All the teachers are very friendly to me.**
(所有教師對我都非常友好。)

be/become friendly with = have/enter the relationship that friends have (作 "交朋友" 解, 例如): 'I've become very friendly with the couple who live opposite.' (我跟住在對面的那對夫婦交上了朋友。)
be friendly to = treat in a kind way (作 "友好對待" 解)

frightened **1** × When I heard the thunder I frightened for a moment.
√ **When I heard the thunder I was frightened for a moment.**
(我聽到了雷聲, 嚇了一跳。)

frighten (transitive 及物動詞) = make (someone) afraid (指 "使人害怕", 例如): 'A strange noise under the bed frightened me.' (床底下有種奇怪的響聲使我害怕。)
be frightened = be afraid (指 "感到害怕")

2 × I was very frightened from his appearance.
√ **I was very frightened by his appearance.**
(他的出現使我驚恐萬分。)

be frightened by someone/something (on one occasion 一次性地)
Compare (比較): **be frightened of** someone/something (habitually 習慣性地, 例如): 'Why are so many people frightened of the dark?' (為什麼有這麼多人怕黑?)

frightening × By this time it had grown dark and he felt very frightening.
√ **By this time it had grown dark and he felt very frightened.**
(這時天色已暗, 他驚恐萬分。)

> 'It is frightening.' = It frightens people (指 "使人驚恐")
> 'They are/feel frightened.' = Someone/something frightens them. (指 "他們對某人某事感到驚恐")

from 1 × I have been studying at London University from 1989.
√ **I have been studying at London University since 1989.**
(我自一九八九年以來一直就讀於倫敦大學。)

> Use **from ... to ...** when you mean 'from one time in the past to another' (用 from ... to ... 指 "從過去一個時間到另一個時間", 例如): 'I studied at Leeds University from 1980 to 1983.' (我從一九八〇年到八三年就讀於里茲大學。)
> Use **since** when you mean 'from a time in the past until now'. (用 since 指 "過去某個時間直到現在"。)

2 × She asked if I'd seen any plays from Shakespeare.
√ **She asked if I'd seen any plays by Shakespeare.**
(她問我是否看過莎士比亞的戲劇。)

> a play, novel, painting, etc. **by** a writer or artist, NOT **from**
> 作家, 藝術家創作的小說、戲劇、繪畫等用 by, 不用 from。

front 1 × The bus stop is in front of the library, outside the post office.
√ **The bus stop is opposite the library, outside the post office.**
(公共汽車站在郵局外面、圖書館對面。)

> **in front of** = in a position directly before (指 "在 ... 前面"): 'There was a bus in front of the car and a truck behind it.' (有輛公共汽車在汽車前面, 後面則是一輛貨車。)
> **opposite** = on the other side of the street, room, etc.; facing (指 "街道、房間等對過的另一邊; 對面的")

2 × He was standing right in the front of the television.
√ **He was standing right in front of the television.**
(他就站在電視機的前面。)

> **in front of** (preposition) WITHOUT **the**
> 上述例句中的 **in front of** 為前置詞片語, 在 **front** 之前不用 **the**。
> Compare (試比較): 'Would you like to sit in the front of the train?' (=the part nearest the front) (你是否要坐在火車前邊的車廂?)

3 See (見) SIDE 1

fruit × The shop sells fruits and vegetables.
√ **The shop sells fruit and vegetables.**
(這家店子出售水果和蔬菜。)

> **Fruit** (=fruit in general) is an uncountable noun.
> **fruit** 泛指水果, 是不可數名詞。
> **Fruits** (=particular types of fruit) is rarely used in British English.
> **fruits** 特指各種水果, 英式英語中不常用。

full 1 × Hospitals today are full with people with heart complaints.
√ **Hospitals today are full of people with heart complaints.**
(如今的醫院有很多心臟病患者。)

> (be) **full of,** NOT **with**
> (be) **full of** 中的 **of** 不可用 **with** 替代。

2 × The person sitting next to the driver was full of mud.
√ **The person sitting next to the driver was covered in mud.**
(坐在駕駛員旁邊的那個人渾身是泥。)

> Compare (試比較): 'The glass was full of wine.' (玻璃杯斟滿了酒。) 'The tablecloth was covered in wine.' (桌布上全是酒。)

fun × On my birthday I had a good fun with my friends.
√ **On my birthday I had some good fun with my friends.**
(在我生日那天, 我同朋友們玩得很高興。)

> **Fun** is an uncountable noun.
> **fun** 是不可數名詞。

furniture

× The room was so full of furnitures it was difficult to move.
√ **The room was so full of furniture it was difficult to move.**
(這房間裏擺滿了傢具, 連走動都困難。)
× At home he felt as if he were a furniture.
√ **At home he felt as if he were a piece of furniture.**
(在家裏, 他感到自己好像是一件傢具。)

Furniture is an uncountable noun.
furniture 是不可數名詞。

gain

× Without a job it is impossible to gain any money.
√ **Without a job it is impossible to earn any money.**
(不做工作就不可能掙錢。)

earn (a sum of) money by working, NOT **gain**
靠工作掙錢用 **earn** money, 不用 **gain** money。

game

√ **AmE I enjoy watching football games.**
(美式英語: 我喜歡看足球比賽。)
√ **BrE I enjoy watching football matches.**
(英式英語: 譯文同上)

In British English, use **a game of football** or **a football match.**
英式英語中, 用 **a game of football** 或 **a football match**。

generally

× The coat is generally green.
√ **The coat is mainly green.**
(這件大衣主要是綠色。)

generally = (1) usually (作 "通常"、"總是" 解, 例如): 'It's generally very hot at this time of year.' (每年這個時候總是很熱。)
(2) in most cases; widely (作 "在多數情況下"、"一般說來" 解, 例如): 'His paintings are generally admired.' (他的畫受到普遍的讚賞。)
mainly = mostly; largely (作 "主要地"、"大體上" 解)

gently

× The shop assistant asked me gently what I wanted.
√ **The shop assistant asked me politely what I wanted.**
(店員很有禮貌地問我要買什麼。)

> **gently** (opposite **roughly**) = in a soft and careful way (**gently** 是 **roughly**〔粗魯地〕的反義詞, 作 "溫文爾雅地" 解, 例如): 'She held the little bird very gently.' (她輕輕地捧着那小鳥。)
> **politely** (opposite **rudely**) = in a way that shows good manners; courteously (**politely** 是 **rudely**〔無禮地〕的反義詞, 作 "有禮貌地"、"客氣地" 解)

get **1** × He got on a taxi and went to the office.
√ **He got in a taxi and went to the office.**
(他上了一輛計程車, 上班去了。)
× Get on the car, and we'll go for a drive.
√ **Get in the car, and we'll go for a drive.**
(上車吧, 咱們兜風去。)

2 × When the bus came by, he got in and rode home.
√ **When the bus came by, he got on and rode home.**
(公共汽車來了, 他上了車回家去。)
× Little Peter got in the plane with excitement.
√ **Little Peter got on the plane with excitement.**
(小彼得興奮地登上飛機。)

> "**Get in**" a car or taxi BUT "**get on**" a bus, tram, train, plane or ferry.
> 根據慣用法、登上小汽車或計程車, 人們用 "**get in**"; 而上公共汽車、電車、火車、飛機、渡船, 則用 "**get on**"。

3 × She got down the bus.
√ **She got off the bus.**
(她下了公共汽車。)

> **Get off** a bus, train, tram, plane and ferry, but **get out of** a car, taxi or lift.
> (譯者按: **Get down** 是中國式英語, 英語不這樣說。)
> 如說下公共汽車, 下火車、電車、飛機或離船上岸, 英語用 **get off**, 但指下小汽車、計程車或升降機則用 **get out of**。

get up See (見) BED 2

girl See (見) FRIEND

give × She gave to him some cheese sandwiches.
√ **She gave him some cheese sandwiches.**
(她給了他一些乳酪三明治。)

> **give** something **to** someone BUT **give** someone something
> 指"給某人某物", 可說 **give** something **to** someone, 也可說 **give** someone something。

glad

× The child's parents were glad having him back safely.

√ **The child's parents were glad to have him back safely.**

(孩子的父母為他安全回來而高興。)

> **glad** + to-v
> **glad** 後接帶 to 的動詞。

glance

× She made a quick glance over her shoulder to see if he was following her.

√ **She gave a quick glance over her shoulder to see if he was following her.**

(她轉過頭去, 很快地看了他一眼, 看他是否跟在她後面。)

> Note the more usual alternative (注意更常見的説法): 'She glanced quickly over her shoulder to see if he was following her.'

glasses

× He wore an old-fashioned glasses and couldn't see very well.

√ **He wore old-fashioned glasses and couldn't see very well.**

(他戴的是舊式眼鏡, 看東西也不清楚。)

> **Glasses** (=spectacles) is a plural noun. Note also (glasses 相當於 spectacles, 是複數名詞。注意也用): 'a pair of glasses' (一副眼鏡).

glory

× I feel glory to be invited to speak at the conference.

√ **I feel proud to be invited to speak at the conference.**

(承邀在大會上講話, 我感到很光榮。)

> "**Feel glory**" is a literal translation from the Chinese "感到光榮". Use "**feel proud**" or "**feel honoured**" or "**feel it a great honour**".
> 按 "**feel glory**" 是從中文的 "感到光榮" 直譯出來的。像這樣的場合, 應該説 "**feel proud**" 或 "**feel honoured**" 或 "**feel it a great honour**"。

go **1** × We go to swim every day on holiday.
√ **We go swimming every day on holiday.**
(我們在假日每天都去游泳。)

> **go** + v-ing = perform an activity (**go** 後接帶 "-ing" 的動詞, 意為 "去從事一項活動", 例如): 'go swimming', 'go cycling', 'go fishing'

2 × The next morning she went to the hotel to visit us.
√ **The next morning she came to the hotel to visit us.**
(第二天早晨, 她到旅館來看我們。)

> **Come** is used for movement towards the place where the speaker is, was, or intends to be.
> **come** 是用以指 "朝着說話人所在的地方或要去的地方過來"。
> **Go** is used for movement in other directions.
> **go** 是用以指 "朝着其他方向過去"

3 See (見) NEAR 2, TO 4

4 See (見) CAR

5 See (見) GO OUT

golden **1** × It's a navy blue coat with golden buttons.
√ **It's a navy blue coat with gold buttons.**
(這件大衣的顏色是海軍藍, 鈕扣是金色。)

> **Golden** is rarely used to mean 'having the colour of gold' except in the phrase 'golden hair'.
> **golden** 很少用來作 "金 (黃) 色" 解, 片語 golden hair (金黃色頭髮) 除外。

2 × It was a very valuable golden ring.
√ **It was a very valuable gold ring.**
(這是一隻非常值錢的金戒指。)

> In modern use, things which are made of gold are described as **gold** rather than **golden.**
> 在現代用法中, 黃金製品用 **gold** 來修飾, 不大用 **golden**。

3 × It was broadcast on television at golden time.
√ **It was broadcast on television at prime time.**
(這電視節目在黃金時間播出。)
× Golden time advertising rates are very high.
√ **Prime-time advertising rates are very high.**
(黃金時間的廣告費非常之高。)

> **Prime time** is "黃金時間" in Chinese. Translated literally into English, it is "golden time".
> 中文的 "黃金時間" 不可直譯作 "golden time", 地道的英文是 **prime time**。

gone √ **AmE 'Have you ever gone to France?' she asked.**
(美式英語: "你是否到過法國?" 她問道。)
√ **BrE 'Have you ever been to France?' she asked.**
(英式英語: 譯文同上)

> In British English, **been** is used when someone has visited a place in the past. **Gone** is used when the person is still in the place they are visiting. Compare (英式英語的 **been** 用以指某人到過某地, 而 **gone** 則表示某人仍在他去的那個地方。試比較): 'Peter has gone to Paris.' (=he has not yet returned [意指他仍在巴黎, 還沒有回來]) 'Peter has been to Paris.' (=he has visited Paris and returned [意指他去過巴黎, 但已經回來了])

good 1 × I don't speak English very good.
√ **I don't speak English very well.**
(我的英語講得不很好。)
× His clothes were freshly ironed and his shoes were good polished.
√ **His clothes were freshly ironed and his shoes were well polished.**
(他的衣服剛剛熨過, 皮鞋也擦得很亮。)

> **Good** is an adjective.
> **good** 是形容詞; 形容詞只修飾名詞。
> **Well** is an adverb.
> **well** 是副詞; 副詞可修飾動詞, 在上兩句, 分別修飾 speak 和 polished。

2 × My mother thinks there's no good putting a very young child in a kindergarten.
√ **My mother thinks it's no good putting a very young child in a kindergarten.**
(我母親認為不宜把年紀很小的孩子放在幼兒園裏。)

it is no good (+v-ing)
it is no good (指 "沒用; 不好、不行、不妥"), 後接帶 "-ing" 的動詞, 句中的 **it is** 不可改為 **there is**。

3 × It's no good to want to help the poor if you don't do anything about it.
√ **It's no good wanting to help the poor if you don't do anything about it.**
(你想要幫助窮人, 就得有實際行動, 否則那又有什麼用呢?)

no good+v-ing
no good 後接帶 "-ing" 的動詞。

good at × He is good in languages.
√ **He is good at languages.**
(他在語言方面很擅長。)

be good at, not **in.**
作 "擅長於" 解的英文片語是 **be good at**, 不是 **be good in**。

goods 1 × The goods was not delivered in time.
√ **The goods were not delivered in time.**
(這批貨物沒有及時送到。)

Goods is a plural noun and takes a plural verb.
goods 是複數名詞, 後接複數動詞。

2 × He had very little money and very few goods.
√ **He had very little money and very few possessions.**
(他沒什麼錢, 財產也不多。)

Goods is most often used to refer to things for sale (goods 常指出售的東西, 例如): 'The supermarket has a wide variety of frozen goods.' (超級市場出售的冷凍商品花色品種不少。) It can also have the meaning of 'personal property' but this is usually in a formal or legal context. (**goods** 也作 "個人財產" 解, 但這個含義通常用於書面語或法律文字中。)
Possessions is a more general word meaning 'all the things a person owns.'
possessions 是個較常用的詞, 作 "個人佔有的財物" 解。

go out

× As soon as the bus stopped, he went out.
√ **As soon as the bus stopped, he got off.**
(公共汽車一停，他就下車。)

> **get on/off** a bus/train/plane etc.
> 上、下公共汽車/火車/飛機等用 **get on/off**
> See (見) **get**

gossip

× She told me gossips about all her relations.
√ **She told me a lot of gossip about all her relations.**
(她對我說了許多關於她所有的親戚的閒話。)

> **gossip** (uncountable 不可數名詞) = talk concerned with people's private lives (指關於他人隱私的流言蜚語)
> Note also (注意也用): 'bits/pieces of gossip'.

got

× I got several friends who don't want children.
√ **I have (got) several friends who don't want children.**
(我有幾個朋友都不要孩子。)

> **Got** is NOT used to replace **have**: 'I have several friends.' 'I've got several friends.' (NOT 'I got several friends.')
> 按 **got** 不可用來替代 **have** 或 **have got**, 可說 'I have several friends.' 或 'I've got several friends.', 但不可說 'I got several friends.'

gracious

× Even as a child, he had admired the dancer's slow, gracious movements.
√ **Even as a child, he had admired the dancer's slow, graceful movements.**
(他那時雖然是個孩子，就已經羨慕那舞蹈者那徐緩而優美的動作了。)

> **gracious** = showing courtesy and kindness (作"有禮貌"、"和藹可親"解): 'The duchess was gracious enough to accept the invitation.' (公爵夫人親切地接受了邀請。)
> **graceful** = having beauty (of movement, form, etc.) ([有關動作、體態等] 優美, 優雅)

grade

× By the end of the war he had been promoted to the grade of captain.
√ **By the end of the war he had been promoted to the rank of captain.**
(在戰爭快結束時，他已晉升為上尉。)

> Soldiers, policemen, etc. have different **ranks**, NOT **grades.**
> 士兵、警察等有不同級別, 用 **ranks** 而不用 **grades**.

grateful See (見) SHALL 2

ground

× On what ground do you think that the money was stolen?

√ **On what grounds do you think that the money was stolen?**
(你根據什麼認為錢是被偷竊的?)

> **grounds** (plural 複數) = a reason or reasons (作 "理由"、"根據" 解, 例如): 'She left him on the grounds of cruelty.' (她以被虐待為理由離開了他。) 'They have no grounds for complaint.' (他們沒有理由投訴。) 'We rejected the proposal on the grounds that it involved further unemployment.' (我們反對這個提案, 理由是這牽涉更多的失業。)

grow

× Many of these children grow in an atmosphere of violence.

√ **Many of these children grow up in an atmosphere of violence.**
(在這些兒童之中, 許多人是在暴力的氣氛中成長的。)

> **grow** = increase in size (作 "變大" 解): 'Mary's little boy grew four centimetres last year.' (瑪麗的小男孩去年長高了四公分。)
> **grow up** = pass from childhood into maturity (作 "成長" 解, 指從童年進入成年)

grow up 1

× Some people think it is the duty of all mothers to stay at home growing up children.

√ **Some people think it is the duty of all mothers to stay at home bringing up children.**
(有人認為, 留在家裏教養孩子是所有母親的責任。)

× My father was grown up in Kyoto.

√ **My father grew up in Kyoto.**

√ **My father was brought up in Kyoto.**
(我父親是在京都長大的。)

> **Grow up** is an intransitive verb.
> **grow up** 是不及物動詞。
> **Bring up** is transitive.
> **bring up** 是及物動詞。

2 × Our production of honey grows up every year.
√ **Our production of honey increases every year.**
(我們的蜂蜜生產逐年增加。)

> **grow up** (of a child 指孩子) = become an adult (作 "長大成人" 解, 例如): 'Tom wants to be a scientist when he grows up.' (湯姆長大後要當科學家。)

guarantee **1** × May I remind you that the cassette recorder is still in guarantee.
√ **May I remind you that the cassette recorder is still under guarantee.**
(我能否提醒你錄音機的保修期限依然有效。)

> **(be) under guarantee,** NOT **in**
> **(be) under guarantee** 中的 **under** 不可用 **in** 替代。

2 √ **AmE I bought the machine just two weeks ago, so it is still under the guarantee.**
(美式英語: 我兩星期前買了這架機器, 其保修期依然有效。)
√ **BrE I bought the machine just two weeks ago, so it is still under guarantee.**
(英式英語: 譯文同上)

> In British English, use **be under guarantee** WITHOUT **the.**
> 英式英語用 **be under guarantee**, 其中沒有 **the**。

guilty × A lot of women feel guilty to leave their children alone or with another person.
√ **A lot of women feel guilty about leaving their children alone or with another person.**
(許多婦女覺得不照管自己的孩子或交給別人照管都是種過錯。)

> feel guilty about (doing) something (指 "因某事或做某事而內疚/問心有愧")

guitar See (見) PLAY 3

habit × It is a habit in Japan to take off your shoes before entering a house.
√ **It is a custom in Japan to take off your shoes before entering a house.**
(日本的風俗習慣是, 進屋前要脫鞋。)

Custom is used of the established practices of a society or very large group.
custom 指社會或一大群人所遵循的風俗習慣。
Habit is used of an individual (按 **habit** 一詞指個人的習慣, 例如): 'Nail-biting is one of her bad habits.' (咬指甲是她的一個壞習慣。)

hair **1** × Her hairs have turned grey.
√ **Her hair has turned grey.**
(她的頭髮已經變得灰白了。)

When **hair** means 'all the hair on a person's head', it is uncountable. However, when it means 'a single hair' or 'several individual hairs', it is countable. Compare (按 hair 一詞用以指人的全部頭髮時是不可數名詞, 但如指一根頭髮或幾根頭髮時則是可數名詞, 試比較): 'There was a long black hair in my soup.' 'She has long black hair.'

2 × His sister is a beautiful dark-hair girl.
√ **His sister is a beautiful dark-haired girl.**
(他妹妹是個美麗的黑髮女郎。)

dark-haired, **fair-haired**, etc.
按 haired 一詞可用以構成複合詞, 作 "... 髮的" 解, 如 **dark-haired** (黑髮的)、**fair-haired** (淺色頭髮的) 等。

half **1** × He agreed to give her the half of the money.
√ **He agreed to give her half of the money.**
(他同意給她一半的錢。)

Do not use **the** before **half** except when talking about a particular half.
不要在 **half** 前面用 the, 除非談及特指的那一半。

2 × We have a break of one and a half hour for lunch.
√ **We have a break of one and a half hours for lunch.**
(我們停工一個半小時吃中飯。)

number greater than one + plural form
一以上的數目後接複數形式

3 × The belt is about one metre and a half long.
√ **The belt is about one and a half metres long.**
(這根腰帶大約一公尺半長。)

> number greater than one + plural form + adjective
> 大於一的數目後接複數形式, 再加接形容詞。(譯者按: 如把錯句改成 " ... about a metre and a half long" 也説得通, 同樣的如 a year and a half, 都是正常的形式, 但目前的趨向, 不如 one and a half metres long 和 one and a half years 更普遍。)

hand **1** × In the hands he was holding a small bird.
√ **In his hands he was holding a small bird.**
(他雙手捧着一隻小鳥。)

> With parts of the body, use **my**, **your**, **his**, etc., NOT **the** (在表示人體某一部份的名詞之前用 **my**、**your**、**his** 等代名詞, 而不用 **the**, 例如): 'He scratched his head.' 'She took him in her arms.' 'They held out their hands.' But it is all right to say (但注意也可以這樣説): "She hit him on the head." and "I slapped him in the face."

2 × In the other hand, many women choose to go out to work.
√ **On the other hand, many women choose to go out to work.**
(另一方面, 許多婦女情願出去做事。)

> **on** the one hand ... **on** the other hand ..., NOT **in**
> **on** the one hand ... **on** the other hand ... 中的 **on** 不可用 **in** 替代

handful × As we came around the corner, we could see a handful people gathered in front of the house.
√ **As we came around the corner, we could see a handful of people gathered in front of the house.**
(我們來到拐角處, 看到一小撮人聚集在屋子前面。)

> **a handful of** + noun
> **a handful of** 作 "少量", "一小撮" 解, 後接名詞。

happen × Something must have happened with George to make him behave in such a way.
√ **Something must have happened to George to make him behave in such a way.**
(一定發生了甚麼事喬治才會做出這樣的行為。)

something **happens to** someone/something, NOT **with**
something **happens to** someone/something 中的 **to** 不可用 **with** 替代。

hardly 1 × It was so dark that we hardly could see.
√ **It was so dark that we could hardly see.**
(天色/光線很暗, 我們幾乎什麼也看不見。)

When there is no auxiliary verb, **hardly** is placed immediately before the main verb (如句中沒有助動詞, **hardly** 應放在主動詞之前, 例如): 'I hardly know her.' However, when the main verb is **be**, **hardly** is placed immediately after it (但如主動詞是 **be**, 則 **hardly** 應緊接在 **be** 之後, 例如): 'Such a small amount of money is hardly worth worrying about.' Otherwise **hardly** goes immediately after the (first) auxiliary verb (如句中有助動詞, **hardly** 應緊接在 (第一個) 助動詞之後, 例如): 'I was so thirsty that I could hardly talk.'

2 × Hardly he had begun to speak when someone interrupted him.
√ **Hardly had he begun to speak when someone interrupted him.**
(他剛開始講話, 就有人打斷他。)

When negative adverbs like **hardly/seldom/never** are used at the beginning of a sentence, the subject and auxiliary verb change places. Note the more common alternative (如否定副詞 **hardly/seldom/never** 用於句首, 則主詞應與助動詞互換位置。請注意較常用的另一種說法): 'He had hardly begun to speak when someone interrupted him.'

3 × The other teacher speaks in a way I can't hardly understand.
√ **The other teacher speaks in a way I can hardly understand.**
(另一位教師的說法, 我簡直聽不懂。)
× The dog looked terrible and couldn't hardly move.
√ **The dog looked terrible and could hardly move.**
(這狗看來很難受, 幾乎不能走動。)

Hardly (= almost not) is NOT used with **never**, **not**, etc.
作 "幾乎不 ..."、"簡直不 ..." 解的 **hardly** 不與 **never**、**not** 等連用。

4 × Society shouldn't punish these people too hardly.
√ **Society shouldn't punish these people too hard.**
(社會不應過份嚴厲懲罰這些人。)

hardly = scarcely; almost not (作 "幾乎不"、"簡直不" 解, 例如): 'I could hardly hear him.' 'I hardly know the woman.'
hard = severe AND severely (作 "嚴厲" 解)

harmful × Traffic fumes are very harmful for our health.
√ **Traffic fumes are very harmful to our health.**
(街上車輛排出的廢氣危害我們的健康。)

(be) harmful to something, NOT **for**
(be) harmful to something 中的 **to** 不可用 **for** 替代。

have 1 × After buying the food, he had not very much money left.
√ **After buying the food, he didn't have very much money left.**
(他買了食品以後, 剩下的錢就不多了。)

When **have** is used as a main verb, the negative and question forms are made with **do**.
(如 **have** 用作主動詞, 則否定式和疑問式要用 **do**。)

2 × I stayed at home yesterday because I was having a bad cold.
√ **I stayed at home yesterday because I had a bad cold.**
(我昨天待在家裏, 因為我得了重感冒。)

When talking about a state or condition, use the simple (NOT progressive) forms of **have** (如 **have** 用來表示一種狀態或情況, 不用進行式而用簡單時態, 例如):
'He has only one arm.' (NOT (不用) 'is having')
'I have just one sister.' (NOT (不用) 'am having')
'We have two dogs and a cat.' (NOT (不用) 'are having')

3 × I don't think that I have to say anything more, so I'll stop now and take this letter to the post office.
√ **I don't think that I have anything more to say, so I'll stop now and take this letter to the post office.**
(我想我已經沒有什麼話要說了, 現在就收筆, 把信拿到郵局去寄。)

> **have to do** something = must do something (作“必須做某事”解, 例如): 'My train leaves in ten minutes so I'll have to go now.'
> **have** something **to do** = have something that you need or intend to do (作“有什麼事你需要做或想去做”解)

4 × He was very hungry but he had no money about him.
√ **He was very hungry but he had no money on him.**
(他很餓, 但是身上沒有錢。)

> **have (got)** something **on** you = have (got) something in your pocket, handbag, etc. (作“你口袋裏或手提包裏有什麼東西”解, 例如): 'Have you (got) a comb on you?'

5 See (見) COLOUR 1

have to × Some wives earn a lot of money and so their husbands haven't to work.
√ **Some wives earn a lot of money and so their husbands don't have to work.**
(有些家庭的妻子賺錢很多, 所以她們的丈夫不必去工作。)

> The negative and question forms of **have to** are formed with **do** (注意: **have to** 的否定式和疑問式要用 do, 例如): 'I don't have to leave just yet.' 'Do you have to leave already?'

he See (見) THEY 1

headache **1** × If I drink coffee I get headache.
√ **If I drink coffee I get a headache.**
(我如果喝了咖啡就會頭痛。)

> **Headache** is a countable noun.
> **headache** 是可數名詞。

2 See (見) BIG 2

health × I hope this letter finds you in a good health.
√ **I hope this letter finds you in good health.**
(我希望你收到此信時身體健康。)

> **Health** is an uncountable noun.
> **health** 是不可數名詞。

hear × They all sat down and heard my story.
√ **They all sat down and listened to my story.**
(他們都坐下來聽我講故事。)

> **listen (to)** = hear and pay attention (to) (作 "用心聽" 解)

help 1 × The girl's parents couldn't help to worry about her.
√ **The girl's parents couldn't help worrying about her.**
(這女孩的父母禁不住為她擔憂。)

> **can't/couldn't help** + v-ing
> **can't/couldn't help** 後接帶 "-ing" 的動詞, 作 "難免", "不禁" 解。

2 × 'Can I help you looking after the animals?' he asked her.
√ **'Can I help you (to) look after the animals?' he asked her.**
("我能幫助你照看這些動物嗎?" 他問她。)

> **help** someone **(to) do** something
> **help** someone 之後可接帶 **to** 的動詞, 也可接不帶 **to** 的動詞。

her See (見) ME 1

here 1 × She comes to here every afternoon to feed the birds.
√ **She comes here every afternoon to feed the birds.**
(她每天下午都到這兒來餵鳥。)

> **There** and **here** cannot follow **to** unless the speaker is indicating or pointing to something (注意: **there** 和 **here** 前面不能用 **to**, 除非說話的人以手指點着某物或某處, 例如): 'When the tide comes in, the water reaches right up to here.' (潮漲時, 水位可達這麼高。)

2 × Here the taxi comes at last!
✓ **Here comes the taxi at last!**
(計程車終於來了!)

Note that the subject and the verb change places after **here/there** (注意: **here/there** 位於句首時, 主詞和動詞應調換位置, 例如): 'Here comes John!' 'There goes the woman I was telling you about.' However, there is no change if the subject is a pronoun (但如句中的主詞是代詞, 則不必改變位置): 'Here he comes!' 'There she goes!'

3 × Here is very stuffy.
✓ **It is very stuffy here.**
(這裡非常悶熱。)

"Here" is an adverb and cannot be used as a subject. It is only placed before the verb is/are when followed by a noun which is the real subject (按 "here" 是個副詞, 不能用作主詞。如後接一作主詞的名詞才可放在 is/are 之前, 例如): 'Here is a restaurant.'

high × Beauvais is very proud of having the highest cathedral in Europe.
✓ **Beauvais is very proud of having the tallest cathedral in Europe.**
(法國的包菲市以擁有歐洲最高的大教堂為榮。)

Use **high** to indicate (a great) distance above the ground (按 **high** 一詞用以表示高出地面多少的距離, 例如): 'a high ceiling', 'a high shelf'.
Tall (NOT **high**) is used of people, trees, and other things which are narrow as well as above average height (注意: **tall** 用以形容人、樹和其他狹長的東西, 例如): 'a tall man', 'a tall chimney', 'a tall house'.

him See (見) ME 1

hire × I am hiring a small house near the university.
✓ **I am renting a small house near the university.**
(我在大學附近租了一個小房子。)

In British English, **hire** means 'obtain the use of something for a short time by paying a sum of money' (在英式英語中, **hire** 指付錢短期租用): 'Let's hire a car for the day.' (我們這一天不妨租一輛汽車。)
Rent usually refers to a series of payments made over a long period of time.
rent 通常指長期支付一系列租費。

his

× The dentist told him he must brush teeth after each meal.
√ **The dentist told him he must brush his teeth after each meal.**
(牙醫告訴他每次飯後都必須刷牙。)

Possessive pronouns like **my**, **your**, **his** and **her** are generally placed before the noun when referring to the parts of the body or personal belongings (英語如表示屬於某人身體的一部份或屬於某人所有之物, 這一名詞之前一般都要加物主代名詞, 如 my、your、his 或 her, 而中文則往往略去, 例如): 'He put his hands into his pockets." (他把手放進口袋裡。)

historic **1**

× She likes reading historic novels.
√ **She likes reading historical novels.**
(她喜歡看歷史小說。)

historic = (1) very important in history (作 "具有歷史意義" 或 "在歷史上佔重要地位" 解, 例如): 'a historic voyage' ("一次具有歷史意義的航程"), 'a historic decision' ("一項帶歷史性的決議")
(2) having a long history (作 "歷史悠久" 解, 例如): 'a historic tradition' ("由來已久的傳統"), 'a historic building' ("歷史悠久的建築物")
historical = of history; in or about the past (有關歷史的, 史學的, 過往的, 例如): 'historical science' (歷史學), 'a historical figure' (歷史人物)

2

× If you have nothing to do, why don't you visit the historic museum?
√ **If you have nothing to do, why don't you visit the history museum?**
(你要是沒事幹, 為什麼不去參觀一下歷史博物館?)

> **a history museum** = a museum dealing with the subject of history (指一所介紹歷史事物 (一所以歷史為題材) 的博物館)
> Compare (試比較): 'a history book', 'a history lesson', 'a history teacher'

historical

× We shall be taking you to see several interesting historical places.
√ **We shall be taking you to see several interesting historic places.**
(我們要帶你去看一些有趣的歷史古跡。)

> **historical** = (1) about or based upon people who actually lived or events that actually happened (有關歷史上某人某事的): 'historical novels', 'historical characters'
> (2) connected with or found in history (有關歷史方面的): 'a historical fact' (史實), 'a historical document' (歷史文件)
> See note at HISTORIC 1
> 見 HISTORIC 1 注意事項

holiday

× She said she was going on holidays to France.
√ **She said she was going on holiday to France.**
(她說她要去法國度假。)
× Some people always seem to be on holidays.
√ **Some people always seem to be on holiday.**
(有些人好像老是在度假。)

> **go/be on holiday**
> 指 "去/在度假", 用 '**go/be on holiday**', 其中前置詞 on 不可用 in 或 for 替代。
> Compare (試比較): 'He's gone on holiday to Spain.' 'He's spending his summer holiday(s) in Spain.'

home

× As soon as I arrived at home, I knew that something was wrong.
√ **As soon as I arrived home, I knew that something was wrong.**
(我一到家就知道出了事。)
× I read the magazine when I returned to my home.
√ **I read the magazine when I returned home.**
(我回到家便看那本雜誌。)

arrive at/return to/go to someone's house BUT **arrive/return/go home**
注意: **arrive at** 或 **return to** 或 **go to** 後接 someone's house, 而 **arrive** 或 **return** 或 **go** 之後接 **home** 則不用 **to** 。

homework 1

× Our grammar teacher gives us a lot of homeworks.
√ **Our grammar teacher gives us a lot of homework.**
(我們的語法教師給我們佈置許多家庭作業。)

Homework is an uncountable noun.
homework 是不可數名詞。

2

× In my opinion, women who go out to work don't have enough time to do the homework.
√ **In my opinion, women who go out to work don't have enough time to do the housework.**
(在我看來, 外出工作的婦女就沒有足夠的時間做家務。)

homework = work that a teacher gives a pupil to do at home (指教師給學生佈置在家做的功課)
housework = all the jobs that have to be done regularly to keep a house or flat clean and tidy (指為了清潔衛生等必須經常做的家務)

honour

× It is an honour to me to welcome you all to Norway.
√ **It is an honour for me to welcome you all to Norway.**
(能歡迎你們各位到挪威來, 是我的榮幸。)

an honour for someone, NOT **to**
注意: **an honour for** someone 中的 **for** 不可用 **to** 替代。

hope 1

× I left the bag on a bus and I have no hope for getting it back.
√ **I left the bag on a bus and I have no hope of getting it back.**
(我把袋子丟在公共汽車裏了, 我不抱失而復得的希望。)

little/no hope of + v-ing NOT **for**
little/no hope of 後接帶 "-ing" 的動詞, 其中的 **of** 不可用 **for** 替代。

2 × I hope you all to have an interesting afternoon.
√ **I hope you all have an interesting afternoon.**
(我希望你們各位下午過得愉快。)

> When there is a change of person before and after **hope**, it cannot be followed by to-v. Instead, the verb is usually in the present simple tense.
> 如 **hope** 的前後是不同的人稱, 後面不接帶 to 的動詞。其次, 所用的動詞通常是一般現在式。)

hospital √ **AmE I've been in the hospital for the last five weeks.**
(美式英語: 近五個星期我一直住在醫院裡。)
√ **BrE I've been in hospital for the last five weeks.**
(英式英語: 譯文同上)

> Note the expressions (注意下列用法): 'be taken to hospital', 'leave hospital', 'be in hospital' WITHOUT **the** (均不用 **the**)
> In British English **the** is used only when talking about a particular hospital.
> 英式英語中只有特指的某一醫院才用 **the**。

hour × It was a twelve hours trip.
√ **It was a twelve-hour trip.**
(這次旅程花了十二小時。)

See note at MONTH
見 MONTH 的注意事項

house 1 × The policeman said he had no more questions and told me to go to my house.
√ **The policeman said he had no more questions and told me to go home.**
(警察説他已沒有其他問題要問, 告訴我可以回家。)

> **go home** = return to the place where you live (作 "回家" 解)

2 × It is believed that the castle was once the house of evil monsters.
√ **It is believed that the castle was once the home of evil monsters.**
(據説, 這城堡一度有鬼怪出現。)

house = a particular type of building, usually lived in by a family (指家庭所居住的單幢房屋, 例如): 'Do you live in a house or a flat?' (你住單幢的房子還是單元住宅?)
home = any building or place in which a person lives (and feels a sense of belonging) 指人生活於其中的"家" (擁有一種歸屬感)

household

× At the weekend they have to do all the household.
√ **At the weekend they have to do all the housework.**
(在週末, 他們必須做所有家務。)

household = all the people living together in a house or flat (指"同住一家的人"): 'Be quiet or you'll wake the whole household.' (安靜一點, 不然你會吵醒全家的人。)
housework = all the jobs that have to be done regularly to keep a house or flat clean and tidy (指為了清潔衛生等必須經常做的家務)
(編譯者按: 美式英語用: On the weekend they....)

housework

× Brian often helps Elisa to do the houseworks.
√ **Brian often helps Elisa to do the housework.**
(布里恩經常幫助伊莉莎做家務。)

Housework is an uncountable noun.
housework 是不可數名詞。

how 1

× Could you describe how the driver looks like?
√ **Could you describe what the driver looks like?**
(你能不能形容一下那司機的樣子?)
× How is Christmas in France?
√ **What is Christmas like in France?**
(法國是怎樣過聖誕節的?)

Use **what** ... **like** (NOT **how**) when asking for a description of someone or something.
如要求別人形容某人或某事某物, 以 **what ... like** 來問, 而不是用 **how**。

2

× Their decision will depend on how good is your offer.
√ **Their decision will depend on how good your offer is.**
(他們如何決定取決於你報價的高低。)

When the object of the sentence is a **wh-**clause, the subject and verb in the **wh-**clause do NOT change places.
如句中的受詞是一個 "wh- 子句" (即以 what、when、where、which 等, 甚至包括 how 作句首的子句), 則子句中主詞和動詞不需調換位置。

3 × I must tell you how I was pleased to receive a letter from you.
√ **I must tell you how pleased I was to receive a letter from you.**
(我一定要跟你說, 收到你的信我不知多麼開心。)

how + adjective/adverb + subject + verb (以 **how** 作句首的句子或子句, 如後接一形容詞或副詞, 則其後才是主詞加動詞, 例如): 'I wonder how far it is.' 'I can't describe how beautifully she played.' 'How clumsy you are!'

4 × How much is the price of this watch?
√ **What's the price of this watch?**
√ **How much does this watch cost?**
(這個手錶要多少錢?)

We say "what is the price" instead of "how much is the price" when we want to know the price of something.
問價錢, 英文習慣用 'What is the price?' 而不用 'How much is the price?'

5 × How to spell 'squirrel'?
√ **How do you spell 'squirrel'?**
('squirrel' [松鼠] 這個字怎麼拼?)

"How to spell 'squirrel'?" is an incomplete sentence, because there is no subject nor predicate in it.
注意: "How to spell 'squirrel'?" 不是一個完整的句子, 因為句中沒有主語和述語。

6 × When the war broke out we didn't know how to do.
√ **When the war broke out we didn't know what to do.**
(戰爭爆發了, 我們不知怎麼辦才好。)

In many cases 'how' is translated into Chinese as "怎麼", such as 'How can I get to Cambridge?' 'I told her how to find me.' However the correct translation of '不知怎麼辦' into English is "do not know what to do".
中文的"怎麼"常常譯作英文的"how", 例如"How can I get to Cambridge?" 可譯作"我怎麼才能到劍橋去?" 又如"I told her how to find me." 可譯作"我告訴她怎麼才能找到我。" 但中文"不知怎麼辦"譯作英文正確的說法應為"do not know what to do"。

hundred 1 ✓ **AmE The magazine has a hundred fifty pages.** (美式英語: 雜誌共有一百五十頁。)
✓ **BrE The magazine has a hundred and fifty pages.** (英式英語: 譯文同上)

In British English, use (英式英語, 在 hundred 之後, 不論接以個位數、十位數或數十位數, 均用 and 連接, 例如): 'a hundred and one', 'five hundred and sixty', etc.

2 × Five hundreds of children are born in the city every day.
✓ **Five hundred children are born in the city every day.** (這城市每天有五百個孩子出生。)

'hundreds of children' BUT 'two hundred children', 'five hundred children', etc.
如說"數百個孩子", 用 hundreds of children, 其中 of 不可少。如說具體數字: 二百個孩子, 五百個孩子, 則不用 of, 直接說 two hundred children, five hundred children。
Dozen, **thousand**, **million**, etc. behave in the same way (注意: **dozen**, **thousand**, **million** 在這方面的用法與 hundred 相同, 例如): 'dozens of eggs'—'two dozen eggs', 'thousands of dollars' —'five thousand dollars', 'millions of tourists' —'several million tourists'

3 See (見) THOUSAND 1

hurry × Tim was in hurry and couldn't stop to talk.
✓ **Tim was in a hurry and couldn't stop to talk.** (丁姆匆忙得很, 無法停下來談話。)

(be) in a hurry
在 **(be) in a hurry** 這一片語中, 不可省略 **a**。

hurt × The driver didn't hurt a lot but his passenger was taken to hospital.

√ **The driver wasn't badly/seriously hurt but his passenger was taken to hospital.**

(駕駛者傷勢並不重, 但同車者則需送醫院。)

> **hurt** = cause (someone) to feel pain (指使人感到疼, 例如): 'These new shoes hurt my feet.' ("新鞋夾疼我的腳。") 'My feet hurt.' ("我的腳感到疼。")
> **be hurt** = be injured (指受傷, 例如): 'Several people were hurt when the wall collapsed.' (牆坍下來, 好幾個人受了傷。)

I × I and some of my classmates publish a monthly magazine.

√ **Some of my classmates and I publish a monthly magazine.**

(我和幾個同班同學一起出版一本月刊。)

> It is usual to mention yourself last: 'You and I ...', NOT 'I and you'; 'my wife and I', NOT 'I and my wife'; 'the General Manager and I', NOT 'I and the General Manager'.
> 雖則中文習慣說 "我和你"、"我和我太太"、"我和總經理", 但英文則說 "you and I"、"my wife and I"、"the General Manager and I"。

if 1 × If it will rain, I shall come and meet you in the car.

√ **If it rains, I shall come and meet you in the car.**

(要是下雨, 我會駕車來接你。)

> When talking about possible or open situations, put the **if** clause in the present tense and use **shall/will** + verb in the main clause.
> 提到可能發生的或未定的情況時, **if** 子句的主動詞用現在式, 主句用 **shall/will** 再接原形動詞。

2 × If there were no unemployment, we will not have the amount of crime we have today.

√ **If there were no unemployment, we would not have the amount of crime we have today.**

(如果沒有失業, 我們就不會有今天這麼多的罪案。)

> When talking about unreal or imaginary situations, put the **if** clause in the past tense and the main clause in the conditional tense.
> 提到與事實不符或不可能發生的情況時, **if** 子句的主動詞用過去式, 主句用表示條件的時態。

3 × If you would have caught the earlier train, we could have travelled together.
√ **If you had caught the earlier train, we could have travelled together.**
(假如你趕上早一班火車, 我們本來是可以同車的。)

> When talking about unfulfilled or impossible situations, put the **if** clause in the past perfect tense and the main clause in the perfect conditional tense.
> 提到沒有做到或不可能發生的情況時, **if** 子句的主動詞用過去完成式, 主句用表示條件的完成式。

4 See (見) WOULD 2

ill × Most of the ill people were very old.
√ **Most of the sick people were very old.**
(大多數的病人年紀都很老。)

> **Ill** (=sick) cannot be placed immediately before a noun. Compare (作 "生病" 解的 ill 不能放在名詞之前, 試比較): 'Many of the old people looked ill.'

imaginary × People tend to become less imaginary as they grow older.
√ **People tend to become less imaginative as they grow older.**
(人們的想像力往往隨着年齡的增長而減退。)

> **imaginary** = existing in or produced by the imagination (作 "憑空想像的"、"虛構的" 解, 例如): 'The characters in the story are entirely imaginary.' (故事中的人物純屬虛構。)
> **imaginative** = having or showing imagination (作 "富於想像力的" 解)

imagine × What about all his friends? He couldn't imagine to leave them all.
√ **What about all his friends? He couldn't imagine leaving them all.**
(所有他那些朋友怎樣呢? 要離開他們, 他簡直無法想像。)

> **imagine** + v-ing
> 注意: **imagine** 後接帶 "-ing" 的動詞。

immediately

× 'Let me know immediately she will arrive,' he shouted.
√ **'Let me know immediately she arrives,' he shouted.**
(“她一到, 你就告訴我,” 他大聲叫道。)

> After **immediately** use the present simple tense for future reference, NOT **shall/will** + verb.
> 在 **immediately** 之後不用將來式的 **shall/will**, 要用一般現在式。注意: immediately 在這個例句中是個連接詞, 相當於 as soon as, 這是英式英語的用法; 美式英語不用 immediately 而用 as soon as 替代。

immigrant

× Japan is contemplating the importation of Vietnamese emigrants to solve the labour problem.
√ **Japan is contemplating the importation of Vietnamese immigrants to solve the labour problem.**
(日本正仔細考慮吸納越南移民以解決勞工不足的問題。)

> **emigrant** = people leaving their own country in order to go and live in another (指自本國向他國移居的移民, 例如): 'Vietnamese emigrants to Japan' (移居日本的越南移民)
> **immigrant** = people coming into a country from abroad to live there (指自外國移居入本國的移民, 例如): 'The Ongs are immigrants from Singapore.' (黃家是從新加坡來的移民。)

important

× He said that money was not important for him.
√ **He said that money was not important to him.**
(他説錢對他並不重要。)
× The pen is very important for me because it was a present from my father.
√ **The pen is very important to me because it was a present from my father.**
(我很看重這枝筆, 因為那是父親送的。)

> When talking about how strongly a person feels about something, use **important to**, NOT **for**.
> 指 “某物對某人來説是重要的”, 用 **important to**, 不用 **important for**。

impression

× He had a deep impression of the old professor.
√ **He was deeply impressed by the old professor.**
(他對那老教授印象很深。)

"to have an impression of someone or **something"** is not an idiomatic expression in English.
注意: **to have an impression of someone** 或 **something** 的說法並不合乎英語的慣用法。

improve See (見) PERFECT 1

improvement
× There has been an improvement on the weather.
√ **There has been an improvement in the weather.**
(天氣越來越好了。)
× Today's weather is an improvement in yesterday's.
√ **Today's weather is an improvement on yesterday's.**
(今天的天氣比昨天的好。)

You can speak of an **improvement in** something if it has got better.
指某方面的事好轉或改善, 可用 improvement in。
You can speak of an **improvement on** something if you compare two things, and the second is better than the first.
如把兩件事作比較, 而後發生的那一件又比早先發生的較為好, 則可用 **improvement on**。

in 1
× In 1st July we went to Italy by car.
√ **On 1st July we went to Italy by car.**
(七月一日我們駕車到意大利。)

on + a day or date, NOT **in**
on 後接 a day (某一天) 或 a date (某日期), 此處的 **on** 不可用 **in** 代替。

2
× In the following morning she called me at the office.
√ **The following morning she called me at the office.**
(第二天早晨她到辦公室來看我。)

'in the morning/afternoon/evening' BUT 'the following morning', 'the next afternoon', 'the previous evening', etc.
表示 "在上午/下午/傍晚", 用 in the morning/afternoon/evening; 而表示 "第二天上午或下午"、"前一晚", 則不用加 in, 如 the following morning、the next afternoon、the previous evening 等。

3 × In the first few days the radio worked very well.
√ **For the first few days the radio worked very well.**
(在剛買回來的頭幾天, 收音機的性能非常好。)

> When talking about how long something lasts or continues, use **for**, NOT **in**.
> 表示某動作持續多長時間, 應用 **for**, 不用 **in**。

4 × In arriving at the airport we discovered that the plane would be late.
√ **On arriving at the airport we discovered that the plane would be late.**
(一到機場, 我們就發覺飛機要晚點。)

> **on/upon** doing something, NOT **in**
> 注意: **on** 或 **upon** 後接帶 "-ing" 的動詞, 表示 "一 ... 就 ..." (亦即 directly after 之意), 不能把 **on** 或 **upon** 改為 **in**。如用 in 後接帶 "-ing" 動詞, 則是表示 when 或 while 之意, 如: "In studying other cultures, you can learn more about your own."

5 × It's a dark brown coat in wool.
√ **It's a dark brown coat made of wool.**
(這是件用羊毛製成的深棕色上衣。)

> **made of** wool/wood etc., NOT **in**
> 注意: **made of** wool/wood, 係毛製或木製之意, **of** 一字不能改作 **in**。但如係指該產品是在何國、何地製造的, 那自然是用 in, 例如: 'Made in Hong Kong/ Taiwan'

6 × I work eight hours in a day.
√ **I work eight hours a day.**
(我每天工作八小時。)

> **In** is NOT used in expressions such as (在下列用法中, 不用 **in**): 'The shop is open six days a week.' 'He visits his father three times a year.' 'Bananas cost fifty pence a pound.' 'I drove to the hospital at ninety miles an hour.'

incapable × Most small children are incapable to sit still for more than five minutes.
√ **Most small children are incapable of sitting still for more than five minutes.**
(大多數的小孩子不能安靜地坐上五分鐘。)

incapable of + v-ing
注意: **incapable** 後不接帶 to 的動詞, 而應接 **of** 再接帶 "-ing" 的動詞。若 incapable 改用 unable, 則後接帶 to 的動詞, 例如: 'He seems unable to understand you.'

include

× The poem includes just two short verses.
√ **The poem consists of just two short verses.**
(這首詩只有兩個詩節。)

include = contain (in addition to something else [作 "包括 … 在內" 解, 指除某些東西外, 還有其他東西。]): 'The United Kingdom **includes** Northern Ireland and Wales.' ("聯合王國包括北愛爾蘭和威爾士在內。" ——即北愛爾蘭和威爾士只是聯合王國的一部份, 此外還有 England 和 Scotland。)
consist of = be made up of ('由 …… 組成' 之意, 例如): 'The United Kingdom **consists of** England, Wales, Scotland and Northern Ireland.' (聯合王國係由英格蘭、威爾士、蘇格蘭和北愛爾蘭組合而成。/ 聯合王國包括英格蘭、威爾士、蘇格蘭和北愛爾蘭四個部份。)

increase

× The increase of crime is accelerating.
√ **The increase in crime is accelerating.**
(罪案的增長正在加快。)

an increase in something, NOT **of**
指 "某事物的增長", 用 **an increase in** something, 其中的 **in** 不可用 **of** 替代。

indeed

× I was having a good time indeed when suddenly the plane started to shake.
√ **I was having a very good time indeed when suddenly the plane started to shake.**
(我當時確實是很高興, 可是飛機突然間開始左右搖動。)

very + adjective + noun + **indeed** (按 **indeed** 用來加強語氣時, 往往與 **very** 接形容詞和名詞這種結構連用, 並放在名詞之後。錯誤的例證中不用 very, 故被視為不妥): 'I thought it was a very clever answer indeed.'
very + adjective/adverb + **indeed** (按 **indeed** 也可用於形容詞或副詞之後以加強語氣): 'The results are very good indeed.' 'She sang very well indeed.'

independent

× Nowadays young people want to be independent from their parents.
√ **Nowadays young people want to be independent of their parents.**
(現今年輕人總是想離開父母過獨立生活。)

> **independent of** someone/something, NOT **from**
> 注意: **independent of** someone/something 中的 **of** 不可用 **from** 替代。

indoor

× As it was raining we decided to stay indoor.
√ **As it was raining we decided to stay indoors.**
(由於下雨, 我們決定留在屋內。)

> **Indoor** is an adjective (按 **indoor** 是形容詞, 只能修飾名詞, 如): 'an indoor swimming pool', 'indoor games'.
> **Indoors** is an adverb. (按 **indoors** 是副詞, 可修飾動詞, 如上句的 indoors 是修飾 to stay 的。)

industrious

× The South has fewer industrious areas.
√ **The South has fewer industrial areas.**
(南部的工業地區較少。)

> **industrious** = hard-working (作 "勤勞的" 解, 例如): 'She's a very industrious student.' (她是個很用功的學生。)
> **industrial** = having or concerning industries (作 "工業的" 解)

industry

× The biggest industries in Jakobsberg are Philips and IBM.
√ **The biggest companies in Jakobsberg are Philips and IBM.**
(瑞典的雅城有兩家最大的企業, 一家是飛利浦, 另一家是 IBM。)

> **industry** = all the people, factories, companies, etc.
> involved in a major area of production (作 "行業"、"企業" 或 "製造業" 解): 'the steel industry' (鋼鐵工業), 'the clothing industry' (服裝製造業)
> Compare (比較): 'IBM is one of the biggest companies in the electronics industry.' (IBM 是電子行業中最大的公司之一。)

inferior

× Some people think that the new system is inferior than the old one.

√ **Some people think that the new system is inferior to the old one.**

(有些人認為新制度比舊制度更差。)

> **inferior to,** NOT **than**
> 我們可以說 **inferior to**, 不可說 **inferior than**。

influence 1

× Finally I asked him not to keep disturbing me, but it had no influence.

√ **Finally I asked him not to keep disturbing me, but it had no effect.**

(最後, 我要求他不要老是干擾我, 但是我的話並不起作用。)

> When talking about the particular result of an action or event, use **effect**, NOT **influence**.
> 表示某一行動或事件導致的具體結果時用 **effect**, 不用 **influence**。
> **effect** = result (作 "結果" 解)
> **influence** = shaping force or power (作 "影響" 解)

2

× I don't think that longer prison sentences would influence on criminals.

√ **I don't think that longer prison sentences would influence criminals.**

(我認為更長的刑期不會對罪犯產生什麼影響。)

> **have an influence on** someone (noun) BUT **influence** someone (verb) WITHOUT **on**
> 表示 "對某人產生影響", 可用 "**have an influence on**", 這裡的 influence 自然是個名詞, 所以後面要用 **on**; 如 influence 用作動詞, 則可直接與 someone 相接, 不必用 **on**。

information 1

× On Friday we'll be able to give you further information of the trip.

√ **On Friday we'll be able to give you further information about the trip.**

(到星期五, 我們就能進一步告訴你關於這次旅行的資料。)

> **information about** something, NOT **of**
> **information about** something 中的 **about** 不可用 **of** 替代。

2 × A journalist often has to travel to get the informations he requires.
√ **A journalist often has to travel to get the information he requires.**
(記者往往要四出奔走才能採訪到所需的新聞。)

> **Information** is an uncountable noun. Note also (按 **information** 是不可數名詞, 不能用複數。注意也說): 'a piece/an item of information'

3 × I asked the salesman to tell me some information about it.
√ **I asked the salesman to give me some information about it.**
(我要求推銷員給我提供有關的資料。)

> **give** someone **information**, NOT **tell**, **say**, etc.
> **give** someone **information** 中的 **give** 不可用 **tell** 或 **say** 替代。

injure **1** × He fell and was injured in the leg.
√ **He fell and injured his leg.**
(他跌了一跤, 腿部受傷。)

> **be shot/wounded in** the leg/arm BUT **be injured** (WITHOUT in the leg/arm) OR **injure** your leg/arm
> 指腿或手臂中彈或受傷, 應説 **be shot/wounded in** the leg/arm; 如用 **be injured**, 後面就不可接 in the leg/arm, 但可説 **injure** your leg/arm。

2 × Fortunately the driver was wearing his seat belt and so he did not injure.
√ **Fortunately the driver was wearing his seat belt and so he wasn't injured.**
(幸虧司機繫着安全帶, 才不致受傷。)

> **injure someone; injure yourself**
> **injure** is NOT intransitive.
> 注意: **injure** 下接 **someone** 和 **yourself**等, 是個及物動詞。

inquire See (見) ENQUIRE

inquiry

× After making several inquiries, I finally discovered his address.
√ **After making several enquiries, I finally discovered his address.**
(我詢問了幾次, 終於找到他的住址。)

Enquiry is more often used for a simple request for information, and **inquiry** for a long serious study. Compare (按 **enquiry** 較常用於簡單的查問, 而 **inquiry** 則指需要時間很長的探究, 試比較): 'a court of inquiry' (調查法庭), 'an inquiry into the cause of the unrest' (對動亂原因的調查)

insecure

× I felt rather insecure of taking the examination.
√ **I felt rather insecure about taking the examination.**
(我對參加這次考試不太有把握。)

insecure about + v-ing, NOT **of**
按 **insecure about** 後接帶 "-ing" 的動詞, 其中的 **about** 不可用 **of** 替代。

inside 1

× It's a dark blue coat with a black inside.
√ **It's a dark blue coat with a black lining.**
(這是一件黑色襯裏的深藍色上衣。)

lining = the material covering the inside of a coat, jacket, etc. (作 "衣服襯裏" 解)

2

× I remember leaving a blue handkerchief inside of the right-hand pocket.
√ **I remember leaving a blue handkerchief inside the right-hand pocket.**
(我記得把一條藍色手帕放在右手口袋裏。)

inside something WITHOUT **of**
按 **inside** 之後不用 **of**, 直接加上 something。但在美式英語中, 尤其口語, 可用 inside of ... 。

insist 1

× The porter insisted to help us with our baggage.
√ **The porter insisted on helping us with our baggage.**
(這個搬運工堅持要幫我們搬行李。)

insist on + v-ing
按 **insist on** 後接帶 "-ing" 的動詞。

2 × She insisted me on carrying her enormous suitcase.
√ **She insisted on me/my carrying her enormous suitcase.**
(她一定要我替她拿她那隻大衣箱。)

insist on (someone('s) doing) something
按 **insist on** 除了後接 something 之外還可後接 someone doing something 或 someone's doing something, 如上例。

3 × We insisted that he wrote the letter.
√ **We insisted that he write the letter.**
(我們一定要他寫這封信。)

In the that-clause that follows such verbs as insist, decide, suggest, intend, suppose, etc., the predicate should be '(**should**) + infinitive WITHOUT to'.
在某些動詞, 諸如 insist、decide、suggest、intend、suppose 等之後所接的 "that-子句" 中, 其動詞部分應用 (**should**) 加原形動詞。注意: **should** 可省略。

in spite of See (見) SPITE

instead × I advised her to go out more instead to stay at home all the time.
√ **I advised her to go out more instead of staying at home all the time.**
(我勸她多出去走走, 不要整天待在家裏。)

instead of (doing) something
按 **instead of** 後接 something 或 doing something。

institute × In my opinion, the monarchy is an old-fashioned institute.
√ **In my opinion, the monarchy is an old-fashioned institution.**
(在我看來, 君主政體是種舊式制度。)

institute = a society or organization set up for a special purpose (作 "學院"、"學會" 等解, 例如): 'He is a member of the Royal Institute of Architects.'
institution = a custom or tradition (作 "風格"、"制度" 等解, 例如): 'Marriage is an institution.' (婚姻是一項制度。)

instruction 1 × I read the instructions book very carefully.
√ **I read the instruction book very carefully.**
(我仔細看了這份說明書。)

Many nouns that are usually plural drop their **-s** when used to modify another noun. Compare (許多複數名詞用來形容另一個名詞時, 通常去掉 **-s**, 試比較): 'a book of instructions' and 'an instruction book', 'a shelf for books' and 'a book shelf', 'a holiday lasting ten days' and 'a ten-day holiday'

2 × The machine is supplied with instructions how to use it.
√ **The machine is supplied with instructions on how to use it.**
(這機器附有使用說明。)

instructions on how to do something
指 "有關做某事的說明或指示", 應說 '**instructions on** how to do something'。
Note that a number of other prepositions can also be used, including **about**, **as to**, **regarding**, and **concerning.**
注意上句中的前置詞除 on 外, 也可用 **about**、**as to**、**regarding** 和 **concerning**。

insure √ **AmE People need a job to insure their independence.**
(美式英語: 人們需要有份工作來確保獨立生活。)
√ **BrE People need a job to ensure their independence.**
(英式英語: 譯文同上)

In both British and American English **ensure** means 'to make certain'. In British English **insure** is only used to mean 'to protect against loss or damage by means of insurance' (在英式和美式英語中, **ensure** 都作 "確保"、"保證" 解。在英式英語中, **insure** 只作 "給 … 買保險" 解): 'She insured her camera for five hundred dollars.' (她給自己的照相機買了五百元保險。) However, in American English **insure** is used with both these meanings. (然而, 在美式英語中, **insure** 則兼有這兩種含義。)

intend × I am intending to stay in England until Christmas.
√ **I intend to stay in England until Christmas.**
(我打算在英國逗留至聖誕節。)

> **intend** is rarely used in the present progressive tense.
> 注意: **intend** 很少用現在進行式。

intention × She said that she hadn't the slightest intention to accept the invitation.
√ **She said that she hadn't the slightest intention of accepting the invitation.**
(她說她一點也沒有接受邀請的意思。)

> have not the slightest **intention of** + v-ing
> 按 have not the slightest **intention** 後接 **of**, 再接帶 "-ing" 的動詞。

interested 1 × It was a very interested idea.
√ **It was a very interesting idea.**
(這個想法很有意思。)

> 'It is interesting.' = It interests people. (作 "令人感興趣" 解。)
> 'They are interested.' = Someone/something interests them. (作 "對某人/某事物感興趣" 解。)

2 × I am not interested about your opinion.
√ **I am not interested in your opinion.**
(我對你的意見不感興趣。)

> **be interested in** (doing) something, NOT **about**
> 按 **be interested in** (doing) something 中的 **in** 不可用 **about** 代替。

3 × I think you will be very interesting in the magazine.
√ **I think you will be very interested in the magazine.**
(我想你會對這本雜誌十分感興趣。)

> Be **interested** in, NOT be interesting in
> "對 ... 感興趣" 應是 be **interested** in, 不是 be interesting in

4 × I was interesting to hear she had got married.
√ **I was interested to hear she had got married.**
(聽說她結了婚, 我對這消息很感興趣。)

See note at 1
見 1 註解

interview × The magazine contains several interviews from famous racing drivers.
√ **The magazine contains several interviews with famous racing drivers.**
(這本雜誌載有幾篇採訪著名賽車手的報導。)

an interview with someone, NOT **from**
注意: **an interview with** someone 中的 **with** 不可用 **from** 替代。

into × Into the right-hand pocket you will find a pair of gloves.
√ **In the right-hand pocket you will find a pair of gloves.**
(你在右手的口袋裏會找到一副手套。)

Into is used with movement (注意: **into** 用於動作, 例如): 'He put his hand into his pocket.'
In can be used with or without movement. Compare (注意: **in** 可用於動作或非動作。試比較): 'He put his hand in his pocket.' 'His hand was in his pocket.'

intrude × I hope I'm not intruding your privacy.
√ **I hope I'm not intruding on your privacy.**
(我沒有打攪您吧?)

When **intrude** means to come in when not wanted, it is intransitive and should be followed by "**on/upon**" (按 **intrude** 一詞, 如屬未經對方同意闖入或打攪對方之意, 是個不及物動詞, 後應跟 **on** 或 **upon**): 'I don't want to intrude on you if you are busy.' 'I'm sorry to intrude on your time.'
Note that it is more natural simply to say (注意: 更自然更簡單的說法是): 'I hope I'm not intruding.'

invent 1 × It will not be long before scientists invent a cure for this terrible disease.

√ **It will not be long before scientists discover a cure for this terrible disease.**

(要不了多久, 科學家就會找到治療這種可怕疾病的方法。)

> **invent** = create (something which has never existed before) for the first time (作 "創造發明" 解, 強調這發明係首次, 例如): 'Who invented the bicycle?'
> **discover** = find or reveal by research (作 "發現"、"找出 ... 方法/對策" 等解, 例如): 'Penicillin was discovered almost by accident.'

2 × I'm sure that your host families will invent lots of interesting things for you to do.

√ **I'm sure that your host families will think of lots of interesting things for you to do.**

(我相信接待你們的那些家庭一定會想出許多有趣的事情讓你們做。)

> **invent** = create (something which has never existed before) for the first time (作 "創造發明" 解, 強調這發明係首次)
> **think of** = produce (something) as an idea or suggestion (作 "想到"、"想出" 解)

invest × Businessmen invest vast amounts on these industries.

√ **Businessmen invest vast amounts in these industries.**

(商人在這些行業中作了大筆投資。)

> **invest** (money etc.) **in** something, NOT **on**
> 注意: **invest** (金錢等) 後接 **in** something, 不可接 **on** something。

invitation See (見) AGREE 5

invite 1 × I don't know why she has invited me her sister's wedding.

√ **I don't know why she has invited me to her sister's wedding.**

(我不知道她為什麼邀請我去參加她妹妹的婚禮。)

> **invite** someone **to** something
> 按 **invite** someone 後接 **to** something。

2 × She invited him for having some ice-cream.
√ **She invited him to have some ice-cream.**
(她邀請他去吃冰淇淋。)

> **invite** someone + to-v
> 按 **invite** someone 後接帶 to 的動詞。

island × I was on holiday with my parents on the island Capri.
√ **I was on holiday with my parents on the island of Capri.**
(我在卡普里島上和父母一起度假。)

> **the island of** + name
> 按 **the island of** 後接名詞 (尤指專有名詞)。

it 1 × At the end of the course, it will be a party at the language school.
√ **At the end of the course, there will be a party at the language school.**
(這門課程結束後, 語言學校將舉行一次聚會。)

> In sentences or clauses which express a state or fact, the subject often comes after the verb **be**. Such statements are introduced by **there** (NOT **it**).
> 在表示狀態或事實的句子或子句裡, 主詞通常位於動詞 **be** 之後。這一類句子不用 **it** 而用 **there** 引導。
> See also (參見) NEED 1, POINT 1

2 × When I turned on the light, it happened the same thing again.
√ **When I turned on the light, the same thing happened again.**
(我開燈時, 又出現同樣情況。)

> **It** is not used as a preparatory subject unless the subject is an infinitive or **that** clause (按 **it** 只有在真正主語是動詞不定式或子句時才用作形式主語): 'It was wonderful to see them again.' (再次見到他們太好了。) 'It is surprising that the letter arrived so quickly.' (信到得這麼快, 這出乎意料之外。) 'It happened that we arrived just as they were leaving.' (巧得很, 我們到達之時也是他們要離開之時。)

3 See (見) THEY

4 See (見) APPRECIATE, FIND 1, LIKE 4

5 See (見) BE 1

it's × The cat sat in front of the fire, cleaning it's whiskers.
√ **The cat sat in front of the fire, cleaning its whiskers.**
(貓蹲在爐火前, 正在舐牠的貓鬚。)

> **its** (WITHOUT an apostrophe) is the possessive form (按 **its** 是 it 的所有格): 'The dog has hurt its nose again.' (狗又把自己的鼻子碰傷了。)
> **it's** (WITH an apostrophe) is a short form (按 **it's** 是個簡略語) = (1) it is: 'it's raining'; (2) it has: 'it's been raining'

jewellery 1 × Women should keep expensive jewelleries in a bank or safe.
√ **Women should keep expensive jewellery in a bank or safe.**
(女士們應把貴重首飾放在銀行或保險箱裡。)

> **Jewellery** is an uncountable noun.
> 按 **jewellery** 是不可數名詞。
> 美式英語寫作 **jewelry**

2 × She and her husband had bought the ring at a jewellery.
√ **She and her husband had bought the ring at a jeweller's.**
(她和丈夫在首飾店買了那枚戒指。)

> **jeweller's** = a shop which sells **jewellery** (gold rings, bracelets, etc.) (作 "首飾店" 解)
> 美式英語寫作 **jeweler's**

joke × He kept saying the same joke again and again.
√ **He kept telling the same joke again and again.**
(他一次又一次地講那笑話。)

> **tell a joke,** NOT **say**
> 我們說 **tell a joke**, 不說 **say** a joke。

journey × It wasn't the first journey he had done to Paris.
√ **It wasn't the first journey he had made to Paris.**
(這不是他第一次去巴黎之行。)

> **make a journey,** NOT **do**
> 我們說 **make a journey**, 不說 **do** a journey。

just 1 × I'd like just to thank you once again for your hospitality.
√ **I'd just like to thank you once again for your hospitality.**
(我只是想再一次感謝你的款待。)

> **Just** usually goes immediately after the (first) auxiliary verb (按 **just** 一般放在 (第一個) 助動詞之後, 例如): 'I'd just like to ask you one more question.' When there is no auxiliary verb, **just** is placed directly before the main verb (句中沒有助動詞時, **just** 緊放在主動詞之前, 例如): 'She just arrived in time.' However, when the main verb is **be**, **just** is placed immediately after it (然而, 句中的主動詞是 **be** 時, **just** 緊放在 **be** 之後, 例如): 'The milk is just outside the door.'

2 × Some people think that mothers should stay at home. I just partly agree with this opinion.
√ **Some people think that mothers should stay at home. I only partly agree with this opinion.**
(有人認為做母親的應該留在家裡, 這意見我只同意一部份。)

> In expressions which mean 'not completely', use **only**, NOT **just** (表示 "不完全" 這一意思, 只用 **only**, 不用 **just**): 'He's only half awake.' 'I only partly believe that.'

kid × On the front of the box was the warning: 'Not suitable for very young kids.'
√ **On the front of the box was the warning: 'Not suitable for very young children.'**
(盒子正面印有警告的字樣: "兒童不宜"。)

> **Kid** is very informal.
> 按 **kid** 是口語用語。

kidnap × We heard on the radio that the plane had been kidnapped by terrorists.
√ **We heard on the radio that the plane had been hijacked by terrorists.**
(我們聽廣播説飛機已遭恐怖分子劫持。)

> **Kidnap** is used only for people.
> 按 **kidnap** ("綁架") 只用於人。

kind 1 × Would you be so kind to arrange for the book to be sent back to me?
√ **Would you be so kind as to arrange for the book to be sent back to me?**
(可否請你費心把書送還給我?)
× If you should find it, would you be so kind as sending it to the following address?
√ **If you should find it, would you be so kind as to send it to the following address?**
(如果你找到了, 可否請你送到下列地址?)

> **be kind enough to do** something (如用 **be kind enough**, 則後接 **to do** something): 'Would you be kind enough to open the door for me?' BUT **be so kind as to** do something (但如用 **be so kind** 這一句式, 後應接 **as to** do something)

2 × All the people he met were very kind with him.
√ **All the people he met were very kind to him.**
(他遇到的人都對他很好。)

> **be kind to** someone, NOT **with**
> 按 **be kind to** someone 中的 **to**, 不可用 **with** 代替。

3 × There are many kind of job for people with qualifications.
√ **There are many kinds of job for people with qualifications.**
(合乎資歷的人士有許多工作可以選擇。)
× I enjoy all kind of sport.
√ **I enjoy all kinds of sport.**
(我喜歡各種各類運動。)

> **Kind** (= type) is a countable noun. Compare (按 kind 作 type —"種類" 解是個可數名詞, 試比較): 'A pineapple is a kind of fruit.' 'Pineapples and oranges are kinds of fruit.'

know 1

× We had only just met, but it was as if we had been knowing each other for years.

√ **We had only just met, but it was as if we had known each other for years.**

(雖然我們剛認識, 但好像我們已經相識好幾年了。)

> **Know** is NOT used in progressive tenses.
> **Know** 不用於進行式。

2

× The best way to know the city is to visit it on foot.

√ **The best way to get to know the city is to visit it on foot.**

(要想了解這城市, 最好的方法是步行瀏覽。)

× When a woman goes out to work, she knows other people.

√ **When a woman goes out to work, she gets to know other people.**

(婦女出去工作, 就會結識到其他人。)

> **know** = be familiar with (作 "知道"、"熟悉" 解): 'I don't know Frankfurt at all.' (我對法蘭克福一無所知。)
> **get to know** = become familiar with (作 "變得熟悉"、"逐漸了解" 解)

knowledge 1

× I have very little knowledge in electricity.

√ **I have very little knowledge of electricity.**

(我對電的知識少之又少。)

> **knowledge of** a subject, NOT **in**
> 按 **knowledge of a** subject (某一學科的知識) 中的 **of** 不可用 **in** 替代。

2

× I am attending a course to improve my knowledges of English.

√ **I am attending a course to improve my knowledge of English.**

(我正參加一個課程, 以增加我的英文知識。)

> **Knowledge** is an uncountable noun.
> 按 **knowledge** 是不可數名詞, 沒有複數。

lack 1

× Doctors can do little when they are lacking proper medical supplies.

√ **Doctors can do little when they lack proper medical supplies.**

(在缺乏適當藥物供應的情況下, 醫生簡直束手無策。)

> **lack** is not usually used in progressive tenses.
> 按 **lack** 一詞通常不用進行式。

2 × At school I used to lack in confidence.
√ **At school I used to lack confidence.**
(我從前讀書, 總是缺乏信心。)
× In those days we lacked of the money to go on holiday.
√ **In those days we lacked the money to go on holiday.**
(那時候, 我們還沒有足夠的錢去度假。)

> **lack** here is a transitive verb which takes a direct object without a preposition
> 上兩句的 **lack** 是及物動詞, 其後緊接受詞, 無需加入前置詞。

3 × Singapore is in lack of natural resources.
√ **Singapore lacks natural resources.**
(新加坡缺乏自然資源。)

> Note the alternative (注意: 可換另一種説法, 例如): 'Singapore suffers from a lack of natural resources.'

landscape × Lots of kings chose to live here because of the beautiful landscape.
√ **Lots of kings chose to live here because of the beautiful scenery.**
(不少國王都喜歡到這裡來定居, 因為此處風景優美。)

> **landscape** = (a view of) a wide stretch of land, especially in the countryside
> 按 **landscape** 一詞雖可譯作 "風景", 但強調的是一大片陸上的景物, 如山林、峽谷、田野、湖泊、瀑布等, 尤指鄉間的風景。風景畫也用此字。
> **scenery** = the natural features of the countryside (hills, valleys, fields, etc.) considered in terms of their beauty
> 按 **scenery** 一詞雖也譯作 "風景", 其實更側重 "景色" 之意, 即從 "美" 的角度去看山林、峽谷、田野、湖泊等優美的自然景色。

last 1 × He looks thinner than when I saw him in the last summer.
√ **He looks thinner than when I saw him last summer.**
(他比我去年夏天看見他時瘦了。)

Do not use a preposition or **the** with 'last week', 'last Tuesday', 'last winter', etc., unless **last** means 'final'. Compare (不要在 last week、last Tuesday、last winter 等前面加前置詞和 **the**, 但如 **last** 解作 "final" — "最後", 則例外, 比較): 'Last week we went to Scotland for a few days.' 'In the last week of her holiday she went to Wales.'

2 × Last evening I went to the cinema with a friend of mine.
√ **Yesterday evening I went to the cinema with a friend of mine.**
(昨天晚上我跟一位朋友去看電影。)

last night or **yesterday evening** BUT NOT **last evening**
説 "昨晚", 應用 **last night** 或 **yesterday evening**, 不用 **last evening**。

3 × Last year we have stayed in the hotel for two weeks.
√ **Last year we stayed in the hotel for two weeks.**
(我們去年在旅館住了兩星期。)

Last night/week/month/year cannot be used with a present perfect tense.
凡是 **last night**、**last week**、**last month**、**last year** 之類已經明確指出是過去的某一時間, 都不能用現在完成式。

4 × First we listened to the tape, then we answered some questions, and at last we wrote the story.
√ **First we listened to the tape, then we answered some questions, and finally we wrote the story.**
(我們先聽錄音帶, 接着回答一些問題, 最後才寫故事。)

At last (= after a long delay; eventually) refers only to time ("指經過一段長時間以後, 終於 ... " 之意 — 只與時間有關, 例如): 'At last the tickets have arrived!'
Finally refers either to time (既指時間, 例如): 'The train finally arrived.' or to sequence (也指先後的順序, 例如): 'Finally, I'd like to thank you all for coming and wish you a safe journey home.'

5 × As a dress designer, I am very interested in the last fashions.
√ **As a dress designer, I am very interested in the latest fashions.**
(作為一個服裝設計師, 我對最新時裝款式很感興趣。)

> **last** = most recent (of a series); previous (作 "最近的一次"、"上一次" 解): 'Our last meeting was in Rome.'
> **latest** = most recent (with an emphasis on newness)
> 作 "新近的"、"最新的"、"最近的" 解

late × My late husband now works for a television company.
√ **My former husband now works for a television company.**
√ **My ex-husband now works for a television company.**
(我的前夫現時在一家電視台工作。)

> **Late** is used (attributively) when talking about someone who has died (作形容詞用時, **late** 一詞表示某人 "已故" 之意): 'his late wife' (他的亡妻), 'the late Mr Flowers' (已故的弗洛士先生)

lately × Lately someone told me that the fire was caused by a cigarette.
√ **Recently someone told me that the fire was caused by a cigarette.**
(最近有人告訴我那次火災是由於煙頭引起的。)

> **Lately** is usually used with the present perfect progressive to refer to a period of time.
> 注意: **lately** 用來指一段時間, 常用現在完成進行式。
> **Recently** can be used in the same way to refer to a period of time. However, it can also refer to a point in time. Compare (注意: **recently** 既可用來指一段時間, 也可指某一時刻, 試比較): 'Just lately/recently I have been wondering whether to look for a new job.' 'Just recently I decided to look for a new job.'

latest × The latest election was won by the socialists.
√ **The last election was won by the socialists.**
(社會黨人士贏得了上次選舉。)

See note at (見) LAST 5

laugh

× I laughed with myself and then explained to him that parents sometimes argue just like children.

√ **I laughed to myself and then explained to him that parents sometimes argue just like children.**
(我暗自笑了起來, 接着向他解釋說: 做父母的有時候也會像孩子一樣爭吵。)

> **laugh/talk to** yourself, NOT **with**
> 注意: **laugh/talk to yourself** 中的 **to** 不可用 **with** 替代。

lay

× We broke down the door and found Mrs Brown laying on the carpet.

√ **We broke down the door and found Mrs Brown lying on the carpet.**
(我們破門而入, 發現白朗夫人躺在地毯上。)

> Do not confuse **lie (lying, lay, lain)** with **lay (laying, laid, laid)**
> 不要把 **lie** 和 **lay** 混淆起來, **lie** 作"躺" 解, 其現在分詞為 **lying**, 過去式為 **lay**, 過去分詞為 **lain**; **lay** 作"放" 解, 其現在分詞為 **laying**, 過去式為 **laid**, 過去分詞為 **laid**。
> **Lie** is ALWAYS intransitive (按 **lie** 一詞總是不及物動詞, 例如): 'He lay on the floor asleep.'
> **Lay** is nearly always transitive (按 **lay** 一詞幾乎總是用作及物動詞): 'She laid her books on the chair.'

lay down

× I just wanted to lay down and have a rest.

√ **I just wanted to lie down and have a rest.**
(我只想躺下休息一下。)

> **lay down** = put something down (作 "把東西放下" 解, 例如): 'Lay the books down on the floor.' (把書放在地板上。)
> **lie down** = put your body into a horizontal position, especially on a bed (作"躺下, 尤指躺在床上" 解)

lead

× Ali asked us if we would lead him to the theatre one night.

√ **Ali asked us if we would take him to the theatre one night.**
(阿里問我們是否會在某個晚上帶他去看場戲。)

> **lead** = show (someone) the way by walking in front, holding by the arm, etc. (指 "走在前面, 挽着別人手臂等給人帶路") 'Some blind people like to be led across the road.' (有些盲人喜歡讓人攙着過馬路。)

learn 1 × Most of the stories are true and we can learn a lot of them.
√ **Most of the stories are true and we can learn a lot from them.**
(大多數的故事都是真實的, 我們可從中學到許多東西。)

> **learn** something **from** a person or thing (NOT = **be taught something** (意為 "從中學到東西" 的片語: **learn** ... **from** ..., 其中的 **from** 不可用 **of** 替代, 例如): 'A child can learn a lot from television.'

2 × His mother learnt her son's success from the newspapers.
√ **His mother learnt of her son's success in the newspapers.**
(他母親從報上得知他成功的消息。)

> **learn of/about** something = to become informed (of) 如說 "得到消息" 或 "獲悉", 應用 **learn of** 或 **learn about**。

leave 1 × I left from the shop without buying anything.
√ **I left the shop without buying anything.**
(我從商店走出來, 什麼東西也沒有買。)

> **leave** somewhere (school, Hong Kong, the States) WITHOUT **from**
> 離開某處 (學校、香港、美國), 可用 **leave**, 後面直接跟 somewhere (school, Hong Kong, the States), 不用 **from**。

2 × Ken's aunt left to New York on 17th April.
√ **Ken's aunt left for New York on 17th April.**
(克恩的姑媽在四月十七日前往紐約。)

> **leave** (somewhere) **for** somewhere else (NOT **to**) (指 " 從某處到某處", 應用 **leave** somewhere **for** somewhere else, 其中 **for**, 不能用 **to** 替代, 例如): 'She left (Leeds) for London on the nine o'clock train.'

lend × Can I lend your pen a minute?
√ **Can I borrow your pen a minute?**
(我能否借你的筆用一用?)

> **lend** = give (someone) the use of (something) for a certain time (作 "借出" 解)
> **borrow** = take or receive (something) for a certain time, intending to return it (作 "借入" 解)

less **1** × Despite the increase in crime, punishments are still less stricter than they should be.
√ **Despite the increase in crime, punishments are still less strict than they should be.**
(儘管犯罪有所增加, 但懲罰仍未到應有的那樣嚴厲。)

> The comparative ending (**-er**) is NEVER used with **less** or **more.**
> 比較級詞尾 **-er** 從來不和 **less** 或 **more** 連用。

2 × If there were less cars on the roads, there would be less accidents.
√ **If there were fewer cars on the roads, there would be fewer accidents.**
(要是路上的汽車少些, 車禍也就會減少。)

> Use **less** with an uncountable noun.
> **less** 用於不可數名詞。
> Use **fewer** with the plural form of a countable noun. Compare (按 **fewer** 一詞用於可數名詞的複數, 試比較): 'Less traffic would mean fewer accidents.' Note that although **less** is widely used in place of **fewer** in conversational English, careful users regard it as non-standard.
> 值得注意的是, 雖說 less 在口語中常用來代替 fewer, 但是用詞講究的人認為不合標準。

level × Pollution today is in a very high level.
√ **Pollution today is at a very high level.**
(現今的污染情況非常嚴重。)

> be/stay/remain etc. **at a particular level,** NOT **in**
> 指 "發展到某一水平/程度" 可用 be/stay/remain 等詞, 後接 **at a particular level,** 其中的前置詞 **at** 不可用 **in** 替代。

lie × I was sure the old woman was saying lies.
√ **I was sure the old woman was telling lies.**
(我肯定那老太婆在說謊。)
× You should not speak lies.
√ **You should not tell lies.**
(你不該說謊。)

> **tell a lie,** NOT **say** or **speak**
> 注意: **tell a lie** 中的動詞 **tell** 不可用 **say** 或 **speak** 替代。

lied × After a while he stopped running and lied down on the ground.

√ **After a while he stopped running and lay down on the ground.**

(他跑了一陣便停下來, 躺在地上。)

> **lied** is the past tense and past participle of **lie** (=to say something which is not true in an attempt to deceive). Compare (注意: **lied** 是 **lie** [說謊] 的過去式和過去分詞, 試比較): **lie (lying, lay, lain) down** (=be in or get into a resting position) (躺下)

like 1 × 'Would you like going for a walk with me?' she asked the little boy.

√ **'Would you like to go for a walk with me?' she asked the little boy.**

("你願意跟我去散步嗎?" 她問那小男孩。)

> **would like**+to-v
> 按 **would like** 後接帶 to 的動詞。

2 × 'Do you like me to show you where to go?' he asked.

√ **'Would you like me to show you where to go?' he asked.**

("我給你領路, 好嗎?" 他問道。)

> Compare (比較): 'Do you like Russian music?' (an enquiry) ("你喜歡俄羅斯音樂嗎?" [詢問])
> 'Would you like to play the piano?' (an invitation) ("請你彈鋼琴, 好嗎?" [邀請])

3 × Not many parents like that their children leave school without any qualifications.

√ **Not many parents like their children to leave school without any qualifications.**

(做父母的都不願意子女離校時連一張證書都沒有。)

> **like**+someone/something+to-v
> 按 **like** someone 或 **like** something 之後應接帶 to 的動詞。

4 × She doesn't like when you use her books.
√ **She doesn't like it when you use her books.**
(她不高興你用她的書。)

like + it + when/if clause (按 **like it** 之後, 如接 **when** 或 **if** 子句, 則這子句實際上是 **like** 的受詞, 例如): 'She won't like it if you arrive late.'

5 × Everyone arrived late like they often do when you don't want them to.
√ **Everyone arrived late as they often do when you don't want them to.**
(所有的人都遲到了, 這同往常一樣: 你不要他們遲到時他們偏偏就遲到。)

Although the use of **like** as a conjuction is becoming fairly common and appears even in formal English, it has not yet been fully accepted by careful users.
儘管 **like** 一詞用作連接詞已經相當普遍, 甚至出現在書面語中。但用詞嚴謹的人對此還不能完全接受。

6 × She spoke very loudly like I was deaf.
√ **She spoke very loudly as if I was deaf.**
(她大聲地說, 好像我是個聾子。)

The use of **like** to mean 'as if' is very informal and is usually regarded as non-standard.
把 **like** 當作 **as if** 來用, 是十分口語體的用法, 因此通常認為不算規範。

7 See (見) SAME 1

8 See (見) SHALL 3

listen 1 × My mother never listens what I say.
√ **My mother never listens to what I say.**
(我母親從來不肯好好聽我說的話。)

listen never takes a direct object, and one **listens to** someone/something.
注意: **listen** 後面不能直接帶一受詞, 只能說 **listen to** someone 或 something。

2 × He doesn't listen very well.
√ **He doesn't hear very well.**
(他的聽覺不怎麼好。)

> To **hear** is to take in sound with the ears, whether one wants to or not.
> 按 **hear** 一詞指用耳朵聽, 至於聽者樂意與否, 耳朵都要聽到。
> To **listen** is to hear with attention. One can listen carefully, but he may hear nothing.
> 按 **listen** 一詞指用心去聽。聽者可以用心去聽, 但不一定能聽到。

lit × All I could see in the darkness was the end of his lit cigarette.
√ **All I could see in the darkness was the end of his lighted cigarette.**
(我在黑暗中能見到的只是他點着的煙頭。)

> In British English **lit** (the past participle of **light**) is NOT used as an attributive adjective. Before a noun, use **lighted.** Compare (英式英語中 **lit** (**light** 的過去分詞) 不作形容詞用, 在名詞前應用 **lighted**, 試比較): 'the cigarette was lit' (這支煙點着了) BUT (但可說) 'a lighted cigarette' (一支點着的煙)

litter 1 × In the cities the streets are full of litters.
√ **In the cities the streets are full of litter.**
(在城市中街上到處是垃圾。)

> **Litter** is an uncountable noun.
> **Litter** 是不可數名詞

2 √ **AmE There would be less litter in the streets if there were more litter baskets.**
(美式英語: 如果垃圾箱多一些, 街上垃圾就會少一些。)
√ **BrE There would be less litter in the streets if there were more litter bins.**
(英式英語: 譯文同上)

> In British English, it is usual to talk about **a wastepaper basket** (usually inside) BUT **a litter bin** (usually outside, in the street).
> 英式英語中指室內的字紙簍常說 **a wastepaper basket**, 而指街上的垃圾箱則說 **a litter bin**。

little 1 × I had never seen a road accident and I was frightened a little.
√ **I had never seen a road accident and I was a little frightened.**
(我以前沒見過車禍, 所以有點害怕。)

When used as an adverb, **a little** ALWAYS comes before the adjective it modifies.
作為副詞, **a little** 只能放在所修飾的形容詞之前。

2 × Today there are too many people for too little jobs.
√ **Today there are too many people for too few jobs.**
(現在人太多, 工作太少了。)

Little is used with uncountable nouns (按 **little** 一詞只能修飾不可數名詞): 'There is too little cake for everyone to have a piece.' (蛋糕太少了, 不夠每人分一塊。)
Few is used with plural countable nouns (注意: **few** 用來修飾可數名詞): 'There are too few sandwiches for all the children to have one.' (三明治太少了, 不夠所有孩子都分一塊。)

live 1 × I love my country and the people who are living in it.
√ **I love my country and the people who live in it.**
(我愛我的國家和生活在其中的同胞。)

Use the present simple tense for a permanent state.
用一般現在式說明永久性狀態。

2 × Whenever we go to the seaside, we live in a hotel.
√ **Whenever we go to the seaside, we stay at a hotel.**
(我們每次去海濱總是住旅館。)
× At the hotel, we lived in room 101.
√ **At the hotel, we stayed in room 101.**
(在這家旅館, 我們住一〇一號房。)

To **live** is to have one's home: "I live in Hong Kong."
注意: **live** 一詞指居住, 例如: "我住在香港"
To **stay** is to live in a place for a while as a visitor or guest (注意: **stay** 一詞指在某處暫作居停或逗留): 'We are staying at a hotel.' 'I stayed the night at a friend's house.' 'My mother is staying (with us) this week.'

lonely √ **AmE Before long he began to feel hungry, lonesome, and helpless.**
(美式英語: 不久他開始感到餓和孤獨無援。)
√ **BrE Before long he began to feel hungry, lonely, and helpless.**
(英式英語: 譯文同上)

> **Lonely** is used in both American and British English.
> 按 **lonely** 一詞在美式、英式英語中都用。
> **Lonesome** is not usually used in British English.
> 按 **lonesome** 一詞一般不用於英式英語中.。

long 1 × He walked along the street as long as the bus stop.
√ **He walked along the street as far as the bus stop.**
(他沿着街往前走, 一直走到公共汽車站。)

> To refer to the furthest point of a distance, use **as far as,** NOT **as long as.**
> 指 "到 … 為止" 可用 **as far as,** 不用 **as long as**。

2 × I am afraid it will take long to improve my English.
√ **I am afraid it will take a long time to improve my English.**
(我的英文恐怕要很長時間才能有進步。)

> **It won't take long.** (negative 用於否定句)
> **Will it take long?** (question 用於疑問句)
> **It will take a long time.** (affirmative 用於肯定句)

look 1 × I stood in front of the window, looking the trees.
√ **I stood in front of the window, looking at the trees.**
(我站在窗前, 望着那些樹。)

> **look at** someone/something
> 用 **look at** someone/something, 其中 **at** 不可缺少。

2 × Someone should inspect the kitchen twice a week to look whether everything is nice and clean.
√ **Someone should inspect the kitchen twice a week to see whether everything is nice and clean.**
(應該有專人每週兩次來檢查廚房, 看看是否一切都保持整潔。)

> **see** = find out (by checking 檢查)
> Compare (比較): 'I looked to see whether it was still raining.'

3 × It looked like hours before the ambulance arrived.
√ **It seemed like hours before the ambulance arrived.**
(好像過了好幾小時救護車才到達。)

look like = show (visible) signs of (有跡像表明): 'It looks like it's going to rain.'
seem (like) = give the feeling or impression of (使人覺得): 'It seems like years since I had a holiday.'

4 See SOUND 4

look after × Having received news of his death, they stopped looking after him.
√ **Having received news of his death, they stopped looking for him.**
(獲悉他的死訊後, 他們便不再尋找他了。)

look after = take care of (作 "照顧" 解): 'Who will look after you if you are ill?'
look for = try to find (作 "尋找" 解): 'I spent a whole hour looking for my keys.'

look at × I stayed in and looked at a film on television.
√ **I stayed in and watched a film on television.**
(我留在家看電視, 看了一部電影。)

look at = turn your eyes to see something (usually briefly) (作 "看"、"望" 解, 看的時間通常較短): 'I looked at the address on the envelope, but didn't recognize it.'
watch = observe closely, often as a spectator or member of an audience (usually for a fairly long period of time)
作 "觀看" 解, 看的人往往是某種場合之觀眾, 看的時間通常較長。

look forward to 1 × I'm looking forwards to seeing you.
√ **I'm looking forward to seeing you.**
(我期待着與您會面。)

look forward to, NOT **forwards**
按 **look forward to** 中的 **forward** 不可用 **forwards** 替代。

2 × I'm looking forward the day I can go home.
√ **I'm looking forward to the day I can go home.**
(我盼望着我能回家的那一天。)
× He said he was looking forward for his holidays.
√ **He said he was looking forward to his holidays.**
(他説他正盼着休假。)

> **look forward to** is a set phrase, from which "to" cannot be left out nor replaced by "for".
> 按 **look forward to** 是個固定詞組, 其中 "**to**" 不能省略, 也不能用 "**for**" 替代。

3 × I'm looking forward to hear from you.
√ **I'm looking forward to hearing from you.**
(佇盼佳音, 幸賜裁答。)

> **look forward to** + v-ing
> **look forward to** 後接帶 "-ing" 的動詞, 不接帶 "to" 的動詞。

look like See (見) HOW 1

lots × She makes us do a lots of homework.
√ **She makes us do a lot of homework.**
√ **She makes us do lots of homework.**
(她叫我們做好多家庭作業。)

> **a lot of,** OR **lots of** WITHOUT **a**
> 指 "許多", 用 **a lot of** 或 **lots of**, 注意 **lots of** 之前不可加 **a**。

love × It was a very unusual gift and I loved it very much.
√ **It was a very unusual gift and I liked it very much.**
(那是一份很不尋常的禮物, 我十分喜歡它。)

> **love someone** very much BUT **like something** very much
> 按 **love** 一般後接 **someone**, 而 **like** 一般後接 **something**。

luck 1 × What a rotten luck! There he was again, sitting right beside me.
√ **What rotten luck! There he was again, sitting right beside me.**
(真倒霉! 他又來了, 還坐在我旁邊。)

> **Luck** is an uncountable noun.
> **luck** 是不可數名詞。

2 × That afternoon she had luck: she found the keys at the bottom of a drawer.
√ **That afternoon she had some luck: she found the keys at the bottom of a drawer.**
(那天下午她還真有點運氣: 她在抽屜底找到了這些鑰匙。)

> Note the alternatives (注意另兩種用法): 'That afternoon she had a piece/stroke of luck ... '
> 'That afternoon she was lucky...'

lucky × It's better to have a lucky family than a lot of money.
√ **It's better to have a happy family than a lot of money.**
(有一個幸福的家庭比有許多錢要好。)

> **lucky** (opposite **unlucky**) = having good luck or good fortune (指 "運氣好" [反義詞為 **unlucky**]): 'You have to be lucky to win a prize.' (你要有好運氣才能贏得獎品。) 'You're lucky the car didn't hit you!' (算你運氣, 汽車沒有撞倒你!)
> **happy** (opposite **sad**) = feeling or showing pleasure or contentment (指 "感到高興或滿足" [反義詞為 **sad**])

luggage 1 × There was no room in the car for all our luggages.
√ **There was no room in the car for all our luggage.**
(汽車裡放不下我們所有的行李。)

> **Luggage** is an uncountable noun.
> **luggage** 是不可數名詞。
> 美式英語用 **baggage**.

2 × I spent the morning packing my luggage.
√ **I spent the morning packing my bags/suitcases.**
(我整個上午忙於裝我的旅行袋/箱子。)

> **pack your bags/suitcases,** NOT **luggage**
> 注意: **pack** 一般不與 **luggage** 連用, 而與 **bags/suitcases** 搭配使用。

lunch × My plan was to visit the library and then have a lunch at a restaurant.
√ **My plan was to visit the library and then have lunch at a restaurant.**
(我的計劃是去圖書館, 然後到一家飯店吃午飯。)

> **have lunch/breakfast/dinner** etc. WITHOUT **a/the**
> 注意: **have** 與 **lunch/breakfast/dinner** etc. 之間不容插入 **a** 或 **the**。

luxury × They don't have any money to spend on luxury things.
√ **They don't have any money to spend on luxuries.**
(他們沒有什麼錢可以花在奢侈品上。)

> **luxuries** (plural of **luxury**) OR **luxury goods, luxury items, but** NOT **luxury things**
> 指 "奢侈品", 可用 **luxuries (**為 **luxury** 的複數), 也可用 **luxury goods** 或 **luxury items**, 而不用 **luxury things**。

machine × Over eighty per cent of these cars are old, and so are their machines.
√ **Over eighty per cent of these cars are old, and so are their engines.**
(這些汽車中百分之八十以上都是舊的, 它們的發動機也如此。)

> **machine** = a device which performs useful work, such as a sewing machine or lawn mower (作 "機器" 解, 如縫紉機, 割草機等。)
> **engine** = a device which provides the power for a motor vehicle, aircraft, etc. (作 "發動機"解, 用於機動車、飛機等。)

made × She claimed that the jumper was made from wool.
√ **She claimed that the jumper was made of wool.**
(她說運動衫是毛織的。)

> Use **made from** when the original materials have been completely changed (原料經加工後完全變了樣者用 **made from**, 例如): 'Bread is made from flour and water.' (麵包是用麵粉和水做的。)
> Use **made of** when the materials in an object can still be recognized as the original materials (原料經加工後仍可辨認者用 **made of**, 例如): 'The table is made of wood and metal.' (這張桌子是用木和金屬製造的。)

magical

× It was a magical stick, and everything it touched turned to gold.

√ **It was a magic stick, and everything it touched turned to gold.**
(這是一根魔杖, 用它一點, 什麼東西都會變成金的。)

> **magical** = produced by or as if by magic; fascinating or enchanting (用 (或好像用) 魔術變成的; 奇妙或迷人的): 'Her first sight of the Taj Mahal was a magical experience.' (她第一次見到泰姬陵時好像着了迷似的。)
> **magic** = able to perform magic; used in magic (指 "會魔術的; 變魔術用的")

mail

√ **AmE It would be quicker to return the book by mail.**
(美式英語: 還書用郵寄更快。)

√ **BrE It would be quicker to return the book by post.**
(英式英語: 譯文同上)

> In American English, use **send/return** something **by mail**.
> 美式英語中, 寄發/寄還物品用 by mail。
> In British English, use **send/return** something **by post**.
> 英式英語中, 寄發/寄還物品用 by post。

majority 1

× People who can read and write are not by the majority in some countries.

√ **People who can read and write are not in the majority in some countries.**
(在某些國家, 能讀能寫的人並不居多數。)

> **in a/the majority** (= the larger number or amount) is a set phrase, in which '**in**' CANNOT be replaced by '**by**'.
> 按 **in a/the majority** 是個 "固定詞組", 作 "大多數" 解, 其中 "**in**" 不能用 "**by**" 替代。

2

× He was elected in a majority of 75 against 42.

√ **He was elected by a majority of 75 against 42.**
(他以 75 對 42 的多數票當選。)

> **by a majority** (= the difference in number between a large and smaller group), NOT '**in**'
> **by a majority** 意為 "大數與小數之差距", 其中 "**by**" 不可用 "**in**" 替代。

make 1
× They made him eating his lunch in silence.
√ **They made him eat his lunch in silence.**
(他們使他吃午飯時不說話。)
× They made her to work hard.
√ **They made her work hard.**
(他們要她努力工作。)

make a person or thing + infinitive WITHOUT **to**
注意: **make** a person or thing 後接不帶 **to** 的動詞。

2
× The government has already made a lot of things in order to solve the problem.
√ **The government has already done a lot of things in order to solve the problem.**
(政府為了解決這個問題已經做了許多事。)
× In Italy we have made a great deal to prevent pollution.
√ **In Italy we have done a great deal to prevent pollution.**
(在意大利我們做了大量工作以防止污染。)

do a great deal/lot/lot of things, NOT **make**
注意: **do a great deal/lot/lot of things** 中的動詞 **do** 不可用 **make** 替代。

3 See (見) BEST 2, DEMONSTRATION, EXPERIENCE 1, GLANCE, PARTY, TEST

male
× She has a deep male voice.
√ **She has a deep masculine voice.**
(她的嗓音低沉得像個男人。)

male = (1) of the sex that does not produce eggs or give birth to young (雄性的): 'a male rabbit', 'a male nurse' (2) for or composed of men or boys (男人或男童的): 'a male choir'
masculine = having qualities or features considered to be suitable for a man (男性的, 有男子氣概的)

man 1
× My man and I have been married since last Christmas.
√ **My husband and I have been married since last Christmas.**
(我和丈夫在去年聖誕節就結婚了。)

husband = the man to whom a woman is married (指 "丈夫"—譯者按: 美式英語, 尤其低下層的人, 會用 my man 指丈夫)

2 × Every day the man is inventing new machines.
√ **Every day man is inventing new machines.**
(人類每天都在發明新機器。)

When using **man** to mean 'the human race', do not use an article.
Man 用來指全人類時, 不用冠詞。

manage **1** × Unfortunately I couldn't manage to pass the exam.
√ **Unfortunately I didn't manage to pass the exam.**
(不幸的是我沒能通過考試。)

Do not place **can** or **could** before **manage** when **manage** means 'succeed'.
按 **manage** 意為 "能做到" 時, 不要在前面加 **can** 或 **could**。

2 × I was told that you might manage repairing it.
√ **I was told that you might manage to repair it.**
(我聽說你有可能把它修好。)

manage + to-v
按 **manage** 一詞後接帶 to 的動詞。

3 × I will manage that the magazine is sent to you every month.
√ **I will arrange for the magazine to be sent to you every month.**
(我將安排每月把雜誌送給你。)

manage = control or be in charge of (a business etc.) (指 "管理" [某種業務]): 'I let my accountant manage all my financial affairs.' (我讓我的會計員管理我一切財務。)
arrange = make plans or preparations (指 "安排" 或 "籌劃")

manifestation × Several manifestations were made, causing the police a lot of problems.
√ **Several demonstrations were held, causing the police a lot of problems.**
(舉行了幾次遊行示威, 給警察造成許多麻煩。)

manifestation = a display, sign, or act of showing (表現、表明): 'The flowers he sent were a clear manifestation of his feelings for her.' (他送去的花清楚地表明了他對她的感情。)

demonstration = a public expression of opinion, usually by a large group of people who feel that something is wrong or unjust (示威遊行): 'a demonstration against nuclear war' (反對核戰爭的示威遊行)

many **1** × It's important to understand why there is so many violence in our world.

√ **It's important to understand why there is so much violence in our world.**
(去了解世界上為什麼有那麼多暴力行為是很重要的。)

Many is used only with countable nouns: 'too many cars' but 'too much traffic'
many 僅用於可數名詞, 如 "too many cars"; 而在不可數名詞之前, 則應用 much, 如 "too much traffic" (交通繁忙)。

2 × One of the policemen started asking me many questions.

√ **One of the policemen started asking me a lot of questions.** (其中的一個警察開始向我問了許多問題。)

Many is used before a noun (or used as a pronoun) mainly in questions and negative sentences (**many** 主要用於問句和否定句的名詞或代詞之前): 'Does he have many friends?' 'He doesn't have many friends.' In affirmative sentences, phrases such as **a lot of** and **plenty of** are used. (在肯定句中, 可用 **a lot of** 或 **plenty of**) Note, however, that **many** is used in affirmative sentences after **too, so,** and **as** (但請注意, **many** 一詞如在 **too**、**so** 和 **as** 之後, 可用於肯定句中, 例如: 'You ask too many questions.') and sometimes in formal contexts (有時也可用於正式的行文中, 例如): 'Many accidents arise as a result of negligence.'

mark **1** × Before buying a cassette recorder, I asked my friend if he could recommend a good mark.

√ **Before buying a cassette recorder, I asked my friend if he could recommend a good make.**
(在買卡式錄音機之前, 我問朋友能否推薦一個好牌子。)

mark (also Mk) = model, type, or version (used chiefly in trade names) (按 **mark** 可略作 "Mk", 意為 "型號", 用於商標名稱, 例如): 'a Mk II Jaguar' (一輛積架二型跑車)
make = brand (of cars, washing machines, refrigerators, etc.) (意為汽車、洗衣機、雪櫃/冰箱等的 "牌子")

2 × Inside the coat there is a mark which says that it is made in Italy.
✓ **Inside the coat there is a label which says that it is made in Italy.**
(外衣的衣裡有個標籤, 說明是意大利製造的。)

> **label** = a small piece of card or material fixed to a garment which gives details about size, manufacture, and cleaning (衣服上的標籤, 說明大小、製造商及洗濯方法, 例如): 'The label says "Dry clean only".'

market × The magazine gives a list of all the computers in the market.
✓ **The magazine gives a list of all the computers on the market.**
(這本雜誌提供了一份在市場上出售的電腦的名單。)

> **on the market** (= available in shops; for sale), NOT **in**
> 注意: **on the market** 指 "店內能買到的; 上市的", 此短語中的前置詞 **on** 不可用 **in** 替代。

marriage × Why didn't you invite me to your marriage?
✓ **Why didn't you invite me to your wedding?**
(為什麼你不請我參加你的婚禮?)

> **marriage** = the ceremony of becoming husband and wife considered from a purely religious or legal point of view (結婚 [指宗教或法律上的關係]): 'Her parents are against the marriage.' (她的父母反對這件婚事。)
> **wedding** = the occasion when this ceremony takes place and the celebrations that follow it (婚禮 [指儀式])

marry 1 × When she met my father, she was about to marry to another man.
✓ **When she met my father, she was about to marry another man.**
(她遇到我父親時, 快要嫁給另一個男人了。)

> **be married to** someone BUT **marry** someone WITHOUT **to**
> 指 "與某人結婚", 用 **be married to** someone, 或用 **marry** someone, 在後一種用法中不用 to。

2 × He is going to ask her to marry with him.
√ **He is going to ask her to marry him.**
(他打算向她求婚。)

> **marry** someone, NOT **marry with**
> 指 "與某人結婚", 用 **marry** someone, 不用 **marry with** someone。

match × The colour of the jacket matches to the trousers.
√ **The colour of the jacket matches the trousers.**
(這件夾克衫的顏色配這條褲子。)

> **match** something WITHOUT **to**
> 按 **match** 一詞作 "與 ... 相配/相稱" 解時, 後接 something, 不可在 something 之前加 **to**。

mathematics × Mathematics are my favourite subject.
√ **Mathematics is my favourite subject.**
(數學是我喜歡的學科。)

> **Mathematics** is ALWAYS singular.
> 注意: **mathematics** 總是作單數用。

matter 1 × The matter is that we won't have enough room in the car to take your mother with us.
√ **The problem is that we won't have enough room in the car to take your mother with us.**
(問題是車內沒有位置能容納你母親, 所以我們無法帶她一起去。)

> **Matter** is used to mean 'problem' or 'trouble' only in questions and negative sentences (注意: **matter** 作 "問題" 或 "麻煩" 解時只用於問句或否定句, 例如): 'What's the matter?' 'Is anything the matter?' 'There's nothing the matter.'

2 × The flight attendant told us that there wasn't any matter; it was just a storm.
√ **The flight attendant told us that nothing was the matter; it was just a storm.**
(空中服務員告訴我們沒出什麼事, 只是遇上了一場風暴。)

> Note the alternatives (注意也可說): 'She told us that there was nothing the matter.' 'She told us that there wasn't anything the matter.'

3 See (見) NO MATTER

matters

× To make the matters worse, the roof leaked and there was no heater in the room.

√ **To make matters worse, the roof leaked and there was no heater in the room.**

(更糟的是, 房頂還漏水, 房裡又沒有暖氣設備。)

> **to make matters worse** WITHOUT **the**
> 注意: **to make matters worse** 中的 matters 一詞之前不可用 **the**。

may be

× May be they have lost our address.

√ **Maybe they have lost our address.**

(也許他們丟失了我們的地址。)

> When you mean 'perhaps', use **maybe,** NOT **may be.**
> Compare (作 "也許" 解時, 用 **maybe**, 不用 **may be**, 比較): 'It may be that they have lost our address.' (他們可能丟失了我們的地址。)

me 1

× I found me a seat and sat down.

√ **I found myself a seat and sat down.**

(我給自己找了個座位坐下。)

× I stayed by the fire to warm me up.

√ **I stayed by the fire to warm myself up.**

(我靠近火爐取暖。)

> When the object or indirect object is the same as the subject, a reflexive pronoun is used (受詞或間接受詞如與主詞是同一人或物, 應用反身代名詞, 例如): 'She got herself a drink.' 'They bought themselves some new clothes.'

2

× I still remember the day me and my sister went to Buenos Aires by bus.

√ **I still remember the day my sister and I went to Buenos Aires by bus.**

(我仍然記得我和妹妹乘長途汽車去布宜諾斯艾利斯的那一天。)

> It is customary to mention yourself last.
> 英文習慣上總是最後提到自己。

meal

√ **AmE We always take our meals in the canteen.**
(美式英語: 我們一向在食堂進餐。)

√ **BrE We always have our meals in the canteen.**
(英式英語: 譯文同上)

In British English, use **have a meal,** NOT **take**.
英式英語中用 **have a meal**, 而不用 **take** a meal。
In American English, you can use **take** OR **have**.
在美式英語中 **have** a meal 和 **take** a meal 均可用。

mean 1

× Being a good flight attendant means to make your passengers feel relaxed.

√ **Being a good flight attendant means making your passengers feel relaxed.**
(作為一個優秀的空中服務員, 你要使乘客感到舒適。)

mean + to-v = intend to do something (**mean** 後接帶 "to" 的動詞, 意為 "打算做什麼", 例如): 'She means to find out who is to blame.' (她意欲弄明白應該歸咎於誰。)
mean + v-ing = involves doing something (注意: **mean** 後接帶 "-ing" 的動詞, 意為 "必須要做某事"、"意味着")

2

× Some people mean that stricter punishments will reduce the amounts of crime.

√ **Some people think/believe that stricter punishments will reduce the amount of crime.**
(有些人認為使用嚴刑就能減少罪案。)

mean (used of people) = intend to say (**mean** 用於人時, 意為 "意思是", 例如): 'I'm not sure what he's saying but I think he means that he can't afford to wait any longer.'

meaning 1

× His meaning was to use the pin to open the lock.

√ **His intention was to use the pin to open the lock.**
(他意圖用這根針把鎖打開。)

meaning = what a word, sign, etc. communicates (意為 "含義"、"意義", 例如): 'If you don't know the meaning of a word, look it up in your dictionary.'
intention = what someone plans or intends to do (意為 "目的"、"企圖")

2 × I asked him to explain what his meaning was.
√ **I asked him to explain what he meant.**
(我要他解釋他什麼意思。)

> **Meaning** (noun) is not usually used of people. Compare (**meaning** 用作名詞時一般不用於人。試比較): 'A word can have several meanings.'

means × He was determined to get the money by all means.
√ **He was determined to get the money by whatever means.**
(他決心要不擇手段把這筆錢弄到手。)

> **by all means** = certainly; please do (mainly used when giving someone permission to do something) (作 "當然; 請這麼辦", 主要用於允許人家做某件事, 例如): 'May I smoke?' 'By all means.' ("我可以吸煙嗎?" "當然可以。")
> Use **by any/whatever means** when you mean 'using whatever methods that are necessary'.
> 作 "採取任何必要手段" 解時, 用 **by any/whatever means**。

measurement × In my opinion, the authorities have to take even stricter measurements to save our archaeological treasures.
√ **In my opinion, the authorities have to take even stricter measures to save our archaeological treasures.**
(我認為當局必須採取更加嚴格的措施來保護我們寶貴的文化遺物。)

> **measurement** = the length, width, etc. of something (意為 "長度"、"寬度", 例如): 'You can't buy new curtains without knowing the measurements of the window.' (你不知道這窗戶的尺寸就不能買新窗簾。)
> **measure** = an action intended to have a particular effect; a law or ruling (意為 "措施; 法令", 例如): 'New measures are to be introduced in the fight against crime.' (在撲滅罪案方面將採取新的措施。)

media × The medias, such as radio and television, tell us what is happening in the world.
√ **The media, such as radio and television, tell us what is happening in the world.**
(傳播媒介, 諸如收音機和電視, 告訴我們世界上正在發生的事。)

× Television is a very powerful media.
√ **Television is a very powerful medium.**
(電視是一種效力強大的傳播媒介。)

Medium is singular.
按 **medium** 是單數。
Media is plural.
按 **media** 是複數。

meet √ **AmE I've arranged to meet with Sarah tomorrow.**
(美式英語: 我安排了明早約見沙拉。)
√ **BrE I've arranged to meet Sarah tomorrow.**
(英式英語: 譯文同上)

meet with someone (mainly American usage) =have a (previously arranged) meeting with (按 **meet with** someone 主要是美式用法, 指 "經安排後約見"): 'We met with their representatives to discuss the problem.'
meet someone (British and American English) =come together (with) by chance or arrangement (按 **meet** someone 在英式和美式英語中均用, 指 "偶然或按事先的安排會面")

melted × The melted steel is then poured into a large tank.
√ **The molten steel is then poured into a large tank.**
(鋼熔化為鋼水後注入一個巨大的砂箱裏。)

'**melted** ice', '**melted** butter' BUT '**molten** steel', '**molten** lava'
指 "溶化的冰/黃油", 用 '**melted** ice/butter'; 指 "熔化的鋼 (即鋼水)/熔岩 (即岩漿)", 用 '**molten** steel/lava'。注意中譯的 melted 用 "溶"; 中譯的 molten 用 "熔"。

memories × Casanova recorded his adventures in his memories.
√ **Casanova recorded his adventures in his memoirs.**
(卡薩諾瓦在他的回憶錄中記下了自己的奇遇。)

memories=things remembered; pictures (of past events) in a person's mind (指 "回憶起的往事", 例如): 'I have many vivid memories of my childhood.' (我的童年生活猶歷歷在目。)
memoirs=a person's written account of (a period in) his or her life (指 "回憶錄")

memorize

× I can remember a poem very quickly.
√ **I can memorize a poem very quickly.**
(我很快就能記住一首詩。)

remember = bring back to one's mind (information, past events, etc.) (指回憶起或想起某事, 例如): 'She suddenly remembered that she had not locked the door.'
memorize = learn and remember on purpose (指有意識地用心去記)

memory

× Each visitor received a small gift as a memory.
√ **Each visitor received a small gift as a souvenir.**
(每位來客都得到一件小禮品作為紀念。)

memory = something remembered (意為 "記憶"、"(憶及的) 往事", 例如): 'I have very few memories of my childhood.'
souvenir = something that is bought or received in a particular place (especially while on holiday) and is kept to remind you of it (帶紀念性質的 "禮品", 尤指在旅遊地所得的那種)

menace

× Nowadays world peace is menaced.
√ **Nowadays world peace is threatened.**
(現在世界和平受到了威脅。)

Menace (verb) is not usually used unless additional information is given about the nature of the danger.
Compare (**menace** (動詞) 一般只是在危險的性質已有說明時才用, 試比較): 'The whole world is threatened/menaced by the risk of nuclear war.' (整個世界都受到核戰爭危險的威脅。)

mention

× My husband has often mentioned about you to me.
√ **My husband has often mentioned you to me.**
(我丈夫經常在我面前提到你。)

mention is a transitive verb which takes a direct object.
注意: **mention** 是一個及物動詞, 可直接帶一個受詞, 無需再帶一個像 about 那樣的前置詞。

middle age × Sitting next to me was a middle age man, probably about forty.
√ **Sitting next to me was a middle-aged man, probably about forty.**
(坐在我身旁的是一位中年男子, 約四十歲左右。)

> **middle-aged** (adjective) = in **middle age** (noun)
> 指 "中年", 英語的形容詞為 **middle-aged**, 名詞為 **middle age**。middle-aged 總是放在名詞之前, 而 middle age 常與 **in** 連用, 作為表語或補語, 如 "He is nearly sixty, but he still considers himself to be in middle age."

Middle Ages × The history of the town dates back to the Middle Age.
√ **The history of the town dates back to the Middle Ages.**
(這座城的歷史追溯到中世紀時代。)

> **middle age** = the period in a person's life between youth and old age (指 "中年")
> **Middle Ages** = the period in European history from about 1100 to 1500 AD (指 "中世紀, 約公元 1100 至 1500 年")

migrate See (見) EMIGRATE

million 1 × Belgium has ten millions inhabitants.
√ **Belgium has ten million inhabitants.**
(比利時有一千萬居民。)
× Brazil has a hundred and twenty millions of inhabitants.
√ **Brazil has a hundred and twenty million inhabitants.**
(巴西有一億二千萬居民。)

See note at (見) HUNDRED 2

2 See (見) THOUSAND 1

mind 1 × Our teacher is very patient and doesn't mind to explain again if we don't understand.
√ **Our teacher is very patient and doesn't mind explaining again if we don't understand.**
(我們的教師很有耐心; 如果我們不明白, 他並不介意再加講解。)

(not) mind + v-ing
注意: **(not) mind** 後接帶 "-ing" 的動詞, **mind** 用於此場合作 "反對; 介意" 解。

2 × It was raining but we didn't mind it.
✓ **It was raining but we didn't mind.**
(那時正在下雨, 但我們不在乎。)

When the object of **mind** can be understood from the context, **mind** is not followed by a pronoun (如在上下文中, mind 的賓語已經很清楚, 這時就可省略): 'Do you mind waiting a few minutes?' 'No, we don't mind.'

3 × I made up my mind going for a swim.
✓ **I made up my mind to go for a swim.**
(我決定去游泳。)

make up your mind + to-v
注意: **make up your mind** 後接帶 "to" 的動詞。

4 × The first thing that comes to my mind when I think about France is wine.
✓ **The first thing that comes to mind when I think about France is wine.**
(一想起法國, 我首先就想到酒。)

come to mind WITHOUT **my, his, their,** etc.
注意: **come to mind** 這個片語中不必插入 **my**, **his**, **their** 等詞。

minute 1 × The train arrived at exactly twelve past three.
✓ **The train arrived at exactly twelve minutes past three.**
(火車正好在三點十二分到達。)

When telling the time, **minutes** must be used after all numbers except **five, ten , twenty** and **twenty-five**.
Compare (提到時間, **minutes** 只有在五、十、二十及二十五分之後才能省略, 試比較): 'It's twenty (minutes) past ten.' (**minutes** can be used) (注意: 有沒 **minutes** 均可)
'It's twenty-three minutes past ten.' (**minutes** must be used) (注意: **minutes** 不可省略)

2 × The college is a twenty minutes bus ride from my flat.
√ **The college is a twenty-minute bus ride from my flat.**
(從我住處乘公共汽車去學院只需二十分鐘。)

See note at (見) MONTH

3 × All I wanted was a few minutes of sleep.
√ **All I wanted was a few minutes' sleep.**
(我所需要的只是睡幾分鐘。)

See note at (見) OF 2

mistake 1 × The man next to me picked up my case in mistake.
√ **The man next to me picked up my case by mistake.**
(我旁邊的那個人誤拿起了我的手提箱。)

> **in error** BUT **by mistake**
> 注意詞語的搭配: 指 "錯誤地", 用 **in error** 或用 **by mistake**。
> See note at (見) ERROR

2 × I rarely do more than three mistakes in an essay.
√ **I rarely make more than three mistakes in an essay.**
(我在一篇文章裏出的錯很少超過三個。)

> **make a mistake,** NOT **do**
> 注意: **make a mistake** 中的動詞 **make** 不可用 **do** 替代。

3 × When I got home with the cassette recorder, it wouldn't work. I tried to find the mistake myself.
√ **When I got home with the cassette recorder, it wouldn't work. I tried to find the fault myself.**
(我把卡式錄音機帶了回家, 發現它不靈了, 我試着自己動手把毛病找出來。)

> A spelling, essay, calculation, decision, etc. may contain a **mistake** (= an error). 拼法、文章、計算、決定等出錯才用 **mistake** (此處也可用 error)。
> A machine or electrical device may have or develop a **fault** (= a weakness or defect).
> 機器或電器產生的毛病用 **fault** (此處也可用 weakness 或 defect)。

Mister 1 × Dear Mister Southcroft …
√ **Dear Mr Southcroft …**
(親愛的薩烏斯克勞夫特先生 …)

Mister is ALWAYS written **Mr**.
按 **Mister** 總是寫作 **Mr**。

2 × Dear Mister,
√ **Dear Sir,**
(親愛的先生:)

In formal letters, write (已知收信人的姓時, 正式稱呼是): **Dear Mr Smith, Dear Ms Jones,** etc. when the surname is known.
When the surname is not known, use (不知收信人的姓時用): **Dear Sir/Madam.**

moment 1 × In that moment the door opened.
√ **At that moment the door opened.**
(就在那個時候門打開了。)

at this/that moment = at this/that particular time
Compare (就在這個/那個時刻, 試比較): **in a moment** = very soon (一會兒, 例如): 'I'll have to go in a moment.'

2 × I'd like to see him in my office the moment he will arrive.
√ **I'd like to see him in my office the moment he arrives.**
(他一到達, 我就要在我的辦公室見他。)

After **the moment,** use the present simple tense for future reference, NOT **shall/will** + verb.
在使用 **the moment** 之後, 如說及將來的事, 應用一般現在式, 不用 **shall/will** 再接原動詞。

momentary × The Pope's visit was a momentary occasion.
√ **The Pope's visit was a momentous occasion.**
(教宗的訪問是件頭等大事。)

momentary = lasting for only a moment (頃刻的, 例如): 'a momentary glance' (瞬間的一瞥), 'momentary hesitation' (片刻的猶豫)
momentous (of events) = very important (重大的, 非常重要的)

money 1 × I wonder where all their money come from.
√ **I wonder where all their money comes from.**
(我弄不清他們所有的錢從哪裡來的。)

> **Money** is an uncountable noun.
> 按 **money** 是不可數名詞，形式上屬單數，故後面的動詞也應用單數形式相呼應。

2 See (見) AFFORD 4

month × The company provides a three months training course.
√ **The company provides a three-month training course.**
(公司提供一個為期三個月的訓練班。)

> Nouns of measurement ('week', 'gram', 'mile', etc.) are always singular when used in compound adjectives (計量名詞，如 week、gram、mile 等，用作複合形容詞時總是單數形式，例如): 'a ten-second silence', 'a six-minute wait', 'a five-mile race'.

mood × I was really not in the mood to listening to the nonsense.
√ **I was really not in the mood to listen to the nonsense.**
(其實我沒心情聽這些胡說八道的話。)

> **In the mood** + to-v
> 注意: **in the mood** 後接帶 to 的動詞，作"高興地，心情愉快"解。

more 1 × I had never seen a more happier child.
√ **I had never seen a happier child.**
(我從未見過比他更快樂的孩子。)

> Never use **more** with the **-er** form of an adjective.
> **more** 不得與 **-er** 形態的形容詞並用。

2 × More of Japanese cars were sold in Europe this year than last year.
√ **More Japanese cars were sold in Europe this year than last year.**
(今年在歐洲銷售的日本汽車比去年要多。)

> Use **more** WITHOUT **of** when the noun that follows is used in a general, unrestricted sense (在一般非限定性的情況下，**more** 後面的名詞前不加 **of**，例如): 'The school should buy more books.'

When talking about a particular group of people or things, use **more of** followed by **the** + noun (指一些特定的人或物時, 應用 **more of the**, 再接名詞, 例如): 'The school should buy more of the books that are written especially for children.'

3 See (見) MUCH 5

4 See (見) NO MORE

more or less

× Some women more or less are forced to work nowadays.

√ **Some women are more or less forced to work nowadays.**

(現在有些婦女或多或少地是被迫外出工作的。)

When there is no auxiliary verb, **more or less** may be placed immediately before the main verb (如句中沒有助動詞, **more or less** 可直接放在主動詞之前, 例如): 'She more or less forced me to invite her.' However, when the main verb is **be,** then the phrase **more or less** is placed immediately after it (但如主動詞是 **be**, 則 **more or less** 應緊接放在其後, 例如): 'Don't stop now! We're more or less there!'
Otherwise **more or less** goes immediately after the (first) auxiliary verb (除此, **more or less** 都應緊接第一個助動詞之後, 例如): 'If you've more or less finished, I'll start clearing up.' Note, however, that in many cases **more or less** may be placed at the end of the clause (但要注意: 在許多情況下, **more or less** 可放在句末, 例如): 'She forced me to invite her, more or less.' 'We're there, more or less!' 'They've finished the job, more or less.'

morning See (見) AFTERNOON, DAY 1

most 1

× Where I come from, the most teachers have to teach at two schools in order to earn enough.

√ **Where I come from, most teachers have to teach at two schools in order to earn enough.**

(在我家鄉, 大多數的教師必須同時在兩所學校任教才能維持生活。)

Do not use **the** before **most** when **most** means 'nearly all'. (如 **most** 意為 "幾乎是全部", 前面不加 **the**。)

2 × I think that pollution is a serious problem in most of the countries nowadays.
√ **I think that pollution is a serious problem in most countries nowadays.**
(我認為在大多數的國家中, 目前污染都很嚴重。)
× Most of the people like to spend Christmas at home.
√ **Most people like to spend Christmas at home.**
(大多數人都喜歡在家裡過聖誕節。)

> Use **most** WITHOUT **of** + determiner when the noun that follows is used in a general, unrestricted sense.
> Compare (如 **most** 所形容的名詞是非限制性的, 則 most 之後緊接該名詞, 如上例 "most people"; 但如該名詞是限制性的, 則 most 之後應加 "**of** the" 才接名詞, 即 most of the people, 例如): 'Most of the people I know like to spend Christmas at home.' (在本句中, people 為 I know 所限制, 故此是限制性的。)

3 × Most of major firms in Japan use word processors.
√ **Most of the major firms in Japan use word processors.**
√ **Most major firms in Japan use word processors.**
(在日本大多數的公司都使用文字處理機。)

> **most of** + determiner (+ adjective) + noun OR
> **most** (+ adjective) + noun
> **most of** 之後應加 the 才接所形容的名詞; 如名詞之前有形容詞, 則緊接 most 之後, 不用 of。

4 × My country is very big and occupies the most part of the continent.
√ **My country is very big and occupies most of the continent.**
√ **My country is very big and occupies the main part of the continent.**
(我的國家幅員廣闊, 佔了本大陸的大部分。)

> **Most** cannot be used as an adjective. (**most** 一詞不能用作形容詞—譯者按: 文法家對 most 一詞的詞性一向存在不同的看法, 有認為 most 以及 any, some, few, much 等是 indefinite determiner, 即所謂 "不定指定詞"; 有認為就是個形容詞。) The only exception is the fixed phrase **for the most part,** meaning 'almost completely; mainly' (唯一例外的是, 作 "幾乎全都是" 或 "主要的" 解的固定詞組 **for the most part** 中的 most, 可算作形容詞, 例如): 'The machines have for the most part been replaced.'

5 × Both girls are clever but Edna is the most intelligent.
√ **Both girls are clever but Edna is the more intelligent.**
(兩個女孩子都很伶俐, 不過艾德娜更為聰明。)

> Use **more** when comparing two people or things.
> 比較兩人或兩物時用 **more**。
> Use **most** when comparing three or more.
> 比較三者或以上時用 **most**。

mother × My mother language is Chinese.
√ **My mother tongue is Chinese.**
√ **My native language is Chinese.**
(我的母語是漢語。)

> **mother language** is a literal translation of "母語". The correct expression is **mother tongue** or **native language.**
> 按 **mother language** 是 "母語" 的中式英文。正確的說法是 **mother tongue** 或 **native language**。

mouse × There were mouses in the canteen.
√ **There were mice in the canteen.**
(食堂裡有老鼠。)

> **Mouse** is singular.
> 按 **mouse** 是單數。
> **Mice** is plural.
> 按 **mice** 是複數。

much 1 × I should like to become an engineer because I know much about engineering.
√ **I should like to become an engineer because I know a lot about engineering.**
(我想成為一個工程師, 因為我對這一行很瞭解。)

> As a noun or pronoun **much** is usually used only in negative sentences and questions (作為名詞或代詞, **much** 一般只用於否定句或問句, 例如): 'He doesn't know much about it.' 'Does he know much about it?' In affirmative sentences, phrases such as **a lot** and **a great deal** are used. (在肯定句中用 **a lot** 及 **a great deal**。)

2 × As a doctor he earns much money.
√ **As a doctor he earns a lot of money.**
(他當醫生賺好多錢。)

Much is used before a noun (or used as a pronoun) mainly in questions and negative sentences (**much** 主要用於問句及否定句中的名詞或代詞之前, 例如): 'Does he earn much money?' 'He doesn't earn much money.' In affirmative sentences, phrases such as **a lot of** and **plenty of** are used. Note, however, that **much** is used in affirmative sentences after **too, so,** and **as** (在肯定句中應用 **a lot of** 及 **plenty of**。然而在肯定句中, **much** 可用在 **too**、**so** 及 **as** 之後, 例如): 'He spends too much money on beer.' and sometimes in formal contexts (有時也用於正式文體中, 例如): 'The country's economy has enjoyed much support from foreign investment.'

3 × British culture is much different from ours.
√ **British culture is very different from ours.**
(英國文化與我國文化有很大的不同。)
× We were much afraid that we would miss the flight.
√ **We were very afraid that we would miss the flight.**
(我們很擔心會誤了班機。)

Much is used before an adjective (1) in questions and negative sentences (**much** 用於形容詞之前的情況有 1. 在問句和否定句中, 例如): 'Is British culture much different from ours?' 'No, it isn't much different.'
(2) before comparative forms (2. 在比較級之前, 例如): 'His last novel was much longer and much more interesting.'
(3) before certian past participles acting as adjectives (3. 在某些作形容詞用的過去分詞之前, 例如): 'Her drawings are much admired.'

4 × There are as much disadvantages as advantages.
√ **There are as many disadvantages as advantages.**
(利與弊一樣多。)

as much + uncountable noun (按 **as much** 後接不可數名詞, 例如): 'You can eat as much food as you like.'
as many + plural form of a countable noun (**as many** 後接可數名詞的複數, 例如): 'You haven't seen as many films as Helen has.'

5 × Nowadays, there are much more criminals than policemen.
√ **Nowadays, there are many/far more criminals than policemen.**
(現今罪犯遠比警察多。)

much more + uncountable noun (按 **much more** 後接不可數名詞, 例如): 'much more traffic'
many/far more + plural countable noun (按 **many/far more** 後接複數可數名詞, 例如): 'far more cars'

6 × He was driving too much fast when the accident happened.
√ **He was driving much too fast when the accident happened.**
(事故發生時, 他駕駛得實在太快了。)

much/far + **too** + adjective/adverb
按 **much/far** 後接 **too**, 再接形容詞/副詞。

7 × I make much too many mistakes.
√ **I make far too many mistakes.**
(我犯的錯誤實在太多了。)

With **too many, too few** and **fewer,** use **far,** NOT **much.**
在 **too many**、**too few** 及 **fewer** 之前用 **far**, 不用 **much**。

music × We tried to listen to a music, but the sound was very bad.
√ **We tried to listen to a piece of music, but the sound was very bad.**
(我們想聽一首樂曲, 但聲音的效果很差。)

Music is an uncountable noun.
按 **music** 是不可數名詞, 前面不能用不定冠詞 "a"。若指 "一首樂曲", 可用 a piece of music。

must 1 × People are not as careful as they must be and drop their litter in the streets.
√ **People are not as careful as they should be and drop their litter in the streets.**
(人們應該留神, 不要在街上亂扔垃圾, 但是他們總是不注意。)

Use **must** to talk about something you are obliged to do, without freedom to choose or decide.
按 **must** 表示必須做或有責任做, 其中並無選擇之餘地。
Use **should** to talk about something you ought to do, but where you have freedom to choose or decide.
按 **should** 表示應該做或有義務做, 其中可有選擇的自由。

2 × The pupils mustn't go to the meeting if they don't want to.
✓ **The pupils needn't go to the meeting if they don't want to.**
(學生如不願參加這次會議, 可不必參加。)

Use **must/mustn't** when you mean 'have to', without freedom to choose or decide.
must/mustn't 作 "必須/不可以" 解, 其中並無選擇之餘地。
Use **needn't** or **don't have to** when there is freedom to choose or decide.
按 **needn't/don't have to** 作 "不必/無需" 解, 其中可有選擇的自由。

3 × If you can't find her, she must hide somewhere.
✓ **If you can't find her, she must be hiding somewhere.**
(如果你找不到她, 那她一定是躲在什麼地方了。)

'She must be hiding somewhere.' (=I conclude that she is hiding) (意為: 我得出結論, 她躲起來了。)
Compare (試比較): 'If you don't want them to find you, you must hide somewhere.' (=you have to hide) (意為: 你必須躲起來。)

myself × Two weeks ago my friend and myself decided to have a picnic.
✓ **Two weeks ago my friend and I decided to have a picnic.**
(兩星期前我和一位朋友決定去野餐。)

Pronouns ending **-self** or **-selves** cannot be placed in the subject position unless they are used for emphasis (字尾是 **-self** 或 **-selves** 的代名詞不能用作主語, 除非是為了加強語氣, 例如): 'I myself have never seen a ghost.' 'They themselves have never been to Italy.'

name

× The magazine is named 'Four Wheels'; it's about cars.
√ **The magazine is called 'Four Wheels'; it's about cars.**
(這本雜誌叫 '四輪', 內容講的是汽車。)

> **name** = (1) give a name to (給取名, 例如): 'They've named the baby Louise.'
> (2) identify by saying or writing the name(s) of (說出或寫出 … 的名字, 例如): 'The students were asked to name the five largest oceans in the world.'
> **call** = (1) give a name to (給 … 取名, 例如): 'They've called the baby Louise.' (2) be known by a particular name ("叫 … 名字", 例如): 'Her mother is also called Louise.'

nation **1**

× I couldn't tell what nation he came from.
√ **I couldn't tell what country he came from.**
(我說不準他是哪個國家的人。)

> **nation** = a large group of people, usually living in one area and having an independent government (可譯作 "國家", 實指聚居在一個地區並擁有一個獨立的政府的民族, 例如): 'The President spoke on radio to the nation.'
> **country** = the area occupied by or associated with a nation (可譯作 "國家", 實指一個民族聚居的地區, 例如): 'Some parts of this country are much warmer than others.'
> Note the alternative (注意另一種說法): 'I couldn't tell his nationality.'

2

× Most former colonies have now become self-governing nations.
√ **Most former colonies have now become self-governing states.**
(昔日大多數的殖民地現在都成為自治的國家。)

> **state** = a country considered as a political organization (可譯作 "國家", 實指一個政體)

nationality **1**

× The harbour was full of ships of different nationalities.
√ **The harbour was full of ships from different countries.**
(港內泊滿了來自各國的輪船。)

> **Nationality** is used only of people.
> 按 **nationality** 一詞意為國籍, 僅用以指人。

2 × The students are from various nationalities.
√ **The students are of various nationalities.**
(這些學生的國籍是不同的。)

> **be of** a particular nationality, NOT **from.**
> "屬於國籍" 可用 **be of** ... nationality, 其中 **of** 不用 **from** 替代。

nationalized × Mabel Wong was born in Hong Kong but she has now become a nationalized British citizen.
√ **Mabel Wong was born in Hong Kong but she has now become a naturalized British citizen.**
(王美寶生於香港, 但現已入了英籍。)

> **nationalized** = owned or controlled by a government (國有化, 國營, 例如): 'Many industries have been nationalized over the last few years.'
> **naturalized** = made a citizen of a country (that is not the country of your birth) (入籍)

nature × I have always found the nature fascinating.
√ **I have always found nature fascinating.**
(我總是感到大自然奇妙無比。)

> **Nature** (= the nature world of birds, trees, rivers, etc.) is NEVER used with **the.**
> 按 **nature** 一詞作 "大自然" 解時不得與 the 並用。

near **1** × He decided to visit a friend who lived very near from where he was at that moment.
√ **He decided to visit a friend who lived very near (to) where he was at that moment.**
(他決定去拜訪一位當時住得很近的朋友。)

> **near (to),** NOT **from**
> 注意: **near** 後接 **to**, 也可省略 **to**, 但不可接 **from**。

2 × I went near to the girl and told her my name.
√ **I went up to the girl and told her my name.**
(我走到女孩跟前, 告訴她我的名字。)

> **go up to** someone = approach someone
> 指 "走近某人", 用 **go up to** someone。

3 × I sometimes meet friends in a near restaurant.
√ **I sometimes meet friends in a nearby restaurant.**
(我有時在附近的一家飯店會見朋友。)
× I ran to the telephone box which was near to call an ambulance.
√ **I ran to the nearby telephone box to call an ambulance.**
(我奔向附近的電話亭叫救護車。)

> **Near** is not used as an attributive adjective except in phrases such as 'a near miss' or 'the near future'. Compare (除在 'a near miss' 或 'the near future' 外, **near** 不用作修飾形容詞, 試比較):
> 'The restaurant is near the town hall.' (preposition) (句中的 near 為前置詞)
> 'The restaurant is quite near.' (predicative adjective) (敍述形容詞)
> 'We went to a nearby restaurant.' (attributive adjective) (修飾形容詞)

nearby × Their house is nearby the new airport.
√ **Their house is near the new airport.**
(他們家就在新機場附近。)

> **Nearby** is used either as an adverb (按 **nearby** 可用作副詞, 例如): 'There is an airport nearby.' or an adjective (或用作形容詞, 例如): 'We flew from a nearby airport.' but NOT as a preposition (但不用作前置詞).

necessary 1 × It is necessary to some people to get more than eight hours' sleep.
√ **It is necessary for some people to get more than eight hours' sleep.**
(有些人必須有八小時以上的睡眠。)

> **necessary for** someone to do something, NOT **to**
> 注意: **necessary for** 後接 someone to do something 時不可用 **to** 替代 **for**。

2 × Many people were necessary to leave their homes during the earthquake.
√ **It was necessary for many people to leave their homes during the earthquake.**
√ **Many people had to leave their homes during the earthquake.**
(地震時許多人必須離開家。)

> Compare (試比較): 'A passport is necessary if you want to travel overseas.'

need **1** × It is no need to tell the police about the accident.
√ **There is no need to tell the police about the accident.**
(沒有必要向警察報告這次事故。)

> **it is not necessary** ... BUT **there is no need** ...
> "沒有必要做 ... ", 既可譯作 "**it is not necessary** ...", 也可譯作 "**there is no need...**"。

2 × There is a great need of international understanding.
√ **There is a great need for international understanding.**
(目前亟需世界各國之間的諒解。)

> **a need for** something, NOT **of**
> 注意: **a need for** (something) 中的前置詞 **for** 不可用 **of** 替代。
> Compare (試比較): **(be) in need of** something (=require 需要): 'The car is in need of a good clean.' 'Are you in need of any assistance?'

3 × Tina needs leave her house at seven o'clock every morning.
√ **Tina needs to leave her house at seven o'clock every morning.**
(蒂娜必須每天早晨七點離開家。)

> Compare: (1) negative form (試比較: 否定式, 例如): 'She doesn't need to stay if she doesn't want to.' 'She needn't stay if she doesn't want.'
> (WITHOUT **to** — 注意在 needn't 之後緊接動詞, 中間不用 **to**)
> (2) question form (疑問式, 例如): 'Does she need to stay any longer?' 'Need she stay any longer?'
> (WITHOUT **to** — 不帶 **to**)

4 × Today's society needs that women work.
√ **Today's society needs women to work.**
(今日的社會需要婦女工作。)

> **need** someone **to do** something, NOT **that**
> **need** 後接 someone **to do** something, 不接帶 **that** 的子句

needn't

× Catherine told her husband he needn't to worry.
√ **Catherine told her husband he needn't worry.**
(凱塞琳告訴丈夫不必擔憂。)

> **needn't** + infinitive WITHOUT **to** (注意: **needn't** 後接原形動詞)
> Note the alternative (注意另一種說法): 'Catherine told her husband that he didn't need to worry.'

neither 1

× Inside the examination room we could neither smoke or talk.
√ **Inside the examination room we could neither smoke nor talk.**
(在考場內, 我們既不能吸烟, 也不能談話。)
× His parents neither shouted at him or smacked him.
√ **His parents neither shouted at him nor smacked him.**
(他的父母既沒有向他叱喝, 也沒有打他。)

> **neither** ... **nor** ..., NOT **neither** ... **or** ...
> 表示 "既不 ... 也不 ..." 用 **neither** ... **nor** ... , 不可用 **neither** ... **or** ...
> Compare (試比較): 'either ... or ...'

2

× Neither John's father nor mine couldn't understand the problem.
√ **Neither John's father nor mine could understand the problem.**
(約翰的父親也好, 我的父親也好, 都弄不懂這個問題。)

> **not/never/rarely** etc. are NOT used after **neither** OR **neither** ... **nor** ...
> 按 **not**, **never**, **rarely** 等詞都不用於 **neither** 或 **neither** ... **nor** ... 之後

3

× Henry neither told Maria nor her sister that he had lost his job.
√ **Henry told neither Maria nor her sister that he had lost his job.**
(亨利既不告訴瑪利亞, 也不告訴她妹妹, 他已失業。)

> **Neither** should be placed immediately before the first of the connected items and **nor** immediately before the second. Compare (按 **neither** 應放在第一個與之相關的詞的緊前面, 如上句的 Maria, 而 **nor** 則放在第二個與之相關的詞的緊前面, 如上句的 her sister 試比較): 'I've seen neither Annie nor Tina.' 'I've neither seen Annie nor written to her.'

4 × In the library I found neither the books I was looking for.
√ **In the library I found neither of the books I was looking for.**
(我要在圖書館找的那兩本書連一本都找不到。)

> **neither** + singular noun form (按 **neither** 後接單數名詞, 意為 "(兩者之中) 哪一個都不 … " 例如): 'Neither camera is suitable.' (這兩個照相機哪一個都不合用。)
> **neither of** + plural noun form (按 neither of 則後接複數名詞, 意為 "兩者都不 … ", 例如): 'Neither of the cameras is suitable.' (兩個照相機全不合用。)

5 × Neither teachers are coming.
√ **Neither teacher is coming.**
√ **Neither of the teachers is/are coming.**
(兩個教師都不會來。)

> When **neither** is used with a singular noun it is followed by a singular verb.
> 如 **neither** 與單數名詞並用, 則應接單數動詞。
> Note that in informed English **neither of** … and **neither** … **nor** are often followed by a plural verb, although this would be considered incorrect in formal writing (注意: 在口語體英語中, **neither of** … 及 **neither** … **nor** 之後常接複數動詞, 雖然在書面英語中認為是錯誤的, 例如): 'Neither Paul nor John is/are coming.'

nervous 1 × The child kept pulling my sleeve, which made me nervous.
√ **The child kept pulling my sleeve, which irritated me.**
(那孩子老是扯我的袖子, 使我很惱火。)

> **nervous** (adjective) = rather afraid (害怕)
> **irritate** (verb) = annoy (使惱火)

2 × Thinking she might be hurt, I felt very nervous.
√ **Thinking she might be hurt, I felt very anxious.**
(想到她可能已受傷, 我感到很着急。)

> **nervous** = rather afraid (害怕, 例如): 'Wouldn't you feel nervous if you had to make a speech to an audience of three hundred people?'
> **anxious** = worried about something which may happen or may have happened (擔心; 着急)

never 1 × I asked him to never arrive late.
√ **I asked him never to arrive late.**
(我要求他以後不再遲到。)

Do not split a **to** infinitive with **never/not.**
不要用 **never/not** 插入 **to** 與動詞不定式之間。

2 × You never can get really good beef in our local supermarket.
√ **You can never get really good beef in our local supermarket.**
(在本地的超級市場, 你絕對找不到真正的好牛肉。)

Never goes immediately after the (first) auxiliary verb (注意 never 緊接 [第一個] 助動詞之後, 例如): 'You should never cross the road without looking.' However, when there is no auxiliary verb, **never** is placed immediately before the main verb (如沒有助動詞, never 放在主動詞之前, 例如): 'She never lies.' When the main verb is **be, never** is placed immediately after it (如主動詞是 **be**, **never** 緊接其後, 例如): 'She is never punctual.'

3 × I did never have time to read the book.
√ **I never had time to read the book.**
(我從沒有時間讀這本書。)

Do is often used with **not** to make negative statements (**do** 常與 **not** 並用, 作為否定語, 例如): 'I didn't answer the letter.' 'She doesn't invite strangers.' However, **do** is NOT used in this way with **never** (但 **do** 與 **never** 不能這樣並用, 例如): 'I never answered the letter.' 'She never invites strangers.'
The exception to this rule is when **do** is used for emphasis (唯一的例外是, 如 **do** 用以加強語就有可能與 **never** 連用, 例如): 'In thirty years I never did have time to read the book.'

4 × She said some of the rudest things I have never heard in all my life.
√ **She said some of the rudest things I have ever heard in all my life.**
(她講出了一些我有生以來聽到的最粗魯的話。)

never = at no time (意為 "從未"、"從不")
ever = at any time (意為 "曾經")

5 × Nobody never tells you the truth.
√ **Nobody ever tells you the truth.**
(誰也不會把真話告訴你。)
× 'Nobody will never find me,' he thought.
√ **'Nobody will ever find me,' he thought.**
('誰也找不到我,' 他想。)

> After **nobody/nothing/rarely** and other words with a negative meaning, use **ever** (NOT **never**) to avoid a double negative.
> 在 **nobody/nothing/rarely** 及其他有否定意思的詞後應用 **ever** (不用 **never**) 以避免雙重否定。

6 × Never I had seen such an ugly face.
√ **Never had I seen such an ugly face.**
(我可從未見過如此醜惡的臉。)

> When negative adverbs such as **never/seldom/hardly/scarcely** are used at the beginning of a sentence, the subject and auxiliary verb change places (凡在句首用 **never/seldom/hardly/scarcely** 等否定副詞時, 主詞與助動詞互換位置。): 'Never have I known him to lose.' 'Rarely do you find such intelligence in a child.'

news × The news are never very good nowadays.
√ **The news is never very good nowadays.**
(如今的消息總是不很好。)
× I'm looking forward to hearing a good news from you.
√ **I'm looking forward to hearing some good news from you.**
(我期望聽到你的好消息。)

> **News** is an uncountable noun.
> 注意: **news** 是不可數名詞。

next 1 × I have some spare time this week but the next week I'll have to start work.
√ **I have some spare time this week but next week I'll have to start work.**
(這星期我還有些空閒時間, 但下星期我就必須開始工作了。)

Do not use **the** in time expressions with **next** when the point or period of time is being considered in relation to the present.
如 **next** 所指的時間與現時有關, 則 **next** 之前不能加 **the**, 以形容時間。
Compare (試比較): 'Next Friday we're going fishing.' (in relation to the present 與現時有關) 'The next afternoon they took us to see the National Gallery.' (in relation to the day before the trip to the National Gallery 與前往 National Gallery 的頭一天有關)

2 × I am looking forward to seeing you on next Sunday.
√ **I am looking foward to seeing you next Sunday.**
(我盼望下星期日與你會面。)

Do not use a preposition to begin a time expression with **next** when the point or period of time is being considered in relation to the present.
如 **next** 所指的時間與現時有關, 則 **next** 之前不能加前置詞表示時間。
See also (也見) ON 1

3 × The next post office is opposite the bus station.
√ **The nearest post office is opposite the bus station.**
(最近的郵局在公共汽車站對面。)

Do not use **next** to mean **nearest.**
不要用 **next** 表示 "最近" 的含義。

nice × Most people like to come home to a nice and tidy house.
√ **Most people like to come home to a house that is nice and tidy.**
(大多數的人都喜歡回到一個十分整潔的家。)

Two-part adjectival phrases with **nice** such as 'nice and tidy', 'nice and clean', and 'nice and smart' are ALWAYS placed after the noun they modify.
注意: (1) 以 **nice** 一詞為首的雙形容詞片語, 如 "nice and tidy"、"nice and clean"、"nice and smart" 等, 總是放在其所修飾的名詞之後; (2) 這類片語中的 **nice and** 實際上作 **very** (很、十分、非常) 解, 如 nice and cool, 意為 "十分涼快", nice and smart, 意為 "相當精明"; 又如 I didn't like the speech, but at least it was nice and short. ——我不喜歡這次的演講, 不過那倒是挺簡短的。

night **1** × He suddenly realized that it was getting dark and it would soon be the night.
√ **He suddenly realized that it was getting dark and it would soon be night.**
(他忽然意識到天色在轉黑, 夜晚即將來臨。)

When **night** means 'the period when it is dark' (as opposed to **day**, 'the period when it is light'), it is usually used WITHOUT **the** (**night** 用作 '黑夜' [與 '白天' 相對] 時, 一般不加 **the**, 例如): 'It would soon be night.' (=It would soon be dark.)

2 × It was about nine o'clock in the night when we heard a noise outside.
√ **It was about nine o'clock at night when we heard a noise outside.**
(大約在晚上九點鐘, 我們聽到外面一片喧鬧聲。)

ten o'clock **in the morning,** two o'clock **in the afternoon,** half-past seven **in the evening,** BUT nine o'clock **at night**
(注意詞的搭配關係: "早上十點鐘" 用 'ten o'clock **in the morning**', "下午兩點鐘" 用 'two o'clock **in the afternoon**', "傍晚七點半鐘" 用 'half-past seven **in the evening**', 而 "晚上九點鐘" 用 'nine o'clock **at night**'。

3 × Night was falling and it started to rain.
√ **It was getting dark and it started to rain.**
(天色漸暗並開始下雨。)

'Night was falling' is not really incorrect but is only used in a literary context.
按 Night was falling 不算錯, 但僅用於文學語體。

nobody **1** × Nobody have complained about the noise.
√ **Nobody has complained about the noise.**
(沒有人抱怨那聲音吵。)
× When I arrived, there were nobody at all in the house.
√ **When I arrived, there was nobody at all in the house.**
(我到達時屋裡根本沒有人。)

nobody/no one + singular verb
nobody/no one 後接單數動詞。

2 × He closed the door quietly so that nobody wouldn't hear him.
√ **He closed the door quietly so that nobody would hear him.**
(他把門輕輕掩上, 不讓別人聽見。)
× Nobody never arrived late.
√ **Nobody ever arrived late.**
(從來沒有人遲到。)

Do not use **not/never/rarely** etc. after **nobody** or **no one.**
在 **nobody** 或 **no one** 後不得用 **not/never/rarely** 等含有否定意思的詞。

3 × Nobody of the children was hurt, but the driver of the car died.
√ **None of/not one of the children was hurt, but the driver of the car died.**
(沒有一個小孩受傷, 但是汽車司機死了。)

Nobody and **no one** cannot be followed by **of** unless the phrase introduced by **of** modifies the preceding noun (注意: **nobody** 與 **no one** 後面不用 **of**, 除非用由 **of** 引導的片語來修飾前面的詞, 例如): 'Nobody/no one of importance attended the meeting.'

4 × We didn't know where to go, and there was no body to ask.
√ **We didn't know where to go, and there was nobody to ask.**
(我們不知該往哪裡走, 也找不到人問路。)

Nobody (pronoun) is ALWAYS one word.
按 **Nobody** 作為代名詞總是一個詞, 不能分開。

noise × I turned on the radio but there was no noise.
√ **I turned on the radio but there was no sound.**
(我擰開收音機, 但聽不到聲音。)

noise = loud unpleasant sounds (意為 "噪音", 例如): 'The noise of the traffic gave me a headache.'
sound = something noticed by the ear (意為 "聲音", 例如): 'the sound of a guitar', 'the sound of a car engine'

no matter 1 × No matter he tries hard, he never succeeds in passing.
√ **No matter how hard he tries, he never succeeds in passing.**
(不管他多麼努力, 他總不能考試及格。)

no matter how much he studies/often he goes/well he plays etc. + main clause
注意: **no matter how** 之後接 much he studies 或 often he goes 或 well he plays 等, 為狀語子句, 其後應接主句。

2 × No matter the recession, sales remained high.
√ **In spite of the recession, sales remained high.**
(儘管經濟出現不景氣, 銷售額仍然很高。)

No matter is ALWAYS followed by **how** or a **wh-** word (注意: **no matter** 總是後接 **how** 或以 **wh-** 開始的詞, 例如): 'No matter what they did, they couldn't put the fire out.'

nominate × Mr Tong was nominated manager of the company in 1984.
√ **Mr Tong was appointed manager of the company in 1984.**
(唐先生在一九八四年被任命為公司經理。)

nominate = suggest someone for election or selection (for a job or position) (提名 … 為候選人)
appoint = give someone a job or position (任命)

no more × My wife had left the hotel and I no more needed a double room.
√ **My wife had left the hotel and I no longer needed a double room.**
(我太太已離開旅館, 我也就不需要住雙人房。)

When talking about time, use **no longer,** NOT **no more.**
Note the alternative (如指時間, 應用 **no longer**, 不用 **no more**, 注意可用另一種說法): 'My wife had left the hotel and I didn't need a double room any more.'

none 1 × None visited the old man for over a week.
√ **Nobody visited the old man for over a week.**
(有一個多星期沒有人來看望這位老人了。)

> Unlike **nobody** and **no one, none** cannot be used of people unless it refers to people who have already been mentioned OR it is followed by **of** (不同於 **nobody** 和 **no one**, **none** 不能用來指人, 除非指前面已提過者, 或其後接 of, 即 **none of** ... , 例如): 'I invited three guests but none (of them) accepted.' 'None of my friends can speak English.'

2 × I told the police officer that in my opinion none of the two drivers was responsible.
√ **I told the police officer that in my opinon neither of the two drivers was responsible.**
(我告訴那警官, 我認為兩名駕駛者都不該負責。)

> When talking about two people or things, use **neither.** For three or more, use **none** (談及兩人或兩物時, 應用 neither; 三者或以上才用 none。)

no one See (見) NOBODY 1, 2, 3

North × I am now living in North England.
√ **I am now living in the north of England.**
(我現時住在英格蘭北部。)

> **North/South/East/West** etc. are usually only used in the names of countries and their internal divisions (**North/South/East/West** 等都只用於國家名稱和國內的地區, 例如): 'North America', 'South Carolina'.
> To refer to approximate locations, use **the north/south of** ... or **northern/southern** etc.
> 如指大致上的位置, 應用 **the north/south of** ... 或 **northern/southern** 等。

no sooner × No sooner we had arrived than it began to rain.
√ **No sooner had we arrived than it began to rain.**
(我們剛一到達, 就開始下雨了。)

> When **no sooner** is placed at the beginning of a sentence, the subject and (auxiliary) verb change places.
> 按 **no sooner** 在句首時, 主詞應同(助)動詞換位。

notice 1 × I wrote him a notice saying that the package had arrived.
√ **I wrote him a note saying that the package had arrived.**
(我給他寫了一個條子說包裹已收到。)

> **notice** = a short written statement giving information or directions, usually found in a public place (通常在公共場所公佈的通知, 例如): 'There was a notice on the wall saying "Private property. No parking." '
> **note** = a short informal letter or written message from one person to another (意為 "便條")

2 × The machine still didn't work, so I re-read the notice.
√ **The machine still didn't work, so I re-read the instructions.**
(機器仍然不動, 所以我重新看了說明書。)

> **notice** = a sign giving information or direcitons, often on a wall in a public place (公共場所的告示, 例如): 'The notice said "No smoking!" '
> **instructions** = a series of directions provided with a new piece of equipment (使用說明)

3 × It was so dark that at first I didn't take any notice of him.
√ **It was so dark that at first I didn't notice him.**
(當時天那麼黑, 我起先沒有覺察到他。)

> **take notice of** = pay attention to (意為: "注意", 例如): 'Nobody took any notice of what I was saying.'
> **notice** = become aware of (意為: "覺察到")

not only 1 × She not only made her own dresses but also her own hats.
√ **She made not only her own dresses but also her own hats.**
(她不僅自己做衣服而且還做帽子。)

> The position of **not only** should be the same as the position of **but also** (i.e. immediately before an object, immediately before a main verb, etc.). 按 **not only** 與 **but also** 的位置應當相同 (即同樣緊接受詞或緊接主動詞等)。

Compare (比較): 'He injured not only his shoulder but also his elbow.' ('his shoulder' and 'his elbow' are both noun phrases 兩者同是名詞片語)
'He not only injured his back but also hurt his head.' ('injured' and 'hurt' are both verbs 兩者同是動詞)

2 × Not only I passed the test, but I got a distinction.
√ **Not only did I pass the test, but I got a distinction.**
(我不僅通過了測試, 而且還獲得了優異的成績。)

When **not only** is used at the beginning of a sentence, the subject and (supplied) auxiliary verb change places (as in the question form) (按 **not only** 在句首時主詞與有時需加上的助動詞換位, 一如問句那樣): 'I passed' becomes (變成) 'did I pass'.

nowadays **1** × Nowaday it is very difficult to find a good job.
√ **Nowadays it is very difficult to find a good job.**
(如今要找一份好的工作實在不容易。)

nowadays (WITH **s**)
注意 **nowadays** 拼法中有個 **s**。

2 × Although she is not very young, she still likes to wear nowadays clothes.
√ **Although she is not very young, she still likes to wear modern/fashionable clothes.**
(她雖然並不年輕, 但還是仍愛穿摩登/時髦的服裝。)

Nowadays (=currently) is an adverb, NOT an adjective.
Nowadays (作 "現在" 解, 相當於 currently 一詞, 是副詞, 不能用作形容詞。)

number **1** × The number of thieves are increasing.
√ **The number of thieves is increasing.**
(竊賊的數目不斷增加。)

the number of ... + singular verb
注意: "the number of ... " 後接單數動詞。

2 × A large number of cars was parked outside the school.
√ **A large number of cars were parked outside the school.**
(大量汽車停在校門外。)

> **a number of** ... + plural verb
> 注意: **a number of** 後接複數動詞。

3 × Harsher punishments will not reduce the number of crime.
√ **Harsher punishments will not reduce the number of crimes.**
(懲罰的手段再嚴厲也不會減少罪案的數量。)

> **the number of** + plural form of a countable noun
> 注意: **the number of** 後接可數名詞的複數形式。

4 See (見) BIG 1

oath × He stated with an oath that he would be loyal to his country and people all his life.
√ **He stated on/under oath that he would be loyal to his country and people all his life.**
(他宣誓說他永遠忠於祖國和人民。)

> **on/under oath** = [law] have made a solemn promise to tell the truth (在法律上意指"已宣誓要說真話")
> **with an oath** = make an expression of strong feeling using religious or sexual words (妄用神名或骯髒字眼咒罵人、詛咒人，例如): 'He loudly exclaimed with an oath against his wife's unfaithfulness.'

obey × He was a very good boy and obeyed to his parents all the time.
√ **He was a very good boy and obeyed his parents all the time.**
(他是個很乖的孩子, 向來聽父母的話。)

> **obey** someone WITHOUT **to**
> 按 **obey** 之後直接跟 someone, 其間不容插入 **to**。

object × Do you object smoking?
√ **Do you object to smoking?**
(你反對抽烟嗎?)

> As a verb, **object** never takes a direct object. One always says **object to** something.
> 作為一個動詞, object 後面不跟直接受詞。表示"反對某事" 應說 **object to** something。

obligation

× My obligations include doing the housework and picking up the children from school.
√ **My duties include doing the housework and picking up the children from school.**
(我的職責是做家務和把孩子從學校接回家。)

obligation = moral duty or responsibility (意為 "義務", 例如): 'Since they had invited us to their wedding, we felt under an obligation to invite them to ours.' (countable 可數名詞)
'You can try the computer in our showroom without any obligation.' (uncountable 不可數名詞)
duty = what you must do in your job or because you think it is right (意為 "責任" 或 "本份", 例如): 'a moral duty'

oblige

× In order to pay the hospital bill, it obliged me to sell my car.
√ **In order to pay the hospital bill, I was obliged to sell my car.**
(為了償付住院費, 我只好把汽車賣掉。)

be obliged + to-v
按 **be obliged** 之後接帶 to 的動詞表示 "不得不 ... " 的意思。

obvious

× The lack of freedom and social justice is obvious for everyone.
√ **The lack of freedom and social justice is obvious to everyone.**
(沒有自由和社會公正的現象是人所共見的。)

obvious to someone, NOT **for**
按 **obvious to** someone 中的前置詞 **to** 不可用 **for** 替代。

occasion

× The scholarship provided me with my first occasion to travel overseas.
√ **The scholarship provided me with my first opportunity to travel overseas.**
(獎學金給了我第一次出洋的機會。)

occasion = the time when an event happens (意為 "時刻"、"時機"、"次(數)", 中文有時也用 "機會" 去表達, 例如): 'I've been to Rome on several occasions.' (= several times)
opportunity = a time when it becomes possible to do something (意為 "機會"、"良機")

occupy × She is very occupied in cooking the dinner.
✓ **She is fully occupied in cooking the dinner.**
(她正忙着做晚飯。)

> **busy** and **occupied** are close in meaning but differ in usage. One can be 'very busy' but NOT 'very occupied'. **fully/solely/wholly/busily** can be used to modify occupied.
> 英文的 **busy** 和 **occupied** 意思相近，但用法不同。我們可以說 very busy 但不可說 very occupied。我們一般地用 **fully**、**solely**、**wholly**、**busily** 這類字眼來修飾 occupied。

o'clock **1** × It was twenty past four o'clock when the train arrived.
✓ **It was twenty past four when the train arrived.**
(火車到達時已經是四點二十分了。)

> **O'clock** may be used in telling the time ONLY for full hours (WITHOUT any minutes following). Compare (按 **o'clock** 只用於正點時刻，不帶分鐘，試比較): 'It's four o'clock.' 'It's ten past four.'

2 × I start work at 9.00 o'clock.
✓ **I start work at 9 o'clock.**
(我每天早上九時開始工作。)

> '5 pm./5.00 p.m.' BUT '5 o'clock' (in the afternoon)
> 表達鐘點有兩種方式，譬如下午五點，既可用 "5 p.m."，也可用 "5.00 p.m."，但如用 "o'clock" 一詞，則應寫作 "5 o'clock" (in the afternoon)。

3 × By seven o'clock p.m. the child had been found.
✓ **By seven p.m. the child had been found.**
✓ **By seven o'clock (in the evening) the child had been found.**
(到了傍晚七點，才找到那孩子。)

> Use either **o'clock** OR **a.m./p.m.,** NOT both.
> 表達鐘點，或用 **o'clock,** 或用 **a.m./p.m.,** 不能兩者同時兼用。

of **1** × The old man didn't give me a minute of peace.
✓ **The old man didn't give me a minute's peace.**
(那老人不讓我有一分鐘的安寧。)

Time expressions are usually formed with **-'s** or **-s'** (表達時間的方式有時用 "**-'s**" 或 "**-s'**" 組成, 例如): 'last week's news', 'three months' leave', etc.

2 × This coat isn't mine. It's of a friend.
√ **This coat isn't mine. It's a friend's.**
(這外衣不是我的, 是我一個朋友的。)

To express human ownership, use **-'s** (NOT **of**). Compare (表示屬人所有的方式可用 "**-'s**", 不用 "**of**", 試比較): 'John's garden' BUT (但可說) 'the roof of the house'

3 × They are both friends of him.
√ **They are both friends of his.**
(他們兩個都是他的朋友。)

a friend **of mine/yours/his/hers/ours/theirs** = one of my/your/his/her/our/their friends (意為 "我的/你的/他的/她的/我們的/他們的一個朋友)
Compare (試比較): 'That's a photograph of him.' (= showing him 照片上有他)
'That's a photograph of his.' (= belonging to or taken by him 照片是他的或他拍攝的)

4 × I don't think the watch is of gold.
√ **I don't think the watch is made of gold.**
(我認為這個錶不是金的。)

(be) made of gold/wood/plastic etc.
表達一件物品是 "由 (金/木/塑膠) 做的", 可用 **(be) made of** 後接 gold/wood/plastic 等。

5 × Arlon is one of the oldest towns of Belgium.
√ **Arlon is one of the oldest towns in Belgium.**
(阿隆是比利時最古老的城鎮之一。)

a town **in** Belgium, a village **in** France, NOT **of**
漢語說 "比利時的市鎮", "法國的村莊", 其中用 "的" 表示從屬關係; 英文則說 a town in Belgium, a village in France, 其中用 "**in**" 表示從屬關係, 不用 "**of**"。

6 × I arrived in London on 25th of November.
√ **I arrived in London on 25th November.**
(我在十一月二十五日抵達倫敦。)

> Say (口頭說) 'the 25th of November' or 'November the 25th' BUT write (但書面用) '25th November' or 'November 25th' WITHOUT **the** or **of** (不用 the 或 of)

7 × The scenery reminded her of a painting of Renoir.
√ **The scenery reminded her of a painting by Renoir.**
(那景色使她想起法國名畫家雷諾瓦畫的一幅畫。)

> **a painting of Renoir** = a picture that someone painted of Renoir (意為 "別人為雷諾瓦畫的一幅肖像")
> **a painting by Renoir** = a picture that Renoir painted (意為 "雷諾瓦畫的一幅作品")

8 × The magazine contains six pages of photographs of the Cup Final of Europe.
√ **The magazine contains six pages of photographs of the European Cup Final.**
(這雜誌有六頁歐洲杯決賽的照片。)

> A phrase beginning with **of** should not be used to modify a noun when there is an adjective available (如可用形容詞修飾名詞, 則不用以 **of** 開始的片語去修飾名詞, 例如): 'Do you like English cheese?' NOT (不說) 'Do you like the cheese of England?'

9 See (見) BEHIND

off **1** × My company gave all the staff an off day to celebrate its fiftieth anniversary.
√ **My company gave all the staff a day off to celebrate its fiftieth anniversary.**
(我的公司給全體職員放假一天, 以慶祝公司成立五十週年。)

> **off** (adjective) = not as good as usual (用作形容詞, 意為 "不如平時表現好", 例如): 'He'll win easily, unless it's one of his off days.' (= a day when he does not play as well as he usually plays) (他一定很輕易就勝出, 除非是他這一天的競技狀態不佳。)
> **off** (adverb) = spent or to be spent as a holiday (用作副詞, 意為 "放假")

2 × Don't forget to off the lights before you go out.
√ **Don't forget to turn/switch off the lights before you go out.**
(上街之前, 不要忘記熄燈。)

> **off** can be an adjective, a preposition or an adverb BUT can never be a verb. You may come across a sentence like this: " 'Off!' he shouted.", and yet, "off" here is an adverb meaning "Get off!" or "Off you go!"
> 按 "off" 一詞可以用作形容詞、前置詞或副詞, 但不可能是動詞。你可能碰到 " 'Off!' he shouted." 這樣一個句子, 但句中的 "off" 是副詞, 意為 "Get off!" 或 "Off you go!"。

3 × The glass fell off of the table.
√ **The glass fell off the table.**
(玻璃杯從桌子上掉了下來。)

> **Off** is NEVER followed by **of.**
> **Off** 之後不接 **of**

offer 1 × The old man then offered something to the little boy to eat.
√ **The old man then offered the little boy something to eat.**
(然後, 老人給那小男孩一點東西吃。)

> With **offer,** the indirect object ('the little boy') comes before the direct object ('something to eat') UNLESS the direct object is a pronoun or is much shorter than the indirect object (用 **offer** 時, 間接受詞 [the little boy] 放在直接受詞 [something to eat] 之前, 除非直接受詞是代詞或比間接受詞要短得多, 例如): 'I offered the apple to the little girl sitting in the corner.'

2 × An old man offered me to go to his house.
√ **An old man invited me to go to his house.**
(一位老人請我去他的家。)

> **offer** to do something (for someone) = express willingness to do something (表示願意為別人做, 例如): 'She offered to help me.'
> **invite** (someone) to (do) something = ask (someone) to a social occasion (表示邀請別人做, 例如): 'He invited her to the party.'

3 × The coat had been offered to me by my wife on my birthday.

√ **The coat had been given to me by my wife on my birthday.**

(這件外套是我太太在我生日時送給我的。)

> Something that is **offered** may or may not be accepted (使用 **offer** 時意指所送出的東西未必被接受, 例如): 'I offered her a cigarette, but she didn't want one.'
> Something that is **given** (such as a birthday present) is accepted (使用 **give** 時意指贈送的東西已被接受, 例如): 'I gave her a cigarette and then lit it for her.'

officer × Most of my friends got jobs as shop assistants or officers.

√ **Most of my friends got jobs as shop assistants or office workers.**

(我大多數的朋友不是當店員就是當辦事員。)

> **officer** = a person having a position of rank or authority (指官員或高級職員, 例如): 'an army officer', 'a police officer', 'a local government officer'
> **office worker** = a person who works in an office (指辦事員)

official × She is good at organizing people without seeming arrogant or official.

√ **She is good at organizing people without seeming arrogant or officious.**

(她善於把人組織起來, 不帶傲氣也不擺官架子。)

> **official** = done by or related to a person or group in authority; formal (指官方的、正式的、例如): 'an official letter', 'an official inquiry', 'official approval'
> **officious** (usually derogatory) = too eager to give orders or exercise authority (指官氣十足的)

old 1 × He fell in love with a young girl of nineteen years old.

√ **He fell in love with a young girl of nineteen.**

(他愛上了一位年方十九的姑娘。)

'a child of five', 'a man of sixty' WITHOUT **years old** 英語 a child of five 或 a man of sixty 後面不必接 **years old**。
Compare (試比較): 'The girl was nineteen years old.'

2 × Rollo Martins is a fifty years-old writer.
√ **Rollo Martins is a fifty-year-old writer.**
(羅洛・馬丁斯是位五十歲的作家。)

Note two hyphens, NOT one. (注意 fifty-year-old 這一片語用兩個連字號。)
Nouns of measurement ('week', 'gram', 'year', etc.) are always singular when used in compound adjectives (在複合形容詞中的計量名詞, 如 week、gram、year 等, 總是用單數, 例如): 'a ten-second silence', 'a six-minute wait', 'a five-mile race'.

old-fashioned × This shirt is rather old-fashion.
√ **This shirt is rather old-fashioned.**
(這件襯衫過時了。)

old-fashioned, NOT **old-fashion**
注意用 **old-fashioned,** 而不用 **old-fashion**。

on 1 × On the next morning he got up and walked down to the river to wash himself.
√ **The next morning he got up and walked down to the river to wash himself.**
(第二天早晨, 他起床後走到河邊去洗澡。)

Do not use a preposition to begin a time expression with **next** when the point of time is being considered in relation to the present (按 **next** 一詞用於時間片語時, 前面不加前置詞, 例如): 'the next morning', 'the next afternoon'.

2 See (見) THING 1, TOP

3 See (見) AFTERNOON 2

once 1 × You may remember that we had once a long talk in the hotel bar.
√ **You may remember that we once had a long talk in the hotel bar.**
(你也許記得, 我們在旅館酒吧曾經有過一次長時間的談話。)

When there is no auxiliary verb, **once** (=on a single occasion in the past) is placed immediately before the main verb (如句中無助動詞, 則作 "過去有一次" 解的 **once** 應直接放在主動詞之前, 例如): 'She once told me she had been married.' Otherwise it goes immediately after the (first) auxiliary verb (如句中有助動詞, 則應緊接在第一個助動詞之後, 例如): 'They had once lived in Chile.' **Once** can also go at the beginning or end of the clause (但 **once** 也可放在句首或句末, 例如): 'Once they had lived in Chile.' 'They had lived in Chile once.'

2 × I hope to see you once next month.
√ **I hope to see you some time next month.**
(我希望下個月能見到你。)

once=on a single occasion in the past, NOT in the future (按 **once** 一詞僅指過去, 不指將來)

3 × Once it will stop raining, we can go out.
√ **Once it stops raining, we can go out.**
√ **Once it has stopped raining, we can go out.**
(雨一停, 我們就能出去。)

After **when/whenever/once/until/after/if,** use the present simple (or present perfect) tense for future reference, NOT **shall/will**+verb.
在 **when/whenever/once/until/after/if** 之後, 只用一般現在式或現在完成式, 以表示未來, 不用 **shall/will** 再接動詞。

one 1 × Outside the house I was stopped by one of my mother's friend.
√ **Outside the house I was stopped by one of my mother's friends.**
(我一走出屋外就被我母親一個朋友叫住了。)

The noun following **one of** has a plural form (在 **one of** 後面的名詞應是複數, 例如): 'one of my friends', 'one of her sisters', 'one of my brother's teachers'.

2 × That hat isn't Angela's—the one of Angela is blue.
√ **That hat isn't Angela's—Angela's is blue.**
(那頂帽子不是安琪拉的, 安琪拉那頂是藍色的。)

When talking about possession, use **-'s/-s',** NOT **the one of.**
表示"屬誰的", 應用 "**-'s**" 或 "**-s'** ", 不用 **the one of**

3 × After we had been to Helen's house, we decided to go to Paul's one.
√ **After we had been to Helen's house, we decided to go to Paul's.**
(去過海倫家以後, 我們決定去保羅家。)
× If you can carry those books, I'll bring these ones.
√ **If you can carry those books, I'll bring these.**
(如果你能拿那些書, 我就拿這些。)

One/ones should not follow words which can themselves be used as pronouns (except in informal conversation).
按 **one** 或 **ones** 不應放在那些可作代名詞用的詞後面 (非正式的口語例外)。

4 × One of the eggs were bad.
√ **One of the eggs was bad.**
(其中的一隻雞蛋壞了。)

A phrase beginning with **one of** takes a singular verb.
以 **one of** 開始的片語用單數動詞。

5 × I'm sharing a flat with one friend who also comes from Hong Kong.
√ **I'm sharing a flat with a friend who also comes from Hong Kong.**
(我和一個也是香港來的朋友同住一個單元住宅。)

Do not use **one** instead of **a** or **an** unless it is used for emphasis. Compare (除非是為了強調, 否則不用 **one** 以取代 **a** 或 **an**。試比較): 'Would you like a cigarette?' 'I said you could take one cigarette, not two!'

6 × One mustn't waste ones time when there is so much to do.
√ **One mustn't waste one's time when there is so much to do.**
(越是忙的時候越不該浪費時間。)

Use **one's** as the possessive form of **one.** Note, however, that there is no apostrophe in **its** (the possessive form of **it**).
如 **one** 的意思是泛指"我們"、"人們",則其所有格應是 **one's**。但要注意, **it** 的所有格是 **its,** 而不是 **it's**。

7 × One cannot succeed unless he works hard.
√ **One cannot succeed unless one works hard.**
(除非努力工作, 否則不會取得成功。)

In British English (unlike American English) it is not usually acceptable to change from **one** to **he, him,** etc. However, most speakers find the repetition of **one** awkward, and try to avoid it (不同於美式英語, 英式英語通常不容許把 **one** 轉為 **he**、**him** 等。但不少人覺得重複 **one** 一詞很不自然, 便採取另一種說法避免重複, 例如): 'One cannot succeed without working hard.'

8 See (見) EVERYONE 1

only **1** × The level of pollution can only be reduced by the introduction of new laws.
√ **The level of pollution can be reduced only by the introduction of new laws.**
(污染的程度只有靠新的立法才能減輕。)

To avoid confusion, **only** should be placed as near as possible to the word or phrase that it modifies.
為避免混淆, **only** 應盡量接近所修飾的詞語。

2 × Only when it started to rain he noticed that he had left his raincoat somewhere.
√ **Only when it started to rain did he notice that he had left his raincoat somewhere.**
(只有到了下雨的時候, 他才發現自己把雨衣忘在別處了。)

After phrases and clauses beginning with **only,** the subject and (supplied) auxiliary verb change places (as in the question form) (如 **Only** 是在句首, 則主詞和助動詞一如問句那樣換位, 例如): 'he noticed' becomes (轉換為) 'did he notice'. Compare (試比較): (1) 'After five days the letter arrived.' 'Only after five days did the letter arrive.' (2) 'When it stopped raining, we set off.' 'Only when it stopped raining did we set off.'

3 × If you only would stay longer, your English would improve.
√ **If only you would stay longer, your English would improve.**
√ **If you would only stay longer, your English would improve.**
(只要你再多待一些時間, 你的英語便會進步。)

> **Only** is rarely placed between the subject and the auxiliary verb.
> **Only** 很少用於主詞和助動詞之間。

4 See (見) NOT ONLY

open **1** × John knocked on the door and his grandfather opened.
√ **John knocked on the door and his grandfather opened it.**
(約翰敲了敲門, 他祖父便把門打開。)

> Compare (比較): (1) 'He opened the door.' 'The door opened.' (2) 'She suddenly opened her eyes.' 'Her eyes suddenly opened.'

2 × I got out of bed and opened the radio to listen to the news.
√ **I got out of bed and turned/switched on the radio to listen to the news.**
(我起了牀, 便開收音機聽新聞。)

> **turn on/off** OR **switch on/off** a light/radio/television, NOT **open**
> 開燈/收音機/電視機用 **turn/switch on,** 不用 **open**。

3 × If someone tried to open a new topic, she would immeditately interrupt.
√ **If someone tried to introduce a new topic, she would immediately interrupt.**
(如果有人想開始一個新話題, 她就馬上打斷他的話。)

> **introduce** a (new) topic/subject/argument, NOT **open**
> 開始或提出一個(新)話題/題目/論點, 用 **introduce,** 不用 **open**。

opened × I couldn't buy a newspaper because the shop wasn't opened.
√ **I couldn't buy a newspaper because the shop wasn't open.**
(我買不到報紙, 因為商店不開門。)

The opposite of **closed** (adjective) is **open** (adjective).
Compare (形容詞 **closed** 的反義詞是 **open**, 試比較): 'The shop was opened by Mary this morning because the manager was ill.'

opinion × According to Henry's opinion, less money should be spent on weapons.
√ **According to Henry, less money should be spent on weapons.**
√ **In Henry's opinion, less money should be spent on weapons.**
(亨利的意見是在武器上要少花錢。)

According to is NOT used with **opinion**.
按 **according to** 一般不與 **opinion** 並用。

opportunity **1** × After ten years I finally had an opportunity for visiting America.
√ **After ten years I finally had an opportunity to visit America.**
(十年以後, 我終於有機會訪美。)

have/get/be **an opportunity** + to-v
按 have/get/be **an opportunity** 後接帶 to 的動詞。

2 × There is an opportunity that David's father will come tonight.
√ **There is a chance that David's father will come tonight.**
(大衛的父親今晚有可能來。)

There is a chance that ... is used to talk about a possibility. (指一種可能性)
Use **opportunity** when the possibility is a favourable one (如表示某一"可能性"是有利於人的, 則可用 **opportunity,** 例如): 'Winning the scholarship gave her the opportunity to visit Paris.'

opposite **1** × I used to think that 'tall' was opposite 'low'.
√ **I used to think that 'tall' was the opposite of 'low'.**
(我以往一直以為 "tall" 的反義詞是 "low"。)

Compare (試比較): 'The bank is opposite (=facing) the post office.'

2 × The opposite woman was knitting a cardigan.
√ **The woman opposite was knitting a cardigan.**
(對過的那位女士正在織一件開襟毛衣。)

Opposite (=facing the speaker or facing the person being talked about) comes after the noun it modifies.
按 **opposite** 一詞意為 "對面"、"對過", 應位於所修飾的名詞之後。

3 × Mary's mother was opposite to her marriage to George.
√ **Mary's mother was opposed to her marriage to George.**
(瑪麗的母親反對女兒嫁給喬治。)

opposite = (1) showing the greatest possible difference (指 "完全不同或相反的", 例如): 'The two men went off in opposite directions.' (=one went to the left and one to the right 即一人向左, 一人向右)
(2) being on the other side of; facing (意為 "對面"、"對過", 例如): 'Her mother lives in the house opposite (mine).'
opposed to = not in favour of; against (意為 "反對")

or **1** × At night we used to go out with our friends or stayed at home listening to music.
√ **At night we used to go out with our friends or stay at home listening to music.**
(從前, 我們晚上不是跟朋友出去就是在家裏聽音樂。)

When you use **or** with two verbs, both verbs should have the same form. Compare (如果要用 **or** 一詞去連接兩個動詞, 這兩個動詞的時態形式必須一致, 上句的 **or** 連接的是 go 和 stay, 錯句用了 stayed, 是過去式, 顯然與現在式的 go 不一致。試比較): 'We used to go to the cinema or watch the television.' 'We went to the cinema or watched the television.' (按美式英語用 watch television)

2 × I think the microphone or the recording mechanism are broken.
√ **I think the microphone or the recording mechanism is broken.**
(我認為擴音機或錄音的設備壞了。)

When each of the nouns joined by **or** is singular, the verb is usually singular.
如 **or** 所連接的名詞都是單數, 則動詞通常也是單數。

3 See (見) NEITHER 1

oral × Her oral English is very fluent and clear.
√ **Her spoken English is very fluent and clear.**
(她的英語口語既流利又清楚。)

The use of **oral** to mean 'spoken' is restricted to certain phrases in education (以 **oral** 來表達 spoken 的含義時, 僅限於教學術語中使用, 例如): 'oral skills', 'an oral examination', etc.

order 1 × Turning on the radio, I noticed immediately that it was out of order.
√ **Turning on the radio, I noticed immediately that it was not working properly.**
(我擰開收音機, 馬上就發現有毛病。)

The phrase **out of order** is used mostly on notices stating that things such as public telephones, ticket machines, etc. are not working.
按 **out of order** 這一片語通常用於通告上, 説明諸如公用電話、自動售票機等失靈。

2 × I was so excited that I forgot to order them to check that the camera was working properly.
√ **I was so excited that I forgot to ask them to check that the camera was working properly.**
(我當時緊張得忘了叫他們檢查攝影機是否有毛病。)

A speaker cannot **order** someone to do something unless he or she has the authority to do so. Compare (除非有職權, 否則一般人不能隨意命令 (**order**) 別人做事, 試比較): 'The teacher ordered the child to sit down.' 'The soldiers were ordered to attack.'

originate × One of our teachers originates from Scotland.
√ **One of our teachers comes from Scotland.**
(我們的一位教師是蘇格蘭人。)

Originate is not usually used of people.
按 **originate** 作 "源自" 解, 一般不用來指人。

other 1 × 'Go and play with some others children,' she said.
√ **'Go and play with some other children,' she said.**
("去和別的孩子一起玩吧," 她說。)

When used before a noun, **other**, as an adjective, has no **s. Others** is a pronoun. Compare (在名詞之前的 **other**, 本身是個形容詞, 不加 **s,** 而 **others** 是代詞。試比較): 'Do you have any other shoes besides the brown ones?' 'Besides the brown shoes, do you have any others?'

2 × They had stolen not just my car but an other car as well.
√ **They had stolen not just my car but another car as well.**
(他們不僅偷了我的汽車, 還偷了另一輛。)

Another (= an other) is ALWAYS one word.
注意: **another** 是一個字。

3 × When Lillian and Janet arrived, I ordered two other cups of coffee.
√ **When Lillian and Janet arrived, I ordered two more cups of coffee.**
(莉蓮和珍娜來了, 我又叫了兩杯咖啡。)

Other means 'more and also different'.
注意: **other** 作 "其他" 解。

otherwise × She'll have to wait for us, or otherwise she won't know where to go.
√ **She'll have to wait for us; otherwise she won't know where to go.**
(她必須等我們, 不然她就不知道該到哪裡去。)

otherwise (= if not) WITHOUT **or**
按 **otherwise** 已含有 "否則"、"不然" 之意, 因此不可再用 **or**。

ought × 'Ought we go now?' she asked me. 'It's getting late.'
√ **'Ought we to go now?' she asked me. 'It's getting late.'**
("我們現在該走了嗎?" 她問我。"時間不早了。")

> **ought** + to-v
> 注意: **ought** 後接帶 to 的動詞

out 1 × She suddenly stood up and ran out from the room.
√ **She suddenly stood up and ran out of the room.**
(她忽然站了起來, 衝出房間。)

> **out of,** NOT **from**
> 句中的 **out of** 不可用 **out from** 替代。

2 × I felt very cold when I went out the room.
√ **I felt very cold when I went out of the room.**
(我一走出房間就感到很冷。)

> **Out** is an adverb (按 **out** 在這裏是個副詞, 例如): 'Alan went out, leaving just the two of us in the room.'
> **Out of** is a preposition
> 按 **out of** 是個前置詞。
> Note that in informal conversation, **out** is sometimes used instead of **out of** (注意: 在日常談話中, 有時用 **out** 代替 **out of,** 例如): 'I saw someone jump out the window.'

outdoor × She makes the dog stay outdoor during the summer.
√ **She makes the dog stay outdoors during the summer.**
(在夏天她把狗放到戶外。)

> **Outdoor** is an adjective (注意: **outdoor** 是形容詞, 例如): 'He enjoys the outdoor life.'
> **Outdoors** is an adverb (注意: **outdoors** 在下句是副詞): 'He likes to work outdoors.'

outside √ **AmE She was listening outside of the door.**
(美式英語: 她在門外注意地聽着。)
√ **BrE She was listening outside the door.**
(英式英語: 譯文同上)

Outside is used in both American and British English.
注意: **outside** 在美式英語和英式英語中都用。
Outside of can be used in informal American English but not in British English. 注意: **outside of** 可用於非正式美式英語, 但不用於英式英語。

outskirts **1** × There are rows of trees fringing the outskirt of the capital.
√ **There are rows of trees fringing the outskirts of the capital.**
(首都的外圍點綴着一排排的樹。)

Outskirts is a plural noun. There is no singular form.
按 **outskirts** 是複數名詞, 沒有單數形式。

2 × I have to take the train because the house is in the outskirts of London.
√ **I have to take the train because the house is on the outskirts of London.**
(因為那房子位於倫敦郊外, 我不得不坐火車去。)

Usually **on the outskirts** means in an outlying distinct, NOT **in**
按 **on the outskirts** 這一片語作 "在郊區" 解, 其中 **on** 通常不能用 **in** 替代

overdue × I suddenly realized that my driving licence was overdue.
√ **I suddenly realized that my driving licence had expired.**
(我忽然發現我的駕駛執照過期了。)

Be/become overdue is used of a bill, payment, library book, etc.
指賬單、支付、圖書館借的書等逾期, 用 **be overdue** 或 **become overdue**。
Expire is used of a licence, contract, library ticket, etc.
指執照、合約、圖書館借書証等期滿, 用 **expire**。

overjoyed × We overjoyed ourselves when we heard the news.
√ **We were overjoyed when we heard the news.**
(聽到這消息後, 我們都十分高興。)

Overjoyed is an adjective. There is no such verb as 'overjoy yourself'.
按 **overjoyed** 是形容詞, 不能用作動詞。

overwork

× He had managed to save a lot of money by overworking.

√ **He had managed to save a lot of money by working overtime.**

(他靠加班加點的收入存了好多錢。)

> **overwork** = work too hard (意為: "操勞過度", 例如): 'The doctor advised him not to overwork.'
> **work overtime** = work beyond the usual time for extra pay (意為: "超時工作" 或 "加班")

own

× I now have enough money to buy an own car.

√ **I now have enough money to buy my own car.**

(我現在有足夠的錢買一輛自己的汽車了。)

> **Own** (determiner/pronoun) ALWAYS follows a possessive form (按 **own** 一詞為 "形容詞" 或 "代詞", 總是接在一個所有格的詞之後, 例如): 'their own children', 'her own flat', 'Tina's own radio'.

pace

× In the silence he thought he heard paces outside the window.

√ **In the silence he thought he heard footsteps outside the window.**

(寂靜中他好像聽到窗外有腳步聲。)

> **pace** = (the distance moved by taking) a single step (一步的距離, 例如): 'The trees were planted ten paces apart.'
> **footstep** = the mark or sound made by a person's step (人的腳印或腳步聲)

painful

× The operation was successful but I still feel very painful.

√ **The operation was successful but I still feel a lot of pain.**

(手術是成功的, 但我還是覺得很疼。)

> **painful** = giving pain (意為 "使 ... 感到疼痛", 例如): 'The finger I trapped in the door is still very painful.'

pair

× The old pair stood up and started to dance.

√ **The old couple stood up and started to dance.**

(這對年老夫婦站起來, 開始跳舞。)

> **couple** = husband and wife, boyfriend and girlfriend, etc. (意為 "夫婦、情侶" 等)

pants

√ **AmE The man was wearing red shoes and bright green pants.**
(美式英語: 那男子穿着紅鞋和鮮綠色的褲子。)

√ **BrE The man was wearing red shoes and bright green trousers.**
(英式英語: 譯文同上)

> **pants** (American English)=trousers (美式英語, 意為"長褲")
> **pants** (British English)=short underclothes covering the lower part of the body; underpants; knickers (英式英語, 意為"短內褲")

paper 1

× Each of us was given a clean paper to write on.

√ **Each of us was given a clean piece/sheet of paper to write on.**
(我們每個人都得到一張乾淨的紙來寫。)

> **Paper** is an uncountable noun.
> 按 **paper** 一詞是不可數名詞。

2

× The last paper of the book was missing.

√ **The last page of the book was missing.**
(書的最後一頁不見了。)

> **page**=a printed sheet in a book, magazine, etc.
> 按 **page** 意為書或雜誌等的一頁。

pardon

× I asked the teacher if I could be pardoned for a few minutes.

√ **I asked the teacher if I could be excused for a few minutes.**
(我問老師可否容許我離開教室幾分鐘。)

> **pardon** (formal)=forgive (意為"寬恕"、"原諒", 例如): 'I'm sure they will pardon the occasional mistake.'
> **excuse**=allow (someone) to leave (a classroom, meeting, etc.) (請求容許離開教室、會議室等之意)

parking

× Several cars were parking outside the building.

√ **Several cars were parked outside the building.**
(有幾輛汽車停在大樓外面。)

> **park** (a vehicle) (of a driver) BUT **be parked** (of a stationary vehicle) (按 **park** 一詞指司機把車停在某處之意, 強調 "停" 這一動作; 而 **be parked** 則是指車輛 "停放着" 這一狀態。)
> Compare (試比較): 'She parks her car outside my house. It is parked there all night.'

part 1 × A part of the difficulty was caused by her poor English.
✓ **Part of the difficulty was caused by her poor English.**
(有一部份困難是她的英語太差造成的。)

> It is unusual to use **a** before **part of** unless **part of** is modified by an adjective. Compare (通常只有在 **part of** 之前有形容詞才用不定冠詞 **"a/an"**, 試比較): 'Lack of money was part of the problem.' 'Lack of money was a large part of the problem.'

2 × Nowadays a large part of women go out to work.
✓ **Nowadays a large number of women go out to work.**
(如今, 大部分的婦女都外出工作。)

> **(a) part of** + uncountable noun/singular form of a countable noun
> 注意: **(a) part of** 後接不可數名詞, 或接可數名詞單數形式。
> Compare (試比較): 'A large part of the population is unemployed.' 'A large number of workers are unemployed.'

3 × He refused to part from his old camera.
✓ **He refused to part with his old camera.**
(他不肯放棄他的舊相機。)

> **part from** (a person) (按 **part from** 意為 "分手"、"分開", 後接人, 例如): 'The two sisters were parted from each other when they were sent to different schools.' BUT **part with** (a thing) (按 **part with** 雖與 **part from** 同義, 但後接物, 如上例)

party × The party was being made at a friend's house.
✓ **The party was being held at a friend's house.**
(聚會正在一位朋友家舉行。)

> **give/hold/throw a party,** NOT **make**
> 注意: **give/hold/throw a party** 中的幾個動詞均不可用 **make** 替代。

pass **1** × We were glad to hear that you had passed in your examination.
✓ **We were glad to hear that you had passed your examination.**
(聽說你通過了考試, 我們很高興。)

> **pass an examination** WITHOUT **in**
> 注意: **pass** 之後不用 **in**, 直接加 **an examination**。

2 × We like to pass our holidays near the sea.
✓ **We like to spend our holidays near the sea.**
(我們喜歡在海濱度假。)

> **spend** your **holidays** somewhere, NOT **pass**
> 注意: **spend** your **holidays** somewhere 中的動詞不可用 **pass** 替代。

3 × We passed the night at a cheap hotel.
✓ **We spent the night at a cheap hotel.**
(我們在一家廉價旅店過夜。)

> **Pass** is usually intransitive when used of time (按 **pass** 一詞通常用於時間, 是不及物動詞, 例如): 'Two weeks passed and there was still no reply.'

4 × I am going to pass my music examination on Thursday.
✓ **I am going to take my music examination on Thursday.**
(我將在星期四參加音樂考試。)

> **pass** (a test or examination) = succeed in (意指通過考試)
> **take** (a test or examination) = undergo (意指參加考試, 例如): 'Of those who took the exam, only fifty per cent passed.'

passed × I bought the car with the money I've earned during the passed twelve months.
✓ **I bought the car with the money I've earned during the past twelve months.**
(我用過去十二個月賺得的錢買了這輛汽車。)

> **Passed** is the past tense and past participle of the verb **pass** and is not used as an adjective. Instead, use **past.**
> 按 **passed** 是動詞 **pass** 的過去式和過去分詞, 不用作形容詞。**past** 才是形容詞。
> Compare (試比較): 'This year has passed quickly.' 'I've been very busy over the past year.'

past

× I was very glad to hear that you past your exams.
√ **I was very glad to hear that you passed your exams.**
(聽說你通過了考試, 我很高興。)

× Several taxis past me without stopping.
√ **Several taxis passed me without stopping.**
(幾輛計程車從我身邊駛過而未停下。)

> **Past** is (1) an adjective (可作形容詞, 例如): 'For the past week he's been ill in bed.'
> (2) a preposition (可作前置詞, 例如): 'She walked past me very quickly.'
> (3) an adverb (可作副詞, 例如): 'She walked past very quickly.'
> (4) a noun (可作名詞, 例如): 'He never speaks about his past.'
> Note that **past** is NOT used as a verb.
> 注意: **past** 不能用作動詞。
> **Passed** is the past tense and past participle of the verb **pass**.
> 按 **passed** 是動詞 **pass** 的過去式和過去分詞。

pay **1**

× 'Who paid the tickets?' I asked.
√ **'Who paid for the tickets?' I asked.**
("是誰出錢買票的?" 我問道。)

> **pay** an amount BUT **pay for** something
> 注意: **pay** 後接一筆錢的數目, 但 **pay for** 則後接所買的東西。

2

× Very few office workers get a good pay.
√ **Very few office workers get good pay.**
(極少辦事員能獲得高工資。)

> **Pay** is an uncountable noun.
> 按 **pay** 是個不可數名詞。

payment

× Dr Schneider charges a high payment but he is very good.
√ **Dr Schneider charges a high fee but he is very good.**
(施乃德醫生收費很貴, 但醫術很高。)

> **payment** = (1) the act of paying (意為 "支付", 例如): 'Here is a cheque in payment of the invoice.' (2) an amount of money (to be) paid (意為 "所支付的金額")
> **fee** = a sum of money paid to a doctor, lawyer, or other professional person (意為: 費用, 即付給醫生、律師或其他專業人士的一筆錢)

peculiar

× She said she liked the jumper because the colour was very peculiar.
√ **She said she liked the jumper because the colour was very unusual.**
(她說她喜歡這件毛衣因為它的顏色與眾不同。)

> **peculiar** (usually derogatory) = odd or strange (按 **peculiar** 一詞往往用作貶義, 作 "古怪的", "怪異的" 解)
> **unusual** = uncommon or rare (意為: "與眾不同的", "不尋常的")

people 1

× Peoples come from all over the world to visit the city.
√ **People come from all over the world to visit the city.**
(人們從世界各地來到這個城市遊覽。)

> **a people** (countable) = a race (按 **a people** 是可數名詞, 指一個民族)
> **people** (uncountable) = men, women, and children (按 **people** 是不可數名詞, 意為 "人們", 與複數動詞連用)

2

× There was few people at the funeral.
√ **There were few people at the funeral.**
(沒有多少人參加這次喪禮。)
× I think people who does these things should be punished.
√ **I think people who do these things should be punished.**
(我認為做這些事的人都應受到懲罰。)

> **People** is a plural noun.
> 按 **people** 一詞是個複數名詞。

3 × Our teacher is quite a young people.
√ **Our teacher is quite a young person.**
(我們的老師是位年輕人。)

> **People** is the plural of **person.**
> 按 **people** 一詞是 **person** 的複數形式。

per cent × A large per cent of the population was against nuclear weapons.
√ **A large percentage of the population was against nuclear weapons.**
(人口中反對核武器者佔很大的百分比。)

> **per cent** = one part in or for each 100 (意為 "百分之 ... ", 例如): 'Seventy per cent of the population was against nuclear weapons.'
> **percentage** = a rate or amount in each 100; proportion (意為 "百分率"、"百分比")

percentage × Only a small percentage of the windmills still works.
√ **Only a small percentage of the windmills still work.**
(仍然可以操作的風車磨坊只佔很小的百分比。)

> **A ... percentage of** does not affect the noun and verb that follow: 'windmills' is plural and so 'work' is also plural.
> 按 **a ... percentage of** 並不影響後面的名詞和動詞: 'windmills' 是複數, 因此後面的動詞 'work' 也是複數形式。同樣地, 如 **percentage of** 後接的名詞是單數, 則動詞也是單數, 例如: 'What percentage of her income is taxable?'

perfect 1 × Each day the weather seemed to become more perfect.
√ **Each day the weather seemed to improve.**
(天氣似乎一天比一天好。)

> Something can be **absolutely perfect** but NOT **very/more/somewhat** (etc.) **perfect**. There are no degrees of perfection.
> 可以說 **absolutely perfect**, 但不能說 **very/more/somewhat perfect**, 因為 "完美" 是不分等級的。

2 × I am pleased to say that the tape recorder now works perfect.
√ **I am pleased to say that the tape recorder now works perfectly.**
(我很高興地説, 錄音機現在一點毛病也沒有了。)

> **Perfect** is an adjective.
> 按 **perfect** 一詞是形容詞。
> **Perfectly** is an adverb.
> 按 **perfectly** 一詞是副詞。

perhaps × If it isn't in the bedroom, perhaps would you have a look in the dining room.
√ **If it isn't in the bedroom, perhaps you would have a look in the dining room.**
(如果它不在寢室, 可否請你到飯廳裡看一下。)

> **Perhaps** does not affect word order. Compare (按 **perhaps** 一詞並不影響句中的詞序, 試比較): 'Would you like to bring your mother with you?' 'Perhaps you would like to bring your mother with you?'

permission 1 × To get a job in Switzerland, foreigners need a special permission.
√ **To get a job in Switzerland, foreigners need special permission.**
(外國人在瑞士找工作需要特別批准。)

> **Permission** is an uncountable noun.
> 按 **permission** 是不可數名詞, 不用不定冠詞 "**a**"。

2 × If you wish to enter another country, you will have to take permission from the authorities.
√ **If you wish to enter another country, you will have to get/obtain permission from the authorities.**
(如果你想進入別的國家, 你必須得到當局的准許。)

> **get/obtain permission,** NOT **take**
> 按 **get/obtain permission** 中的動詞 **get/obtain** 不可用 **take** 替代。

person × Her husband talked so much that all the other persons in the room had to keep quiet.
√ **Her husband talked so much that all the other people in the room had to keep quiet.**
(她丈夫講話滔滔不絕, 室內其他的人只好不作聲。)

Person is singular.
按 **person** 一詞是單數。
People is plural.
按 **people** 一詞是複數。
Note that **persons** is rarely used except in public notices and other formal contexts (除公告或正式文字外, 一般很少使用 **persons** 一詞, 例如): 'Seating capacity: twelve persons.'

personality

× He is a man of strong personality who will fight for what is right.
√ **He is a man of strong character who will fight for what is right.**
(他是一個性格剛強的人, 願意為正義而戰鬥。)

When talking about a person's moral quality, use **character**, NOT **personality**.
指 "性格", 用 **character**, 不用 **personality** (個性)。
Compare (試比較): 'For a career in sales, you need a forceful personality.' (從事推銷這個行業, 需要有堅強的個性。) 'People of character and integrity never turn their backs on the truth.' (一個正直誠實的人是不會背棄真理的。)

phenomena

× There has never been a serious study of this phenomena.
√ **There has never been a serious study of this phenomenon.**
(對這種現象從來沒有認真研究過。)
√ **There has never been a serious study of these phenomena.**
(對這些現象從來沒有認真研究過。)

Phenomenon is singular.
按 **phenomenon** 是單數。
Phenomena is plural.
按 **phenomena** 是複數。

phone 1

√ **AmE I talked to him for a long time by phone last night.**
(美式英語: 昨晚我在電話上跟他講了很長時間。)
√ **BrE I talked to him for a long time on/over the phone last night.**
(英式英語: 譯文同上)

In American English, use (美式英語用) **talk/speak** to someone **by/on/over the phone**.
In British English, use (英式英語用) **talk/speak** to someone **on/over the phone**, NOT (不用) **by phone**.

2 × She phoned to the hospital to ask about her husband.
√ **She phoned the hospital to ask about her husband.**
(她打電話到醫院詢問她丈夫的病情。)

phone someone/somewhere WITHOUT **to**
按 **phone** 之後, 直接用 **someone/somewhere,** 不必用 **to**。

piano See (見) PLAY 3

piece 1 × The pencils were free and so I took two pieces.
√ **The pencils were free and so I took two.**
(鉛筆是免費的, 所以我拿了兩枝。)

Piece is NOT used with countable nouns.
按 **piece** 不與可數名詞連用。

2 × Helen cut the bread and gave me two.
√ **Helen cut the bread and gave me two pieces.**
(海倫把麵包切開, 給了我兩塊。)

Bread is uncountable when speaking about whole loaves or bread in general. A part of a loaf is **a piece or slice of bread.** Some uncountable nouns also go with **piece** (上句說的麵包, 指整個而言; 如說一塊麵包, 英文是 **a piece/slice of bread**。有些不可數名詞也同 **piece** 連用, 例如): 'a piece of cheese', 'a piece of furniture', 'a piece of information', 'a piece of luck', etc.

pitiful × We both felt pitiful when we saw how lonely she was.
√ **We both felt pity for her when we saw how lonely she was.**
(見到她那麼孤獨, 我倆都動了惻隱之心。)

pity (noun)=sorrow for the suffering of others
(按 **pity** 是名詞, 作 "同情" 解)
pitiful (adjective)=deserving or arousing pity (按 **pitiful** 是形容詞, 作 "可憐的" 解, 例如): 'He had lost all his hair in the fire and was a pitiful sight.'

pity × She expected me to feel pity on her and help her.
√ **She expected me to take pity on her and help her.**
√ **She expected me to feel pity for her and help her.**
(她期待我會可憐她並會幫助她。)

> **take pity on** BUT **feel pity for**
> 注意詞語的搭配關係, 指 "對 ... 表示同情", 用 **take pity on**, 也可用 **feel pity for**。

place **1** × He was looking for a place where to spend the night.
√ **He was looking for somewhere to spend the night.**
(他在找一個可以過夜的地方。)

> look for/find etc. **somewhere** + to-v (如說 "找個什麼地方 ... ", 可用 look for 或 find **somewhere**, 後接帶 to 的動詞, 例如): 'She is looking for somewhere to live.' Compare (試比較另一種句型): 'He was looking for a place where he could spend the night.' 'She's looking for a place where she can live.'

2 × When I lived at home, my father did not let me go to any place on my own.
√ **When I lived at home, my father did not let me go anywhere on my own.**
(我在家住的時候, 父親不讓我獨自到任何地方去。)

> Use **anywhere** when you mean 'in/to any place'.
> 如果你是指 "在任何地方" 或 "到任何地方", 應用 **anywhere**。

3 × I left the coat in my room but it may not be in that place any longer.
√ **I left the coat in my room but it may not be there any longer.**
(我把外衣留在房間, 可是現在也許不在那兒了。)

> Use **there** when you mean 'in/to that place'.
> 如果你是指 "在那地方" 或 "到那地方", 應用 **there**。

4 × The old man laughed and answered, 'There's enough place in the wardrobe for all your clothes.'
√ **The old man laughed and answered, 'There's enough room in the wardrobe for all your clothes.'**
(老人笑着答道: "衣櫃裡有的是地方, 把你所有的衣服放進去都行。")

> **place** = a position or particular part of some space (意為一個空間、一塊地方, 例如): 'The best place to sit is right in front of the stage.'
> **room** = a space which is big enough for something (意為空出的一塊地方、餘地, 例如): 'There's room in the back seat for all three of you.'

play **1** × My favourite play is chess.
√ **My favourite game is chess.**
(我喜歡的遊戲是下棋。)

> **play** (verb) = take part in (a sport or game) (意為 "參加運動或遊戲", 是個動詞, 例如): 'She plays tennis every Saturday.'
> **game** (noun) = something you do for enjoyment or sport (意為 "遊戲", 是個名詞)
> Compare (試比較): 'Which game would you like to play, chess or draughts?'

2 × At the cinema they were playing an action film.
√ **At the cinema they were showing an action film.**
(電影院裏正放映一部動作片。)

> **show a film**, NOT **play**
> 注意: 放電影英文是 **show a film** 而不是 **play a film**

3 √ **AmE I've been playing piano since I was eight.**
(美式英語: 我從八歲起就彈鋼琴了。)
√ **BrE I've been playing the piano since I was eight.**
(英式英語: 譯文同上)

> In American English **the** is optional when talking about musical instruments.
> 美式英語提到樂器時, 既可用 **the**, 也可省略不用。
> In British English, use **play** football/tennis/chess BUT **play the** piano/guitar/violin.
> 英式英語用 **play** 與 football/tennis/chess 連用時不用 **the**, 但與 piano/guitar/violin 連用時, 必須用 **the**。

please × Please, as soon as the radio has been repaired, let me know.
√ **As soon as the radio has been repaired, please let me know.**
(收音機一修好, 請立即通知我。)

Please is NEVER used before a subordinate clause.
注意: **please** 從不用於子句之首。
Note the common patterns (注意常用句型):
'Please let me know as soon as you can.' 'Will you please let me know as soon as you can?'
'Will you let me know as soon as you can, please?'

pleasure **1** × As mayor of this town, it gives me a great pleasure to welcome you.
√ **As mayor of this town, it gives me great pleasure to welcome you.**
(作為本市的市長, 我非常高興地對你表示歡迎。)

give someone **(great) pleasure** WITHOUT **a**
注意: **give** someone (**great**) **pleasure** 中不用冠詞 "**a**"
Compare (試比較): 'It is a great pleasure for me to welcome you.'

2 × A lot of people work for their pleasure, not because of financial obligations.
√ **A lot of people work for pleasure, not because of financial obligations.**
(很多人工作是為了樂趣, 而不是迫於經濟負擔。)

do something **for pleasure** WITHOUT **his/our/their** etc.
在 **do** something **for pleasure** 這一片語中, **pleasure** 之前不加 **his/our/their** 之類的物主代詞。

3 × It's the first time that I've had the pleasure to meet her.
√ **It's the first time that I've had the pleasure of meeting her.**
(這是我第一次有幸會見她。)

be pleased + to-v BUT **have the pleasure of** + v-ing
按 **be pleased** 後接帶 to 的動詞, 而 **have the pleasure of** 後接帶 "-ing" 的動詞。

p.m. **1** × The fight will be shown on television at 7:30 p.m. in the evening.
√ **The fight will be shown on television at 7:30 p.m.**
√ **The fight will be shown on television at 7:30 in the evening.**
(今天晚上七點半電視會播出這場拳擊賽。)

'at 7:30 p.m.' OR 'at 7:30 in the evening'
注意: 表示 "午後", 英文可用 "p.m." 或 "in the evening", 兩者只用其一, 不能同時用, 因 p.m. (post meridiem) 本身已是 "午後" (after midday) 之意。

2 See (見) O'CLOCK 3

pocket × He was leaning against the wall with his hands in the pockets.
✓ **He was leaning against the wall with his hands in his pockets.**
(他背靠着牆, 雙手插在口袋裡。)

When talking about the position of a person's hands, use **my/your/his** etc. (NOT **the**) with **pocket**.
指雙手的位置時, **pocket** 前應用 **my/your/his** 等, 不用 **the**。

poetry × In my spare time I like writing poetries.
✓ **In my spare time I like writing poetry.**
(我閑着的時候喜歡寫詩。)

Poetry is an uncountable noun.
注意: **poetry** 是不可數名詞。

point 1 × The meal was terrible but it was no point in complaining.
✓ **The meal was terrible but there was no point in complaining.**
(這頓飯太糟了, 不過抱怨也沒用。)

there is little/no point (in) + v-ing, NOT **it**
按 **there** is little point 或 no point 意為 "沒有用"、"沒有效果", 其中 **there** 不能寫作 **it**; 又 little 或 no point 之後可接 in, 或省略也可, 再加帶 "-ing" 的動詞。

2 × There is no point to complain about the service.
✓ **There is no point (in) complaining about the service.**
(對服務提出投訴是毫無用處的。)

there is little/no point (in) + v-ing, NOT + to-v
按 **there is little/no point (in)** 應後接帶 "-ing" 的動詞, 而不接帶 to 的動詞。

3 × I had to spend forty-eight hours listening to him with a gun pointed to my head.
√ **I had to spend forty-eight hours listening to him with a gun pointed at my head.**
(在槍口對着腦袋的情況下, 我不得不連續四十八小時聽他說話。)

> **point at** (NOT **to**) = aim (something) in a particular direction
> 按 **point at** 作 "對準" 解, 其中的 **at** 不能用 **to** 替代。

point of view 1 × My point of view is that married women with young children should be able to work if they wish.
√ **My opinion/view is that married women with young children should be able to work if they wish.**
(我的看法是, 如果有小孩的已婚婦女想要工作, 那麼她們是應當能夠去工作的。)

> **point of view** = the position or angle from which someone approaches a problem or situation (指 "看問題的角度", 例如): 'A good salesman should try to see things from the customer's point of view.' (一個好的售貨員應該從顧客的角度去考慮。)
> **opinion/view** = what a person thinks about something
> Note that **point of view** is usually used when referring to other people's opinions, NOT your own. (指 "看法"、"見解"。注意: **point of view** 通常用來指別人的看法而不是自己的看法。)
> Compare (試比較): 'in her opinion/from her point of view' BUT 'in my opinion'

2 × In her point of view, there is only one solution.
√ **From her point of view, there is only one solution.**
(從她的觀點看, 解決辦法只有一個。)

> **in her view/opinion** BUT **from her point of view**
> 在 her view 或 opinion 之前用 **in**; 在 her point of view 之前用 **from**。

police 1 × The police was not able to find anything.
√ **The police were not able to find anything.**
(警方找不到任何線索。)

> **Police** is ALWAYS used with a plural verb.
> **police** 總是用複數動詞。

2 × He was charged with shooting a police.
√ **He was charged with shooting a policeman.**
(他被控向一名警察開槍。)

> **policeman** = a member of the police force (意為: "警務人員")
> **police** = the police force in general (意為: "警察部隊")

3 × The woman took the lost child to the nearest police office.
√ **The woman took the lost child to the nearest police station.**
(那婦人把迷了路的小孩帶到鄰近的警察局去。)

> **police station,** NOT **office**
> 警察局是 **police station**, 而不是 **police office**。

politics × One of the main politics of the government is to reduce unemployment.
√ **One of the main policies of the government is to reduce unemployment.**
(政府的主要政策之一是減少失業。)

> **politics** = (1) the art and science of governing a country (指治理國家的藝術和科學, 例如): 'He has chosen a career in politics.'
> (2) political affairs (指政治事務, 例如): 'I'm not interested in politics.'
> (3) political opinions (指政治見解, 例如): 'Nobody knows much about his politics.'
> **policy** = a plan or course of action (taken by a government, political party, business, etc.) (指政府、政黨、商業等的政策; 方針)

pollution × There is a pollution everywhere, even in the countryside.
√ **There is pollution everywhere, even in the countryside.**
(到處都有污染, 甚至在農村都有。)

> **Pollution** is an uncountable noun.
> 按 **pollution** 是個不可數名詞, 前面不用不定冠詞 "**a**"。

ponder

× It is a very delicate question and we have to ponder the advantages against the disadvantages.
√ **It is a very delicate question and we have to weigh the advantages against the disadvantages.**
(這是一個很微妙的問題, 我們必須權衡利弊。)

> **ponder** = spend time considering (指 "仔細考慮", 例如): 'He was standing by the car, pondering how to get into it without a key.'
> **weigh** = compare or measure (指 "比較" 或 "衡量")

position

× I should like to explain our government's position about nuclear weapons.
√ **I should like to explain our government's position on nuclear weapons.**
(我想解釋一下我國政府關於核武器的立場。)

> **position on** something, NOT **about**
> 指 "關於某事的立場" 可用 **position on** something, 其中的前置詞 **on** 不可用 **about** 替代。

possibility 1

× We are considering the possibility to do the job ourselves.
√ **We are considering the possibility of doing the job ourselves.**
(我們正在考慮自己來做這件事的可能性。)

> **be possible** + to-v (按 **be possible** 後接帶 to 的動詞, 例如): 'It may be possible to do the job ourselves.' BUT **the possibility** of + v-ing (但 **the possibility of** 後要接帶 "-ing" 的動詞)

2

× My visit to Tokyo was a good possibility for me to learn Japanese.
√ **My visit to Tokyo gave me a good opportunity to learn Japanese.**
(訪問東京給了我一個學習日語的好機會。)
× A person who wants to go out to work should be given the possibility to do so.
√ **A person who wants to go out to work should be given the opportunity to do so.**
(一個想出去工作的人應當有機會這麼做。)

> Use **opportunity** to talk about a favourable moment or occasion to do something.
> 談及有利的時機應用 **opportunity**。
> Compare (試比較): 'There's a possibility that I'll be late.'

possible **1** × If you find my book, could you possible return it to me?
✓ **If you find my book, could you possibly return it to me?**
(如果你找到我的書, 能否還給我?)

> **Possible** is an adjective.
> 按 **possible** 是形容詞, 修飾的是名詞。
> **Possibly** is an adverb.
> 按 **possibly** 是副詞, 修飾的是動詞、形容詞或另一個副詞。

2 × Is it possible that you can send me the coat this week?
✓ **Is it possible for you to send me the coat this week?**
(你能否在本週內給我把這件大衣送來嗎?)

> **possible** (for someone) + to-v
> 按 **possible** (for someone) 後接帶 to 的動詞。

3 See (見) EVER 3

post × I refused to return the book unless they agreed to pay the cost of the post.
✓ **I refused to return the book unless they agreed to pay the cost of the postage.**
(我拒絕送還這書, 除非他們答應支付郵費。)

> **post** (British English)/**mail** (American English) = the official system for sending letters and parcels (意為 "郵政")
> **postage** = the charge for sending a letter or parcel by post (意為 "郵費")

power × The illness has left her with very little power.
✓ **The illness has left her with very little strength/energy.**
(這場病使她體力/活力消失。)

> A person's **power** refers to their social or political influence, NOT to their physical **strength**. Compare (人的 **power** 指政治權力或社會影響力而不是指體力 **strength**, 試比較): 'The British royal family has very little power these days.' 'I seem to have lost all the strength in my left arm, doctor.'

practice ✓ **AmE I had to practice for half an hour every evening.**
(美式英語: 我必須每晚練習半小時。)
✓ **BrE I had to practise for half an hour every evening.**
(英式英語: 譯文同上)

> In American English **practice** (**ce**) is the most usual form for both noun and verb. However, **practise** (**se**) may also be used for both.
> 在美式英語中, **practice** (注意最後兩個字母是 **ce**) 一詞通常是既可作名詞, 也可作動詞。**practise** (注意最後兩個字母是 **se**) 一詞也是如此。
> In British English **practise** (**se**) is the verb and **practice** (**ce**) is the noun.
> 在英式英語中, **practise** (注意最後兩個字母是 **se**) 一詞只用作動詞, 而 **practice** (注意最後兩個字母是 **ce**) 一詞只用作名詞。

prefer **1** × I preferred to stay out in the cold rather than spending the night there.
✓ **I preferred to stay out in the cold rather than spend the night there.**
(我寧願不顧寒冷在外露宿, 也不在那地方過夜。)

> **prefer** to do A **(rather) than** do B (在這個句型裏, 注意 **rather than** 之後要接不帶 **to** 的動詞。)

2 × Why do you prefer the theatre than the cinema?
✓ **Why do you prefer the theatre to the cinema?**
(為什麼你寧願看戲而不看電影?)
× I prefer drawing than painting.
✓ **I prefer drawing to painting.**
(比起油畫, 我更喜歡素描。)

> **prefer** A **to** B, NOT **than**
> 指 "喜歡甲多於乙" 可用 **prefer** A **to** B, 其中的 **to** 不能用 **than** 替代。

3 × He prefers living in Hong Kong more than living in Taiwan.
✓ **He prefers living in Hong Kong to living in Taiwan.**
(他認為住在香港比住在台灣好。)

> **Prefer** is NOT used with **more than**.
> 按 **prefer** 一詞不與 **more than** 連用。

preferable

× Going swimming is more preferable than playing football.

✓ **Going swimming is preferable to playing football.**
(寧可去游泳而不玩足球。)

> An adjective which contains the sense 'more' as part of its meaning cannot be used with **more**.
> 形容詞本身已有 "更加" 這樣一個含義時, 不與 **more** 並用。

present **1**

× This tie was a present of my wife.

✓ **This tie was a present from my wife.**
(這條領帶是我太太送的禮物。)

> **(receive) a present from** somebody, NOT **of**
> 由某人處收到禮物用 (**receive**) **a present from** somebody, 其中的 **from** 不能換作 **of**。

2

× Before leaving the examination room we had to present our answer papers.

✓ **Before leaving the examination room we had to hand in our answer papers.**
(離開考場前我們必須交上自己的試卷。)

> **present** = give or award, especially in a formal or ceremonial way (意為: 贈送; 授予; 出示, 例如): 'The prizes are usually presented by the headmaster.'
> **hand in** = give (something) to another person, especially by passing it to them by hand (意為: 交上)

3

× It was the first time I had been present to a road accident.

✓ **It was the first time I had been present at a road accident.**
(這是我第一次碰上交通事故。)

> **be present at** an event, NOT **to**
> 指 "在某事件發生的現場", 用 '**be present at** an event', 其中 **at** 不可用 **to** 替代。

presently

✓ **AmE Presently, nearly every machine used in the home is made of plastic.**
(美式英語: 目前, 幾乎所有的家用機器都是用塑膠製的。)

✓ **BrE At present, nearly every machine used in the home is made of plastic.**
(英式英語: 譯文同上)

Presently can mean 'soon' in both British and American English (按 **presently** 一詞在英式和美式英語中都有"即將"的含義, 例如): 'The car will arrive presently to take Her Majesty back to the palace.'
Note that in American English **presently** can also mean 'at present; currently' (美式英語中 **presently** 也有"現在"的含義, 例如): 'The President is presently undergoing minor surgery.'
The American usage is gradually becoming accepted outside the USA, although careful users of British English consider it to be non-standard.
美式的用法正逐漸為美國國外所接受, 但審慎的英式英語使用者認為這樣是不合標準的。

prevent **1** × His parents tried to prevent him to join the army.
√ **His parents tried to prevent him from joining the army.**
(他的父母竭力阻止他參軍。)

prevent someone **(from)** + v-ing
按 **prevent** someone (**from**) 後接帶"-ing"的動詞。

2 × Stricter punishments would prevent people from doing these things.
√ **Stricter punishments would deter people from doing these things.**
(採取更嚴厲的懲罰可以制止人做這種事情。)

prevent = stop (someone doing something) (意為"阻止", 例如): 'They locked all the doors to prevent him from escaping.'
deter = discourage (意為"使人不敢")

3 × Stricter punishments may help to prevent society from serious crime.
√ **Stricter punishments may help to protect society from serious crime.**
(採取更嚴厲的懲罰有助於保護社會免受嚴重罪案之害。)

prevent = stop (something happening) (意為"阻止", 例如): 'Bad weather prevented the plane from taking off.' 'Good tyres help to prevent accidents.'
protect = guard or keep safe (意為"保護")

prevention

× I decided to take a big stick with me, just as a prevention.

√ **I decided to take a big stick with me, just as a precaution.**

(為安全起見, 我決定帶上一根粗棍子。)

prevention = the act of preventing (stopping something from happening) (意為: "防止"、"預防", 例如): 'The police are concerned with the prevention of crime.'
precaution = an action taken in an attempt to avoid possible danger, injury, etc. (意為: "安全措施"、"防範行動")

price

× The price of keeping a person in prison for a year is enormous.

√ **The cost of keeping a person in prison for a year is enormous.**

(監禁一個人一年的費用是鉅大的。)

price = the amount of money asked for something which is for sale (意為: "價格")
cost = the expense of doing something or having something done (意為: "費用"、"成本")

pride

× They take great pride of their daughter who is now a famous scientist.

√ **They take great pride in their daughter who is now a famous scientist.**

(他們深以女兒為榮, 因為女兒現在已經成了一位著名的科學家了。)

take pride in, NOT **of**
注意: **take pride in** (以 ... 為榮) 中的前置詞 in 不能用 **of** 替代

print

× The magazine is printed every month.

√ **The magazine is published every month.**

(這份雜誌每月出版。)

print = produce many copies of a book, newspaper, etc. by using machines (意為: "印刷", 例如): 'Due to increased demand, another six thousand copies are to be printed.'
publish = produce and distribute (a book, newspaper, etc.) for sale to the public (意為: 出版[書、報等])

prison

× Sending people to the prison is not the way to reduce crime.

√ **Sending people to prison is not the way to reduce crime.**
(把人送進監獄不是減少罪案的辦法。)

> Use **go to prison**, **send** someone **to prison**, be **put in prison** WITHOUT **the**.
> 在 **go to prison**, **send someone to prison**, **put in prison** 等短語中均不用 **the**。
> Only use **the** when talking about a particular prison (只有提及某一特定的監獄時才用 **the**, 例如): 'The prison in this town is a big one.'

probation

× You'll be in probation for the first three months.

√ **You'll be on probation for the first three months.**
(你的頭三個月是試用期。)

> **on probation**, NOT **in**
> 注意: **on probation** (試用) 中的前置詞 **on** 不可用 **in** 替代

probably

× They probably will understand and try to help you.

√ **They will probably understand and try to help you.**
(他們大概會諒解並會設法幫助你。)

> **Probably** usually goes immediately after the (first) auxiliary verb (按 **probably** 通常緊接第一個助動詞之後, 例如): 'They have probably finished the meeting.' When there is no auxiliary verb, **probably** is usually placed immediately before the main verb (如沒有助動詞, **probably** 緊放在主動詞之前, 例如): 'She probably knows.' However, when the main verb is **be, probably** is placed immediately after it (但如主動詞是 **be**, **probably** 就緊接其後, 例如): 'He is probably ill.' Note that **probably** can also come at the beginning of a sentence, though this is less common. (注意 **probably** 也可放在句首, 然而並不那麼常用。)

problem 1

× I experienced problems to find the right accommodation.

√ **I experienced problems in finding the right accommodation.**
(我在尋找合適住處時遇上了各種問題。)

> **a problem/problems in** + v-ing
> 注意: **a problem/problems in** 後接帶 "-ing" 的動詞。

2 × If their children are at school all day, I see no problem why both parents should not go to work if they want to.

√ **If their children are at school all day, I see no reason why both parents should not go to work if they want to.**
(如果子女全日上學, 而做父母的也願意工作, 我看不出有什麼道理他們不應該一同出去工作。)

> **reason why**, NOT **problem**
> 按 **reason** 後接由 **why** 引導的子句, 而 **problem** 之後則不能用帶 why 的子句。

proceed × The main film was proceeded by a short cartoon.

√ **The main film was preceded by a short cartoon.**
(放映主片之前先放映了一部短的卡通片。)

> **proceed** = begin and continue (意為 "進行", 例如): 'After a five-minute delay, the lecture proceeded.'
> **precede** = come, go, or happen (immediately) before (在 ... 之前發生或進行)

professor × He has applied for a job as a professor in a language school.

√ **He has applied for a job as a teacher in a language school.**
(他申請當語言學校的教師。)

> **professor** = the most senior teacher in a university (意為: 大學教授)

program √ **AmE Every Friday we receive a program of the following week's events.**
(美式英語: 每星期五我們都收到一份下週活動的計劃。)

√ **BrE Every Friday we receive a programme of the following week's events.**
(英式英語: 譯文同上)

> **Program** is the usual American English spelling.
> 美式英語習慣的拼法是 "**program**"。
> **Programme** is the British English spelling.
> 英式英語的拼法是 "**programme**"。
> Note, however, that **a computer program** has the same spelling in both American and British English.
> 注意: **a computer program** 中的 "**program**" 在英、美式英語中的拼法是一致的。

progress

× I did little progress at the start of the course.
√ **I made little progress at the start of the course.**
(在課程剛開始時我進步甚小。)

> **make progress**, NOT **do**
> 注意: **make progress** 中的動詞 **make** 不可用 **do** 替代。

prohibit

× Even the teachers were prohibited to walk on the lawn.
√ **Even the teachers were prohibited from walking on the lawn.**
(就是教師也禁止在草地上走。)

> **prohibit** someone **from** + v-ing
> 注意: **prohibit** someone **from** 後接帶 "-ing" 的動詞。

promise

× Jimmy promised to his parents not to run away again.
√ **Jimmy promised his parents not to run away again.**
(吉米向父母保証不再逃跑。)

> **promise** someone something WITHOUT **to**
> 如說 "答應某人做某事", 可用 **promise,** 後緊接 "某人" — someone, 再接 "做某事" — something, 其中 **promise** 之後不帶 **to**。

proof

× Today we have scientific proofs that tobacco is harmful.
√ **Today we have scientific proof that tobacco is harmful.**
(今天我們經過科學分析, 証明煙草是有害的。)

> **Proof** is an uncountable noun.
> 按 **proof** 一詞是不可數名詞, 不用複數。

propaganda

× The television company receives most of its money from propaganda.
√ **The television company receives most of its money from advertising.**
(電視公司的收入主要來自廣告。)

> **Propaganda** is used in a political context.
> 按 **propaganda** 一詞屬政治範疇, 意為 "宣傳"。
> **Advertising** is used in a commercial context.
> 按 **advertising** 一詞屬商業範疇, 意為 "廣告"。

properties

× The police eventually found most of the stolen properties.

√ **The police eventually found most of the stolen property.**

(警方最終找到了大部分贓物。)

> **Property** (=possessions or belongings) is an uncountable noun.
> 按 **property** 作 "財產" 解是不可數名詞。

propose

× It was proposed all members of staff to start work an hour earlier.

√ **It was proposed that all members of staff (should) start work an hour earlier.**

(有人提議全體人員提早一小時開始工作。)

> **propose that** someone **(should) do** something
> 注意: **propose** 後接由 **that** 引導的子句, 句中的主動詞必須用其原形, 即使用不帶 to 的動詞, 或在主動詞之前加上 **should**。

prospect

× There were very few prospects to get a job.

√ **There were very few prospects of getting a job.**

(找到工作的希望甚微。)

> **prospects of** + v-ing
> 注意: **prospects of** 後接帶 "-ing" 的動詞。

protection

× Wanting a military protection is not the same as wanting a war.

√ **Wanting military protection is not the same as wanting a war.**

(需要軍事保護並不等於想要戰爭。)

> **Protection** is an uncountable noun.
> 按 **protection** 一詞是不可數名詞, 前面不能用不定冠詞 "**a**"。

protest

× She told the shop assistant that she wanted to protest about the cardigan she had bought.

√ **She told the shop assistant that she wanted to complain about the cardigan she had bought.**

(她跟店員說關於那件買了的毛衣, 她要提出投訴。)

Protest is used when a person feels very strongly that something is wrong or unjust (按 protest 一詞作 "抗議" 解, 表示強烈反對之意, 例如): 'The crowds were protesting about the government's purchase of nuclear weapons.'
Complain is used to express feelings of annoyance, dissatisfaction, unhappiness, etc.
按 **complain** 一詞作 "投訴"、"埋怨"、"抱怨" 解, 表示受到騷擾、不滿、不高興之意。

prove × This new engine has not been properly proved.
√ **This new engine has not been properly tested.**
(這台發動機尚未很好地試驗過。)

prove = provide proof or be proof of (something) (按 **prove** 一詞, 作 "證明" 解, 例如): 'Can you prove to the court that you are telling the truth?'
test = try; do experiments on (something) in order to discover how good or bad it is (按 **test** 一詞, 意為 "測試"、"檢驗" 之意。)

provide **1** × My job provides me the opportunity to meet new people every day.
√ **My job provides me with the opportunity to meet new people every day.**
(我的工作使我有機會每天接觸不同的人。)

provide someone **with** (a chance or opportunity to do something) (按 **provide** someone **with** 意為 "向某人提供機會或做某事的機會")
Note the alternative (請注意另一種說法): 'My job gives me the opportunity to meet new people every day.'

2 × In my view, a father should provide his family.
√ **In my view, a father should provide for his family.**
(我認為, 做父親的有責任養家。)

provide for someone = support someone (buy their food, clothes, etc.) (意為 "供養某人")

3 × I was very pleased with the room you provided to me.
√ **I was very pleased with the room you provided for me.**
√ **I was very pleased with the room you provided me with.**
(對你提供給我的房間我很滿意。)

provide (a room, accommodation, etc.) **for** someone OR **provide** someone with (a room, accommodation, etc.), NOT **to**
注意: 指 "為人提供諸如房間、住宿的地方等", 有兩種表達方式, 一種是 '**provide** (a room, accommodation 等等) **for** someone'; 另一種是 '**provide** someone **with** (a room, accommodation 等等)。這兩種方式中的 **for** 或 **with** 不可用 **to** 替代。

public

× The play was so boring that some of the public got up and left.
√ **The play was so boring that some of the audience got up and left.**
(這齣戲枯燥乏味, 所以一些觀眾站起來走了。)

public = people in general (意為 "公眾", 例如): 'The British public has been shocked by the incident.'
audience = people who (pay to) attend a performance at a cinema, theatre, etc. (意為 "觀眾", "聽眾")

punishment

× For certain crimes, the punishment should be very strong.
√ **For certain crimes, the punishment should be very severe.**
(對某些罪行應嚴加懲處。)

a **severe/harsh punishment**, NOT **strong**
指 "嚴厲的懲罰", 用 '**a severe/harsh punishment**', 其中的形容詞 **severe/harsh** 不可用 **strong** 替代。

put off

× Once indoors, he immediately put off his wet clothes and dried himself.
√ **Once indoors, he immediately took off his wet clothes and dried himself.**
(一進門, 他馬上脫掉身上的濕衣服, 把身體揩乾。)

take off your clothes, NOT **put off**
按 **take off** your clothes 中的動詞 **take off** 不可用 **put off** 替代。

qualification

× I am taking another course to improve my qualification.
√ **I am taking another course to improve my qualifications.**
(我正在進修一門課以提高自己的資歷。)

qualifications = the necessary ability, examination passes, experience, etc. (for a particular job) (意為“資歷”, 例如): 'We decided to appoint her because she had the right qualifications for the job.'
qualification = a BA, MSc, or other examination pass (意為“資格”、“身份”, 例如): 'She has gained a medical qualification.' (她獲得了當醫生的資格。)

quality
× Switzerland produces goods with a very high quality.
√ **Switzerland produces goods of a very high quality.**
(瑞士的產品質量很高。)

of (a) high/low/poor **quality,** NOT **with**
注意: **of (a)** high/low/poor **quality** 中的前置詞 of 不可用 **with** 替代。

quarrel
× At the end of the quarrel Paul was badly hurt and I had to take him to hospital.
√ **At the end of the fight Paul was badly hurt and I had to take him to hospital.**
(打完架後保羅受傷不輕, 我只得把他送往醫院。)

quarrel = an argument; a verbal conflict (意為“吵架”)
fight = a physical conflict involving the use of violence, weapons, blows, etc. (意為“打架”)

question
× Today it is out of the question that the first years of a child's life are very important.
√ **Today it is beyond question that the first years of a child's life are very important.**
(小孩剛出世那幾年是非常重要的, 這一點現在已毫無疑問了。)

out of the question (used especially of proposals) = completely impossible (意為“完全不可能”, 尤其用於建議方面, 例如): 'To ask the men to work seven days a week is out of the question.'
beyond question = beyond doubt (意為“毫無疑問”)

quick
× We were expected to answer each question very quick.
√ **We were expected to answer each question very quickly.**
(我們必須很快地回答每道題。)

Quick is an adjective.
按 **quick** 是形容詞。
Quickly is an adverb.
按 **quickly** 是副詞。

quiet × I went up the stairs as quiet as I could.
√ **I went up the stairs as quietly as I could.**
(我盡可能小聲地上樓梯。)

Quiet is an adjective.
按 **quiet** 是形容詞。
Quietly is an adverb.
按 **quietly** 是副詞。

quite 1 × I've quite grown used to living on my own.
√ **I've grown quite used to living on my own.**
(我已經很習慣於獨自生活了。)

Quite is placed immediately before the word or phrase it modifies.
按 **quite** 應直接放在所修飾的詞或片語之前。

2 × In the circumstances, it was a quite rude answer.
√ **In the circumstances, it was quite a rude answer.**
(在當時的情況下, 這是個相當粗魯的回答。)

quite + **a/an** + adjective + noun
按 **quite a/an** 後接形容詞, 再接名詞, 本是一種句式結構, 其中 **a/an** 不能放在 **quite** 之前。

3 × This year the work at university is quite harder than last year.
√ **This year the work at university is rather harder than last year.**
(大學裏的功課今年比去年要難得多。)

Quite is NOT used before comparative adjectives/adverbs.
按 **quite** 一詞不用於比較形容詞或副詞之前。

radio × I was listening to the news in the radio.
√ **I was listening to the news on the radio.**
(我那時正在聽新聞廣播。)

on the radio/television, NOT **in**
按 **on the radio/television** 中的前置詞 **on** 不可用 **in** 替代。

raincoat × It's a black rain coat with red buttons.
√ **It's a black raincoat with red buttons.**
(那是一件帶紅扣子的黑色雨衣。)

> **Raincoat** is ALWAYS one word.
> 按 **raincoat** 是一個詞, 不能把 rain 和 coat 分開寫。

raise 1 √ **AmE My husband has just been given a big raise.**
(美式英語: 我丈夫的薪金最近增加了很多。)
√ **BrE My husband has just been given a big pay rise.**
(英式英語: 譯文同上)

> When the meaning is 'an increase in wages', use **raise** in American English and **rise** in British English.
> 指"工資增加", 美式英語用 **raise,** 英式英語用 **rise**。

2 See (見) CRITICISM

rare × Water is very rare in some parts of the country.
√ **Water is very scarce in some parts of the country.**
(鄉村有些地方是很缺水的。)

> **rare** (of unusual things and events) = uncommon (意為"罕見的"、"珍奇的", 通常指少有之物或事, 例如): 'a rare coin', 'a rare bird', 'a rare visit'
> **scarce** (of things which are usually common) = in short supply (意為"短缺的", 通常指尋常之物。)

rarely See (見) NEVER 5, 6

rather 1 × I told her I would rather to go by train than to fly.
√ **I told her I would rather go by train than fly.**
(我告訴她我寧願坐火車, 不願乘飛機。)

> **would rather** + infinitive WITHOUT **to**
> 注意: **would rather** 後接不帶 **to** 的動詞。

2 × I would rather you shouldn't invite too many people.
√ **I would rather you didn't invite too many people.**
(我倒希望你沒有邀請太多的人。)

> Do not follow **would rather** with **should/would.**
> 注意: **would rather** 作"希望"解, 相當於 wish, 後接子句時, 動詞用過去式, 而不用 **should/would**。

reach 1 × When the blue car reached to the corner, it stopped.
✓ **When the blue car reached the corner, it stopped.**
(那藍色汽車駛到拐角處就停下。)

> **reach** somewhere/something WITHOUT **to**
> 指 "到達某地"、"伸手觸及某物", 可用 '**reach** somewhere/something', 在 **reach** 之後不可用 **to**。

2 See (見) AIM 2

real ✓ **AmE I'm real sorry to hear that.**
(美式英語: 聽到那消息, 我真的非常難過。)
✓ **BrE I'm really sorry to hear that.**
(英式英語: 譯文同上)

> When the meaning is 'very', use **really** (NOT **real**) in British English.
> 如那形容詞本身含有 very (非常、十分) 之意, 則英式英語用 **really** 而不是 **real** 去修飾。
> In American English, both **really** and **real** are possible but **real** is more informal.
> 在同樣的情況下, 美式英語既可用 **really** 也可用 **real** 去修飾, 但用 **real** 則屬口語體。

realize 1 × The headmaster realized his threat and sent the children home.
✓ **The headmaster carried out his threat and sent the children home.**
(校長警告過孩子們, 要打發他們回家去。結果他真的這麼做了。)

> **Realize** (=to make something happen or become real) is usually used with words such as 'hope', 'ambition', and 'intention'.
> 按 **realize** 作 "實現" 解, 通常與 "希望"、"抱負" 同用 (注意 **carry out** 作 "實行"、"執行" 解)

2 × Nobody realized whether he was coming.
✓ **Nobody knew whether he was coming.**
(誰也不知道他來不來。)

Realize (=to become aware of) is used when talking about something which is factual or certain, NOT something uncertain.
按 **realize** 如作"認識到"解, 則所指的應是實在的或肯定有的事, 而不是未確定的事。
Compare (試比較): 'Nobody realized that he was coming.' (He was coming but nobody was aware of it.)

really 1 × It was only a short trip but we had really a good time.
✓ **It was only a short trip but we had a really good time.**
✓ **It was only a short trip but we really had a good time.**
(那只是一次短程的旅行, 但我們確實過得很愉快。)

Really (=very; extremely) usually comes immediately before the adjective or adverb it qualifies. Otherwise its position is a matter of emphasis. It is commonly placed immediately before the verb. When a verb has several parts, **really** is usually placed immediately after the (first) auxiliary (按 **really** 一詞意為"非常"、"極其", 通常直接放在所修飾的形容詞或副詞之前。在其他情況下, **really** 這個詞放在哪個詞之前, 就是要加重哪個詞的語氣。通常則直接放在動詞之前。如主動詞帶有助動詞, **really** 一般緊放在第一個助動詞之後, 例如): 'We're really enjoying ourselves.'

2 × To his great amazement, little Nicola really won the race.
✓ **To his great amazement, little Nicola actually won the race.**
(使他大為驚訝的是, 小尼古拉竟然在賽跑中獲勝。)

Really and **actually** are sometimes interchangeable, but NOT when the meaning is 'strange as it may seem'. For this meaning, use **actually.**
按 **really** 和 **actually** 有時可以交替使用, 但如作"居然"、"竟然"解, 則只用 **actually** 一詞。

reason 1 × The reason I didn't buy the car was because I thought it was too expensive.
✓ **The reason I didn't buy the car was that I thought it was too expensive.**
(我不買這輛車的原因是我認為它太貴了。)

The use of a **because** clause after **reason** is regarded by careful users as non-standard.
在 **reason** 後用 **because** 子句, 文字嚴謹的人認為不夠規範。

2 × There are many good reasons to thinking like this.
√ **There are many good reasons for thinking like this.**
(有好多理由使人這麼想。)
× What is the reason of your long silence?
√ **What is the reason for your long silence?**
(什麼原因使你沉默很久?)

reason for (doing) something, NOT **to** OR **of**
按 **reason for** (doing) something 中的 **for,** 不可用 **to** 或 **of** 替代。

reasonable × I was far too upset and emotional to make a reasonable decision.
√ **I was far too upset and emotional to make a rational decision.**
(我當時心裏太煩和太衝動了, 無法作出理智的決定。)

reasonable = fair, sensible, or acceptable (意為合理的; 可接受的, 例如): 'a reasonable offer/suggestion'
rational = produced by means of careful, logical thinking (意為: 理智的; 合乎理性的, 例如): 'a rational conclusion/argument/explanation'

recognize × On the plane home, I suddenly recognized that I had left my coat at the hotel.
√ **On the plane home, I suddenly realized that I had left my coat at the hotel.**
(在回程的飛機上, 我忽然意識到我把大衣忘在旅店了。)

recognize = know again (someone or something you have seen, heard, or met before) (意為 "認出", 例如): 'She had changed so much over the years that I hardly recognized her.'
realize = be/become aware of something (意為: 認識到)

recommend

× I recommend you a walk along the Seine.
√ **I recommend a walk along the Seine.**
√ **I recommend (that) you take a walk along the Seine.**
√ **I recommend taking a walk along the Seine.**
(我提議你到塞納河邊去散步。)

> **Recommend** is used in the following patterns to mean 'advise or suggest' (按 recommend 意為"提議; 推薦"時, 有下列句型): 'recommend a person/thing', 'recommend (that) someone (should) do something', 'recommend doing something'.
> Note that in British English there is also the pattern (注意英式英語中也有這類句型): 'recommend someone to do something'. However, this pattern can sound awkward and is less common. (但這類句型欠自然, 不常用。)

refrain

× We all refrained telling her what we really thought.
√ **We all refrained from telling her what we really thought.**
(我們都不告訴她我們的真實想法。)

> **refrain from** + v-ing
> 按 **refrain from** 作"克制; 避免"解, 後接帶"-ing"的動詞。

refuse

× I expect that the younger generation will refuse these old-fashioned ideas.
√ **I expect that the younger generation will reject these old-fashioned ideas.**
(我估計年青一代會拒絕接受這些老思想。)

> **refuse an invitation** = decline an invitation (意為"拒絕/謝絕邀請")
> **refuse/reject an offer** = decline an offer (意為"不接受提議")
> **reject an idea/philosophy** = dismiss an idea/philosophy because you are not in agreement with it (拒絕接受某種意見、看法或哲學觀點)

regard 1

× Please give your sister my warmest regard.
√ **Please give your sister my warmest regards.**
(請替我向令姐致以最熱誠的問候。)

> **regard** = (1) consideration (意為 "尊敬"、"重視", 例如): 'You have no regard for my feelings.'
> (2) respect (意為 "尊敬", 例如): 'He had a high regard for his teacher.' 'I hold her in the highest regard.'
> **regards** = greetings; good wishes (意為 "問候"、"致意")

2 × He shows no regard to other people.
✓ **He shows no regard for other people.**
(他對別人漠不關心。)

> **regard for** (the feelings of) someone, NOT **to**
> 注意: **regard for** 意為 "尊重"、"關心", 其中 **for** 不可用 **to** 替代。

3 × He is generally regarded to be one of the world's finest physicists.
✓ **He is generally regarded as one of the world's finest physicists.**
(他被公認為世界最優秀的物理學家之一。)

> **regard** a person or thing **as** (being) something, NOT **to** be
> 指 "把某人或某物視為 ...", 可用 "**regard** a person or thing **as** ..." 其中 **as** 不能用 **to** 替代。

regret **1** × He soon began to regret to have run away from home.
✓ **He soon began to regret having run away from home.**
(他不久就開始後悔從家裏出走。)

> **regret** + v-ing
> 按 **regret** 一詞後接帶 "-ing" 的動詞。

2 × I am regretful to inform you that your application for the position has been unsuccessful.
✓ **I regret to inform you that your application for the position has been unsuccessful.**
(我很抱歉地通知你, 你的申請未獲批准。)

> **Regretful** is usually used to describe real feelings (按 **regretful** 一詞通常用來表達內心真實的感受, 例如): 'I felt rather regretful that I couldn't go with them.' 'She gave me a regretful look.'

I/We regret to ... is a polite expression used chiefly in formal letters.
按 **I** 或 **We regret** 後接帶 to 的動詞是正式函件的客套話, 口語體不用; 日常口語可能會說: 'I'm afraid you didn't get the job.'

regretful × I made several regretful mistakes.
√ **I made several regrettable mistakes.**
(我犯了一些令我悔恨的錯誤。)

regretful = feeling or expressing regret (意為 "惋惜", 例如): 'She said goodbye to her old home with many regretful glances." (她帶着依依不捨的眼光看了故居好幾眼才離去。)
regrettable = to be regretted (意為 "感到遺憾或懊悔")

related × All the other problems are related with the economic one.
√ **All the other problems are related to the economic one.**
(所有其他問題都與經濟問題有關。)

A is **related to** B, NOT **with**
指 "甲與乙有關", 用 'A is **related to** B', 其中前置詞 to 不可用 **with** 替代。

relax × I usually relax myself by taking a hot bath.
√ **I usually relax by taking a hot bath.**
(我通常是洗熱水澡來鬆弛身心。)

Relax is NOT a reflexive verb.
按 **relax** 不是反身動詞, 其後不必用反身代詞 (如 myself, yourself 等)。

relieve × His fear immediately changed to relieve.
√ **His fear immediately changed to relief.**
(他的恐懼立刻就消除了。)

Relieve is a verb. (按此為動詞)
Relief is a noun. (按此為名詞)

remember 1 × I am remembering leaving a map of Rome in the pocket.
√ **I remember leaving a map of Rome in the pocket.**
(我記得我把一張羅馬地圖放在口袋裏。)

Remember is NOT used in progressive tenses.
按 **remember** 一詞不可用進行式。

2 × I did not remember to meet her before but I pretended I knew her.
✓ **I did not remember meeting her before but I pretended I knew her.**
(我記不起曾經見過她, 不過我裝作是認識她的。)

remember + to-v = not forget (如 **remember** 後接帶 to 的動詞, 意為 "不要忘記"、"沒有忘記", 例如):
'Please remember to feed the cat.'
remember + v-ing = recall (如 **remember** 後接帶 "-ing" 的動詞, 意為 "想起"、"回憶起")

3 × I would like to remember you that the machine is still under guarantee.
✓ **I would like to remind you that the machine is still under guarantee.**
(我想提醒你, 這機器仍未過保修期限。)

remind someone = cause someone to remember
(按 **remind someone** 意為 "提醒某人" 或 "使想起")

remind **1** × The flowers reminded him his garden.
✓ **The flowers reminded him of his garden.**
(這些花使他想起了自己的花園。)

remind someone **of** something = cause someone to think about something (意為 "使人想起某事", 其中 of 不能缺)

2 × I wish you had reminded me of phoning her.
✓ **I wish you had reminded me to phone her.**
(你當時要能提醒我打電話給她就好了。)

remind someone **to do** something = tell someone that there is something he or she ought to do (意為 "提醒某人做某事" — **remind** someone 之後接帶 **to** 的動詞)

3 × I remind the happy days we spent together at college.
✓ **I remember the happy days we spent together at college.**
(我記得我們一起在大學那段快樂的日子。)

remind = cause (someone) to remember (意為“使人回憶起”)
Compare (試比較): ‘I was reminded of the happy days we spent together at college.’ (= something caused me to remember ...) (促使我回憶起)

remove

× My family removed into the suburbs when I was five years old.
√ **My family moved into the suburbs when I was five years old.**
(我五歲時, 我家遷到郊區去了。)

Some people used to use **remove** when talking about people moving to another house but this is now considered very old-fashioned.
有人用 **remove** 表達“搬遷”, 但這種用法今天已認為過時。

rent

× If you like riding, there are horses you can rent.
√ **If you like riding, there are horses you can hire.**
(如果你愛騎馬, 出租的馬有的是。)

In British English, **hire** usually refers to a single payment made for the temporary use of something (英式英語中 **hire** 指一次付款的臨時租用, 例如): ‘hire a tennis racket/wedding dress/car’. **Rent** usually refers to a regular series of payments made over a long period of time (按 **rent** 指長期的按期付款, 例如): ‘rent a house/flat’. Note, however, that in American English, a person **rents** a car, a horse, a boat, a flat, a house, a video, etc.
(注意: 美式英語則用 **rent** a car, a horse, a boat, a flat, a house, a video 等。)

replace

× I told him he would have to replace the broken lid by a new one.
√ **I told him he would have to replace the broken lid with a new one.**
(我告訴他, 他必須用一個新蓋子替換那打破的蓋子。)

replace something **with** something else, NOT **by**
指“以一物替代另一物”, 用 ‘**replace** something **with** something else’, 其中前置詞 **with** 不可用 **by** 替代。

request × We had to request for more help.
√ **We had to request more help.**
(我們必須請求更多的援助。)

> **request** something WITHOUT **for**
> 按 **request** 係及物動詞, 其後直接跟 something, 不用前置詞 **for**。

research **1** × I'm doing some researches on the industrial development of my country.
√ **I'm doing some research on the industrial development of my country.**
(我正在做一些我國工業發展的研究。)

> **Research** is an uncountable noun.
> 按 **research** 作 "研究" 解時是不可數名詞, 沒有複數形式。

2 × A lot of money is spent on research against the causes of cancer.
√ **A lot of money is spent on research into the causes of cancer.**
(研究癌症起因耗資很大。)

> (do) **research into** something, NOT **against**
> 按 **research** 作名詞用, 後接前置詞 **into,** 而不用 **against,** 如 '(do) research into something'。

3 × More police were sent to join in the research but the child was never found.
√ **More police were sent to join in the search but the child was never found.**
(已派更多警察參加搜尋, 但孩子始終沒有找到。)

> **research** = advanced study which aims to discover new knowledge (意為 "研究工作", 例如): 'cancer research', 'She's doing research into the causes of crime.'
> **search** = the act of looking for (someone or something) by carefully examining a place or area (意為 "搜尋")

resist × She couldn't resist his rudeness any longer and walked out of the room.
√ **She couldn't tolerate his rudeness any longer and walked out of the room.**
(她再也受不了他那粗暴的態度, 於是走出房間。)

resist = fight against; oppose (意為: "抵抗", 例如): 'resist an enemy attack'
tolerate = stand; bear; put up with (意為: "忍受"、"容忍")

respectful

× Some former prisoners are now respectful citizens.
√ **Some former prisoners are now respectable citizens.**
(有些從前是囚犯的人現在成了受尊敬的公民。)
× If you want to make a good impression, you'll have to look a bit more respectful.
√ **If you want to make a good impression, you'll have to look a bit more respectable.**
(如果你要給人好印象, 就必須打扮得更體面一些。)

respectful = having or showing respect (意為: "表示敬意的"、"有禮的", 例如): 'a respectful attitude'
respectable = displaying socially acceptable standards in appearance or behaviour; deserving respect (意為: "應受尊敬的"、"體面的")

responsible **1**

× I'm writing to you as you are the responsible person for customer relations.
√ **I'm writing to you as you are the person responsible for customer relations.**
(由於你是顧客關係部的負責人, 我特此寫信給你。)

a responsible person = a trustworthy person (意為 "可信賴的人"、"可靠的人")
the person responsible (for something) = the person whose duty it is to deal with or look after something (意為 "負責人"、"主管人")

2

× I am also responsible to decide on the best way to manufacture a product.
√ **I am also responsible for deciding on the best way to manufacture a product.**
(產品製造的方式也由我決定。)

responsible for + v-ing
"負責做某事" 或 "對 … 負責" 可用 **responsible for** 後接帶 "-ing" 的動詞。

3 × The dealer is responsible of any fault in the product.
√ **The dealer is responsible for any fault in the product.**
(經銷商對產品的任何毛病都負有責任。)

> **responsible for** something, NOT **of**
> 按 **responsible for** something 中的前置詞 **for** 不可用 **of** 替代

rest × Whenever we rest in Milan, we always go to the opera.
√ **Whenever we stay in Milan, we always go to the opera.**
(我們每次在米蘭逗留, 總是去看歌劇。)

> **rest** = stop an activity in order to recover your energy (意為 "休息", 例如): 'After climbing for two hours, we decided to stop and rest.'
> **stay** = spend time (in a place), especially one or more nights (意為 "逗留", 尤指留下住宿)

result × Nowadays we hear a lot about pollution and its results on our health.
√ **Nowadays we hear a lot about pollution and its effects on our health.**
(今天我們聽到許多關於污染及其影響我們健康的事。)

> **result** = the outcome of an action or state of affairs (意為: "結果", 例如): 'His poverty was the result of gambling.' 'Her first book was the result of a trip to Africa.' 'The anti-smoking campaign has produced excellent results.'
> **effect** (on someone/something) = a change in condition brought about by a cause (意為: "影響", 例如): 'The drug had no effect on him.' (= there was no change in his condition)
> 'Wine always had an effect on me — it makes me want to sing.'

return 1 × She returned back after half an hour.
√ **She returned after half an hour.**
(她半小時以後就回來了。)

× When are you going to return back the money you owe me?
✓ **When are you going to return the money you owe me?**
(你什麼時候把欠款還我?)

Back is NOT used with **return** because **return** means (按 **back** 一詞不與 **return** 連用, 因為 return 本身含有): 'come/go/give/send back' (回來/回去/還給/送回) 之意。

2 × In my opinion the government should return capital punishment.
✓ **In my opinion the government should restore/bring back/reintroduce capital punishment.**
(我認為政府應恢復死刑。)

return = give or send back (意為 "歸還"、"退回", 例如): 'Please return the photographs as soon as possible.'

3 See (見) HOME

reward × Two of the German films were given rewards.
✓ **Two of the German films were given awards.**
(德國電影中有兩部獲獎。)

reward = a sum of money offered for helping the police, finding and returning lost possessions, etc. (意為: "報酬"、"酬金", 例如): 'The bank is offering a reward of a thousand pounds.'
award = a prize given for merit (意為: "獎品/金")

ride × He spends all his time riding his new car.
✓ **He spends all his time driving his new car.**
(他把所有時間都花在駕駛新車上了。)

ride a horse/bicycle BUT **drive** a car/van/train
注意詞語的搭配關係, **ride** 作 "騎、乘" 解時與 a horse/bicycle 等詞連用, **drive** 作 "駕駛" 解時, 與 a car/van/train 等詞連用。

ring × I rang to the college to explain my absence.
✓ **I rang the college to explain my absence.**
(我打電話到學院解釋缺課的原因。)

ring a person/place WITHOUT **to**
注意: **ring** 作 "給 … 打電話" 解時, 直接跟 a person/place, 而不用 **to**。

rise × Many firms try to survive by rising productivity.
√ **Many firms try to survive by raising productivity.**
(許多公司力圖提高生產率以渡過難關。)

Rise is an intransitive verb (按 **rise** 一詞是不及物動詞, 其後不接受詞, 例如): 'Prices rose.' (=Prices increased.)
Raise is a transitive verb (按 **raise** 一詞是及物動詞, 其後接受詞, 例如): 'They raised the prices.' (=They increased the prices.)

risk × Not one of us would risk to go out on our own.
√ **Not one of us would risk going out on our own.**
(我們誰也不願意冒險單獨出去。)

risk + v-ing
按 risk 作 "冒 … 的危險" 解時, 後接帶 "-ing" 的動詞。

rob × While he was asleep, she robbed him his watch.
√ **While he was asleep, she stole his watch.**
√ **While he was asleep, she robbed him of his watch.**
(她趁他睡着時偷了他的錶。)
× The wicked old man robbed all my money.
√ **The wicked old man stole all my money.**
√ **The wicked old man robbed me of all my money.**
(那壞老頭偷走了/搶走了我所有的錢。)

steal something (**from** someone) OR (less common) **rob** someone (**of** something)
指 "偷 (某人的) 東西", 用 '**steal** something (**from** someone)', 另一形式是 '**rob** someone (**of** something)' — 意為 "搶了某人 (的東西)", 但此用法不常見。

round × The accident happened round three o'clock.
√ **The accident happened around three o'clock.**
(事故發生在三點鐘左右。)

around (NOT **round**) = (at) about/approximately
注意: **around** 作 "… 前後或左右; 大約" 解時, 相當於 (at) about/approximately。而 **round** 無上述意義, 不容與 **around** 混淆。

rude × The shop assistant was very rude with me.
√ **The shop assistant was very rude to me.**
(那店員對我很無禮。)

> (be) **rude to** someone, NOT **with**
> 指 "對某人無禮", 用 '(be) **rude to** someone', 其中前置詞 **to** 不可用 **with** 替代。

run × The car was running too fast for me to see the number plate.
√ **The car was moving too fast for me to see the number plate.**
(那輛車子開得太快, 我看不清車牌。)

> A vehicle **travels, moves,** or **goes** at a certain speed in a certain direction.
> 指 "車輛以某種速度行駛", 可用 **travel, move, go** 等動詞。

's × Some of the tree's leaves had fallen on top of the car.
√ **Some of the leaves from the tree had fallen on top of the car.**
(樹上的一些葉子落在車頂上。)

> Compare (試比較): 'All her father's tools were missing.' (NOT 不作 'tools of her father')
> 'The handles of the tools were made of wood.' (NOT 不作 '... tools' handles ...').
> The possessive **'s/s'** is commonly used with human and animal nouns but not with inanimate nouns.
> 所有式的 **'s/s'** 通常與人和動物有關的名詞連用而不與無生命的名詞連用。

sack 1 × When I took the two oranges out of the sack, I discovered that one of them was bad.
√ **When I took the two oranges out of the bag, I discovered that one of them was bad.**
(我從袋子裏取出兩個橘子, 發覺其中一個爛了。)

> **sack** = a very large strong bag (指可裝重物的大袋): 'a sack of coal'
> **bag** = a container made of cloth, paper, leather, etc. (指由布、紙、皮革等製成的袋或提包, 例如): 'a bag of sweets', 'a shopping bag'

2 × My new coat has a belt and two large sacks.
√ **My new coat has a belt and two large pockets.**
(我的新上衣有一條腰帶和兩個大口袋。)

> **sack** = a very large strong bag (指可裝重物的大袋)
> **pocket** = a small flat cloth bag sewn into or onto a garment, used for keeping small items in (指衣服的口袋)

salary × His salary is about a hundred and fifty pounds a week.
√ **His wage is about a hundred and fifty pounds a week.**
(他的工資約為每週一百五十鎊。)

> A **salary** is usually paid monthly but a **wage** is usually paid weekly.
> 按 **salary** 指 "月薪", 一般按月支付; **wage** 則指 "週薪", 一般按週支付。

sale × I bought both pairs of shoes on a sale.
√ **I bought both pairs of shoes at/in a sale.**
(這兩雙鞋都是我在一次大減價時買的。)

> buy something **at/in a sale,** NOT **on**
> buy something **at/in a sale** 中的前置詞 **at/in** 不可用 **on** 替代。但指 "出售; 待售", 可說 '**on sale**', 例如: Video recorders are now on sale. (現有錄影機出售。) 注意美式英語中 **on sale** 也作 "大減價" 解。

salute × A group of officials were at the airport to salute the visitors.
√ **A group of officials were at the airport to greet/welcome the visitors.**
(一群官員在機場歡迎來賓。)

> **salute** (of members of the armed forces) = make a formal sign of respect, especially by raising the right arm (指軍人舉右手致敬禮, 例如): 'Always salute a superior officer.'
> **greet/welcome** = express pleasure on meeting someone (表示歡迎)

same 1 × Paris has the same level of pollution with Los Angeles.
√ **Paris has the same level of pollution as Los Angeles.**
(巴黎和洛杉磯的污染程度一樣。)
× The belt is made of the same material like the coat.
√ **The belt is made of the same material as the coat.**
(腰帶所用的質料與上衣所用的相同。)

> **the same … as,** NOT **with** or **like**
> 注意: **the same … as** 中的 **as** 不可用 **with** 或 **like** 替代。

2 See (見) THAN 1

satisfactory × For many people, a part-time job can be very satisfactory.
√ **For many people, a part-time job can be very satisfying.**
(對許多人來說, 一份非全職的工作也能給人滿足感。)

> **satisfactory** = good enough to satisfy or be acceptable (意為 "令人滿意的", 例如): 'Some of the students are asked to leave the college if their work is not satisfactory.' (有的學生如果功課不能令人滿意, 就得被迫退學。)
> **satisfying** = giving pleasure or contentment (意為: "令人滿足的")

satisfied × I was completely satisfied of the quality of her work.
√ **I was completely satisfied with the quality of her work.**
(我對她的工作質量完全滿意。)

> **satisfied with** someone/something, NOT **of**
> 指 "對人或物滿意", 用 **(be) satisfied with** someone/ something, 其中前置詞 **with** 不可用 **of** 替代。

save × The police telephoned his parents to tell them that he was save.
√ **The police telephoned his parents to tell them that he was safe.**
(警察打電話告訴他父母他很安全。)

> **Save** is a verb.
> **save** 是動詞。
> **Safe** is an adjective
> **safe** 是形容詞。

scarce × Chocolate was very rare during the war.
✓ **Chocolate was very scarce during the war.**
(巧克力糖在戰時十分短缺。)

> **scarce** (of things which are usually common) = in short supply (意為: "短缺的")
> **rare** (of unusual things and events) = uncommon (意為: "罕見的")

scarcely See (見) NEVER 6

scene 1 × From the window, there was a beautiful scene of the lake.
✓ **From the window, there was a beautiful view of the lake.**
(窗外可見一片秀麗的湖泊風光。)

> **scene** = a view presented by a particular situation or setting; picture
> (由某一特定環境呈現的) 景色 (如街景之類)
> **view** = the area within your vision when you are in a particular place
> (從遠處看到的) 風景

2 × The driver stopped now and again so that we could enjoy the scene.
✓ **The driver stopped now and again so that we could enjoy the scenery.**
(司機一再把車子停下來, 讓我們飽覽沿途的風景。)

> **scene** = a view presented by a particular situation or setting; picture (由某一特定環境呈現的景色, 例如): 'The old man chasing the dog made a very amusing scene.' (那老人追着狗跑的情景使人發噱。)
> **scenery** = the natural features of the countryside (指 "郊野的自然景色")

scenery

× What a beautiful scenery!
√ **What beautiful scenery!**
(多麼美麗的景色!)

> **Scenery** is an uncountable noun.
> 按 **scenery** 是不可數名詞, 前面不能加不定冠詞 "**a**"。

school 1

√ **AmE Most Norwegians speak English quite well because everybody has to learn English in school.**
(美式英語: 大多數的挪威人都能講相當流利的英語, 因為人人都要在學校學英語。)
√ **BrE Most Norwegians speak English quite well because everybody has to learn English at school.**
(英式英語: 譯文同上)

> In American English, use **in/at school.**
> 美式英語用 **in school** 或 **at school**
> **In British English, use at school,** NOT **in.**
> 英式英語用 **at school,** 不用 **in school**

2

× She said that her daughter wanted to leave the school and get married.
√ **She said that her daughter wanted to leave school and get married.**
(她說她女兒想輟學去結婚。)
× He still isn't old enough to go to a school.
√ **He still isn't old enough to go to school.**
(他還沒有達到學齡。)

> Use **leave school, start school, go to school** (WITHOUT **a** or **the**) when referring to school as an institution and not to one school in particular. Compare (如指 "上學"、"輟學" 這一類概念而不是指到某一特定的學校去, 則 **leave school** (輟學)、**start school** (開學)、**go to school** (上學) 等用語都不應加冠詞 "**a**" 或 "**the**"。試比較): 'She goes to a very good school.'

scissors

× First cut along the dotted line with a scissors.
√ **First cut along the dotted line with a pair of scissors.**
√ **First cut along the dotted line with some scissors.**
(先用剪刀沿着虛綫剪開。)

> **Scissors** is a plural noun.
> 按 **scissors** 是複數名詞。

search 1

× A police patrol was organized to search Tom.
√ **A police patrol was organized to search for Tom.**
(一支警察巡邏隊經已組成並派出搜尋湯姆。)
× An old lady saw Tom and realized that he was the little boy who was searched by the police.
√ **An old lady saw Tom and realized that he was the little boy the police were searching for.**
√ **An old lady saw Tom and realized that he was the little boy who was sought by the police.**
(一位老太太看見湯姆便認出他正是警察搜尋的那個小男孩。)

> **search someone** = examine someone's clothing or pockets to discover whether he or she is carrying a gun, drugs, stolen goods, etc. (指"搜身", 例如): 'They searched him but couldn't find the film.'
> **search for** or **seek** (formal) = try to find someone/something 注意 **search for** 或 **seek** 均作"搜尋"之意。後者是書面用語。

2

× I searched my passport everywhere but couldn't find it.
√ **I searched for my passport everywhere but couldn't find it.**
(我到處找我的護照, 可是找不到。)

> **search a place** = examine a place carefully to try to find something (意為"搜查", 例如): 'I searched the room but couldn't find my passport.'
> **search for something** = try to find something (usually something that has been lost or hidden) 按 **search for something** 意為尋找 (失去了的或藏起來的東西)

second See (見) MONTH

see 1

× I saw a large blue car to drive past on the other side of the road.
√ **I saw a large blue car drive past on the other side of the road.**
(我看見一輛藍色的大轎車在馬路那一邊駛過。)

> **see** a person/thing + infinitive WITHOUT **to**
> see a person 或 thing 後接不帶 to 的動詞。

2 × He sat seeing the planes taking off.
√ **He sat watching the planes taking off.**
(他坐在那裏看着一架架飛機起飛。)
× The lecturer asked us to see carefully what he was doing.
√ **The lecturer asked us to look carefully at what he was doing.**
(那講師叫我們仔細地看他在做什麼。)

> **see** = experience with the eyes (without concentrating or paying attention) (沒有特別注意地看, 例如): 'Did you see anyone go out?' 'Turn the light on if you can't see.'
> **watch** = use the eyes to observe something, especially for a long time
> 按 **watch** 意為 "注視"、"長時間地觀看"
> **look at** = use the eyes to observe something, usually for a short time
> 按 **look at** 意為: "觀看", 一般時間不長。

3 × I have sent you the magazine so you can see by yourself how beautiful our country is.
√ **I have sent you the magazine so you can see for yourself how beautiful our country is.**
(我把雜誌寄給你了, 讓你自己看看我們的國家有多麼美。)

> **see for yourself** (NOT **by**) = see (something) with your own eyes
> 按 **see for yourself** 意為 "親眼目睹", 其中 **for** 不能用 **by** 替代。
> Compare (試比較): 'If everybody is busy, you'll have to go by yourself.' (= alone)

4 × Do you see this kind of magazine?
√ **Do you read this kind of magazine?**
(你看不看這一類雜誌?)

> **Read a magazine/book/novel/newspaper.** NOT **see**
> 按中文習慣說 "看報"、"看小說、"看雜誌", 其實這 "看" 是 "讀" 的意思, 英文習慣說 **read a magazine/book/novel/newspaper** 而不用 **see a magazine** 等。

5 See DREAM 3

seek 1 × He sat nearer the tree, seeking for protection.
√ **He sat nearer the tree, seeking protection.**
(為了尋求保護, 他靠近那棵樹坐。)

> **seek** someone/something WITHOUT **for**
> 按 **seek** 作 "尋求" 解, 緊接受詞: someone 或 something, 不用 **for**。

2 × We are often accused of seeking for to destroy the countryside.
√ **We are often accused of seeking to destroy the countryside.**
(我們經常受到譴責, 說我們企圖破壞農村。)

> **seek to do** something WITHOUT **for**
> **seek to do** something 作 "企圖/試圖做某事" 解, **seek** 後不接 **for**。

seem 1 × The woman who was shouting seemed the owner of the car.
√ **The woman who was shouting seemed to be the owner of the car.**
(那個正在呼喊的女人似乎是車主。)

> When the noun phrase following **seem** does not contain an adjective, **seem** is usually followed by **to be.** Compare (如 **seem** 後面連接的名詞片語中沒有形容詞, 則 **seem** 後一般都要加 **to be,** 試比較): 'She seemed (to be) angry.' 'She seemed (to be) an intelligent woman.' 'She seemed to be the leader of the group.'

2 × You should give help to anyone who seems that he needs it.
√ **You should give help to anyone who seems to need it.**
(你應當幫助那些看來需要幫助的人。)

> **it** (preparatory subject) + **seem** + **that** clause
> This is the only pattern in which **seem** may be followed by a **that** clause. Compare (注意: **seem** 如後接以 **that** 開始的子句, 則 **seem** 的主詞必須是作為 "先行主詞" 的 **it**。上面的錯句並非如此。試比較): 'It seems that John needs help.' 'John seems to need help.'

seldom See (見) NEVER 6

semester

√ **AmE Last semester there were a lot of complaints.**
(美式英語: 上學期人們有很多的不滿意見。)
√ **BrE Last term there were a lot of complaints.**
(英式英語; 譯文同上)

> The American school year is usually divided into two **semesters,** although it is also sometimes divided into three or four **terms.**
> 美國的學校一學年一般分為兩個 semester, 但有時也分為三或四個 **terms**。
> In Britain, the school year is usually divided into three **terms**.
> 英國的學校一學年一般分為三個 **terms**。

send

× I'll send you to the gate.
√ **I'll see you to the gate.**
(我送你到門口。)

> **send** = to cause to go or be taken to a place (意為: "派遣"、"傳遞")
> **see** (= to go with) someone to a place (意為: "陪送")

serious

× If we're serious in reducing the amount of crime, there should be stricter punishments.
√ **If we're serious about reducing the amount of crime, there should be stricter punishments.**
(如果我們要認真減少罪案發生, 就應當施行更為嚴厲的刑罰。)

> **be serious about** (doing) something, NOT **in**
> 注意: **be serious about** something 作 "認真對待某事" 解, be serious about doing something 作 "認真地做某事" 解, 這裡前置詞 **about** 不可用 **in** 替代。

shadow

× If the sun is too hot, perhaps you would like to sit in the shadow?
√ **If the sun is too hot, perhaps you would like to sit in the shade?**
(如果現在太陽太熱, 也許你願意坐到樹蔭下去吧?)

> **shade** = any area sheltered from the sun (有遮蔭的地方)
> **shadow** = a clear shape made by the shade of a particular person or thing (陰影)
> Compare (比較): 'The leafy branches provide plenty of shade.' 'The little boy saw his shadow on the ground.'

shall 1 × The next meeting of the heads of state shall take place in Vienna.
√ **The next meeting of the heads of state will take place in Vienna.**
(下屆國家首腦會議將在維也納舉行。)

For future reference, use **will** with the second and third person. **Shall** is used only with the first person (I/we).
第二、三人稱用的將來時態是 **will;** 只有第一人稱 (I/we) 用 **shall**。

2 × I shall be very grateful if you could help me with my problem.
√ **I should be very grateful if you could help me with my problem.**
(如果你能幫我解決問題, 我當十分感激。)

I should/would/'d be very grateful/pleased etc. if you could ..., NOT **shall**
在虛擬語氣中, 主句中的 **should/would/'d** 不可用 **shall** 替代。

3 × Finally, I'll like to thank you again for your hospitality.
√ **Finally, I'd like to thank you again for your hospitality.**
(最後, 我要再次感謝你的款待。)

I should/would/'d like to thank/ask etc. (polite) = I want to thank/ask etc. (意為: "我想感謝"、"我想請求" 等)

4 See (見) AFTER 6, AS LONG AS 1, CASE 2, IF 1, IMMEDIATELY 2, MOMENT 2, ONCE 3, UNTIL 2, WHEN 1, WHENEVER

shaved × He had a clean-shaved face.
√ **He had a clean-shaven face.**
(他的臉刮得很乾淨。)

The adjective, especially when used in compounds, is **shaven.** The past participle is usually **shaved** (注意: **shaven** 常用作形容詞, 用於複合詞中尤為明顯。**shave** 的過去分詞一般用 **shaved,** 例如): 'Have you shaved today?'

she See (見) THEY 1

sheep × A lot of cows and sheeps died because of the polluted water.
√ **A lot of cows and sheep died because of the polluted water.**
(很多牛羊因水的污染而死亡。)

> **Sheep** is the singular AND plural form.
> 注意: **sheep** 既是單數也是複數名詞。

shopping 1 × This morning I went for shopping.
√ **This morning I went shopping.**
(今天早晨我出去買東西了。)

> **go** + v-ing
> 按 **go** 後接帶 "-ing" 的動詞。
> Compare (比較): 'go fishing', 'go swimming', etc.

2 × It happened in the supermarket while I was doing my shoppings.
√ **It happened in the supermarket while I was doing my shopping.**
(這事發生的時候我正在超級市場買東西。)

> **Shopping** is an uncountable noun.
> 按 **shopping** 是不可數名詞

shortly 1 × She spoke very shortly about how they had lived during the war.
√ **She spoke very briefly about how they had lived during the war.**
(她很簡短地講了一下他們戰爭年代的生活情況。)

> **shortly** = impatiently; not politely (意為: "不耐煩地"; "不客氣地", 例如): 'He answered rather shortly that he was not the slightest bit interested.'
> **briefly** = for a short time (意為: "簡短地")

2 × Shortly, he said that the repair was not his responsibility.
√ **In short, he said that the repair was not his responsibility.**
(總而言之, 他説這次修理不在他的職責範圍之內。)

> **shortly** = soon (意為: "不久", 例如): 'I'll be back shortly.'
> **in short** = to sum up in a few words (意為: "簡言之")

shorts × He packed two shirts and a shorts.
√ **he packed two shirts and a pair of shorts.**
(他在箱子裡放進了兩件襯衣和一條短褲。)

> **Shorts** is a plural noun. Note the alternative (按 **shorts** 是複數名詞。注意另一種說法): 'some shorts'.

shout 1 × She made me so annoyed I felt like shouting to her.
√ **She made me so annoyed I felt like shouting at her.**
(她使我厭煩得簡直想對她大聲叫嚷。)

> **shout to** someone = call someone to attract their attention (指高聲呼喚以引人注意)
> **shout at** someone = speak to someone in a very loud voice, especially when angry (指大聲叫嚷, 尤其在憤怒時。)

side 1 × On the back side of the coat there were some dirty marks.
√ **On the back of the coat there were some dirty marks.**
(外衣的背部有些污漬。)
× You will find my name and address on the back side of this sheet.
√ **You will find my name and address on the back of this sheet.**
(在這張紙的背面, 你可找到我的名字和地址。)

> **on the back/front** of something (WITHOUT **side**)
> 在 **on the back/front** of something 中不用 **side**
> Note that if a thing has only two sides it is possible to say **on the other side** (注意: 如某物只有兩面, 那便可用 **on the other side,** 例如): 'My favourite songs are on the other side (of the record).'

2 × On the other side, I can understand why she feels disappointed.
√ **On the other hand, I can understand why she feels disappointed.**
(另一方面, 我能理解她所以感到失望的原因。)

> **on the one hand** … **/on the other hand** …, NOT **side**
> 漢語說的: "一方面 …, 另一方面 …", 英語應說: **on the one hand** …, **on the other hand,** 其中 **hand** 不可用 **side** 替代。

sightseeing × We are going to do a sightseeing tomorrow.
√ **We are going to do some sightseeing tomorrow.**
(我們明天要去遊覽。)

> **Sightseeing** is an uncountable noun.
> 按 **sightseeing** 是不可數名詞, 前面不加不定冠詞 "**a**"。

sign × One of her hobbies is collecting the signs of famous singers.
√ **One of her hobbies is collecting the signatures of famous singers.**
(她的一個愛好是收集著名歌星的簽名。)

> **sign** = something which is understood as having a particular meaning (意為: "記號", "標誌", 例如): 'a road sign'
> **signature** = a person's name written in that person's own handwriting on a cheque, formal letter, etc. (意為: "簽名")

since 1 × I am studying law since 1988.
√ **I have been studying law since 1988.**
(自一九八八年以來, 我一直在攻讀法律。)
× Since that journey, I never sailed again.
√ **Since that journey, I have never sailed again.**
(自從那次旅行以後, 我再也沒有乘船出海了。)

> When talking about an action or state which began in the past and continues into the present, use a present perfect tense.
> 談及從過去開始一直延續到現在的動作或狀態, 應用現在完成式。

2 × I have been living in London since four weeks now.
√ **I have been living in London for four weeks now.**
(我在倫敦已經住了四個星期了。)

since + beginning of period (按 **since** 後接一段時間中開始的那一點)
for + length of period (按 **for** 後接一段時間的長度)
Compare (試比較): 'I have been living in London for almost two years, since October 1988.' (自從一九八八年十月以來, 我已經在倫敦住了差不多兩年了。)

3 × I stayed in your hotel for three nights, since 23rd November to 26th November.
√ **I stayed in your hotel for three nights, from 23rd November to 26th November.**
(從十一月二十三日到二十六日, 我在你的旅館住了三晚。)

from ... to ... (從 ... 到 ..., 應用 **from ... to ...**, 例如): 'from Monday to Wednesday', 'from 7 a.m. to 3 p.m.', 'from 1947 to 1966'

4 × Since the last few years, unemployment has been increasing.
√ **Over/during the last few years, unemployment has been increasing.**
(近幾年, 失業率不斷上升。)

Since is used to indicate a point of time in the past (i.e. the starting point for an action or state which is still continuing in the present) (用 **since** 指從過去某一點時間開始但延續至現在, 例如): 'I've been living in Paris since July.'
Use **over/during** to talk about the period of time within which an action happens. (用 **over/during** 指一段時間中發生的動作。)

sincerely × Dear John, ... Yours sincerely ...
√ **Dear John, ... Yours/With love/With best wishes ...**
(親愛的約翰, ... 你的/愛你的/祝好 ...)

When writing to a friend or relative, do not end your letter **Yours sincerely** or **Yours faithfully.** These phrases are usually used in more formal letters.
寫信給朋友或親戚時, 結尾不要用 **Yours sincerely** 或 **Yours faithfully**。這些詞一般用於較正式的信件。

sit 1 × I looked for an empty sit at the other end of the plane.
√ **I looked for an empty seat at the other end of the plane.**
(我在機艙另一端找一個空位。)

> **Seat** /sit/ is a noun.
> 按 **seat** 是名詞。
> **Sit** /sɪt/ is a verb.
> 按 **sit** 是動詞。

2 See (見) ARMCHAIR

skilful × 'You are lucky to have such a skilful child,' she said.
√ **'You are lucky to have such a talented child,' she said.**
("你有這麼一個能幹的孩子真是幸運", 她說。)

> **skilful** = having or showing skill (gained from instruction and experience) (意為: "靈巧的", "有手藝的")
> **talented** = having or showing a natural ability to do something well (意為: "能幹的", "有才華的")

sleep 1 × I slept at ten o'clock last night.
√ **I went to sleep at ten o'clock last night.**
(我昨天晚上十點鐘入睡。)

> **sleep** = remain in the state of being asleep (睡着)
> **go to sleep** = fall asleep (i.e. enter the state of being asleep) (意為: "入睡")
> Compare (試比較): 'I went to bed at nine, went to sleep at ten, and slept until six this morning.' (我九點鐘就寢, 十點鐘入睡, 一覺睡到第二天早晨六點。)

2 × After showing the conductor my ticket, I started sleeping again.
√ **After showing the conductor my ticket, I went back to sleep.**
(給列車員看過車票後, 我又睡着了。)

> **go back to sleep** = fall asleep again (after an interruption) (意為: "又睡着了")

3 × I felt warm and relaxed and was almost sleeping when suddenly the telephone rang.

√ **I felt warm and relaxed and was almost asleep when suddenly the telephone rang.**
(我感到又溫暖又舒服, 剛要睡着, 電話鈴突然響了。)

> **Asleep** (adjective) can be used with **almost, nearly,** etc. when talking about a partial state.
> 按 **asleep** (形容詞) 可與 **almost, nearly** 並用, 說明 "快要睡着" 狀態。
> **Sleep** (verb) always refers to a complete state and cannot be qualified in this way.
> 按 **sleep** (動詞) 總是指 "完全睡着" 狀態, 不可用 **almost, nearly** 等詞修飾。

4 × I started sleeping and didn't wake up till the next morning.

√ **I fell asleep and didn't wake up till the next morning.**
(我睡着了, 並且一直睡到第二天早晨。)

> **Fall asleep** and **go to sleep** are the usual expressions.
> 按 **fall asleep** 和 **go to sleep** 是慣常用語。

5 × The child fell into sleep as soon as he got into bed.

√ **The child fell asleep as soon as he got into bed.**
(孩子一上牀就睡着了。)

> **fall asleep,** NOT **into**
> 按 **fall** 和 **asleep** 之間不可插入 **into**。

slide × One or two cars were sliding when they tried to stop because of the ice.

√ **One or two cars were skidding when they tried to stop because of the ice.**
(因為路面有冰, 有一、兩輛汽車在煞車時打滑了。)

> **slide** = to go smoothly over a surface (意為: "平穩而順暢地滑行", 例如): 'The children were happily sliding on the ice.'
> **skid** = to slide out of control, especially of a vehicle when the driver tries to stop quickly (意為: "失去控制的滑動, 尤指汽車煞不住車")

small

× Even his wife said he was a selfish, bad-tempered small man.

√ **Even his wife said he was a selfish, bad-tempered little man.**
(連他的妻子也說他這個小個子是個自私而又脾氣很壞的人。)

Unlike **small, little** can be used to express approval or disapproval (不同於 **small, little** 可用來表示褒義或貶義, 例如): 'a nasty little man', 'a beautiful little car'.

smash

× He ran out of the house and smashed the door behind him.

√ **He ran out of the house and slammed the door behind him.**
(他跑出房子, 使勁把門砰一聲關上。)

smash = break into pieces (意為: "打碎", 例如): 'I'm amazed that the plate didn't smash when you dropped it.' 'Those naughty children have smashed the window with their cricket ball.'
slam = (of a door, drawer, etc.) shut violently with a bang (意為: "砰一聲猛然關上")

smell

× Travelling can be very unpleasant, especially if the person sitting next to you smells garlic and old cheese.

√ **Travelling can be very unpleasant, especially if the person sitting next to you smells of garlic and old cheese.**
(旅行可以使人很不愉快, 如果坐在你旁邊的人帶着一身的大蒜和臭乾酪氣味時, 尤其如此。)

smell = perceive or recognize something by means of the nose (意為: "嗅到", 例如): 'I can smell smoke.'
smell of (onions etc.) = have or give off the smell of (onions etc.) (意為: "帶有/發出 … 氣味)

smile

× She smiled to me as if she knew me.

√ **She smiled at me as if she knew me.**
(她對我微笑, 好像認識我。)

× I thought I saw him smile on her.

√ **I thought I saw him smile at her.**
(我想我看見他對她笑了一笑。)

smile at someone, NOT **to** OR **on**
注意: **smile** 後接 **at** someone, 其中前置詞 **at** 不可用 **to** 或 **on** 替代。

smoke × We could see a thick black smoke coming out of the window.
√ **We could see thick black smoke coming out of the window.**
(我們可以看到一股濃黑的煙冒出窗外。)

Smoke is an uncountable noun.
按 **smoke** 一詞屬不可數名詞, 前面不可加不定冠詞 "**a**", 雖則在漢語裏, (濃) 煙之前, 可加 "一股"。

so 1 × The coat is new and is so in very good condition.
√ **The coat is new and so is in very good condition.**
(這外衣是新的, 所以這麼筆挺。)

When used as a conjunction, **so** must be placed at the beginning of the clause. Note the alternative (作為連接詞使用時, so 必須放在子句之首。注意可用另一種說法): 'The coat is new and is therefore in very good condition.'

2 × My English is so poor so my wife has to translate everything.
√ **My English is so poor that my wife has to translate everything.**
(我的英語很差, 所以我太太不得不翻譯每一句話。)

"so ... that ..." = to such a degree (意為: "如此 ... 乃至於 ...", 例如): 'She was so clever that all the universities wanted her.' 'The pianist played so badly that the audience walked out.'
Compare (試比較): 'My English is very poor so my wife has to translate everything.'

3 × I'm sure you'd never find so bad food in any other canteen.
√ **I'm sure you'd never find such bad food in any other canteen.**
(我相信無論你在哪一個食堂也找不到這麼差的飯菜。)

So cannot be used before an adjective which is immediately followed by a noun.
如果一個形容詞後面緊接着名詞, 則這個形容詞之前不能用 so。)
Compare (試比較): 'The food was so bad that nobody could eat it.' 'Nobody had ever tasted such bad food.'

4 See THAT 4

social **1** × The next election was won by the Social Party.
√ **The next election was won by the Socialist Party.**
(社會黨取得了下一屆選舉的勝利。)

social = concerning (life in a) society (意為: "社會的", 例如): 'The two children have different social backgrounds.'
socialist = concerning socialism (the political system that favours equality of opportunity and public as opposed to private ownership) (意為: "社會主義的")

2 × Our new neighbours are not very social.
√ **Our new neighbours are not very sociable.**
(我們的鄰居不愛交際。)

social = concerning (life in a) society (意為: "社會的")
sociable = friendly (意為: "友善的"; "愛交際的")

society × I was asked to give a talk about women and their role in the society.
√ **I was asked to give a talk about women and their role in society.**
(我應邀作了一次關於婦女和她們的社會作用的談話。)

Do not use **the** with **society** when it means 'people in general, considered as a single group'.
Compare (按 **society** 指整個社會時前面不加 **the,** 試比較): 'He joined the drama society.' (= a particular organization) (意為: "協會")

soft × She spoke very soft and nobody could hear her.
√ **She spoke very softly and nobody could hear her.**
(她說話聲音很小, 誰也聽不見。)

Soft is an adjective.
按 **soft** 是形容詞。
Softly is an adverb.
按 **softly** 是副詞。

solution × The ideal solution of this problem is for his wife to get a part-time job.
√ **The ideal solution to this problem is for his wife to get a part-time job.**
(解決這個問題的理想辦法是讓他妻子找一份半職的工作。)

a solution to a problem, NOT **of**
注意: **a solution** 後接 **to a problem,** 其中前置詞 **to** 不可用 **of** 替代。

some 1 × The rewind button worked properly for only some hours.
√ **The rewind button worked properly for only a few hours.**
(這個倒退按鈕只正常地工作了幾小時。)

some = several (意為: "一些")
a few = not many (意為: "不多", "三幾個")

2 × Do you have some questions?
√ **Do you have any questions?**
(你有什麼問題嗎?)

In questions and negative sentences, use **any,** NOT **some.**
問句和否定句中用 **any,** 不用 some。

somebody See (見) SOMEONE

someone 1 × There are someones who aren't afraid of punishment at all.
√ **There are some people who aren't afraid of punishment at all.**
(有些人根本就不怕懲罰。)

Someone and **somebody** do NOT have plural forms.
按 **someone** 和 **somebody** 沒有複數形式

2 × She hadn't seen someone for over a week.
√ **She hadn't seen anyone for over a week.**
(她有一個多星期沒見任何人。)
× Somehow he had to get on the train without being seen by someone.
√ **Somehow he had to get on the train without being seen by anyone.**
(無論如何, 他上火車的時候不能讓人發現。)

In a negative context, use **anyone/anybody,** NOT **someone/somebody.**
在否定句中應用 **anyone** 或 **anybody,** 而不用 **someone** 或 **somebody**。

3 × I ran over to the car to see if someone was injured.
√ **I ran over to the car to see if anyone was injured.**
(我向汽車跑過去, 看看有沒有人受傷。)

When talking about something unknown or uncertain, use **anyone/anybody,** NOT **someone/somebody** (如指的是未知或未肯定的事, 應用 **anyone** 或 **anybody,** 而不用 **someone** 或 **somebody,** 例如): 'Did you see anyone?' 'I doubt if anybody will object.'

4 × Perhaps someone of your staff has already found it.
√ **Perhaps one of your staff has already found it.**
(也許你的員工中已經有人找到了。)

one of + plural countable noun, NOT **someone of**
Note the alternative (注意: **one of** 之後可接複數可數名詞, 而 **someone of** 之後則不可。注意另一種説法): 'Perhaps someone on your staff has already found it.'

something 1 × By six o'clock I am too tired to do something else.
√ **By six o'clock I am too tired to do anything else.**
(到了六點鐘, 我已經累得什麼事也做不了。)

Note that **anything** is used in affirmative sentences which actually express a negative meaning (注意在肯定句中的 **anything** 實含否定意義, 例如): 'By six o'clock I am too tired to do anything else.' (= By six o'clock I am so tired that I cannot do anything else.)
Compare (試比較): 'too ill to eat any food', 'too busy to see anyone'

2 × At first we couldn't see something suspicious.
√ **At first we couldn't see anything suspicious.**
(起初我們看不出任何可疑的地方。)
× Does your country export something?
√ **Does your country export anything?**
(你們國家有什麼東西出口嗎?)

Something is usually used in affirmative sentences (**something** 一般用於肯定句, 例如): 'We could see something.'
Anything is usually used in negative sentences and questions (**anything** 一般用於否定句和問句, 例如): 'We couldn't see anything.' 'Can you see anything?'

3 × If the cassette is stuck, you'll have to use a knife or something like that.
√ **If the cassette is stuck, you'll have to use a knife or something.**
(如果磁帶卡住了, 你就必須用一把小刀之類的東西。)

... or something is an informal expression meaning '... or something like that' (**... or something** 屬口語體, 意為: "... 之類的東西", 例如): 'Why don't you buy her a book or something?'

somewhere × The bus service is so bad that it's almost impossible to get somewhere.
√ **The bus service is so bad that it's almost impossible to get anywhere.**
(公共汽車的服務很差; 你要是依賴它, 簡直是哪兒也去不成。)

Use **anywhere** (NOT **somewhere**) in a negative context.
在否定句中用 **anywhere**, 不用 **somewhere**。

soon × As it soon will be Christmas, I'm anxious to get the television repaired as quickly as possible.
√ **As it will soon be Christmas, I'm anxious to get the television repaired as quickly as possible.**
(聖誕節快到了, 我急於找人盡快把電視機修好。)

Soon is usually placed immediately after the (first) auxiliary verb (通常地, **soon** 緊接在第一個助動詞之後, 例如): 'Ann said she would soon have enough money to go on holiday.' When there is no auxiliary verb,

> **soon** is usually placed immediately before the main verb (如沒有助動詞, **soon** 一般放在主動詞之前, 例如): 'She soon had enough money.' However, when the main verb is **be**, **soon** is placed immediately after it (如主動詞是 **be**, 則 **soon** 緊接在主動詞之後, 例如): 'She was soon fit and well again.'

sooner See (見) NO SOONER

sorry × I really sorry about all the trouble I have caused you.
√ **I am really sorry about all the trouble I have caused you.**
(我給你帶來了那麼多的麻煩, 真是非常抱歉。)

> **Sorry** is an adjective, NOT a verb (按 **sorry** 是形容詞, 不是動詞, 例如): 'be sorry', 'feel sorry', 'look sorry', etc.

so that × He hadn't taken any warm clothes so that he felt cold.
√ **He hadn't taken any warm clothes so he felt cold.**
(他沒有帶什麼保暖衣服, 所以覺得冷了。)

> **So that** is used to express purpose (按 **so that** 用來表示目的, 例如): 'He took some warm clothes so that he wouldn't be cold.'
> **So** is used to talk about the result of an action.
> 按 **so** 用來説明行動的結果。

South See (見) NORTH

space × There are hundreds of millions of stars in the space.
√ **There are hundreds of millions of stars in space.**
(太空中有數以億計的恒星。)

> Do not use **the** when using **space** to mean 'everything beyond the Earth's atmosphere'.
> 按 **space** 指宇宙、太空時不用 **the**。

spare × They spare as much money as they can for their holidays.
√ **They save as much money as they can for their holidays.**
(他們盡量把錢省下來, 以作度假之用。)

spare = (1) have in excess and available (意指 1. "有剩餘可供使用", 例如): 'Do we have any money to spare this week? The baby could do with some new clothes.' (這星期我們有多餘的錢剩下來嗎? 嬰兒需要買一些新衣服了。)
(2) afford (to give) (2. "撥出, 勻出, 拿出", 例如): 'I'd like to watch the film but I can't spare the time.' (我倒是想看這電影, 可就是抽不出時間。)
save = set aside (意指 "節省, 儲存")

speak 1 × Only eight per cent of all Swiss are speaking Italian.
√ **Only eight per cent of all Swiss speak Italian.**
(全部瑞士人中只有百分之八講意大利語。)

Use the present simple tense for habitual actions.
表示習慣行動時用一般現在式。

2 × Neither of my parents speaks in English.
√ **Neither of my parents speaks English.**
(我父母都不會講英語。)

speak (English) = know (English) and use it habitually (意指講英語)
speak in (English) = use (English) to communicate on a particular occasion (意指用英語交談)
Compare (試比較): 'The guide speaks English, German, and Spanish but he'll be speaking in Spanish this afternoon because most of the visitors are from Spain.'

3 × She spoke that she would visit England in July.
√ **She said that she would visit England in July.**
(她說她將在七月訪英。)

Speak is NOT used as a reporting verb.
按 **speak** 不能用作一個傳意動詞。

4 × I could hear her speaking with herself in the kitchen.
√ **I could hear her talking to herself in the kitchen.**
(我能聽見她在廚房裏自言自語。)

talk to yourself, NOT **speak with**
按 **talk to** yourself 中的 **talk to** 不可用 **speak with** 替代。

5 See (見) LIE

specially

× I was surprised that she was late, specially since she usually arrived early.

√ **I was surprised that she was late, especially since she usually arrived early.**
(我對她這次遲到覺得很意外, 特別是因為她通常都是早到的。)

× A woman who works sometimes neglects her family, specially the children.

√ **A woman who works sometimes neglects her family, especially the children.**
(一個出來社會做事的女人有時會忽略了她的家人, 尤其是孩子。)

> **specially** = for a single special purpose (意為 "特殊地"、"專門地", 例如): 'The course has been specially prepared for young beginners.' 'I came here specially to see you.'
> **especially** = (1) particularly (意為 "特別是"、"尤其是", 例如): 'You need extra heating in the house—especially during the winter months.'
> (2) to an exceptional degree (意為 "格外地"、"份外地", 例如): 'The film will be especially interesting to those who are fond of water sports.'

spectacle

× On the first day of the holiday I broke my spectacle.

√ **On the first day of the holiday I broke my spectacles.**
(在假期的第一天我把眼鏡打破了。)

> **Spectacles** (= glasses) is a plural noun.
> 按 **spectacles** 是複數名詞。
> Compare (試比較): 'a pair of spectacles'.

speech

× I was invited to make a speech on the radio.

√ **I was invited to give a talk on the radio.**
(我應邀在廣播電台作一次講話。)

> A **speech** is usually made by a politician or by an important person at a meeting, social occasion, or dinner (作 "演說" 解, 例如): 'The Prime Minister's speech included a fierce attack on the unions.'
> A **talk** is usually informative, and often given by a lecturer (意為: "專題講話", 例如): 'The subject of Dr Chase's talk is "Solar Energy and the Nuclear Debate".'

speed 1 × Despite the traffic lights ahead, the car continued with the same speed.
√ **Despite the traffic lights ahead, the car continued at the same speed.**
(儘管前面有交通燈, 汽車繼續以同樣速度行駛。)

> **travel/move** etc. **at** (a certain) speed, NOT **with**
> 注意: **travel**、**move** 等詞與 **at** (a certain) speed 連用時, 前置詞 **at** 不可用 **with** 替代。

2 × The police stopped several drivers for overspeeding.
√ **The police stopped several drivers for speeding.**
(警察截住幾名超速的駕駛者。)

> **speeding** = driving faster than the speed limit (超速)
> There is no such verb as 'overspeed'.
> 英語中沒有 **overspeed** 這個動詞。

spend 1 × They don't have any money to spend for luxuries.
√ **They don't have any money to spend on luxuries.**
(他們沒什麼錢可以花在奢侈品上。)

> **spend** (an amount of) money **on** something, NOT **for**
> 指 "把 (一筆) 錢花在某物上" 用 '**spend** (an amount of) money **on** something', 其中前置詞 **on** 不可用 **for** 替代。

2 × Thank you for spending so much time to listen to our complaints.
√ **Thank you for spending so much time listening to our complaints.**
(感謝你花了這麼多時間聽取我們的投訴。)

> **spend time** + v-ing
> 按 **spend time** 後接帶 "-ing" 的動詞。

3 × We went to the cinema to spend the time until the train arrived.
√ **We went to the cinema to pass the time until the train arrived.**
(在火車到達之前我們去看電影消磨時間。)

> **pass (the) time** = do something in order to avoid doing nothing and being bored (意為消磨時間, 例如): 'On long train journeys the children pass the time by playing cards.'

4 × She spends most of her free time on reading.
√ **She spends most of her free time reading.**
(她大部份的空閑時間花在看書上。)
× We spent the whole day in shopping.
√ **We spent the whole day shopping.**
(我們花了一整天的時間買東西。)

> **spend** (a period of) **time** + v-ing WITHOUT **on** OR **in**
> 花時間於...上, 用 **spend** (a period of) **time** 後接帶 "-ing" 的動詞, 動詞前不用加 **on** 或 **in** 。

5 × We spent a very good time in New York.
√ **We had a very good time in New York.**
(我們在紐約過得很愉快。)

> **have a good time** (= enjoy yourself), NOT **spend**
> 按 **have a good time** 相當於 enjoy yourself, 其中的動詞 **have** 不可用 **spend** 替代。

spite **1** × Inspite of our advice, she agreed to marry him.
√ **In spite of our advice, she agreed to marry him.**
(她不理會我們的勸告, 答應了嫁給他。)

> **In spite of** is ALWAYS three words.
> 按 **in spite of** 總是分開寫的三個詞, 不應寫成 inspite of。

2 × They refused to play in the rain in spite of the crowd protested.
√ **They refused to play in the rain in spite of the crowd's protests.**
(他們不顧廣大觀眾的抗議, 拒絕在雨中比賽。)

> **In spite of** is a preposition (NOT a conjunction) and cannot be followed by a subject and verb.
> 按 **in spite of** 是由詞組構成的前置詞, 而不是連接詞, 因此其後不能接一個子句; 只能接名詞或片語。

3 × I believe that every crime, in spite of the circumstances, should be severely punished.
√ **I believe that every crime, regardless of the circumstances, should be severely punished.**
(我認為任何一種犯罪, 不論情況如何, 都應嚴加懲處。)

In spite of = despite (意為: "不管"、"不顧", 例如): 'The plane took off in spite of the bad weather.' (= although the weather was bad)
regardless of = without considering or taking notice of (意為 "不考慮"、"不在乎"、"無論", 例如): 'The plane will take off, regardless of the weather.' (= no matter whether the weather is good or bad)

sport **1** × The magazine is about sports.
√ **The magazine is about sport.**
(這是一本體育雜誌。)

sport/s (countable) = a particular type of sport (是個可數名詞, 意為一項或多項運動, 例如): 'Football and tennis are popular sports.'
sport (uncountable) = sport in general (是個不可數名詞, 意為 "體育運動", 是個總稱, 例如): 'Sport is good for your health.'

2 × She bought a bright red sport car.
√ **She bought a bright red sports car.**
(她買了一輛鮮紅色的賽車。)

In most compounds, use **sports**, NOT **sport** (在與其他詞構成複合詞中, 大都用 **sports**, 不用 **sport**, 例如): 'sports centre', 'sports jacket'.
Note, however, that in some American English compounds, both are possible (但應注意, 有些美式英語的複合詞, 兩者都可以用, 例如): 'sport(s) center', 'sport(s) jacket'.

spring See (見) SUMMER

staff × There are over eighty staffs at the new college.
√ **There are over eighty members of staff at the new college.**
(這所新學校有八十多名教職員工。)

Staff refers not to a single person but to a group. 按 **staff** 不是指個人而是一個群體。
Note the alternative (注意另一種說法, 例如): 'The new college has a staff of over eighty.'

stand × She's always very impatient and can't stand to have to wait.
√ **She's always very impatient and can't stand having to wait.**
(她總是非常不耐煩, 一等人就受不了。)

> **can't/couldn't stand** + v-ing
> 按 **can't (couldn't) stand** 後接帶 "-ing" 的動詞, 這裡 **stand** 作 "忍受, 忍耐" 解。

start See (見) SLEEP 2, 4

statistic × Many statistic studies show that the more sophisticated a society, the smaller the number of housewives.
√ **Many statistical studies show that the more sophisticated a society, the smaller the number of housewives.**
(很多統計研究表明, 社會越先進, 家庭主婦的人數就越少。)

> **Statistic** is a noun.
> 按 **statistic** 是名詞。
> **Statistical** is an adjective.
> 按 **statistical** 是形容詞。

steal 1 × They can't afford to buy food and so they steal people.
√ **They can't afford to buy food and so they steal from people.**
(他們買不起食品就偷人家的。)

> Note the alternative (注意另一種說法): 'They can't afford to buy food and so they steal.'

2 × The bank in our town has been stolen twice this year.
√ **The bank in our town has been robbed twice this year.**
(我們鎮上的銀行今年已經兩次被搶劫。)

> **steal** money, a watch, etc, BUT **rob** a person, a bank, or a post office
> 注意: "偷錢"、"偷錶" 等用 **steal**, 但 "搶劫人、銀行或郵局" 用 **rob**。

still

× It is my first time abroad and so I feel still excited and confused.

√ **It is my first time abroad and so I still feel excited and confused.**
(這是我第一次到國外，所以我仍然感到興奮和手足無措。)

× My country still is not very rich, but at least everyone has enough food to eat.

√ **My country is still not very rich, but at least everyone has enough food to eat.**
(我國還不很富裕，但至少每個人都能吃飽。)

When there is no auxiliary verb, **still** is placed immediately before the main verb (沒有助動詞時，**still** 緊放在主動詞之前，例如): 'I still feel excited.' If the main verb is **be, still** is placed immediately after it (如主動詞是 **be, still** 就緊接其後，例如): 'It's still dark outside.' Otherwise **still** goes immediately after the (first) auxiliary verb (在其他場合 **still** 緊接 (第一個) 助動詞之後，例如): 'You can't still be feeling tired.'

stimulus

× Coffee is quite a strong stimulus.

√ **Coffee is quite a strong stimulant.**
(咖啡是一種相當強的興奮劑。)

stimulus (non-medical 非藥物的) = something which causes or encourages activity or greater effort (意為:
"刺激"，例如): 'The new textbook provided a good stimulus for both teachers and students.'
stimulant (medical 藥物的) = a drug, medicine, etc. which causes or encourages activity in the mind or body (意為: "興奮劑")

stop 1

× He was very tired but that didn't stop him to walk even further.

√ **He was very tired but that didn't stop him from walking even further.**
(他已經很累了，但也沒有使他停下腳步。)

stop someone (**from**) + v-ing = prevent someone (from) doing something (意為 "阻止某人做某事")

2

× The child couldn't stop from talking.

√ **The child couldn't stop talking.**
(那孩子無法停止說話。)

stop + v-ing (WITHOUT **from**) = cease an activity (按 **stop** 後接帶 "-ing" 的動詞, 不必插入 **from**, 意為 "停止做某事"): 'I've stopped smoking.'
Compare (試比較): 'The rain stopped us from going out.' (= prevented us from going out) (意為 "阻止我們出去")

3 × I stopped to play the piano at the age of eight.
√ **I stopped playing the piano at the age of eight.**
(我到了八歲就沒有彈鋼琴了。)
× The child loved toys and couldn't stop to look at them.
√ **The child loved toys and couldn't stop looking at them.**
(那孩子喜歡玩具, 一刻不停地看着它們。)

stop + v-ing = cease or discontinue an activity (**stop** 後接帶 "-ing" 的動詞表示 "停止或不再繼續去做一個動作"。)
stop + to-v = halt or pause (in order to do something) (**stop** 後接帶 to 的動詞, 表示 "停下來去做某一件事", 如): 'Although I was in a hurry, I stopped to talk to
him.' (雖然我很匆忙, 我還是停下來跟他說話。)

storey × They live on the second storey.
√ **They live on the second floor.**
(他們住在三樓。)

A building has (a number of) **storeys** or **floors**. However, it is usual to say that a person lives on a particular **floor**, NOT **storey** (說一幢大廈有好幾層樓, 可用 **storeys** 或 **floor** 以表達 "層樓" 這概念。但一般說住在幾樓用 **floor**, 不用 **storey**, 例如): 'My flat is on the seventh floor.'
Note the American spelling (注意美式拼法是): **story**.

strange × I'm sure you will recognize the coat because it is very strange.
√ **I'm sure you will recognize the coat because it is very unusual.**
(我肯定你會認出這件上衣, 因為它很特別。)

strange (usually derogatory) = odd; peculiar (意為: "奇怪的")
unusual = uncommon; rare (意為: "與眾不同的"; "少見的")

strong See (見) PUNISHMENT

strongly

× When the plane took off, she held my hand strongly and began to cry.

√ **When the plane took off, she held my hand tightly and began to cry.**
(飛機起飛時, 她使勁握我的手, 哭了起來。)

> **hold/grasp/grip** something **tightly**, NOT **strongly**
> 指 "緊緊地握住某物", 用 **'hold/grasp/grip** something **tightly'**, 這裡 **tightly** 不可用 **strongly** 替代。
> **strongly** = (1) noticeably (顯著地, 例如): 'He smelt strongly of beer.'
> = (2) urgently (意為: "懇切地", "極力地", 例如): 'I strongly advise you to think again.'

studio

√ **AmE She lives in a small studio in London.**
(美式英語: 在倫敦, 她住在一個小房間內。)

√ **BrE She lives in a small bedsitter in London.**
(英式英語: 譯文同上)

> **studio** (American English)/**bedsitter** (British English) = a single rented room in which a person lives and sleeps (房間)
> Note that in British English **studio** means 'a room where a painter or photographer works' or '(a part of) a building where a film is made.'
> 注意英式英語中的 **studio** 指 "畫家或攝影家的工作室" 或 "攝影棚"。

subconscious

× The driver of the car was taken to hospital subconscious.

√ **The driver of the car was taken to hospital unconscious.**
(送去醫院時, 駕車者已失去知覺。)

> **subconscious** (of thoughts or desires) = existing or occurring in the mind without the person being aware of it (意為: "下意識的", 例如): 'His dream about crossing the ocean single-handed probably arose from a subconscious desire for fame.'
> **unconscious** (of a person) = without consciousness (沒有知覺的)

subject

× The subject of my thesis is about women in the popular press.
√ **The subject of my thesis is women in the popular press.**
(我的論文主題是大眾新聞中的婦女。)

> **Subject** is NOT followed by **about**.
> 在 **subject** 一詞之後不接 **about**。
> Note the alternative (注意另一種説法): 'My thesis is about women in the popular press.'

succeed

× Not many of us succeed to achieve our ambitions.
√ **Not many of us succeed in achieving our ambitions.**
(我們之中沒有多少人能實現自己的抱負。)

> To express the idea of having the ability to do something, you can use both **manage to** (do something) and **succeed in** (doing something). The latter is rather formal.
> 如需表示自己有能力做好某事, 可使用 **manage to** (後接原形動詞) 和 **succeed in** (後接帶 "-ing" 的動詞) 這兩個動詞片語。後者是較正規的書面用語。

successful

× Has the regime been successful to reform the society?
√ **Has the regime been successful in reforming the society?**
(這個政權在社會改革方面已取得成功了嗎?)

> **(be) successful in** + v-ing
> 按 **(be) successful in** 後接帶 "-ing" 的動詞。

such 1

× I was such in a hurry that I forgot my coat.
√ **I was in such a hurry that I forgot my coat.**
(我匆忙得連上衣都忘了。)

> When used as a predeterminer, **such** is placed immediately before **a/an**. It NEVER comes before a preposition.
> 作為前置限定詞, **such** 應緊放在 **a/an** 之前, 而從不位於介詞之前。

2 × She was always a such intelligent woman.
✓ **She was always such an intelligent woman.**
(她向來是一個這麼聰敏的女人。)

such + **a/an** + adjective + noun
注意以下詞語排列的順序: **such** 先接 **a/an**, 然後接形容詞, 再接名詞。

suddenly × Late one evening, as I was getting into the bath, suddenly I heard a strange noise.
✓ **Late one evening, as I was getting into the bath, I suddenly heard a strange noise.**
(一天深夜, 我正要跨進浴缸時忽然聽見奇怪的響聲。)

When there is no auxiliary verb, **suddenly** is placed immediately before the main verb (沒有助動詞時, **suddenly** 緊放在主動詞之前): 'He suddenly stopped talking.' If the main verb is **be**, **suddenly** is placed immediately after it (如果主動詞是 **be**, **suddenly** 就緊接其後): 'He was suddenly all alone.' Otherwise **suddenly** goes immediately after the (first) auxiliary verb (在其他情況中 **suddenly** 應緊接(第一個) 助動詞之後): 'He has suddenly stopped smoking.'
Note also the use of **suddenly** at the beginning of a sentence, where it tends to have a more dramatic effect (注意 **suddenly** 位於句首具有更加生動的效果): 'Suddenly, there was a loud crash.' 'Suddenly, two strange men appeared in the room.'

suffer × The woman was so unpleasant that not one of us could suffer her.
✓ **The woman was so unpleasant that not one of us could tolerate her.**
(這女人令人討厭得我們誰也受不了。)

Suffer is no longer used with the meaning 'tolerate' except in a literary or religious context.
除了在文學作品或宗教語境中外, **suffer** 現已不含 "tolerate (忍受)" 之意。

suggest 1 × She suggested to go to the zoo.
✓ **She suggested going to the zoo.**
(她建議去動物園。)

suggest + v-ing
按 **suggest** 後接帶 "-ing" 的動詞。

2 × I suggest you buying the magazine too.
√ **I suggest you buy the magazine too.**
(我建議你也買這本雜志。)
× I suggest you to take more exercise.
√ **I suggest you take more exercise.**
(我建議你多做體操。)

> **suggest** (that) someone **do** something
> 按 **suggest** 後接受賓語從句時, 從句中的主動詞總是用其原型, 即不帶 to 的動詞。

suit 1 × All the rooms in the hotel were occupied except for the honeymoon suit.
√ **All the rooms in the hotel were occupied except for the honeymoon suite.**
(除了蜜月套房以外, 旅館里所有的房間已住滿。)

> **a suit** /sut/ **of clothes** BUT **a suite** /swit/ **of rooms** (in a hotel)
> 指 "一套服裝", 用 '**a suit of clothes**', 指 "(旅館的)套房", 用 **a suite of rooms**。

2 × This type of work suits to many people.
√ **This type of work suits many people.**
(這種工作適合許多人做。)

> something **suits** someone WITHOUT **to**
> 指 "某物適合某人", 用 'something **suits** someone', 不用 **to**。

suitable × I did not feel suitable to a career in medicine.
√ **I did not feel suited to a career in medicine.**
(我覺得自己不能適應醫藥這一行業。)

> **suitable (for)**=right or appropriate (意為: "對 ... 適合", "適合於", 例如): 'The film isn't really suitable for children.' 'We would like to give her the job but her qualifications aren't suitable.'
> **(be/feel) suited to**=(be/feel) the right or appropriate person for a particular situation (意為: "對 ... 感到適應", 例如): 'He's not suited to live in a big city.'

summer × In Norway the weather in the summers is usually about the same as in England.
√ **In Norway the weather in (the) summer is usually about the same as in England.**
(在挪威, 夏天的天氣通常和英國的一樣。)

in (the) spring/summer/autumn/winter = each spring/summer/autumn/winter (泛指春/夏/秋/冬)

sunken × Within three minutes the ship had sunken.
√ **Within three minutes the ship had sunk.**
(三分鐘內這艘船就沉下去了。)

sink, sinking, sank, sunk
按 **sink** 的現在分詞為 **sinking**, 過去式為 **sank**, 過去分詞為 **sunk**。
Sunken is the adjective (**sunken** 是形容詞, 例如): 'a sunken ship'.

superior 1 × The second hotel was superior than the first one.
√ **The second hotel was superior to the first one.**
(第二家旅館比第一家要高級。)

superior to something, NOT **than**
指 "比某事物好/強的", 用 '**superior to** something', 其中前置詞 **to** 不可用 **than** 替代。

2 × It was difficult to decide which of the designs was more superior.
√ **It was difficult to decide which of the designs was superior.**
(很難決定究竟哪一種設計要好些。)

Superior has no comparative form.
按 **superior** 沒有比較級形式。

supply × We shall supply you everything you need.
√ **We shall supply you with everything you need.**
(我們將向您提供您所需要的一切物品。)

supply someone **with** something
指 "向某人提供某物", 用 '**supply** someone **with** something', 注意前置詞要用 **with**。

support

× He couldn't support the way his father used to shout at him.

√ **He couldn't tolerate the way his father used to shout at him.**

(他受不了父親老是向他大叫大嚷的態度。)

> **Support** is NOT used with the meaning 'tolerate' or 'put up with'.
> **support** 不含"忍受"之意。

suppose **1**

× My wife supposes to have left her coat in the cloakroom.

√ **My wife supposes that she has left her coat in the cloakroom.**

(我太太以為把上衣忘在衣帽間了。)

> **suppose + that** clause
> 按 **suppose** 後接以 **that** 開始的子句。

2

× All their products are suppose to be guaranteed for six months.

√ **All their products are supposed to be guaranteed for six months.**

(他們所有的產品理應保用六個月。)

> **be supposed** (WITH final **d**) to be/do something
> 按 **be supposed** (以 **d** 結尾) 後接 to be/do something, 作"應該","理應"解。

3

× It is a very unusual coat so I suppose you will not have any trouble finding it.

√ **It is a very unusual coat so I don't suppose you will have any trouble finding it.**

(這是一件與眾不同的上衣, 所以我認為你要找到它不會有什麼困難。)

> When the clause following **suppose** contains a negative idea, **suppose** is made negative and the verb that follows is positive.
> 按 **suppose** 後的從句是否定的時候, 否定詞應與 **suppose** 並用, 後面的動詞則是肯定的。

4 × Since the machine is still under guarantee, I suppose I won't be charged for the repairs.

✓ **Since the machine is still under guarantee, I assume I won't be charged for the repairs.**
(由於機器仍在受保期間, 我認為我不用付修理費。)

> **suppose** = think something is likely; imagine (意為: "猜想"、"以為", 例如): 'If she's lost her umbrella, I suppose I'll have to lend her mine.'
> **assume** = accept that something is true (without being told) and behave or act accordingly (意為: "認定"、"推想")

sure × I always buy my ticket in advance to make sure about getting a seat.

✓ **I always buy my ticket in advance to make sure of getting a seat.**
(我是一定要有座位的, 所以總是預先購票。)

> **make sure of** (doing) something, NOT **about**
> 注意: **make sure of** 作 "將 ... 拿到手; 將 ... 弄明白" 解, 後接 something 或 doing something, 前置詞 **of** 不可用 **about** 替代。

surely 1 × It was an absolutely terrible flight. The next time I go to Rio, I will surely go by train.

✓ **It was an absolutely terrible flight. The next time I go to Rio, I will definitely go by train.**
(那次坐飛機去里約熱內盧可怕極了, 下次再去我肯定會坐火車。)

> **Surely** is used to express a strong belief (or disbelief) in the likelihood of something and often to encourage the listener to express agreement (按 **surely** 一詞意為 "必然", "一定", 用以表示對某事深信不疑或全然不信, 往往是要對方同意自己, 例如): 'Surely they should have arrived by now!' 'A twenty-dollar parking fine! Surely someone's made a mistake!' 'Surely a man like Harry couldn't have done such a terrible thing!'
> **Definitely** expresses a sense of certainty about a fact or facts. (按 **definitely** 一詞意為 "肯定地", "必定", 用以表示對某事或某些事情有絕對把握, 例如: 'That answer is definitely true.' 'That was definitely the best play I've seen all year.')

2 × He said he felt nervous because of all the recent air disasters. Surely I became worried too.
√ **He said he felt nervous because of all the recent air disasters. Naturally I became worried too.**
(他說因為最近發生這麼多空難，他很害怕。我自然也感到擔心。)

> **surely** = I feel sure that (意為: "一定"、"必然")
> **naturally** = as one would expect; of course (意為: "當然"、"自然")

surprise 1 × The young woman looked very surprise to see me.
√ **The young woman looked very surprised to see me.**
(這位年青女子見到我顯得大為驚訝。)

> **Surprise** is a verb and a noun.
> **surprise** 是動詞也是名詞。
> **Surprised** is an adjective.
> **surprised** 是形容詞。

2 × That these people commit crimes is not surprising me.
√ **That these people commit crimes does not surprise me.**
(這些人犯罪並不使我感到意外。)

> The verb **surprise** is NOT used in progressive tenses.
> 動詞 **surprise** 不用進行式。
> Compare (比較): 'That these people commit crimes is not surprising.'
> **Surprising** is an adjective.
> 按 **surprising** 是形容詞。

3 × At my surprise, the whole house was empty.
√ **To my surprise, the whole house was empty.**
(使我驚奇的是，整所房子竟是空的。)

> **to** my/his/their etc. **surprise**, NOT **at**
> 注意: **to** my/his/their 等後接 **surprise**, 用以修飾整個句子, 作 "使某人驚奇的是" 解, 前置詞 **to** 不可用 **at** 替代。

surprised

× I was very surprised learning that you had decided to go to medical school.

√ **I was very surprised to learn that you had decided to go to medical school.**

(聽說你決定要學醫, 我大為驚訝。)

> **be surprised** + to-v
> 注意: **be surprised** 後接帶 to 的動詞。

sympathetic

× He's a selfish, greedy man and not at all sympathetic.

√ **He's a selfish, greedy man and not at all likeable.**

(他是個自私、貪婪的人, 一點也不叫人喜歡。)

> **sympathetic** = feeling or showing sympathy (有同情心的): 'He expected people to be sympathetic because he was an orphan.'
> **likeable** = easy to like (令人喜歡的)

take 1

× A few minutes later an ambulance arrived and took the injured man.

√ **A few minutes later an ambulance arrived and took the injured man away.**

(幾分鐘以後, 來了一輛救護車, 把傷者接走了。)

> **Take** (= carry, lead, or move) is used with adverbs such as **away**, **out**, etc. or with a phrase that refers to a place (注意: **take** 解作 "搬、拿" 解時, 應與 **away**、**out** 等副詞或與表示地點的片語連用): 'I took her to the cinema.'
> Note the alternative (注意: 也可換另一說法): 'A few minutes later an ambulance arrived and collected the injured man.'

2

× Unfortunately my studies take a lot of time.

√ **Unfortunately my studies take up a lot of time.**

(遺憾的是, 我的學業佔了很多時間。)

> **take up** an amount of time or space = occupy an amount of time or space
> 注意: 指佔用時間或空間應用 **take up**。

3 × When you come to dinner on Sunday, take your fiancée with you so I can meet her.
√ **When you come to dinner on Sunday, bring your fiancée with you so I can meet her.**
(星期天你來吃飯的時候, 把你的未婚妻帶來, 讓我見見她。)

> **Bring** is used for movement towards the place where the speaker is, was, or intends to be (or towards the person being talked about) (按 **bring** 意為 "帶來", 例如): 'She asked the nurse to bring her a drink of water.'
> **Take** is used for movement in other directions.
> 注意: **take** 意為 "帶走" 或 "帶到別處去"。

4 See DINNER, MEAL, PERMISSION 2

take notice of See (見) NOTICE 3

take up × As soon as the plane took up, I realized I had forgotten my coat.
√ **As soon as the plane took off, I realized I had forgotten my coat.**
(飛機一起飛, 我就意識到忘記了帶大衣了。)

> **take off** (of an aeroplane/airplane) = leave the ground, NOT **take up**
> 指 "(飛機) 起飛", 用 **take off**; **take off** 不可用 **take up** 替代。

talk 1 √ **AmE I didn't want to talk with him because I was in a hurry.**
(美式英語: 我當時很匆忙, 所以不想跟他說話。)
√ **BrE I didn't want to talk to him because I was in a hurry.**
(英式英語: 譯文同上)

> In British English, use **talk to** someone (**about** something), NOT **with**.
> 注意: 如説 "(就某事) 跟某人談話", 英式英語只用 **talk to** someone (about something), 不用 **talk with**。
> In American English, both **to** and **with** are possible.
> 注意: 美式英語則 **talk to** 和 **talk with** someone 都用。

2 × He talked that he had just arrived from Beijing.
√ **He said that he had just arrived from Beijing.**
(他説他剛從北京來。)

Talk is NOT used as a reporting verb.
注意: **talk** 一詞不可用作傳意動詞, 即其後不接受詞子句。

tall × I prefer rooms with tall ceilings.
√ **I prefer rooms with high ceilings.**
(我喜歡天花板高的房間。)

tall = the distance from bottom to top (指 "從底到頂的距離", 例如): 'a tall person', 'a tall tree'
high = the distance (of the uppermost point) above the ground (指 "從地面到最高點", 例如): 'a high shelf', 'a high altitude', 'a high mountain'

taste 1 × I buy all my family's clothes because my husband has such a bad taste.
√ **I buy all my family's clothes because my husband has such bad taste.**
(全家的衣服都由我買, 因為我丈夫的審美觀極差。)

(have/show) **excellent/good/poor taste** WITHOUT **a**
按 **taste** 作 "審美觀"、"欣賞力" 解是不可數名詞, 如與 (have/show) **excellent/good/poor** 連用, 則形容詞之前不能加冠詞 "**a**"。

2 See (見) SOUND 4

tasteful × The food was excellent and very tasteful.
√ **The food was excellent and very tasty.**
(菜餚十分精美可口。)

tasteful = approved by people with good taste (i. e. people who have the ability to choose or recognize good art, music, clothes, style, behaviour, etc.) (意為: "高格調的", "雅致的", "有欣賞力的", 例如): 'The design of the room was very tasteful—pale colours, matching fabrics, and soft corner lighting.' (房間的佈置很雅致: 清淡的色調、配搭適宜的窗簾和牆角落柔和的燈光。)
tasty (of food) = having a pleasant taste (i.e. a pleasant sensation on the tongue) (指食物 "美味的", "可口的", 例如): 'a tasty meal'

tax × Too many people are given taxes instead of being sent to prison.

√ **Too many people are given fines instead of being sent to prison.**
(很多人只被處以罰款, 而未被監禁。)

> **tax** = a sum of money paid to the government according to the amount a person earns and the things a person buys (意為: "稅", 例如): 'The tax on wine has been increased.' 'income tax'
> **fine** = a sum of money paid as a penalty by a person who breaks the law (意為: "罰款", 例如): 'a parking fine'

teach × We are taught in reading, writing, and in English grammar.

√ **We are taught reading, writing, and English grammar.**
(老師教我們讀、寫和英文文法。)

> **be taught** something WITHOUT **in**
> 按 **be taught** 後接 something, 不必用 **in**。

technique × The main cause of unemployment is modern technique.

√ **The main cause of unemployment is modern technology.**
(引致失業的主要原因是現代科技的發展。)

> **technique** = a (skilled) way of doing something (指某種專門技術)
> **technology** = all the scientific theories, methods, and processes that are used in industry (指整體的科學技術)

telephone See (見) PHONE

television See (見) RADIO

tell 1 × He told that he hadn't eaten anything for over a week.

√ **He told them that he hadn't eaten anything for over a week.**
(他告訴他們, 他有一個多星期沒吃東西了。)

√ **He said that he hadn't eaten anything for over a week.**
(他說他有一個多星期沒吃東西了。)

× He had been married twice, he told, and had four children.

√ **He had been married twice, he told me, and had four children.**
(他告訴我, 他結過兩次婚而且有四個孩子。)

√ **He had been married twice, he said, and had four children.**
(他說他結過兩次婚而且有四個孩子。)

> Unlike **say**, **tell** (as a reporting verb) is used with an indirect object.
> 注意: **tell** 和 **say** 的用法不同: **say** 之後可直接用受詞子句, 而 **tell** (用作傳意動詞時) 之後要用一間接受詞。

2 × John said that he was trying to get to London. 'That's where I'm going,' told the man.

√ **John said that he was trying to get to London. 'That's where I'm going,' said the man.**
(約翰說他正設法前往倫敦。那男子便說: "這正是我要去的地方。")

> **Tell** must be followed by a grammatical object and is usually used with indirect (reported) speech (注意: **tell** 必須後接受詞, 而且通常與間接引語並用, 例如): 'The man told John (that) he was going to London.'

3 × Please tell to Mr Young that I am looking forward to meeting him.

√ **Please tell Mr Young that I am looking forward to meeting him.**
(請告訴楊先生我希望和他會晤。)

> **tell** something **to** someone (指 "告知某人某事", 既可用 **tell** something **to** someone, 例如): 'Please tell the news to Mrs Patel.' BUT **tell** someone something WITHOUT **to** (也可用 **tell** someone something, 但其中不需加 **to**, 例如): 'They've told Mrs Patel the news.'

4 × Can you tell me where should I go to buy a ticket?

√ **Can you tell me where I should go to buy a ticket?**
(你能告訴我該去哪裏買票嗎?)

When the object of the sentence is a **wh-** clause, the subject and verb in the **wh-** clause do NOT change places.
如句中的受詞是一個以 "wh-" 的詞開始的子句, 則這子句的主語和動詞無需調換位置。

5 × My teacher told me not feel shy.
√ **My teacher told me not to feel shy.**
(我老師叫我不要怕羞。)

tell someone **(not) to do** something
"叫別人 (不要) 做某事", 可用 **tell** someone (**not**) **to do** something。注意: **tell** someone 之後接帶 **to** 的動詞。

6 × Kitty was always telling about herself and her problems.
√ **Kitty was always talking about herself and her problems.**
(吉蒂老是講自己的事情和她的難題。)

tell someone **about** something BUT **talk about** something
注意: "告知某人某事", 可用 **tell** someone **about** something, 如說 "談論某事", 則用 **talk about** something。

tempo × He stopped running when he saw the dog and then continued in a slower tempo.
√ **He stopped running when he saw the dog and then continued at a slower pace.**
(他看見那狗就停止跑步, 然後放慢腳步繼續走路。)

tempo = the speed at which a piece of music is/should be played (意為: 音樂的節拍, 例如): 'Suddenly the band broke into a faster tempo.'
pace = the speed at which a person walks or runs (意為: 人走路或跑步的速度)

term See (見) SEMESTER

test × On my first day at the school, I had to join a test.
√ **On my first day at the school, I had to take a test.**
(我第一天上學時, 必須參加一次測試。)

take/do a test, NOT **join**
(**take/do a test** 中動詞 **take** 或 **do** 不可用 **join** 替代。)

than 1 × Women have the same abilities than men.
√ **Women have the same abilities as men.**
(婦女具有與男人同樣的能力。)

> **the same ... as**, NOT **than**
> 用了 **the same**, 其後必須用 **as** 而不用 **than**。

2 See (見) PREFER 3, 4

thank 1 × I thank you very much for your last letter.
√ **Thank you very much for your last letter.**
(謝謝你最近的來信。)

> **I** and **we** are used with **thank** only in a rather formal context (**I** 和 **we** 只在正式的語境中才與 **thank** 一起使用, 例如): 'I should like to thank you for all your help.' 'We can't thank you enough.'

2 × First, I thank you for answering my letter.
√ **First, I should like to thank you for answering my letter.**
√ **First, may I thank you for answering my letter.**
(首先, 承蒙作答, 不勝感謝。)

> Note the less formal alternative (注意: 較隨便的方式是): 'Thank you for answering my letter.'

3 × Thank you very much that you have agreed to help us.
√ **Thank you very much for agreeing to help us.**
(感謝你同意幫助我們。)

> **thank** someone **for** + v-ing
> 注意: **thank** someone **for** 後接帶 "-ing" 的動詞。

thanks × First of all, thanks for your most interesting question.
√ **First of all, thank you for your most interesting question.**
(首先, 感謝你提了極有趣的問題。)

> **Thanks** is informal.
> 用 **thanks** 時, 語氣隨便。
> **Thank you** is more formal.
> **thank you** 的用法較為正式。

that 1 × The weather has been very good, except for two days that it rained.

√ **The weather has been very good, except for two days when it rained.**

(天氣一直都很好, 就是有兩天下了雨。)

When the meaning is 'on/in/during which' (referring to time), use **when**, NOT **that**. Compare (如與時間有關而本意又相當於 on/in/during which, 即 "當其時" 之意, 則子句應用以 **when** 開始的句型而不用以 **that** 開始的句型, 試比較): 'I shall always remember the two days that I spent in Paris.'

2 × I was shocked by the sight that I could hardly speak.

√ **I was so shocked by the sight that I could hardly speak.**

(看到這情景我大為震驚, 簡直說不出話來了。)

so + adjective/adverb + **that** clause (表示 "如此 … 以致於 …", 可用 **so** 後接形容詞或副詞再接以 **that** 開始的子句, 例如): 'I'm so tired that I can't keep awake.' 'He spoke so quickly that nobody could understand him.'

3 × He closed the door quietly that nobody would hear him.

√ **He closed the door quietly so that nobody would hear him.**

(他輕輕地關上門, 不讓任何人聽見。)

Use **so that** to express purpose, NOT **that**.
如要表示 "目的", 可用 **so that** 這一片語, 不是用 **that**。

4 × Children are not as easy to please nowadays that they were in the past.

√ **Children are not as easy to please nowadays as they were in the past.**

(現在的小孩不像從前那麼容易哄了。)

When making a comparison, use **(not) as/so … as** (NOT **that**) (比較兩種情況, 可用 **(not) as/so … as** 這一句型, 例如): 'It's as hard to get into university today as it was ten years ago.'

5 × It worried me that the letter had not arrived, especially that it had never happened before.
√ **It worried me that the letter had not arrived, especially since/as it had never happened before.**
(這封信一直沒有送到, 我感到很擔心, 因為這樣的事從來沒有發生過。)

When giving a reason for something, use **since** or **as**, NOT **that**
說明理由或表示 "為什麼", 應用 **since** 或 **as**, 不用 **that**。

6 × It is two months now that I left Germany.
√ **It is two months now since I left Germany.**
(我離開德國到現在, 已經有兩個月了。)

Note, however, that you can sometimes use **that** with **ago** (注意: 有時可用 **that** 與 **ago** 搭配, 例如): 'It was ten years ago that I first came to England.'

7 × Next to me was an old lady that seemed to be sound asleep.
√ **Next to me was an old lady who seemed to be sound asleep.**
(我身旁有位老太太, 似乎睡得很香。)

That can only be used to introduce an identifying relative clause (one which identifies, defines, or restricts the preceding noun) (按 **that** 只能用以引導限定性形容詞子句, 即限定前面名詞的子句, 例如): 'The woman that is sitting behind us is Tom's mother.' 'The man that I marry will have lots of money.' **That** cannot be used to introduce a non-identifying relative clause (one which simply adds more information about the noun and which is preceded by a comma.) (按 **that** 不能用以引導非限定性形容詞子句, 即僅僅是增加前面名詞的內容的子句或句前有逗號那種子句。)

8 × If you haven't sent it yet, I'd be pleased if you would do that as soon as possible.
√ **If you haven't sent it yet, I'd be pleased if you would do so as soon as possible.**
(如你尚未送出, 我希望你能盡快地把它送出去。)

To make a precise reference to a previously mentioned action, use **do so**, NOT **do that**.
為了確切表示已提過的行動, 可用 **do so**, 而不是 **do that**。

the **1** × She is arriving on March the 25th.
✓ **She is arriving on March 25th.**
(她將在三月二十五日抵達。)

When speaking, use (在口語中, 日期前用 **the**): 'March the twenty-fifth' OR 'the twenty-fifth of March'.
When writing, use (在書面語中, 不用 **the** 和 **of**): 'March 25th' OR '25th March' (WITHOUT **the** and **of**).

2 × Very few people can speak the English well in Japan.
✓ **Very few people can speak English well in Japan.**
(在日本, 英文說得好的人極少。)

Do not use **the** with the names of languages (提到某一語言的時候, 如 English、French、Chinese 之類, 前面不用 **the**, 例如): 'speak English', 'learn French', 'understand Chinese', etc.
Use **the** when talking about the people who live in a particular country (如用 English、French、Chinese 等詞表達該國家的人, 則應加 **the,** 例如): 'the English', 'the French', 'the Chinese'.

3 × I have just seen a new magazine about the computers.
✓ **I have just seen a new magazine about computers.**
(我剛才見到一本電腦雜誌。)

Do not use **the** with the plural form of a countable noun when used in a general sense. 用作泛指的可數名詞, 複數前不用 **the**。
Compare (試比較): 'She likes cats.' (=cats in general) (泛指貓) 'The cats we saw in Venice looked very hungry.' (=a particular group of cats) (特指某一類的貓)

4 × Some people have more contact with the violence and it becomes a part of their lives.
✓ **Some people have more contact with violence and it becomes a part of their lives.**
(有的人與暴力接觸多了, 結果暴力也就成了他們生活的一部分。)
× Nowadays the pollution is a very serious problem.
✓ **Nowadays pollution is a very serious problem.**
(今天污染是個很嚴重的問題。)

Do not use **the** with an uncountable noun when talking in a general sense (用作泛指的不可數名詞, 不加 **the,** 例如): 'He hates dishonesty.' 'Power doesn't interest him.'
The is used when the sense is restricted (凡表示其含義非泛指而限於一定範圍之內的詞都加 **the,** 如下句的 dishonesty, 限於是 the man 的品質, 所以要加 **the**; 另一句的 power 則限於是 politicians 所能享有的, 也需加 **the**): 'She hates the dishonesty of the man.' 'The power enjoyed by politicians doesn't interest him.'

5 × Our plane arrived at the Hong Kong Airport.
√ **Our plane arrived at Hong Kong Airport.**
(我們的飛機降落在香港飛機場。)

Do not use **the** before the names of airports and railway stations (按機場名稱和火車站名稱均不加 **the**): 'Charles de Gaulle (Airport)', 'Narita (Airport)', 'Charing Cross (Station)'.

6 × The language school is situated in a big building in the Malibu Street.
√ **The language school is situated in a big building in Malibu Street.**
(這所語言學校座落在馬力布大街的一幢大樓裡。)

Do not use **the** with the names of streets and roads (在街道名稱和馬路名稱之前不用 **the**, 例如): 'Oxford Street', 'Fifth Avenue', 'Fir Tree Avenue', 'Blue Pool Road'.

7 × Climbing the Mount Fuji in winter can be very dangerous.
√ **Climbing Mount Fuji in winter can be very dangerous.**
(冬天爬富士山可能非常危險。)

Do not use **the** with the name of a mountain (不應在山名之前加 **the**, 例如): 'Mount Everest', 'Mount Fuji', 'Mount Olympus'. Note, however, that **the** is used with the names of groups of mountains (但需注意: 山脈名稱之前則要加 **the**, 例如): 'the Alps', 'the Andes', 'the Himalayas'.

8 × Yellow River has caused many terrible floods.
√ **The Yellow River has caused many terrible floods.**
(黃河曾帶來許多次可怕的水災。)

Always use **the** with the names of canals, rivers, and seas (運河、江河以及海洋的名稱之前都應加 **the**, 例如): 'the Suez Canal', 'the Ganges', 'the Thames', 'the Atlantic', 'the Mediterranean'.

9 × It is more than ten years since I visited West Indies.
√ **It is more than ten years since I visited the West Indies.**
(我訪問西印度群島至今已有十幾年了。)

Most plural proper nouns begin with **the** (複數的專有名詞之前大都加 **the**, 例如): 'the Bahamas', 'the Himalayas', 'the United States'.

10 × This is my second visit to UK.
√ **This is my second visit to the UK.**
(這是我第二次遊覽英國。)

Use **the** with any country whose name includes 'states', 'union', 'republic', etc. (凡是帶有 'states'、'union'、'republic' 等詞的國名, 前面都加 **the**, 例如): 'the UK', 'the United Kingdom', 'the USA', 'the United States', 'the USSR', 'the Union of Soviet Socialist Republics'.

11 × Only very wealthy tourists can afford to stay at Imperial Hotel.
√ **Only very wealthy tourists can afford to stay at the Imperial Hotel.**
(只有很有錢的遊客才住得起帝國大飯店。)

The is usually used with the names of hotels and restaurants unless the name is a possessive form. Compare (通常旅館和飯店的名字之前都加 **the**, 但如名字本身為名詞所有格的則不用, 試比較): 'the Hilton', 'the Mandarin', 'the Sheraton' BUT 'Claridge's', 'Salvo's', 'Tiffany's'

12 See (見) CHURCH, COLLEGE, HALF 1, HOSPITAL, PLAY 3, SCHOOL 2

them See (見) ME 1

then 1

× We took a bus to the city centre then caught a train to London.

√ **We took a bus to the city centre and then caught a train to London.**
(我們乘公共汽車去市中心, 然後搭火車去倫敦。)

> **Then** is NOT a conjunction.
> 注意: **then** 不是連接詞。

2

× After my father retires, then I shall help him financially.

√ **After my father retires, I shall help him financially.**
(我父親退休後, 我將在經濟上幫助他。)

> **Then** (= at that time) is only used after a time clause when it introduces a result or consequence. Compare (按 **then** 作 "屆時" 解時, 僅用於時間子句之後, 引導表示結果或後果的主句, 試比較): 'When you've seen the trees, then you'll know why I came to live here.' (= as a result of seeing the trees) (子句表示原因, 主句表示結果)

there 1

× My sister often goes to a swimming pool at the end of the road but I don't like going to there.

√ **My sister often goes to a swimming pool at the end of the road but I don't like going there.**
(我姐姐常去這馬路盡頭的游泳池游泳, 不過我不喜歡去那裏。)

> **There** and **here** cannot follow **to** unless the speaker is indicating or pointing to something (注意: **there** 和 **here** 之前不應加 **to**, 除非說話的人手指着某一點說話, 例如): 'When the tide comes in, the water reaches right up to there.'

2

× There was four people in the car.

√ **There were four people in the car.**
(車上有四個人。)

> **there is/was** + EITHER the singular form of a countable noun OR an uncountable noun (按 **there is/was** 之後既接單數可數名詞, 或是不可數名詞, 例如): 'There was a letter on the mat.' 'There was smoke coming under the door.'
> **there are/were** + the plural forms of a countable noun (按 **there are/were** 之後應接複數可數名詞, 例如): 'There were babies crying in every room.'

3 × Suddenly he remembered the little lake, there his mother used to take him.
√ **Suddenly he remembered the little lake, where his mother used to take him.**
(突然間, 他想起了那個小湖; 從前, 他媽媽常帶他到那兒去。)

> **There** is an adverb.
> 注意: **there** 是副詞。
> **Where** is a conjunction.
> 注意: **where** 是連接詞。

4 × There are exactly two weeks since I last went to New York.
√ **It is exactly two weeks since I last went to New York.**
(我上次去紐約, 至今已有整整兩個星期了。)

> **It is** + time phrase + **since** + clause
> 注意: **it is** 後接時間短語 (如 two weeks), 再接以 **since** 引導的子句。這是一種特定句型, 其中 **it** 不可用 **there** 替代。

5 See (見) GOOD 2

6 See (見) WHERE

they 1 × As far as I can see, the two wheels which are supposed to turn around/round they do not turn around/round.
√ **As far as I can see, the two wheels which are supposed to turn around/round do not turn around/round.**
(就我所看到的, 這兩個理應轉過來的輪子並沒有轉過來。)

> Do not repeat the subject (by using a pronoun) after a relative clause. The subject of 'do not turn around/round' is 'the two wheels'.
> 不要在關係子句 (如上句的 which-clause) 之後再用代名詞重複主語。句中 "do not turn around/round" 的主語是 "the two wheels"。

2 × They are several activities arranged for you.
√ **There are several activities arranged for you.**
(有幾項活動已經為你安排好了。)

In many sentences the verb **be** is used to express a state or fact. If the subject has not been mentioned before, it is placed immediately after the verb and the sentence begins with **there** (NOT **they** or **it**) (動詞 **be** 往往用以表示一種靜止狀態或一個事實。如主語未曾在前面出現過, 則句子應以 **there** 開始, 而不應以 **they** 或 **it** 開始, 同時主語應與動詞調換位置, 即主語緊接在動詞之後, 例如): 'There are too many chairs in the room.' 'There's a bottle of wine in the cupboard.'

thing 1 × The only bad thing on him was that he never stopped talking.
√ **The only bad thing about him was that he never stopped talking.**
(他身上唯一的缺點是不停嘴地說話。)

a good/bad thing about someone/something, NOT **on**
如要表示某人的優點或缺點、某物的好處或壞處, 可用 **a good/bad thing about** someone/something, 其中 **about** 不可用 **on** 代替, 雖則中文的説法可能用"身上"。

2 See (見) EVERY **2**

think 1 × I am often thinking about these problems.
√ **I often think about these problems.**
(我經常考慮這些問題。)

Use the present simple tense when talking about an action which happens regularly or often. **Think** (=give thought to) is not usually used in the progressive unless it refers to a current activity (如表示的是一個經常發生的動作, 可用一般現在式。**think** 一詞, 如作"考慮"、"思索"解, 一般不用進行式, 除非是指目前正進行的活動, 例如): 'Be quiet, I'm thinking.'

2 × I think she didn't understand what you said.
√ **I don't think she understood what you said.**
(我看她並不明白你說的話。)

Note that when the clause following **think** contains a negative idea, **think** is made negative and the verb that follows is positive.
注意: 如 **think** 後接的子句含否定之意, 英語的習慣表達方式是, 把否定詞放在 **think** 之前, 後接的子句中動詞用肯定形式。請注意錯句的表達方式頗符合中國人的思維邏輯, 中國學生特別要注意中英語的不同表達方式。

3 × We should spend more time thinking why people do such terrible things.
√ **We should spend more time thinking about why people do such terrible things.**
(我們應該多花些時間想想, 為什麼有些人會做出這種可怕的事。)

think about = consider (意為: "考慮"、"想一想")

4 × People without a job try not to think on the future.
√ **People without a job try not to think about/of the future.**
(沒有工作的人不敢去想及將來的事。)

think about/of someone/something = form ideas in your mind about someone/something (意為: "考慮到"、"想及" 某人或某事)

5 × I am thinking to make another trip to Italy next year.
√ **I am thinking of making another trip to Italy next year.**
(我在計劃明年再去一次意大利。)
× I was thinking to wear the trousers so I took them out of the suitcase.
√ **I was thinking of wearing the trousers so I took them out of the suitcase.**
(我打算穿這條褲子, 所以就從箱子裏把它取出來了。)

think of + v-ing = intend or plan
按 **think of** 後接帶 "-ing" 的動詞, 相當於 "有意"、"打算"、"計劃" 之意。

6 × 'I must be getting old', I thought myself.
√ **'I must be getting old', I thought to myself.**
("我一定是老了," 我心裏琢磨着。)

× 'I can't stay here all night,' he thought by himself.
√ **'I can't stay here all night,' he thought to himself.**
(“我不可能整晚留在這裏,” 他心裏想。)

> **think to** yourself, NOT **by**
> 注意: **think** to yourself 中的 **to** 不可用 **by** 替代。

7 × I was thinking if you would like to have lunch before visiting the museum.
√ **I was wondering if you would like to have lunch before visiting the museum.**
(不知道你是否願意先吃午飯再參觀博物館。)

> **I was wondering if/whether** is often used to introduce polite invitations and requests (注意: **I was wondering if/whether** 這一句型常用以表達客氣的邀請和請求, 例如): 'I was wondering if you'd like to play tennis on Saturday.' 'I was wondering whether you could give me some advice.'

this × During this next five weeks I will be staying with an English family.
√ **During these next five weeks I will be staying with an English family.**
(在隨後的五個星期裡, 我將和一個英國家庭一起住。)

> **This** /ðɪs/ is singular.
> 注意: **this** 是單數。
> **These** /ðiz/ is plural.
> 注意: **these** 是複數。
> The use of **this** or **these** depends upon whether the noun that follows is singular or plural. Compare (用 **this** 或 **these** 取決於後面的名詞是單數還是複數, 試比較): 'this book' BUT 'these books'

thousand 1 × There were more than thousand people in the audience.
√ **There were more than a thousand people in the audience.**
(聽眾有一千多人。)

> **Hundred**, **thousand**, **million**, etc. cannot be used in the singular without **a** or **one**.
> 注意: **hundred**, **thousand**, **million** 等前面必須有 **a** 或 **one**, 才能用單數形式。

2 ✓ **AmE We received exactly two thousand thirty replies.**
✓ **BrE We received exactly two thousand and thirty replies.**
(我們收到整整二千零三十封回信。)

In British English, use (注意英式英語如下用法): 'one thousand and nine', 'eight thousand and sixty-two' BUT (但是) 'five thousand six hundred', 'three thousand two hundred and nine'.

3 See (見) HUNDRED

threaten 1 × She threatened leaving without him if he didn't hurry.
✓ **She threatened to leave without him if he didn't hurry.**
(她威脅着說, 如果他再不趕快, 她就一個人走了。)

threaten + to-v
按 **threaten** 後接帶 to 的動詞, 不接帶 "-ing" 的動詞

2 × He heard his father threatening his mother of leaving her.
✓ **He heard his father threatening his mother with leaving her.**
(他聽到父親威脅母親說要拋棄她。)

threaten someone **with** something, NOT **of**
threaten someone with something 作 "以某事威脅某人" 解, 注意其中前置詞 **with** 不可用 **of** 替代。

thunder × I heard a terribly loud noise, like a thunder, as the vehicles crashed into each other.
✓ **I heard a terribly loud noise, like thunder, as the vehicles crashed into each other.**
(兩輛車相撞時, 我聽到一聲雷鳴般的巨響。)

Thunder is an uncountable noun
按 **thunder** 是不可數名詞。

till × I managed to drive the car till the nearest hospital.
✓ **I managed to drive the car to the nearest hospital.**
✓ **I managed to drive the car as far as the nearest hospital.**
(我設法把車開到最近的醫院。)

Till and **until** are usually used when talking about time, NOT distance, area, or scope.
按 **till** 和 **until** 一般用來指時間, 不指距離、面積或範圍。

time 1 × They walked along the beach for long time.
√ **They walked along the beach for a long time.**
(他們沿着海灘走了很長時間。)

a long time WITH **a**
注意 **a long time** 中 **a** 不能省略

2 × I'm sorry I've not had a time to write to you until now.
√ **I'm sorry I've not had time to write to you until now.**
(很抱歉, 我一直拖到現在才有空給你寫信。)

(not) have time (to do something) WITHOUT a
在 **(not) have time** (to do something) 中 **time** 之前不用 **a**。

3 × The course in electrical engineering takes four years time.
√ **The course in electrical engineering takes four years.**
(讀電子工程要花四年時間。)

When talking about how long something takes or lasts, do not use **time** with a time phrase (談及做某事需多長時間或某物可支持多長時間, 不要在用了時間片語的同時又加 **time** 一詞, 例如): 'Each letter took one hour to write.' 'The battery will last seven days.'
Note, however, that in phrases which begin with **in**, the word **time** may be included (注意在以 **in** 開始的片語中可以用 **time** 這個詞, 例如): 'I'll have finished my course in four years' time.' 'Bill is due to arrive in three weeks' time.'

4 × Parents should spend more time to look after their children.
√ **Parents should spend more time looking after their children.**
(做父母的應該多花點時間照顧自己的子女。)

spend time + v-ing
指 "花時間做 …", 用 **spend time** 後接帶 "-ing" 的動詞。

5 × On the last time I went shopping I bought a cassette recorder.

✓ **The last time I went shopping I bought a cassette recorder.**
(我上次去買東西時, 買了一架卡式錄音機。)

> **the next time**, **the first time**, etc. WITHOUT **on**
> 注意: **the next time**, **the first time** 之前不用 **on**。

6 × The fire brigade arrived just on time, before the fire could spread.

✓ **The fire brigade arrvied just in time, before the fire could spread.**
(消防隊及時趕到, 未讓火勢蔓延。)

> **on time** = (arriving) at the right time; punctual(ly) (意為: "準時", 例如): 'The train arrived at 17:28; it was exactly on time.'
> **in time** = not late; early enough (意為: "及時", 例如): 'Make sure you arrive in time to see the beginning of the film.'

7 × It didn't take a long time before we were back home again.

✓ **It didn't take long before we were back home again.**
(沒多久, 我們又回到家了。)

> **not take long** WITHOUT **time** OR **a**
> 按 **not take long** 中不用 **time**, 也不用 **a**。但 "過了很久" 卻用 "it takes a long time"。

times × He couldn't see where he was going and fell down many times.

✓ **He couldn't see where he was going and kept falling down.**
(他看不見去路, 所以不斷摔倒。)

> 'To do something many times' (= keep doing something) is not actually wrong but sounds unnatural.
> to do something many times 相當於 keep doing something, 雖然不算錯, 只是聽來欠自然。

tired

× By the time we arrived in Rio I was feeling completely tired.

√ **By the time we arrived in Rio I was feeling completely exhausted.**

(我們到達里約熱內盧的時候, 我已感到筋疲力盡。)

Although usage varies, an adjective which does not contain the sense 'very', 'extremely', or '100%' as part of its meaning is NOT usually used with **absolutely** or **completely**. To intensify such adjectives, use **very** or **extremely**.
雖然用法不是一成不變, 但凡是不帶 very (非常)、extremely (極其) 和 100% (百分之百) 這類含義的形容詞, 一般在加強語氣時均不與 absolutely 和 completely 連用, 而用 very 或 extremely 來修飾。
Compare (試比較): 'completely exhausted' BUT (但可以說) 'very tired' (**exhausted** = 'very tired')
'completely soaked' BUT (但可以說) 'very wet' (**soaked** = 'very wet')
'absolutely filthy' BUT (但可以說) 'very dirty' (**filthy** = 'very dirty')
'absolutely frantic' BUT (但可以說) 'very anxious' (**frantic** = 'very anxious')

tiresome

× The flight from Hong Kong to London was very tiresome.

√ **The flight from Hong Kong to London was very tiring.**

(從香港飛往倫敦的航程使人感到很疲勞。)

tiresome = annoying or irritating (意為: "令人感到討厭的"): 'That tiresome child never gives me a minute's peace.'
tiring = causing tiredness; exhausting (意為: "使人疲勞的")

title 1

× The new magazine is titled 'Computer News'.

√ **The new magazine is called 'Computer News'.**

(這本新雜誌名叫 "電腦新聞"。)

Title is a noun, NOT a verb.
按 **title** 是名詞, 不能用作動詞, title 的動詞為 entitle。

2 × The newspaper titles were all about the earthquake.
√ **The newspaper headlines were all about the earthquake.**
(報紙的標題全是關於這次地震的。)

> **title** = name of a book, play, painting, piece of music, etc. (意為: 書畫、戲劇、樂曲的名稱)
> **headline** = heading above a story in a newspaper (意為: 報紙報導的標題)

to **1** × At that moment he noticed a man running to him.
√ **At that moment he noticed a man running towards him.**
(就在那個時候, 他注意到有一個男人向他跑過來。)

> Use **to** when you want to emphasize the destination.
> 強調目的地時用 **to**
> Use **towards** when you want to emphasize the direction.
> 強調方向時用 **towards**
> Compare (試比較): 'John drove to the station.' (We know he stopped at the station.) (意為: 我們知道他的車子開到火車站前停下來。)
> 'John drove towards the station.' (We don't know where he stopped.) (意為: 我們並不知道他會在什麼地方停下來。)

2 × He came into the shop and went to the woman behind the counter.
√ **He came into the shop and went up/over to the woman behind the counter.**
(他進了商店, 逕直走到櫃枱後面的那個女人跟前。)
× The old lady stood up, went to John, and asked him what he was doing there.
√ **The old lady stood up, went up/over to John, and asked him what he was doing there.**
(老太太站起來, 走到約翰跟前, 問他在那兒做什麼。)

> To describe the action of deliberately moving towards and stopping in front of a person, use **go up/over to**, NOT **go to**.
> 說明有目的地向某人走過去並停在他跟前, 用 **go up to** 或 **go over to**, 而不用 **go to**。

3 × Each time I tried to close my eyes and to relax, the young man said something to me.
√ **Each time I tried to close my eyes and relax, the young man said something to me.**
(每次我要閉目養神, 那年輕人就對我講話。)

When two infinitives are joined by **and**, **to** is usually used only before the first one.
如兩個帶 **tc** 的動詞是由 **and** 來連接的話, 通常只有前一個動詞帶 **to**, 後面的一個可略去 **to**。

4 See (見) NOT 1

to and fro × The teacher walked to-and-fro in front of the class as he talked.
√ **The teacher walked to and fro in front of the class as he talked.**
(教師一邊講一邊在學生面前走來走去。)

to-and-fro is an adjective modifying a noun (按 **to-and-fro** 是形容詞, 修飾名詞, 例如): 'a to-and-fro movement'.
to and fro is an adverb modifying a verb
按 **to and fro** 是副詞, 修飾動詞。

toast × I usually have a cup of coffee and a toast for breakfast.
√ **I usually have a cup of coffee and a piece of toast for breakfast.**
(早餐的時候, 我通常喝一杯咖啡和吃一塊烤麵包。)

Toast is an uncountable noun.
按 **toast** 是不可數名詞。

today × As I told you in our today's telephone conversation, I think I left my coat at your hotel.
√ **As I told you in today's telephone conversation, I think I left my coat at your hotel.**
(我今天打電話時告訴過你, 我想我是把上衣遺留在你那間旅店裡了。)

Do not use a determiner before **today's**, **yesterday's**, etc. (在 **today's**, **yesterday's** 之前不要用限定詞) Note the alternative (注意另一種說法): 'As I told you (earlier) today in our telephone conversation ...'

too 1 × In my opinion, this is a too traditional approach.
√ **In my opinion, this is too traditional an approach.**
(依我看, 這種方法太因循守舊了。)

> **too** + adjective + **a/an** + noun
> 形容詞一般放在 **a/an** 和名詞之間, 但與 **too** 連用時, 就放在 a/an 之前。

2 × I was too happy when I received your letter today.
√ **I was very happy when I received your letter today.**
(今天收到你的信, 我感到非常高興。)

> **too** = more than enough; more than is good or acceptable (意為: "過於"、"太", 例如): 'You are driving too fast! Stop and let me get out.' 'The meat was too tough to eat.'
> **very** = extremely (意為: "非常"、"十分")
> Compare (試比較): 'It was very cold but not too cold to go out.'

3 × I don't like football and my brother doesn't too.
√ **I don't like football and my brother doesn't either.**
(我不喜歡足球, 我弟弟也不喜歡。)

> When using **too** and **either** as adverbs, use **too** in affirmative statements and **either** in negative statements. Compare (以 **too** 或 **either** 作為副詞時, **too** 用在肯定句中, **either** 用在否定句中, 試比較): 'I can read and my sister can too.' 'I can't swim and my sister can't either.'

4 × Too, I would like to know more about the British way of life.
√ **Also, I would like to know more about the British way of life.**
(此外, 我想多知道一些關於英國的生活方式。)

> Unlike **also** and **in addition**, **too** is NEVER used at the beginning of a sentence. Compare (與 **also** 及 **in addition** 不同, **too** 不能用於句首, 試比較): 'I would like to know more about the British way of life, too.'

5 See (見) MUCH 6

too many

× It's an interesting magazine with too many good ideas.

√ **It's an interesting magazine with a lot of good ideas.**
(這是一本精彩的雜誌, 有很多精到的見解。)

> **too many** = more than is acceptable or required
> (意為: "過多"、"太多")

too much **1**

× 'If you are too much selfish, nobody will like you,' she said.

√ **'If you are too selfish, nobody will like you,' she said.**
("如果你太自私, 誰也不會喜歡你," 她說。)

> **too** + adjective WITHOUT **much**
> 按 **too** 後接形容詞, 不用 **much**。

2

× I noticed that he had had a couple of drinks too much.

√ **I noticed that he had had a couple of drinks too many.**
(我注意到他太貪杯了。)

> countable noun + **too many**
> 按可數名詞後接 **too many**。

3 See (見) MUCH 6

top

× You will find my address on top of the letter.

√ **You will find my address at the top of the letter.**
(你可以在信的上端找到我的地址。)

> Compare (試比較): 'The book is on top of the television.' (= resting on the surface of the television) (放在電視機上面)

touch

× It is good for a person to go out to work because they get in touch with other people.

√ **It is good for a person to go out to work because they come into contact with other people.**
(到社會上工作對個人有好處, 因為他們會接觸到其他人。)

get in touch with = communicate with (someone) by letter or telephone (意為: "與 ... 聯絡", 指用通信或打電話的方法, 例如): 'Don't wait until Christmas before you get in touch.'
come into contact with = meet (意為: "與 ... 接觸", 指會見)

translate

× The magazine has just been translated to Greek.
✓ **The magazine has just been translated into Greek.**
(這本雜誌剛被譯成希臘語。)

translate something (from one language) **into** another, NOT **to**
如要說 "把什麼 (某種語言) 翻譯成別的語言", 可用 **translate** something (from one language) **into** another, 其中前置詞 **into** 不可用 **to** 替代。

travel

× He began to tell me about the first travel he had done by plane.
✓ **He began to tell me about the first journey he had made by plane.**
(他開始跟我講他第一次乘飛機旅行的經歷。)

travel (uncountable) = the general activity of moving about the world or from place to place (按 **travel** 一詞是不可數名詞, 意為 "遊歷", 強調的是從一地到另一地的活動, 例如): 'She enjoys foreign travel.'
journey (countable) = a trip from one place to another (按 **journey** 一詞是可數名詞, 意為: "旅行", 強調從一地到另一地的一次旅行, 也可解作 "旅程", 強調從一地到另一地所需的時間和距離。)

trouble

× I'm sorry to cause you so many troubles.
✓ **I'm sorry to cause you so much trouble.**
(我很抱歉給你增添這麼多麻煩。)

Trouble is an uncountable noun here.
按 **trouble** 在上例中是不可數名詞。

trousers

× He bought himself a new trousers.
✓ **He bought himself a new pair of trousers.**
(他給自己買了一條新褲子。)

Trousers is a plural noun. (按 **trousers** 是複數名詞)

true

× I hope my dream becomes true.
√ **I hope my dream comes true.**
(我希望自己的夢想能變成現實。)

> **come true**, NOT **become**
> 按 **come true** 指 "(願望、夢想等) 實現", 是固定詞組, 其中動詞 come 不可用 **become** 替代。

trust

× After he was caught stealing, nobody trusted in him.
√ **After he was caught stealing, nobody trusted him.**
(他偷竊時給人抓住, 從此誰也不信任他了。)

> **trust in** = have faith in (意為: "信奉"、"對 ... 有信心", 例如): 'trust in God'
> **trust** = rely on someone to be honest (意為: "信任"、"信賴")

turn back

× Hearing a crash, I quickly turned back and saw that a car had hit a lamp post.
√ **Hearing a crash, I quickly turned round/around and saw that a car had hit a lamp post.**
(聽到砰一聲響, 我馬上轉過身, 看見一輛汽車撞在電燈柱上。)
× Having woken up, he sat up in his seat and turned back to see who was making all the noise.
√ **Having woken up, he sat up in his seat and turned round/around to see who was making all the noise.**
(他被吵醒以後, 在椅子上坐了起來, 轉過身去看是誰弄的這麼大的聲音。)

> **turn back** = stop and begin to return to the place you started from (意為: "轉回去"、"由原路折回", 例如): 'If the bridge has been destroyed, we'll have to turn back.'
> **turn round/around** = move so that you face in the opposite direction (意為: "轉過身去"、"調頭")

turn up

× George turned up to be the brother of one of my old schoolfriends.
√ **George turned out to be the brother of one of my old schoolfriends.**
(喬治原來是我一位老同學的兄弟。)

turn up = arrive, appear, or be found (意為: "出現"、"被找到", 例如): 'He turned up at the party dressed in pink pyjamas!' 'I can't find my keys, but I expect they'll turn up somewhere.'
turn out = prove to be (意為: "原來是"、"結果是", 例如): 'After a bad start, the party turned out to be a great success.'

two See (見) BOTH 4

type × The manager of the shop told me that he was not responsible for these type of fault.
√ **The manager of the shop told me that he was not responsible for these types of fault.**
(這店的經理告訴我, 對這類毛病他概不負責。)

these types of fault (OR **these types of faults**) BUT **this type of fault**
指 "這些毛病/缺陷", 有兩種說法: 一種是 '**these types of fault**'; 另一種是 '**these types of faults**'。指 "這種毛病/缺陷", 用 'this type of fault'。
Note the alternative (注意另一種說法): 'faults of this type'

UK × I have an uncle who lives in UK.
√ **I have an uncle who lives in the UK.**
(我有位伯父住在英國。)

See (見) note at THE 10

ultimately × Ultimately there has been another increase in the number of violent crimes.
√ **Lately there has been another increase in the number of violent crimes.**
(最近暴力案件又有所增加。)

ultimately = in the end (意為: "最終"、"最後", 例如): 'Naturally I can give you some advice but ultimately it's your decision.'
lately = in the recent past (意為: "最近"、"近來")

understand **1**

× Until I saw the clock I hadn't understood how late it was.

√ **Until I saw the clock I hadn't realized how late it was.**

(在看鐘以前, 我還沒有意識到時間有多晚了。)

> **understand** = know or grasp the meaning of something (意為: "明白"、"懂得", 例如): 'I found the lecture hard to understand.'
> **realize** = become aware (of something) (意為: "意識到")

2

× As you understand, I don't have much free time.

√ **As you know, I don't have much free time.**

(你知道, 我沒有很多空閒時間。)

> **as you (will) know/appreciate/realize/gather,** NOT **understand**
> 一般用 **as you (will) know/appreciate/realize/gather,** 而不用 **as you understand**。

unique

× It is one of the most unique pieces of architecture in Spain.

√ **It is one of the rarest pieces of architecture in Spain.**

(這是在西班牙最難得見到的建築之一。)

> Something can be **absolutely unique** or **totally unique** but NOT **very/more/most/somewhat** (etc.) **unique**. There are no degrees of uniqueness when **unique** means 'the only one of its kind'.
> (注意: **unique** 只能用 **absolutely** 或 **totally** 修飾, 不用 **very/more/most/somewhat** 等, 因為 **unique** 原意是 "獨一無二", 所以也就沒有程度之分。)

United States

× I met people from Canada and United States.

√ **I met people from Canada and the United States.**

(我會見了從加拿大和美國來的人。)

See (見) note at THE 10

university

× I am about to start studying at the Leeds University.

√ **I am about to start studying at Leeds University.**

(我就快要在里茲大學讀書了。)

Leeds University BUT **the University of Leeds**
London University BUT **the Unviersity of London**
指里茲大學, 可説 '**Leeds University**' 或 '**the University of Leeds**'; 指倫敦大學也是如此, 可説 '**London University**' 或説 '**the University of London**'。
Note that the usual written form is (注意平常的書寫格式是) '**the University of Leeds/London etc.**'.

unless **1** × You'll fail your exams unless if you work harder.
✓ **You'll fail your exams unless you work harder.**
(除非你再加努力, 否則你就考不及格。)

Unless is NOT used with **if.**
注意: **unless** 一詞不與 **if** 連用。

2 × It would have been a wonderful holiday unless Ali had come with us.
✓ **It would have been a wonderful holiday if Ali hadn't come with us.**
(如果阿里當時沒有跟我們來, 這個假日本來會過得很好的。)

Unless cannot introduce an impossible condition. Compare (按 **unless** 不能用於不可能發生的情況, 試比較): 'I'll go out tonight if it doesn't rain.' OR 'I'll go out tonight unless it rains.' (It is possible that it may rain 有可能下雨)
'I'd go out tonight if I didn't have so much work to do.' (NOT 不用 **unless**)
'I'd have gone out last night if I hadn't had so much work to do.' (NOT 不用 **unless**)

until **1** × I shall wait here until you will return.
✓ **I shall wait here until you return.**
(我會在這兒等你回來。)

After **until/when/whenever/once/after/if,** use the present simple tense (or present perfect) for future reference, NOT **shall/will** + verb.
在 **until**、**when**、**whenever**、**once**、**after**、**if** 等引導的子句中, 用一般現在式或現在完成式以表示將來, 不用 **shall** 或 **will** 接動詞。

2 × I will have finished this book until tomorrow.
√ **I will have finished this book by tomorrow.**
(到了明天我一定會把這本書看完。)

> **Until** is used for an action or state continuing up to a certain time.
> 注意: **until** 表示一種連續的行動或狀態, 一直持續到某一時間。
> **By** is used for an action which happens at or before a certain time. Compare (按 **by** 一詞表示一個動作發生在某一時間或在某一時間之前, 試比較):
> 'I have to keep writing until the end of next year.'
> 'My book will be finished by the end of next year.'

3 × The magazine covers everything from politics until what's happening in Hollywood.
√ **The magazine covers everything from politics to what's happening in Hollywood.**
(這本雜誌包羅萬象, 從政治到好萊塢的新聞, 應有盡有。)

> **Until** and **till** are usually used when talking about time, NOT distance, area, or scope.
> 注意: **until** 和 **till** 通常用於時間方面, 不涉及距離、面積或範圍。

upstairs See (見) DOWNSTAIRS

us See (見) ME 1

USA × I was travelling on a flight from USA to Paris.
√ **I was travelling on a flight from the USA to Paris.**
(我正乘一架班機從美國飛往巴黎。)

See (見) note at THE 10

use 1 × In my previous job I use to travel a lot.
√ **In my previous job I used to travel a lot.**
(在我上一任的工作中我經常出差。)

> **used to** (WITH silent **d**)
> 注意: **used to** 中的 **d** 不發音。
> Compare (試比較): 'I used to use a fountain pen.'

2 × It took a long time for me to get use to the local accent.
√ **It took a long time for me to get used to the local accent.**
(我過了很久才習慣當地的口音。)

> **get used to** something (WITH silent **d**) = become accustomed to something
> (意指 "習慣於某事物", 注意 **used** 中的 **d** 不發音)

used 1 × The shoes under the bed were used and had holes in them.
√ **The shoes under the bed were worn-out and had holes in them.**
(牀下的那雙鞋已經穿壞了, 還穿破了洞。)

> **used** = not brand new; second-hand (指 "舊的", "用過的", "二手的", 例如): 'He is looking for a good, used car for his daughter.'
> **worn-out** = reduced to an unusable state by continuous use or wear (指 "穿破了的"、"用壞了的")

2 × People are used to consider women inferior to men.
√ **People are used to considering women inferior to men.**
(人們慣性地認為女性比男性低下。)

> **used to do** something = did something regularly in the past but not any more (意指過去經常做某事, 但現已不做)
> **be used to doing** something = be in the habit of doing something (意指習慣於做某事)

usual 1 × In Finland it is very usual that women go out to work.
√ **In Finland it is very usual for women to go out to work.**
(在芬蘭, 婦女出去工作是很平常的事。)

> **usual for** someone **to do** something, NOT **that**
> 按 **usual for** 後接 someone **to do** something。注意 usual 之後不接以 **that** 引導的子句。

2 × I thought it was just a usual doll but then it began to sing.
√ **I thought it was just an ordinary doll but then it began to sing.**
(我當時以為這不過是個普通的洋娃娃, 可是緊接着這洋娃娃就開始唱起來了。)

usual (opposite **unusual**) = customary (意為: "慣常的", 其反義詞是 **unusual**, 例如): 'We arranged to meet at the usual time.' 'It's usual to thank people for their help.'
ordinary (opposite **special**) = without any special features or qualities (意為: "普通的"、"平常的", 其反義詞是 **special**)

usually × As usually, he arrived five minutes late.
√ **As usual, he arrived five minutes late.**
(跟平常一樣, 他遲到了五分鐘。)

Note the fixed phrase: **as usual.**
注意 **as usual** 是固定詞組。

variety × We would like to see a greater variety in dishes on the menu.
√ **We would like to see a greater variety of dishes on the menu.**
(我們希望在菜單上看到更多菜式的選擇。)

variety of, NOT **in**
注意: **variety of** 中的前置詞 **of** 不可用 **in** 替代。

vegetable × I buy a lot of fresh fruit and vegetable.
√ **I buy a lot of fresh fruit and vegetables.**
(我買好多鮮果和蔬菜。)

Unlike **fruit, vegetable** is a countable noun.
不同於 **fruit, vegetable** 是可數名詞。

very 1 × He looked very funny that I couldn't help laughing.
√ **He looked so funny that I couldn't help laughing.**
(他那樣子真滑稽, 我忍不住大笑起來。)

so + adjective/adverb + **that** clause
so 後接形容詞/副詞, 再接用 **that** 的子句, 是一種常用的句型, 表示 to such a degree (達到如此程度, 乃致於 ...) 之意。

2 × She was very admired and respected by all the pupils' parents.
√ **She was greatly/much admired and respected by all the pupils' parents.**
(所有的學生家長都對她十分讚賞和尊敬。)

> Past participles with a strongly passive meaning are usually modified by **greatly** or **much,** NOT **very.** Note that **very** is chiefly used with adjectives and past participles that are like adjectives and refer to a state of mind or emotional condition (含有明顯被動意思的過去分詞, 一般用 **greatly** 或 **much** 修飾, 不用 **very**。注意 very 主要用於形容詞和作用與形容詞相似並表現思想狀態或情緒的過去分詞, 例如): 'very bored/worried/interested/pleased'.

3 × Although he was very in love with Marianne, he wanted to marry a rich heiress.
√ **Although he was deeply in love with Marianne, he wanted to marry a rich heiress.**
(儘管他很愛瑪莉安, 但他卻要娶一位很有錢的女繼承人。)

> **Very** cannot usually be used before a phrase beginning with a preposition (such as 'in love with', 'in need of', 'at odds with', etc. which require different adverbs to express the meaning of '**very**', e.g. '**deeply** in love with', '**badly** in need of', '**acutely** at odds with'). However, in such cases it is often possible to use **very much** (注意 **very** 一般不能用來修飾前置詞片語, 如 in love with, in need of, at odds with 等, 此等片語如要表達 '十分'、'非常' 的意思, 須用不同的副詞, 如 **deeply** in love with, **badly** in need of, **acutely** at odds with 等, 但也可以用 **very much** 來代替, 例如): 'Although he was very much in love with Marianne, he wanted to marry a rich heiress.'

4 See (見) note at CERTAIN 1

very much × I like very much beaches.
√ **I like beaches very much.**
(我很喜歡海灘。)

> A verb and its direct object are not usually separated by an adverb or adverbial phrase.
> 一般來説, 不要用副詞或副詞片語把動詞與直接受詞分開。

victim × Only two people died in the fire but there were a lot of victims.
√ **Only two people died in the fire but there were a lot of casualties.**
(在這場火災中, 只有兩人死亡, 但有很多人受傷。)

If you wish to refer only to those people who are injured in an accident, use **casualties**. If you wish to refer to all the people who suffer in an accident, both the dead and injured, use **victims**.
如果只指事故中的受傷者用 **casualties;** 如果指事故中所有受害者 (指受傷者又指死亡者) 則用 **victims**。但 **casualties** 作為軍事用語指 "傷亡人數"。

view 1 × The view of all the blood on the ground made her feel ill.
√ **The sight of all the blood on the ground made her feel ill.**
(見到一地都是血, 她覺得噁心。)

Note that **view** is usually used of something distant (注意 **view** 一般指遠景, 例如): 'To get a better view of the valley, we climbed to the top of the hill.'

2 See (見) POINT OF VIEW

visit × We decided to do another visit the next day.
√ **We decided to pay another visit the next day.**
(我們決定第二天再去訪問。)

pay (someone/something) **a visit** OR **pay a visit** (to someone/something), NOT **do**
pay (someone/something) **a visit** 或 **pay a visit** (to someone/something) 中的動詞 **pay** 不可用 **do** 替代。

voice 1 × He continued speaking with a very loud voice.
√ **He continued speaking in a very loud voice.**
(他繼續大聲説話。)

speak/talk in a loud/quiet voice, NOT **with**
speak/talk in a loud/quiet voice 中的前置詞 **in** 不可用 **with** 替代。

2 × The film was very interesting, even though there was no voice.
√ **The film was very interesting, even though there was no sound.**
(這部電影儘管沒有聲音, 還是很有趣。)

> **voice** = the sound produced by a person when speaking or singing (是人說話或唱歌的聲音)
> **sound** = something that is heard (是聽到的任何聲音, 包括人聲、音樂聲、飛機引擎聲等)
> Compare: (試比較) 'The only sound I could hear was a child's voice.'

wait × I stopped and waited the truck to pass.
√ **I stopped and waited for the truck to pass.**
(我站住等那輛卡車過去。)

> **wait for** a person/thing (to do something)
> 指 "等待某人/某物 (做某事)", 用 '**wait for** a person/thing (to do something)'

want 1 × My parents wanted that I should go to a different university.
√ **My parents wanted me to go to a different university.**
(我父母要我上另一所大學。)
× 'Do you want I take you to his house?' she asked.
√ **'Do you want me to take you to his house?' she asked.**
("你要我帶你上他家去嗎?" 她問道。)

> **want me/him/her/it/us/them/you to do** something
> 指 "要某人做某事", 用 **want me/him/her/it/us/them/you to do** something, 即 **want** 之後應接代名詞的受詞, 而不是主格的 **I/he/she** 等。

2 × I want you to send me the coat if you find it.
√ **I would like you to send me the coat if you find it.**
(如果你找到那件上衣, 請把它送來。)

> 'I want you to send me the coat' is grammatically correct but in many situations it would be considered to be too direct. 'I would like you to ...' is more polite.
> 按 "I want you to send me the coat" 在文法上並不錯, 但在許多情況下, 語氣似嫌過於直率, 用 "I would like you to ..." 則語氣較為客氣。

3 × The whole house wanted to be painted.
√ **The whole house wanted painting.**
(這房子整幢需要油漆。)

> **Want** is followed by v-ing when it is used with the meaning 'need' (如 **want** 的含意等於 need, 後接帶 "-ing" 的動詞, 例如): 'The grass wants/needs cutting once a week.'

4 × Just as he wanted to leave the bank, a detective grabbed him by the arm.
√ **Just as he was about to leave the bank, a detective grabbed him by the arm.**
(他正要離開銀行, 一個偵探一把抓住他的手臂。)

> **be about** + to-v (NOT **want**) = be on the point of doing something
> 按 **be about** 後接帶 to 的動詞, 相當於 be on the point of doing something, 即 "正要做什麼" 的意思。

watch **1** × The purpose of the trip was to watch the ancient Egyptian temples.
√ **The purpose of the trip was to see the ancient Egyptian temples.**
(這次旅行的目的是要參觀古埃及廟宇。)

> **watch** = observe an activity or event (i.e. something which includes motion or change) (注視某種活動或事件): 'We sat on the beach and watched the sun go down.'
> **see** = experience something visually (看見, 見到): 'Have you ever seen a giant turtle?'

2 × We spent the afternoon watching paintings.
√ **We spent the afternoon looking at paintings.**
(我們整個下午都在看畫。)

> **watch** = observe an activity or event (注視某種活動或事件)
> **look at** = direct your gaze at; examine (把目光集中在 …, 觀察)

way **1** × In the way to the airport we got caught in a traffic jam.
√ **On the way to the airport we got caught in a traffic jam.**
(去機場途中我們遇到了交通阻塞。)

> **on the way to** a place, NOT **in**
> 注意: **on the way to** a place 中的 **to** 不可用 **in** 替代。

2 × For some people, crime is just another way to make a living.
√ **For some people, crime is just another way of making a living.**
(對有些人來說, 犯罪不過是另一種謀生之計。)

> **a way** (= means) **of** + v-ing
> 按 **a way** (相當於 means — 手段) **of** 後接帶 "-ing" 的動詞。

weather × We had a miserable weather while on holiday.
√ **We had miserable weather while on holiday.**
(我們度假時遇上了壞天氣。)

> **Weather** is an uncountable noun.
> 按 **weather** 是不可數名詞, 前面不能加不定冠詞 "**a**"。

week **1** × We knew that a four weeks holiday would bring us closer together.
√ **We knew that a four-week holiday would bring us closer together.**
(我們知道為期四週的假期會使我們的關係更加密切。)

See (見) note at MONTH

2 See (見) IN 6

welcome **1** × As mayor, I would like to welcome you all in our town.
√ **As mayor, I would like to welcome you all to our town.**
(作為市長, 我歡迎你們各位來到我們這個城市。)

> **welcome** someone **to** a place, NOT **in**
> 指 "歡迎某人來某地", 用 **welcome** someone **to** a place, 其中前置詞 **to** 不可用 **in** 替代。

2 × You can bring as many friends to the party as you like. Everyone is welcomed.
✓ **You can bring as many friends to the party as you like. Everyone is welcome.**
(你願意帶多少朋友來參加晚會都可以, 每一個人都會受到歡迎。)

> **welcome** (verb) = greet a guest or visitor in a friendly way when he or she arrives (作動詞用時, 表示以友善的態度接待來訪的客人)
> **welcome** (adjective) = warmly invited (作形容詞用時, 表示 "深受歡迎")

well **1** × Everything was well until somebody came and sat in the seat next to mine.
✓ **Everything was fine until somebody came and sat in the seat next to mine.**
(開頭一切都挺好的, 後來有人坐到我旁邊的座位上, 情況就不一樣了。)
× His table manners were not very well.
✓ **His table manners were not very good.**
(他吃飯時的舉止不很雅觀。)

> **Well** is usually used as an adverb (按 **well** 一般用作副詞, 例如): 'The team played well on Saturday.' As an adjective, **well** usually means 'in good health' (按 **well** 用作形容詞含 "健康" 之意, 例如): 'George can't come because he's not very well.' 'You're looking well after your holiday.'

2 × He knew well where he wanted to go.
✓ **He knew exactly/precisely where he wanted to go.**
(他很清楚自己要去什麼地方。)

> **know** someone/something **well** = be fully familiar with (意為: "熟悉"): 'After living in Florence for two years, I know the city very well.'

well-known × Both these singers are very well-known.
✓ **Both these singers are very well known.**
(這兩個歌手都很有名。)

> Compare (試比較): 'a well-known singer' (hyphenated before a noun 置於名詞之前, 用連字號 "-") BUT (但是) 'the singer is well known' (two separate words when used predicatively) (按 well known 是兩個詞, well 是副詞, known 是敍述形容詞, 不能放在名詞之前。)

West See (見) NORTH

when 1 × When I'll return home, I'll look for a better job.
✓ **When I return home, I'll look for a better job.**
(我回家以後, 會找一份更好的工作。)

After **when/whenever/once/until/after/if**, use the present simple (or present perfect) tense for future reference, NOT **shall/will** + verb.
在 **when/whenever/once/until/after/if** 之後, 用一般現在式或現在完成式, 以表示將來, 不用 **shall** 或 **will**。

2 × When arriving home, I wrote down everything I had seen.
✓ **On/Upon arriving home, I wrote down everything I had seen.**
(一回到家, 我就寫下自己看到的一切。)

To express the meaning 'immediately after (doing something)' use **on/upon** + v-ing, NOT **when**.
表示 "一做完某事, 立即就 ..." 可用 **on/upon**, 後接帶 "-ing" 的動詞, 不用 **when**。

where × He wanted to get to Paris, where he had an uncle living there.
✓ **He wanted to get to Paris, where he had an uncle living.**
(他要去巴黎, 因為他有一位舅父住在那裡。)

When **where** is used as a relative pronoun, it is NOT followed by **there**. Compare (用 **where** 作關係代名詞時, 後面不跟 **there**, 試比較): 'He lives in London. He has a house there.' 'He lives in London, where he has a house.'

whole × As a whole, I am very happy here.
✓ **On the whole, I am very happy here.**
(總的說來, 我在這裡很快樂。)

as a whole = considered as a single body or unit (作為一個整體): 'The college as a whole supports the principal.'
on the whole = taking all things into consideration (總的說來): 'On the whole, the results are very good.'

why See (見) AS 5

winter See (見) SUMMER

wish 1

× He wishes he can drive a car; taxis are so expensive.

√ **He wishes he could drive a car; taxis are so expensive.**

(他真希望自己會開汽車; 現在計程車收費太高了。)

With **wish**, a past tense is used to express a present meaning. (在 **wish** 之後的句子裏, 如所希望的情況是不真實的或很少能實現的, 則應用過去式以表示現在): 'I wish I knew how to play the guitar.'

2

× I wished him to go away because I was tired and needed some sleep.

√ **I wanted him to go away because I was tired and needed some sleep.**

√ **I wished that he would go away because I was tired and needed some sleep.**

(我希望他離開, 因為我累了, 需要睡一會。)

want someone **to do** something BUT **wish (that)** someone **would do** something
指 "要或希望某人做某事", 可用 "**want** someone **to do** something, 但如用 wish 一詞, 則說 **wish (that)** someone **would do** something。

3

× I wish you will have an enjoyable and unforgettable stay.

√ **I hope you (will) have an enjoyable and unforgettable stay.**

(祝你玩得開心, 將來回味無窮。)

To express hopes and wishes for the future, do not use **wish** followed by **will** + verb. However, **wish** can be followed by a noun or noun phrase (如要表示對於將來的希望, 不能用了 **wish** 後接 "**will** + 動詞"。但是 **wish** 後可接名詞或名詞片語): 'I wish you an enjoyable and unforgettable stay.' 'We'd like to wish you a very merry Christmas.'

within × I promised to return the record within next weekend.
√ **I promised to return the record by next weekend.**
(我答應在下週末歸還這張唱片。)

> **within** = before (a day, week, etc.) is over (在 [一天、一週等] 之內): 'I promised to return the record within a week.' (我答應在一週之內歸還這張唱片。)
> **by** = no later than (意為: "在…的時候", "不遲於…")
> Note that **within** is followed by an expression which describes a period of time (a day, five hours, etc.) whereas **by** is followed by a time or date.
> 注意: **within** 之後接的是表示一段時間的詞, 如一天、五小時之類; 而 **by** 之後接的是某一時間或某個日期。

without × He went out with not a coat.
√ **He went out without a coat.**
(他不穿大衣就出去了。)

> **with not** is not an idiomatic expression for "not having".
> 按 "**with not**" 並不是 "not having" 這個意思的英語慣常表達方式。

wonder × I wonder that the machine has other faults I haven't noticed.
√ **I wonder whether the machine has other faults I haven't noticed.**
(我懷疑這機器 (是否) 還有別的毛病我沒注意到。)

> **wonder + (that)–clause** = to be surprised and want to know why (按 **wonder** 後接由 **that** 引導的子句意為 "覺得驚奇並想知道為什麼, 例如): 'I wonder (**that**) he dares to show his face here again after the way he behaved!' (他那樣子表現以後, 我倒是想知道他還敢不敢在這兒露臉兒!)
> **wonder whether/if** = to suggest or think (something) that is not so; doubt (意為暗示或心裏想某事不一定如此, 或心裏懷疑是否如此)

wood × The coat has a leather belt and three brown wood buttons.
√ **The coat has a leather belt and three brown wooden buttons.**
(這件外套有條皮腰帶和三粒棕色木鈕扣。)

The adjective meaning 'made of wood' is usually **wooden**, NOT **wood**.
作"木製的"解的形容詞一般用 **wooden**, 不用 **wood**。

work 1
× Without a full-time work, some people think it is not worth living.
√ **Without full-time work, some people think it is not worth living.**
√ **Without a full-time job, some people think it is not worth living.**
(如果不是做全職的工作, 有的人就認為沒法過日子。)
× I have come to England to do a research work in civil engineering.
√ **I have come to England to do research work in civil engineering.**
(我來英國的目的是從事土木工程研究。)

Work is an uncountable noun.
work 是個不可數名詞, 前面不可與不定冠詞 "a" 連用。

2
× I got up and got ready to go to my work.
√ **I got up and got ready to go to work.**
(我起牀後準備去上班。)

go to work WITHOUT **my/your/his** etc.
go to work 作"上班"解時, 其中不容插入 **my/you/his** 等。
Compare (比較): 'go to school', 'go to church'

3
× These days a lot of women go to work outside.
√ **These days a lot of women go out to work.**
(現今好多婦女到社會上去工作。)

go out to work = have a job outside your home
(意為: "到社會上去工作")

world 1
× The sewing machine is one of the most widely used products of the world.
√ **The sewing machine is one of the most widely used products in the world.**
(縫紉機是世界上使用最廣的產品之一。)

superlative adjective + **in the world**, NOT **of**
最高級形容詞後接 **in the world**, 不可接 **of the world**。

2 × Rio is known in the world for its beautiful beaches.
√ **Rio is known throughout the world for its beautiful beaches.**
(里約熱內盧海灘之美是舉世聞名的。)

> known/spoken/understood etc. **throughout the world**, NOT **in**
> 按 known/spoken/understood 等一般與 **throughout the world** 連用, 不與 **in the world** 並用。

worse × It was the worse journey I have ever made.
√ **It was the worst journey I have ever made.**
(這是我歷次旅行最糟的一次。)
× People's lack of responsibility makes the problem even more worse.
√ **People's lack of responsibility makes the problem even worse.**
(由於人們缺乏責任感, 問題變得更為嚴重。)

> **bad, worse, worst**
> 按 **bad** 的比較級為 **worse**, 最高級為 **worst**。

worst × The next time I saw her she looked even worst.
√ **The next time I saw her she looked even worse.**
(我第二次見她時, 她的神情看來更差了。)

> **bad, worse, worst**
> 按 **bad** 的比較級為 **worse**, 最高級為 **worst**。

worth 1 × The missing ring worths about two thousand pounds.
√ **The missing ring is worth about two thousand pounds.**
(那隻丢失了的戒指大約價值兩千鎊。)

> **Worth** is an adjective/preposition, NOT a verb.
> **worth** 可作表語形容詞, 也可作前置詞, 但不作動詞。

2 × That new magazine is certainly worth its money.
√ **That new magazine is certainly worth the money.**
(那本新出的雜誌無疑是物有所值的。)

> **be worth the money,** NOT **its**
> **be worth the money** 中的 **the**, 不可用 **its** 來替代。

3 × That ring has great sentimental worth.
√ **That ring has great sentimental value.**
(那隻戒指帶有濃厚的感情意義, 十分可貴)

> Compare (試比較): 'That watch is worth fifty pounds.' 'That watch has a value of fifty pounds.'

would 1 × Some people might argue that a woman wouldn't work if she has children.
√ **Some people might argue that a woman shouldn't work if she has children.**
(有人也許要爭辯說, 有孩子的婦女不該外出工作。)

> Use **should** (NOT **would**) to express obligation or duty.
> 表示責任和應該做的事, 用 **should**, 不用 **would**。

2 × If you would have any more questions, I'll do my best to answer them.
√ **If you should have any more questions, I'll do my best to answer them.**
(如果你還有什麼問題, 我將盡力回答。)

> When talking about something which is unlikely or improbable, use **if ... should**, NOT **if ... would**.
> 作假設時指不太可能發生或做到的事, 用 **if** ... **should**, 不用 **if** ... **would**。

wound × Only the driver was wounded in the accident.
√ **Only the driver was injured/hurt in the accident.**
(只有駕車的人在事故中受了傷。)

> **wound** = cause injury to (someone) by using a weapon
> 按 **wound** 一詞意指為武器所致的傷。

write 1 √ **AmE I want to apologize for not having written you before.**
√ **BrE I want to apologize for not having written to you before.**
(十分抱歉, 未能及早給你寫信。)

> **write to** a person or place (British English 英式英語)
> **write (to)** a person or place (American English 美式英語)

2 × Dear … I write to you to ask for your advice.
√ **Dear … I am writing to you to ask for your advice.**
(親愛的 … 我現在給你寫信, 想徵詢你的意見。)

The present progressive tense is used for actions which are happening at the time when they are mentioned.
現在進行式是用以表達當時提及的那個時刻正在做的動作。

year 1 × Robert was a little boy of ten years.
√ **Robert was a little boy of ten.**
(羅伯特是個十歲的小男孩。)

'a child of six', 'a man of fifty', etc. WITHOUT **years**
'a child of six', 'a man of fifty' 等, 都不需加 **years** 一詞。
Compare (比較): 'Robert was ten years old.'
See also (也參見) OLD

2 See (見) IN 6

yet 1 × He left the house at five in the morning, when the family was yet asleep.
√ **He left the house at five in the morning, when the family was still asleep.**
(他在清晨五點離家, 當時全家還沒有起床。)

Yet is mainly used in questions and negative sentences and is used to ask whether something has happened (**yet** 主要用於問句、否定句以及問某事是否已發生, 例如): 'Have they woken up yet?' (=Are they still asleep?) or to say that something has not happened (或用以說某事尚未發生, 例如): 'They haven't woken up yet.' (=They are still asleep.)
Still is mainly used to talk about actions or states which are continuing in the present (**still** 主要用於表示現在仍然在進行的事, 例如): 'I'm still hungry.' 'She still goes to the same school.' However, **still** can also be used with a negative verb to say that something has not happened (但是, **still** 也可用於否定句, 說明某事尚未發生, 例如): 'I still haven't passed my driving test.' (=It's taking a long time.)

2 × I remember that you used to be fond of water sports. Are you yet?
√ **I remember that you used to be fond of water sports. Are you still?**
(我記得你過去一向喜愛水上運動, 現在仍然如此嗎?)

> Use **still** when talking about something which is continuing. Compare (用 **still** 說明現正進行的事, 試比較): I'm still reading the book you lent me.' 'Haven't you finished it yet?'

3 See (見) ALTHOUGH 1

you See (見) ME 1

yours **1** × Dear Sir, ...Yours,
√ **Dear Sir, ...Yours faithfully,**
某某先生大鑒, ...您忠實的; 謹啟

> When writing a formal letter beginning **Dear Sir** or **Dear Madam,** you should end it with **Yours faithfully.**
> 正式信件開始時用 **Dear Sir** 或 **Dear Madam**, 其結尾應用 **Yours faithfully**。

2 × Dear Mum and Dad, ...Yours, Erich
√ **Dear Mum and Dad, ...Love, Erich**
親愛的媽媽, 爸爸, ...愛您們的阿歷

> **Yours** is often used at the end of letters to friends but NOT to parents and close relatives.
> **Yours** 用於致朋友的信末, 但不能用於致父母或近親的信末。

Glossary 文法術語表

active — 主動語態 See (見) PASSIVE

adjective — 形容詞 a word which describes a noun or pronoun 用於修飾名詞或代名詞: 'He bought himself a new tie.' 'The university is fairly new.' 'She is quite tall.'

adverb — 副詞 a word which describes or adds to the meaning of a verb 用於修飾動詞 (例如: 'drink it slowly'), adjective 修飾形容詞 (例如: 'extremely cold'), another adverb 修飾另一個副詞 (例如: 'very quickly') or sentence 也可修飾句子 (例如 'Unfortunately there was nowhere to sit.')

affirmative — 肯定式 (also 也用 **positive**) See (見) NEGATIVE

article — 冠詞 'a/an' or 'the'

attributive — 定語 An attributive adjective is one that is placed before the noun it describes 用作修飾語的形容詞一般位於它所修飾的名詞之前, 例如: 'a green raincoat', 'a serious disease', 'a large brown envelope'. A predicative adjective is one that is used after a verb such as 'be/seem/appear/look/become' etc. 用作述語的形容詞總是位於be/seen/appear/look/become 等動詞之後, 例如: 'We were afraid of missing the plane.' 'Her father looks very ill.' Many (but not all) adjectives can be used both attributively and predicatively. 許多 (但不是所有) 形容詞既能用作修飾語又能用作述語。

auxiliary — 助動詞 See (見) MAIN VERB

clause — 分句; 子句 a group of words containing a subject and a verb, which either forms a sentence by itself 含有主語和動詞的一組詞, 或獨自成句 (例如: 'I'm going out tonight.') or forms part of a sentence 或作為句子的一部分 (例如: 'if it doesn't rain').
See also (參見) MAIN CLAUSE, SUBORDINATE CLAUSE

colloquial — 口語的 See (見) INFORMAL

common noun — 普通名詞 See (見) PROPER NOUN

comparative — 比較級 the form of an adjective or adverb that is used to express a greater or smaller degree. Most comparatives end in '-er' or are formed with 'more' or 'less' 指形容詞或副詞用來表示較大較小程度的一種形式, 大多數比較級以 -er 結尾, 或者前面加上 more 或 less, 例如: 'Her work is better than it used to be.' 'The problem was more difficult than I thought.' 'John always speaks more politely than his brother.'

compound — 複合詞 A compound word is one that is made up of two or more parts 複合詞由兩個或兩個以上的詞構成, 例如: 'boyfriend', 'fingertip', 'six-foot', 'second-hand', 'mother-in-law', 'cassette recorder', 'training college'.

conditional 條件子句; 條件句; 條件詞 **1** a clause beginning with a word such as 'if' or 'unless', or a sentence containing such a clause 以 if 或 unless 這類連接詞開頭的子句, 或者含有條件子句的句子 **2** a form of the verb made with 'would/should' and the infinitive (WITHOUT 'to') 由 would/should 後接不帶 to 的不定式構成的一種動詞形式, 例如: 'I would like to see that film again.' 'Would you like a cup of tea?'

conjunction 連接詞 a word like 'and/but/since/when/if/although which joins words, phrases or clauses together, or shows how they are related to each other 諸如 and/but/since/when/if/although 之類的詞, 用來連接詞與詞、短語與短語、或子句與子句, 或者表示所連接的部分之間的關係, 例如: 'He was a very good boy and obeyed his parents all the time.' 'Although I was frightened, I couldn't scream.'

context — 上下文; 前後關係 **1** the word or words which come immediately before and/or after a word or phrase 前後相關的詞或詞語 **2** the situation in which language is used 上下文; 語境

contraction — 縮略 a short form used in everyday conversation, informal letters, etc. 日常談話、非正式信件中使用的縮略形式, 例如: 'isn't', 'he'll', 'they've' (compare 比較: 'is not', 'he will', 'they have')

countable — 可數名詞 A countable noun is a noun which has both singular and plural forms 可數名詞有單複數兩種形式, 例如: 'tree–trees', 'apple–apples', 'man–men'. The singular form may follow 'a/an' 單數前可用 a/an, 例如: 'a tree', 'an apple', 'a man'.

derogatory — 貶義 (詞) expressing an unfavourable quality, attitude or opinion 貶義的

determiner 限定詞 a word like 'a/an/my/this/some/every' that limits the meaning of a noun or noun phrase 諸如 a/an/my/this/some/every 之類的詞, 限定名詞或名詞短語的意義, 例如: 'an apple', 'my house', 'every member of staff'.

direct object — 直接受詞 See (見) OBJECT

direct speech — 直接引語 speech that is written down in the exact words of the original speaker, without changing tenses, pronouns, adverbs, etc. 原語照引, 所用時態、代名詞、副詞等不作更改 Compare 比較: "My parents were killed in a road accident." (direct speech 直接引語): She said that her parents had been killed in a road accident. (reported speech 間接引語). Direct speech is usually shown by inverted commas. 直接引語通常用引號表示。
See also (參見) REPORTED SPEECH

double negative — 重複否定 the use of two

negative words when only one is required. 只需用一個否定詞時卻用了兩個。

emphasis — 加強語氣 the special force that is sometimes given to a word or phrase to draw it to the listener's or reader's attention. 有時為了引起聽者或讀者的注意, 可對某詞或短語加以強調, 例如: 'I do hope your mother gets better soon. ' 'She's really enjoying her stay in London.' 'They themselves have never been to Italy.'

fixed phrase — 固定詞組 two or more words which are always used together and which cannot be changed in any way 兩個或兩個以上的詞, 總是一起使用, 不能加以絲毫改動, 例如: 'on the contrary' (not 不用 'on a contrary', 'on the contraries', etc.)

formal — 書面用語 Formal language is the type of language that is used in official reports, public speeches, business letters, etc. 指官方報告、公眾演講、商業函件等使用的正規語體。
See also (參見) INFORMAL

full infinitive — 帶 to 的不定式 See INFINITIVE

future — 將來式 There are several ways of talking about the future in English. One of these is often called the 'future tense'. This is formed with 'will/shall' and the infinitive (WITHOUT 'to') 英語中有幾種表達將來的方式, 其中一種通常叫做 "將來式", 它由 will/shall 後接不帶 to 的不定式構成, 例如: 'will send', 'shall go', 等。
See also (參見) PROGRESSIVE

identifying relative clause — 限制性修飾語子句 See (見) RELATIVE CLAUSE.

indirect object — 間接受詞 See (見) OBJECT

indirect question — 間接疑問句 An indirect question is the form that is used to report a question that has been asked previously. 指原先已問過的問題再複述一遍。Compare 比較: "What's the time?" (direct question 直接疑問句); She asked me what the time was. (indirect quesiton 間接疑問句)

infinitive — (動詞) 不定式 the form of a verb that is shown in a dictionary. There are two types of infinitive, the 'full infinitive' shown in this book as 'to-v' ('to come', 'to take', 'to send') and the 'bare infinitive' ('come', 'take', 'send') 指詞典上使用的那種動詞形式。不定詞有兩種: "帶 to 的不定詞" (本書中用 to-v), 如 to come, to take, to send; "不帶 to 的不定詞", 如 come, take, send。

informal — 口語體 (的) informal or colloquial language is the language that is used in everyday conversation, for example between friends or members of a family. 親朋間日常談話所用的非正規語體式口語
Compare 比較: 'I regret to inform you that your application for a position with our company has been unsuccessful.' (formal 書面用語); 'I'm afraid you didn't get the job.' (informal 口語體)
See also (參見) FORMAL

intensify — 強化 Words like 'very/extremely/absolutely' are used to make adjectives stronger. These words are known as 'intensifiers' because they are used to 'intensify' (= make stronger) 像 very/extremely/absolutely 這類詞用來加強形容詞, 它們叫做 "強化詞", 因為其作用便是 "強化"。

intransitive — 不及物動詞 An intransitive verb is a verb that is used without an object 指不用賓語的動詞, 例如: 'The man suddenly disappeared.'

irregular — 不規則 (動詞或名詞) not following the usual pattern or rules. For example, the past tense of an irregular verb does NOT end in '-ed' 指不按常規變形, 例如, 不規則動詞的過去式不以 -ed 結尾, 如 ('went', 'took', 'gave'). Similarly, the plural form of an irregular noun does NOT end in '-s' 同樣, 不規則名詞的複數不以 -s 結尾, 如 ('children', 'mice', 'criteria').

main clause (also 也作 **independent clause**) — 主句 a group of words containing a subject and verb, which can form a sentence 含有主語和動詞, 可以單獨成句的一組詞, 例如: 'I'm going out tonight, if it doesn't rain.'
See also (參見) SUBORDINATE CLAUSE

main verb — 主要動詞 a verb like 'speak/take/go' which can be used as the only verb in a sentence 像 speak/take/go 這類動詞可在句中單獨用作動詞, 例如: 'She speaks German and Russian.' 'He took her to the cinema.' 'They went on holiday in April.' A main verb is often used with an auxiliary verb such as 'be/do/have' in order to form a tense, question, passive form, etc. 主要動詞常跟 be/do/ have 等助動詞連用, 構成某種時態, 疑問句, 被動語態等, 例如: 'My husband is learning English.' 'Do you speak French?' 'The car was stolen during the night.'

modify (also 也作 **qualify**) — 修飾 A word is often used with one or more other words which provide additional information about it or limit its meaning. In such cases the word is said to be 'modified'. For example, in the sentence 'Japanese cars are quite cheap', the noun 'cars' is modified by the adjective 'Japanese' and the adjective 'cheap' is modified by the adverb 'quite'. 詞常與詞連用, 從中充實其含義, 或其含義受到限定, 在這種情況下, 我們說此詞受到彼詞的 "修飾"。例如, 在 Japanese cars are quite cheap 這句

中, 名詞 cars 受形容詞 Japanese 的修飾, 而形容詞 cheap 則受副詞 quite 的修飾。

negative — 否定式 A verb is negative when it is used with a word like 'not/never/rarely' etc. 否定式動詞指的是和 not/never/rarely 等連用的動詞, 例如: 'She never answers my questions.' A clause or sentence containing a negative verb is also negative. 含有否定式動詞的子句或句子便是否定句。Compare 比較: 'He wanted to go to bed.' (affirmative verb/sentence 肯定式動詞/肯定句); 'He didn't want to go to bed.' (negative verb/sentence 否定式動詞/否定句)

non-identifying relative clause — 非限制性修飾語子句 See (見) RELATIVE CLAUSE

noun — 名詞 a word used to name a person, animal, place, thing, etc. which can be used with an article or a determiner 表示人、動物、地方、東西等的詞叫名詞, 前面可加冠詞或限定詞, 例如: 'Each visitor received a small gift.'

noun phrase — 名詞片語 a group of words which is used like a noun or pronoun 指和名詞或代名詞用法相同的一組詞, 例如: 'Each visitor received a small gift.'

object — 受詞 the word or group of words affected by the action of the verb, usually placed immediately after the verb. There are two types of object. A 'direct object' is affected directly by the verb: 指受動詞動作影響的詞或一組詞, 通常緊接在動詞之後。受詞有兩種。"直接受詞" 直接受動詞的影響, 例如: 'She opened the door.' 'she wrote a long letter.' A sentence which has a direct object can also have an 'indirect object' (= an object that is affected indirectly by the verb) 帶有直接受詞的句子也可有 "間接受詞" (受動詞間接影響的受詞), 例如: 'She wrote me a long letter.' 'They have sent him an invitation.'

participle — 分詞 See (見) PAST PARTICIPLE, PRESENT PARTICIPLE

passive — 被動語態 When the subject of a sentence performs the action expressed by the verb, the verb is said to be 'active' 凡是句子主語進行動詞所表示的動作, 那麼, 這動詞就叫做 "主動語態", 例如: 'The government spends a lot of money on cancer research.' However, when the subject does not perform the action expressed by the verb but is affected by it, the verb is said to be 'passive'. 然而, 如果主語不進行動詞所表示的動作, 而是受動詞所影響, 那麼, 這動詞叫做 "被動語態", 例如: 'A lot of money is spent on cancer research.' We use the passive when we are interested in knowing what is done, not who or what is doing it. The passive is also used when we do not know who or what has performed the action 我們所以要用被動語態是因為我們着眼於所做的事情, 而不是誰或什麼東西在做這事。如果我們不知道誰或什麼東西做了某動作, 也可用被動語態, 例如: 'My watch has been stolen.'

past participle — 過去分詞 the verb form that is used to make the present perfect and past perfect 用於構成現在完成式和過去完成式的一種動詞形式, 例如: 'kicked', 'gone', 'fallen'. Some past participles are also used as adjecives 有些過去分詞也用作形容詞, 例如: 'a frightened cat', 'a folded newspaper'.

past perfect — 過去完成式 the form of the verb that is made with 'had' and the past participle 由 "had + 過去分詞" 所構成的一種動詞形式, 例如: 'After she had picked the flowers, she got back into the car.' 'If I'd known your address, I would've come to see you.'
See also (參見) PROGRESSIVE

past tense 過去式 The past tense of a regular verb is the same as the past participle ('-ed') 規則動詞的過去式和過去分詞相同, 都以 -ed 結尾, 例如: 'cooked', 'thanked', 'opened'. The past tense of an irregular verb is formed in many different ways: 不規則動詞過去式的構成有許多不同方式, 例如: 'went', 'took', 'saw', 'thought', 'found', 'left', 'spoke'.
See also (參見) PROGRESSIVE

perfect conditional — 條件完成式 the form of the verb that is made with 'would/should have' and the past participle 指由 would/should have + 過去分詞所構成的一種詞形式: 'would have opened', 'should have sent'.
See also (參見) PROGRESSIVE

phrase — 片語/詞組 a group of words which may be used like a noun 指一組詞, 其作用如名詞 ('many people'), a verb 如動詞 ('has been working'), an adjective 如形容詞 ('very interesting') or an adverb 或者用作副詞 ('in the summer').

plural — 複數 the form of a word that is used when talking about two or more people, things, etc. 指兩個或兩個以上的人、東西等。
See also (參見) SINGULAR

plural noun — 複數名詞 a noun that is always used with a plural verb: 指和動詞連用時總是作為複數對待的名詞, 例如: 'trousers', 'scissors', 'police', 'goods'.

possessive — 所有格 the form of a word which expresses ownership or connection 表示所有權和所屬關係, 例如: 'Have you met my wife?' 'It wasn't the driver's fault.' 'She said that the book wasn't hers.' The possessive is also used in time expressions 所有格也用於表達時間, 例如: 'She'll be back in two days' time.'

predeterminer — 前指定詞 a word like 'such/half/quite/both/all' that can be used before 'a/an' or 'the' 指 such/half/quite/both/all 等可以位於 a/an 或 the 之前的這些詞, 例如: 'David is such a good boy.' 'All the other children are very naughty.'

predicative — 述語 See (見) ATTRIBUTIVE

preparatory subject — 形式主語 Instead of using a clause or infinitive structure as the subject of a sentence, it is often better to begin the sentence with 'it' and put the clause or infinitive structure towards the end of the sentence 句子的主語一般不用子句和不定式結構, 通常宜改用 it, 把它放在句首而把子句或不定結構移在句末, 例如: 'It is impossible to see in the dark.' 'It's a pity that she couldn't come.' In these cases 'it' is known as a preparatory subject. 上述兩句中的 it 叫做形式主語。'There' is sometimes used in a similar way to introduce a new piece of information 按 there 有時也有類似用法, 引述一項新信息, 例如: 'There is a bottle of milk in the fridge.'

preparatory object — 形式受詞 instead of using a clause or infinitive structure as the object of a sentence. It is often better to use 'it' as a preparatory object and put the clause or infinitive structure towards the end of the sentence 句中的動詞後面一般不緊接子句和不定式結構作受詞, 通常宜改用 it 作形式受詞, 而把子句和不定式結構移至句末, 例如: 'He found it impossible to leave the office before six o'clock.' 'They made it clear that he was not welcome.'

preposition — 前置詞 a word such as 'in/over/of/through/at/for' which is used before a noun, pronoun, etc. to show its connection with a previous word 指用於名詞、代詞等前面的 in/ over/of/through/at/for 這類詞, 表示和它前面出現的詞的關係, 例如: 'I spoke to the man sitting behind me.' 'He was born in a town just outside Paris.' 'We were afraid of missing the plane.'

present participle — 現在分詞 the '-ing' form of a verb 動詞的 -ing 形式; 如: 'coming', 'speaking'.

present perfect — 現在完成式 the present perfect tense is made with 'have/has' and the past participle 它由 "have/has + 過去分詞" 構成, 例如: 'I've seen the new Mercedes but I haven't seen the new Datsun.' 'Have you seen it?'
See also (參見) PROGRESSIVE

present progressive (also 也用 **present continuous**) — 現在進行式 The present progressive tense is made with 'be' and the present participle 它由 "be + 現在分詞" 構成, 例如: 'I'm waiting for a taxi.' 'Are you waiting for a taxi too?'

present simple — 一般現在式 Unlike the present progresive tense, the present simple is made WITHOUT 'be' 不同於現在進行式, 一般現在式不用 be: 'I like fish but I don't like meat.' 'Do you like meat?'

progressive (also 也作 **continuous**) 進行式 a form of the verb made with 'be' and the present participle 由 "be + 現在分詞" 構成的一種動詞形式, 例如: 'It was raining this morning.' (past progressive 過去進行式) 'Are you coming with us tonight?' (present progressive — 現在進行式) 'I've been waiting here for an hour.' (present perfect progressive 現在完成進行式) 'Where had you been living before you moved to London?' (past perfect progressive 過去完成進行式) 'At six o'clck I shall be waiting for you outside the station.' (future progressive 將來進行式)
See also (參見) SIMPLE

pronoun — 代名詞 a word like 'he/her/mine/themselves' that is used in place of a noun or noun phrase 諸如 he/her/mine/themselves 之類的詞, 用於代替名詞或名詞片語, 例如: 'Ann spoke very softly and nobody could hear her.' ('her' is the pronoun for 'Ann' 按: her 是代名詞, 替代 Ann): 'The little girl fell over and hurt herself.' ('herself' is the pronoun for 'the little girl' 按 herself 是代名詞, 替代 the little girl)

proper noun — 專有名詞 the name of a particular person, place, or thing 指人、地方或東西的專名, 例如: 'Mary', 'Oxford', 'Daily Telegraph'. A proper noun always begins with a capital letter. All other nouns are common nouns 專有名詞的第一個字母總是大寫。所有其他名詞都是普通名詞, 如: 'letter', 'table', 'cassette recorder', 'state'.

qualify (見) See MODIFY

reflexive pronoun — 反身代名詞 A reflexive pronoun is used when talking about the subject doing something to himself or herself 它用於主語的動作對自身所產生的影響, 例如: 'Henry has hurt himself.' 'I found myself a seat and sat down.'

reflexive verb — 反身動詞 A reflexive verb is a verb that is used with a reflexive pronoun 指和反身代名詞連用的那種動詞, 例如: 'We all enjoyed ourselves.' 'You mustn't blame yourself for the accident.'

relative clause — 修飾語子句 a descriptive clause usually beginning with 'that/who/whom/whose' or 'which'. There are two types of relative clause, 'identifying' and 'non-identifying'. An identifying relative clause answers the question 'which?' It identifies or defines the preceding noun 指通常以 that/who/whom/whose 或 which 開頭的一種修飾性子句。修飾語子句分 "限制性" 和 "非限制性" 兩種。限制性修飾語子句往往可用 "哪一個" 來提問和回答, 它限定前面所修飾的名詞, 例如: 'The man who was carrying a torch showed us to our seats.' (Which man? The man carrying the torch.) A non-identifying relative clause does not identify or define the preceding noun but merely adds further information 非限制性修飾語子句並不限定前面所修飾的名詞,只是補充說明情況, 例如: 'The man, who was carrying a torch, showed us to our seats.'

relative pronoun — 關係代名詞 'that/who/whom/whose' or 'which', used to introduce a relative clause 指 that/who/whom/whose

或 which 這些詞, 用來引導修飾語子句
See also (參見) RELATIVE CLAUSE

reported speech (also 也作 **indirect speech**) — 間接引語 someone's words reported indirectly, with changes of tense, pronouns, adverbs, etc. 間接引述人們的話, 對時態、代詞、副詞等需作必要的改變
See also (參見) DIRECT SPEECH

reporting verb — 傳意動詞 a verb like 'say/answer/ask' which is used when reporting what someone has said, asked, etc. 指像 say/answer/ask 等用來引出間接引語的動詞: 'She said that she needed more time.'

simple — 一般時態 These are simple verb forms 下列各句的動詞都屬一般時態: 'Yesterday it rained all day.' (past simple 一般過去式) 'What time does the postman come?' (present simple 一般現在時). 'I've sent your sister an invitation.' (present perfect simple 一般現在完成式)
See also (參見) PROGRESSIVE

singular — 單數 the form of a word that is used to refer to one person, thing, etc. 指用來表示一個人、一件東西等的名詞。
Compare 比較: 'This pen was made in Japan.' (singular 單數): 'These pens were made in Japan.' (plural 複數)

subject — 主詞; 主語 the word or group of words in a sentence about which something is said. In a statement, the subject usually appears at the beginning of the sentence and is followed by the verb 指句中和動詞有密切關係的詞或一組詞。主語通常位於句首後接動詞, 例如: 'Parents should spend more time looking after their children.' 'The way he dresses is rather unusual.' 'Fighting crime keeps the police very busy.'

subordinate clause (also 也作 **dependent clause**) — 從句 a clause that cannot be used by itself as a sentence but depends grammatically on a main clause 指不能單獨成句, 語法上依賴主句: 'If the sun is too hot perhaps you would like to sit in the shade.' (subordinate clause + main clause). A subordinate clause often begins with a word like 'if/when/although/since/that' etc. 子句往往以 if/when/although/since/that 等詞開頭。
See also (參見) MAIN CLAUSE

suffix — 後綴 A group of letters added to the end of a word to change its use or meaning 指加在詞尾的一組字母, 從而改變原詞的詞性和含義, 例如: 'friendly', 'delightful', 'kindness'.

superlative — 最高級 the form of an adjective or adverb that is used to express the greatest or smallest degree. Most superlative forms end in '-est' or are formed with 'most' or 'least' 指表示最大或最小程度的形容詞或副詞的一種形式。形容詞或副詞的最高級多半以 -est 結尾或前面加上 most 或 least, 例如: 'She's the prettiest baby I've ever seen.' 'We all agreed that the first of the three questions was the most difficult.'

to-v — to + 動詞原形 See (見) INFINITIVE

transitive — 及物動詞 A transitive verb is a verb that is used with an object 指後接受詞的動詞, 例如: 'She opened the drawer and took out a knife.'

uncountable — 不可數名詞 An uncountable noun is a noun which has no plural form and which is not usually preceded by 'a/an' 指沒有複數形式、通常前面不加 a/an 的名詞, 例如: 'accommodation', 'research', 'furniture', 'information', 'luggage', 'advice'.

verb — 動詞 a word expressing an action or state 指表示行動或狀態的詞, 例如: 'I visited her in London.' 'He knows a lot about engineering.'

v-ing — 以 ing 結尾的動詞 the '-ing' form of a verb, often used like a noun 動詞的這種形式通常用作名詞, 例如: 'I enjoy speaking foreign languages.' 'Please forgive me for interrupting you.'

vowel — 元音 a speech sound made when the breath escapes freely, without being blocked or restricted in the mouth or throat, such as /i/ as in 'key' /ki/, or /ɑ/ as in 'car' /kɑr/. The letters of the alphabet which stand for these sounds ('a', 'e', 'i', 'o', 'u') are known as 'vowels'. 指自由送氣、不受嘴喉阻塞的音素, 如 key /ki/ 中的 /i/, 或 car /kɑr/ 中的 /ɑ/ 。用 a, e, i, o, u 這些字母表示的音素叫做元音。

wh- — 以 wh- 開頭的詞 'When/where/why/how/who/whom/ whose/what/which/whether' are commonly known as 'wh-words'. A clause beginning with one of these words is a 'wh- clause' 指 when/where/why/ how/who/whom/whose/what/which/whether 這些詞。以這類詞開頭的子句叫做 wh- 子句, 例如: 'I didn't know what to do.' 'She told me where he was.'

或 which 這些詞, 用來引導修飾語子句
See also (參見) RELATIVE CLAUSE

reported speech (also 也作 **indirect speech)** — 間接引語 someone's words reported indirectly, with changes of tense, pronouns, adverbs, etc. 間接引述人們的話, 對時態、代詞、副詞等需作必要的改變
See also (參見) DIRECT SPEECH

reporting verb — 傳意動詞 a verb like 'say/answer/ask' which is used when reporting what someone has said, asked, etc. 指像 say/answer/ask 等用來引出間接引語的動詞: 'She said that she needed more time.'

simple — 一般時態 These are simple verb forms 下列各句的動詞都屬一般時態: 'Yesterday it rained all day.' (past simple 一般過去式) 'What time does the postman come?' (present simple 一般現在時). 'I've sent your sister an invitation.' (present perfect simple 一般現在完成式)
See also (參見) PROGRESSIVE

singular — 單數 the form of a word that is used to refer to one person, thing, etc. 指用來表示一個人、一件東西等的名詞。
Compare 比較: 'This pen was made in Japan.' (singular 單數): 'These pens were made in Japan.' (plural 複數)

subject — 主詞; 主語 the word or group of words in a sentence about which something is said. In a statement, the subject usually appears at the beginning of the sentence and is followed by the verb 指句中和動詞有密切關係的詞或一組詞。主語通常位於句首後接動詞, 例如: 'Parents should spend more time looking after their children.' 'The way he dresses is rather unusual.' 'Fighting crime keeps the police very busy.'

subordinate clause (also 也作 **dependent clause)** — 從句 a clause that cannot be used by itself as a sentence but depends grammatically on a main clause 指不能單獨成句, 語法上依賴主句: 'If the sun is too hot perhaps you would like to sit in the shade.' (subordinate clause + main clause). A subordinate clause often begins with a word like 'if/when/although/since/that' etc. 子句往往以 if/when/although/since/that 等詞開頭。
See also (參見) MAIN CLAUSE

suffix — 後綴 A group of letters added to the end of a word to change its use or meaning 指加在詞尾的一組字母, 從而改變原詞的詞性和含義, 例如: 'friendly', 'delightful', 'kindness'.

superlative — 最高級 the form of an adjective or adverb that is used to express the greatest or smallest degree. Most superlative forms end in '-est' or are formed with 'most' or 'least' 指表示最大或最小程度的形容詞或副詞的一種形式。形容詞或副詞的最高級多半以 -est 結尾或前面加上 most 或 least, 例如: 'She's the prettiest baby I've ever seen.' 'We all agreed that the first of the three questions was the most difficult.'

to-v — to + 動詞原形 See (見) INFINITIVE

transitive — 及物動詞 A transitive verb is a verb that is used with an object 指後接受詞的動詞, 例如: 'She opened the drawer and took out a knife.'

uncountable — 不可數名詞 An uncountable noun is a noun which has no plural form and which is not usually preceded by 'a/an' 指沒有複數形式、通常前面不加 a/an 的名詞, 例如: 'accommodation', 'research', 'furniture', 'information', 'luggage', 'advice'.

verb — 動詞 a word expressing an action or state 指表示行動或狀態的詞, 例如: 'I visited her in London.' 'He knows a lot about engineering.'

v-ing — 以 ing 結尾的動詞 the '-ing' form of a verb, often used like a noun 動詞的這種形式通常用作名詞, 例如: 'I enjoy speaking foreign languages.' 'Please forgive me for interrupting you.'

vowel — 元音 a speech sound made when the breath escapes freely, without being blocked or restricted in the mouth or throat, such as /i/ as in 'key' /ki/, or /ɑ/ as in 'car' /kɑr/. The letters of the alphabet which stand for these sounds ('a', 'e', 'i', 'o', 'u') are known as 'vowels'. 指自由送氣、不受嘴喉阻塞的音素, 如 key /ki/ 中的 /i/, 或 car /kɑr/ 中的 /ɑ/。用 a, e, i, o, u 這些字母表示的音素叫做元音。

wh- — 以 wh- 開頭的詞 'When/where/why/how/who/whom/ whose/what/which/whether' are commonly known as 'wh-words'. A clause beginning with one of these words is a 'wh- clause' 指 when/where/why/ how/who/whom/whose/what/which/whether 這些詞。以這類詞開頭的子句叫做 wh- 子句, 例如: 'I didn't know what to do.' 'She told me where he was.'